# About This Book

## Why Is This Topic Important?

This book explores the realities of e-learning at several different levels: how e-learning is being used in different environments, the technologies of e-learning, design challenges raised by e-learning, learning theory and research affected by e-learning, and the economics of e-learning. With organizations investing thousands, even millions, of dollars in e-learning, this realistic portrait of e-learning provides executives, managers, and senior practitioners with an independent and balanced perspective on which to determine their investments, and researchers, instructors, and students with a broad picture with which to assess e-learning.

## What Can You Achieve with This Book?

With this book, readers can achieve one of two things:

- Executives, managers, and senior practitioners who have responsibility for e-learning can build a practical, holistic view of the field on which to assess future plans for their technology investments and designs for e-learning.

- Researchers, instructors, and students can critically assess e-learning in general and suggested implementations in particular.

## How Is This Book Organized?

This book has sixteen chapters spread among six parts, each of which looks at e-learning from a different perspective and is written by an expert in that topic. Our contributors represent both academe and industry. After Part I, which sets the context, the following broad areas are explored: The Reality Versus the Hype of e-Learning, Technology Issues, Design Issues, Issues of Theory and Research, Economic Issues and Moving Forward. Brief biographical information on each contributor is included at the end of the book.

# About Pfeiffer

Pfeiffer serves the professional development and hands-on resource needs of training and human resource practitioners and gives them products to do their jobs better. We deliver proven ideas and solutions from experts in HR development and HR management, and we offer effective and customizable tools to improve workplace performance. From novice to seasoned professional, Pfeiffer is the source you can trust to make yourself and your organization more successful.

**Essential Knowledge** Pfeiffer produces insightful, practical, and comprehensive materials on topics that matter the most to training and HR professionals. Our Essential Knowledge resources translate the expertise of seasoned professionals into practical, how-to guidance on critical workplace issues and problems. These resources are supported by case studies, worksheets, and job aids and are frequently supplemented with CD-ROMs, websites, and other means of making the content easier to read, understand, and use.

**Essential Tools** Pfeiffer's Essential Tools resources save time and expense by offering proven, ready-to-use materials—including exercises, activities, games, instruments, and assessments—for use during a training or-team-learning event. These resources are frequently offered in looseleaf or CD-ROM format to facilitate copying and customization of the material.

Pfeiffer also recognizes the remarkable power of new technologies in expanding the reach and effectiveness of training. While e-hype has often created whizbang solutions in search of a problem, we are dedicated to bringing convenience and enhancements to proven training solutions. All our e-tools comply with rigorous functionality standards. The most appropriate technology wrapped around essential content yields the perfect solution for today's on-the-go trainers and human resource professionals.

**Pfeiffer** *Essential resources for training and HR professionals*
www.pfeiffer.com

*This book is dedicated to our parents, Bob and Beverly Oringel and Louis Carliner and Jodean Rubin, who instilled in us a love of learning and a desire to use that love to make the world a little better.*

*From Patti: My parents, both gone now, were writers, teachers, and lifelong learners. Bob Oringel wrote audio engineering textbooks and mentored new audio engineers. Beverly Oringel was a high school history teacher whose students kept in contact with her over many, many years. What they taught me influences my career and life every day.*

*From Saul: My father, Louis Carliner, had strong values around education, which are among his best-known lessons to me over forty years after his passing. Although she thought she was starting a second career for herself, in the process of doing so, Jodean Rubin introduced me to the field of training and development, which is where I have made my career.*

*Patti Shank and Saul Carliner*

SAUL CARLINER
AND PATTI SHANK
EDITORS

# THE
# e-Learning
## HANDBOOK

Past Promises,
Present Challenges

**Pfeiffer**
A Wiley Imprint
www.pfeiffer.com

Published by Pfeiffer
An Imprint of Wiley
989 Market Street, San Francisco, CA 94103-1741
www.pfeiffer.com

Limit of Liability/Disclaimer of Warranty: While the publisher and author have used their best efforts in preparing this book, they make no representations or warranties with respect to the accuracy or completeness of the contents of this book and specifically disclaim any implied warranties of merchantability or fitness for a particular purpose. No warranty may be created or extended by sales representatives or written sales materials. The advice and strategies contained herein may not be suitable for your situation. You should consult with a professional where appropriate. Neither the publisher nor author shall be liable for any loss of profit or any other commercial damages, including but not limited to special, incidental, consequential, or other damages.

Readers should be aware that Internet websites offered as citations and/or sources for further information may have changed or disappeared between the time this was written and when it is read.

For additional copies/bulk purchases of this book in the U.S. please contact 800-274-4434.

Pfeiffer books and products are available through most bookstores. To contact Pfeiffer directly call our Customer Care Department within the U.S. at 800-274-4434, outside the U.S. at 317-572-3985, fax 317-572-4002, or visit www.pfeiffer.com.

Pfeiffer also publishes its books in a variety of electronic formats. Some content that appears in print may not be available in electronic books.

Library of Congress Cataloging-in-Publication Data

    The e-learning handbook : past promises, present challenges / Saul Carliner and Patti Shank, editors.
      p.  cm.
    Includes bibliographical references and index.
    ISBN 978-0-7879-7831-0 (cloth)
      1. Computer-assisted instruction.   2. Internet in education.   3. Instructional systems—Design.
  I. Carliner, Saul.  II. Shank, Patti.
  LB1028.5.E165  2008
  371.33'44678—dc22

                                                    2007049557

Acquiring Editor: Matthew Davis
Director of Development: Kathleen Dolan Davies
Developmental Editor: Susan Rachmeler

Production Editor: Dawn Kilgore
Editor: Rebecca Taff
Manufacturing Supervisor: Becky Morgan

Printed in the United States of America
Printing-10-9-8-7-6-5-4-3-2-1

# Contents

# Preface

Toward the end of 2004, I came up with what I thought was a bright idea. For an article I was writing about the state of the industry, I surveyed people considered to be "thought leaders" in this industry. I wanted to see whether my experiences as a practitioner were mirrored by others. I sent a request for opinions and attitudes; I asked respondents to share their thoughts about trends affecting the field, frustrations working in the field, and rays of sunshine we could expect to see in future years. Responses arrived rapidly; I especially appreciated their candor. What was especially rewarding was the level of sharing and conversation among people whose work I admire. I synthesized their thoughts and added my own in an article published in the *eLearning Developers Journal* (Shank, 2004).

In fact, that conversation actually began many years earlier, but I didn't realize it at the time. I had heard of Saul Carliner and very much enjoyed his writing but hadn't met him until about seven years ago at an industry conference. After his presentation, I went up to introduce myself. We shared some laughs about the absurdities of the field and Ph.D. study, and promised to keep in touch.

It's hard to appreciate at the time what influence any conversation will have on the course of your work or life. Saul and I kept in touch and developed a friendship over email, phone conversations, and meetings at industry events. He offered a great deal of heartfelt empathy and good advice while I worked through my Ph.D., a rare and precious gift. And we have since shared views, resources, and strong opinions about everything from stupid practices in the field to the best places to shop (and have even gone shopping together at the Container Store and Target).

Saul included me on emails soliciting input from others whose names I knew but had never met in person. Over time, I got to know some of these people as well by sharing resources and meeting them in person at industry events. One thing led to another and I asked many of them to contribute to the *eLearning Developers Journal* article. And many of them have written chapters for this book.

For the *eLearning Developers Journal* article, Saul questioned the "industryness" of this industry, saying that e-learning was being integrated into education and training and should no longer be seen as separate from it. In his view, this indicated its success, not demise, because the use of technology truly needs to be part of the everyday thought processes of people in the business of building learning. I couldn't agree more. Much silliness (or worse) was done while online learning went from a (lunatic) fringe element to part of the everyday way of thinking about instructional delivery (and unfortunately, much of that silliness still prevails). If we no longer consider use of a technology for learning an either/or proposition, things are moving in the right direction. Instructional technology can, hopefully, be used to augment the whole spectrum of teaching and learning, from putting syllabi and references online to support a classroom-based course to self-contained tutorials on Microsoft Excel. We can have conversations among co-learners (including the instructor) during and in-between "class," and extend learning beyond the classroom, where it can flourish beyond the content, activities, and assessments common to formal learning environments.

Technology needs to support informal learning as well, as this is how the bulk of learning occurs. The goal with informal learning is not to deliver instructional content but to help build competence and means to live our lives. When we see ourselves as builders of content, we too often kill the natural desire to learn. We need to support learning anywhere and everywhere competence is needed to solve life's problems, even where there are no plugs and computers.

Sometime during 2002, Saul and I started talking about co-editing a collection of original essays on the business, technological, design, research, and philosophical issues underlying e-learning. We looked for writers who could provide critical assessments of the industry (or non-industry, as it were) for both academic and corporate e-learning professionals. This book started as a result of these conversations.

Continuing conversations molded the book and the ideas of the people who wrote these chapters and, hopefully, these conversations will initiate other conversations that mold where we are going next. Saul and I both feel this is greatly needed and hope these conversations will lead to changes in our field.

Patti Shank
January, 2008

# Introduction

On one hand, online learning is real, it's happening, and its use is increasing.

On the other hand, online learning isn't being adopted as widely or as quickly as some of the enthusiastic analysts have predicted. Consider the following:

- Actual adoption is significantly slower than predicted. For example, one organization predicted in 1998 that 50 percent of all workplace training would be delivered online by 2003. The actual percentage in 2005 was closer to 15 to 20 percent, depending on the survey.

- Similarly, although online learning has delivered the promised return on investment in industry by eliminating training-related travel costs (according to a 2002 report from IDC), online learning has not offered similar returns to academe. At the institutional level, many online ventures that started to great fanfare in the late 1990s folded or were scaled back by 2002. Examples include the failed NYU Online, Fathom.com—an online venture housed at Columbia University that was a partnership of many schools and cultural institutions—and the scaled-back Unext.com (a company that purchases the online rights to courses from leading business schools).

- Although online learning promised to improve the quality and efficiency of teaching in universities, the actual results have shown something different. Although studies, such as Sitzmann and Wisher (2005) and Bernard, Abrami, Lou, Borokhovski, Wade, Wozney, Wallet, Fiset, and Huang (2004), have demonstrated that online and classroom learning are essentially equally effective, other evidence suggests that instructors find teaching online courses to be more time-consuming than teaching the same course in a traditional classroom, and some economic studies suggest that, because of their labor-intensity, online courses in an academic setting are more costly to teach than classroom courses.

- After the technology vendors promised that better tools and management systems would improve the quality, speed of development, and ease of deployment of online learning, training managers and instructional designers are realizing that the real issues are offline, such as the quality of content, the processes administering online learning, and providing support for online learners. (Perhaps these issues were acknowledged, but the extent of their significance is only now being addressed.) For example, great concern is now being expressed over the quality of the content of online lessons; much of it disappoints learners, sponsors, and instructional designers.

- Although some people believe that standards will solve many problems with online learning, the standards are still a mess in this industry. For example, SCORM-compliant content doesn't always allow people to exchange data as it should. Other standards are ignored, such as the standards for quality content.

- Most fundamentally, many of the learning professionals charged with choosing and implementing technology don't really understand it. As a result, they make expensive mistakes in purchasing and make plans for uses of technology that aren't going to work, such as reusable learning objects.

This edited collection of original essays takes a critical look at economic, technological, instructional design, business, evaluation, research, and philosophical issues underlying e-learning, like those just described. Each chapter is written by an expert in that area and addresses a different issue, such as the struggle to implement standards, the practicalities in implementing learning objects, the business failures of many e-learning start-ups, the high dropout rates in e-learning, and the economic viability of online learning.

## Who Should Read This Book

This book is intended both for the academic community and for experienced professionals.

- The academic community might use it as:
  - A textbook for courses and seminars on distance education, instructional design (such as an advanced instructional design seminar or a seminar on special topics in instructional design), educational leadership, and managing training programs.
  - A research reference.
- Experienced professionals will use this book to inform their long-term strategy regarding e-learning. Specific readers that we have targeted among experienced professionals include:
  - Decision makers about e-learning strategies and technologies, such as chief learning officers, human resources executives, and training managers and
  - Experienced developers of e-learning (people who have developed at least five e-learning programs).

## How This Book Is Organized

This book has sixteen chapters spread among six parts, each of which looks at e-learning from a different perspective. Each chapter is written by an expert in that topic. Our contributors represent both academe and industry. They also represent four continents: Asia, Australia, Europe, and North America.

Some of the authors critically analyze a situation, others analyze and advocate for evolutionary change, and still others analyze the situation and advocate for revolutionary change, such as a major facelift to instructional systems design (the bedrock of most design approaches) and an entirely new approach to research on learning, resulting from a need to change the approach to researching e-learning.

Regardless of approach, each chapter offers the following features:

- A brief opening box describing "About This Chapter," so you can quickly determine whether you are interested in reading further.

- The following features at closing:

  ▪ Concluding thoughts about the topic;

  ▪ A chart summarizing the key points to take away from the discussion in the chapter;

  ▪ Guiding questions for discussion, which are especially intended for people planning to use the content in this book in the classroom; and

  ▪ "Learn More About It," a chart suggesting links, books, papers, reports, and articles where you might find additional information and examples of interest on the topic discussed in the chapter.

The following sections describe the structure of this book in more detail.

## Part I: The Context for e-Learning

This section has one chapter, Chapter 1, Thinking Critically to Move e-Learning Forward, written by co-editor Patti Shank, which explores where we are and where we've been, and why we need to consider these issues before moving forward. Specifically, this chapter introduces the landscape of e-learning today and why it's in a slump. Next, it explores the boom-and-bust cycle of e-learning (previous booms of hype in the mid-1980s and early 1990s), how technology advances rapidly but the design of learning content moves much more slowly (although, with learning objects and shuttleware, some design changes occurred this time around), and introduces some of the debates in the field. Last, it explores what academics and corporate practitioners can learn from each other.

## Part II: The Reality Versus the Hype of e-Learning

This part critically explores the e-learning that was proposed by the proponents of e-learning in its infancy in the late 1990s and the early part of the millennium, and the reality that ultimately resulted. As contributor Margaret Driscoll notes, the difference between the initial hype and the current reality of e-learning is not as black and white as many people suppose. Chapters in this part include:

- Chapter 2, Hype Versus Reality in the Boardroom: Why e-Learning Hasn't Lived Up to Its Initial Projections for Penetrating the Corporate Environment by Margaret Driscoll, which explores the challenges of making e-learning work in the corporate world. Specifically, this chapter contrasts the optimistic predictions of e-learning use and projections of e-learning growth with the reality experienced in the middle of the first decade of the millennium, identifies where e-learning has been successful, and places the reality of e-learning in the workplace in the broader context of long-term change.

- Chapter 3, Hype Versus Reality on the Campus: Why e-Learning Isn't Likely to Replace a Professor Any Time Soon by Brent Wilson and Lee Christopher, which provides a similar exploration of the challenges of making e-learning work in the academic world. Focusing on the role of the professor who is asked to teach online courses, the chapter explores some of the challenges that professors have encountered and, like the previous chapter, places the reality of e-learning on campus into the broader context of long-term change.

- Chapter 4, Knowledge Management: From the Graveyard of Good Ideas, by William Horton, which explores why one of the most promising forms of informal e-learning— knowledge management—has failed to achieve its potential by describing the challenges with technology and project management.

## Part III: Technology Issues

This part explores some of the technical challenges that have affected the growth of e-learning in academic and corporate environments. Chapters in this part include:

- Chapter 5, Infrastructure for Learning: Options for Today or Screw-Ups for Tomorrow, by Patti Shank, L. Wayne Precht, Harvey Singh, Jim Everidge, and Jane Bozarth, which addresses the challenges of preparing an infrastructure for e-learning in organizations. This chapter addresses specifically questions such as: How do needs vary with different phases in the use of e-learning in an organization? What infrastructure is essential? What's nice to have? What challenges should people be aware of, such as obsolete file formats? Is technology for learning likely to merge with similar technologies in other fields, such as a merger of learning content management systems with more widely available content management systems? Last, this chapter considers why technology is so complicated that the industry has had to spawn a sub-industry of people who advise others on how to choose and implement the infrastructure.

- Chapter 6, e-Learning Standards: A Framework for Enabling the Creation and Distribution of High-Quality, Cost-Effective, Web-Delivered Instruction by Pat Brogan, which critically examines standards. After a quick survey of the standards, this chapter explores issues such as the ongoing problems with interoperability—even after products conform to standards, the IMS bite off more than it could chew with the terminology issue, and the realistic prognosis for learning objects. This chapter also addresses issues such as whether these standards protect current e-learning developers from the problems of obsolete file formats that existed before and whether standards really matter to smaller organizations, who aren't developing or purchasing large libraries of e-learning.

- Chapter 7, Learning with Objects by Patrick Parrish, which explores the challenges of reusable learning objects. After describing what learning objects are (so readers have a common definition of the concept as definitions are a challenge in this area), this chapter presents two paradigms for exploring learning objects. From each perspective, the assumptions underlying and ignored by the paradigm and the resulting effect on how learning objects affect work and everyday life. The chapter closes with a brief description of a promising effort to employ learning objects in a professional development context.

- Chapter 8, Web 2.0 and Beyond: The Changing Needs of Learners, New Tools, and Ways to Learn by co-editor Patti Shank, which explores Web 2.0, the emerging generation of software driving the web in general and e-learning in particular. After defining Web 2.0, this chapter explores the changing nature of information and learning, then considers the changing nature of learners (especially those who have grown up with the Internet). Next, it explores the response to these changes by providing an inventory of the software tools that characterize Web 2.0, such as blogs, wikis, "google jockeying," and "mashups." Then the chapter considers how Web 2.0 is creating new ways to learn and closes by considering these changes within the broader context of e-learning.

- Chapter 9, Locked Out: Bridging the Divide Between Training and Information Technology by Marc J. Rosenberg and Steve Foreman, which addresses personnel challenges associated with learning technology, such as: Are training organizations capable of managing new learning technologies in ways that are consistent with corporate Information Technology (IT) requirements? and Are IT organizations capable of responding to the unique requirements that new learning technologies present? Some of the challenges result from the learning staff's limited understanding of the technology; some of the challenges result from the IT organization's lack of understanding of the changing role of the learning staff. This chapter explores these problems and suggests ways to address them.

## Part IV: Design Issues

This part explores some of the design challenges that have arisen as our collective experience with e-learning has expanded. Chapters in this part include:

- Chapter 10, A Holistic Framework of Instructional Design for e-Learning by co-editor Saul Carliner, which argues that ISD is a value system. The author believes that the value system, developed in the 1940s with few major changes since then, no longer reflects the value systems of practicing instructional designers in industry, limits practice, does it address project management for e-learning. But because of its wide recognition and its flexibility in research, perhaps the model can be updated. This chapter then proposes a new model called a framework, because ISD is a methodology, not a model. The framework consists of three parts: design philosophies and theories, general design methodology, and instructional considerations. Among the implications of adopting this framework are a stronger focus on human performance, teaching based on real-world problems, and research that is focused on case studies of real e-learning projects.

- Chapter 11, Converting $e_3$-Learning to $e^3$-Learning: An Alternative Instructional Design Method by M. David Merrill, which illustrates those instructional principles that can help designers avoid *enervative, endless,* or *empty* $e_3$-learning (pronounced e sub-three learning) and replace it with *effective, efficient,* and *engaging* $e^3$-learning (pronounced e to the third power learning). This chapter then describes these first principles of instruction, which include the *activation* principle, the *demonstration* principle, the *application* principle, the *task-centered* principle, and the *integration* principle. This chapter concludes with a brief description of an alternative method for designing more effective, efficient, and enabling e³ instruction.

- Chapter 12, Design with the Learning in Mind by Patricia McGee, which addresses the challenges of providing learners with the support needed to succeed in e-learning courses. Specifically, this chapter addresses the pedagogical, interpersonal, and cognitive supports that can assist online learners. Within each area, this chapter illustrates how strategies, tactics, and organization can be enacted.

## Part V: Issues of Theory and Research

This part explores some of the challenges that arise in transferring learning theory, which has primarily been developed for application in the classroom, to the online environment, as well as issues with the research—including a call for a radically different approach to research on e-learning. Chapters in this part include:

- Chapter 13, Revisiting Learning Theory for e-Learning by Gretchen Lowerison, Roger Côté, Philip C. Abrami, and Marie-Claude Lavoie, which explores the ways that learning theories have had to be adjusted to the realities of teaching online and whether certain popular approaches to learning, such as constructivism, can effectively work in a self-study online environment.

- Chapter 14, Design Research: A Better Approach to Improving Online Learning by Thomas C. Reeves, Jan Herrington, and Ron Oliver, which explores what should happen with research in online learning in the light of several major meta-analyses that have essentially concluded that "no significant differences" exist between distance and classroom instruction, the authors add that "It hardly needs saying that the largely pseudoscientific research studies reviewed for these meta-analyses fail to provide practitioners with much-needed guidance for improving the design and use of online learning." In this chapter, the authors propose a different approach to research called design research, which (1) addresses pressing complex problems in real contexts in close collaboration with practitioners; (2) integrates known and hypothetical design principles with technological affordances to render plausible solutions to these real-world problems; and (3) involves conducting cycles of rigorous and reflective inquiry to test and refine innovative learning environments as well as to define new design principles. This chapter explores what design research is, provides a rationale for it, presents strategies for conducting it, and suggests ways to overcome challenges to design research.

## Part VI: Economic Issues and Moving Forward

This part explores some of the economic issues that have affected the growth of e-learning in academic and corporate environments, as well as predictions for the future of e-learning. Chapters in this part include:

- Chapter 15, Is e-Learning Economically Viable? by Patrick Lambe, which explores how the evaluation of e-learning and its economic impact have evolved over the past several years from simplistic ROI considerations to metrics that are closely aligned to a business strategy, and thereby can be justified and tracked over time. Specifically, this chapter explores the following topics over a range of different applications of e-learning: why investments in training and e-learning are not equivalent; the need for infrastructure investments in e-learning; and a variety of economic benefits to e-learning, including productivity and quality improvement, a market requirement, access to new markets, a means of leveraging human capital, and a means of reducing business risk.

- Chapter 16, e-Learning: Today's Challenge, Tomorrow's Reality by co-editor Saul Carliner, which explores ways that organizations are currently using e-learning in academic and workplace contexts and, given the issues raised in this book, how e-learning might make a difference in the future.

# References

Bernard, R.M., Abrami, P.C., Lou, Y., Borokhovski, E., Wade, A., Wozney, L., Wallet, P.A., Fiset, M., & Huang, B. (2004). How does distance education compare to classroom instruction? A meta-analysis of the empirical literature. *Review of Educational Research, 74*(3), 379–439.

Sitzmann, T.M., & Wisher, R. (2005). The effectiveness of web-based training compared to classroom instruction: A meta-analysis. In *Proceedings at the ASTD Research-to-Practice Conference-Within-a-Conference.* Alexandria, VA: ASTD Press.

# Part I

# The Context for e-Learning

This section has one chapter, Chapter 1, Thinking Critically to Move e-Learning Forward, written by co-editor Patti Shank, which explores where we are, where we've been, and why we need to consider these issues before moving forward. Specifically, this chapter introduces the landscape of e-learning today and why there's still so much controversy about it. Next, it explores the boom and bust cycle of e-learning (previous booms of hype occurred in the mid-1980s and early 1990s), how technology advances rapidly but the design of learning content moves much more slowly, and introduces some of the debates in the field. Last, it explores what academics and corporate practitioners of e-learning can learn from one another.

# Chapter 1

# Thinking Critically to Move e-Learning Forward

*Patti Shank,*
*Learning Peaks, LLC*

**About This Chapter**

This chapter answers the question: "Why should people think critically about e-learning?" Education, in general, and e-learning, in particular, suffer from a strong case of hyperbole. Strong claims are made that are neither rooted in solid research nor borne out by practice. Consider, for example, the unrealistic projections for growth in e-learning. Growth of e-learning in the workplace, universities, or schools has not met the unrealistic projections of the dot-com era. Executives and administrators do not understand learning or e-learning and, as a result, many have made poor purchases of e-learning infrastructure and applications and have been prey for less-than-scrupulous vendors. Because of close relationships between vendors and the press, the trade press has not always been as forthcoming as it could be about the claims made by e-learning vendors. Most significantly, many e-learning implementations in universities and workplaces have failed to meet expectations.

Yet, e-learning has certainly enjoyed some success as well. Students taking online courses from universities, especially non-traditional students (those who do not live on campus and who typically have family or work responsibilities) appreciate the fact that online courses and degree programs allow them to reap the benefits of higher education.

In both universities and workplaces, use of e-learning grows, even if slower than original projections. e-Learning has found significant success in particular niches, such as e-portfolios in schools, course management systems in universities, and blended learning in workplaces. e-Learning has moved past the initial hype. During this period, realistic and sustainable uses of e-learning are being realized. Each chapter in this book explores lessons learned as e-learning moves past the hype to integration into the daily fabric of teaching and learning in all kinds of settings.

# The Bad News

Education in general, and e-learning in particular, suffer from a strong case of hyperbole. Strong claims are made that are neither rooted in solid research nor borne out by practice. Consider, for example, the unrealistic projections for growth in e-learning. According to one estimate made in 2000, 53 percent of all corporate learning would be online by 2003. Studies conducted since then suggest that actual adoption is proceeding more slowly—only representing 10 to 20 percent of all corporate learning (Dolazelek, 2004; Sugrue & Rivera, 2005). In the university sector, once touted as a strong candidate for e-learning, high-profile launches of e-university efforts, like Columbia University's FATHOM and New York University's NYU Online, met equally high-profile crashes soon after the dot-bomb in 2001–2002.

Studies indicating satisfaction with e-learning applications are similarly suspect. For example, participants may be hand-selected by vendors, so the opinions of extremely dissatisfied customers are not likely to be included. Even claims about the effectiveness of online teaching are overly exaggerated and lack an understanding about how people learn. Consider, for example, claims by some proponents of e-learning that it is significantly more effective. Several meta-analyses of comparisons between e-learning and classroom learning have concluded that media and technologies make little difference in learning outcomes (Bernard, Abrami, Lou, Borokhovski, Wade, Wozney, Wallet, Fiset, & Huang, 2004; Russell, 2005).

Many people don't understand basic definitions or key concepts of e-learning. For example, according to an annual study of training directors, only about one-third feel comfortable describing terms like knowledge management, learning content management systems, and performance technology to people outside of the training function (Carliner, Groshens, Chapman, & Gery, 2005). Yet these people must secure the funding needed to implement e-learning in an organization.

Vendors of e-learning applications and development services have preyed on this naïvete. Some vendors push a one-size-fits-all approach to take advantage of clients' lack of understanding. Sometimes, they promote false or insignificant distinctions in technology to differentiate themselves from their competitors or use phrases like "SCORM-compliant" without explaining the underlying "gotchas." For example, one vendor claimed to be the only vendor of "true" e-learning because its software ran on the client PC while its competitors' primarily ran on the server. To most users, the distinction is non-existent. Another hyped its unique directory structure that wasn't really all that unique; any vendor could offer it but, as a result of customer requests, most chose not to (Carliner, 2003).

Seeking to entice readers in an era during which people are desperately searching for the "next big thing" to follow the admittedly watershed emergence of the Internet, our trade press has only magnified the problem, publishing ideas of dubious value and articles of similarly dubious research. For example, the concept of workflow-based training is essentially a repackaging of a 1990s-era concept, electronic performance support systems (EPSS) with an admittedly clearer name (Gery, 1991), but none of the first articles about workflow-based training cited Gery's watershed book on electronic performance support systems, giving the false impression that a derivative concept was actually original. More seriously, because they are a significant source of advertising dollars, the trade press has been reluctant to take on vendors, even when customers complain about the technology, service, and integrity of their vendors.

On a practical level, this failure to think critically and to publish and act without performing due diligence (also known as research) has proven to be dangerous.

How dangerous? You decide. Some clients want quick answers. The vice president of training for a Fortune 100 corporation called a consultant asking for a recommendation of an authoring tool and was dismayed when the consultant advised him that she needed more information before doing so. The vice president replied that he would ask someone else who would give him what he wants. Executives like him are finding consultants to give them easy answers, but the results are troubling. For example, one engineering firm chose a rapid e-learning solution—one in which they could develop a brief lecture in PowerPoint, record narration, and make the recording available through a learning management system. The system ensured on-demand training that the staff could develop at a low cost and short lead times. But after a year and a half and the development of fifty-four courses, only 194 course completions had been recorded. (That is, each course had been viewed, on average, slightly less than four times.)

Universities and schools face similar challenges. For example, one private university launched an e-degree just before the Internet boom. But when the university staff wanted to update the software a couple of years later to match current industry standards, they could not do so. The administration gave the contract for hosting and tracking the courses to a public relations firm, whose president served on the university's board of directors. Similarly, schools feel challenged to integrate technology into the classroom, but it's only partially integrated. Part of the problem may lie in schools' insistence on using traditional models of professional development to introduce teachers to the technology. These models often require weeks of training during the summer or two days of training during the school year, and ongoing support throughout the school year. Perhaps school systems need to borrow ideas from the workplace like just-in-time and build in ongoing support, because isolated workshops, no matter how long, are unlikely to impact teaching habits in any meaningful way.

Clients may want an online learning strategy that simplifies moving content online and tracking learners, but if they are looking for *really* reduced training costs and effective learning, many are setting themselves up for disappointment. Consider, for example, one study that found that, rather than reduce costs, online courses at universities are actually about $100 (Canadian) more expensive to offer per student than classroom courses (Qayyum, n.d.). Although e-learning courses do not require traditional classrooms and buildings, they are often more resource intensive to produce and deliver because of the need for instructional designers, media developers, course management system administrators, infrastructure and other technology, and increased hand-holding provided for new online students.

The workplace has faced similarly disappointing outcomes. Vendors and executives hear the right word—effectiveness—but get the concept wrong. As one blogger observed:

> (T)he canned-learning supply chain is easy to manage and control, which is more important than any ultimate impact on business performance. After all, we are judged on measurable results, so we shoot for measurable goals. And that learning supply chain, with which we are now all so comfortable, is just loaded with measurability—especially now that we have an LMS to automate the work for us. (Parkin, 2005)

Delivering instructional content online (or elsewhere) is insufficient to produce learning or usable skills. Desirable outcomes require far more effort than building instructional content.

Learning professionals have bought into simplistic half-truths that are easy to digest but lead to less-than-satisfying outcomes. In fact, when training professionals primarily from countries in the European Union (EU) were surveyed about their views of the quality of e-learning based on usability, design, content, and interactivity (Massey, 2002), more than half felt the quality of existing e-learning was poor or fair. Only 6 percent rated it as very good or excellent. Similarly, according to another study, about 75 percent of workplace implementations of e-learning have proven less than satisfying (Van Buren & Sloman, 2003). We believe that the results are similar in university and school environments.

## The Good News

If Van Buren and Sloman found that 75 percent of all workplace implementations of e-learning have proven disappointing, they also found that 25 percent were satisfying. Despite strong evidence that the average, everyday implementation of e-learning has fallen short of expectations, evidence also exists that some e-learning has been successful, although often different than predicted in the claims in the initial hype.

Consider adoption. Although adoption has not grown as rapidly as predicted, it has grown—and at rates that most business people would call respectable. Even during the economic downfall of 2001 through 2004 that caused a two-year drop in spending on corporate training (Dolezalek, 2004), and significant drops in public funding for education in the United States, e-learning spending and usage grew.

In the higher-education sector, the Sloan Consortium (2004) reports growth of online enrollments in higher-education courses at greater than 20 percent. Furthermore, the Sloan Consortium found that students are as satisfied with online courses as they are with classroom-based courses and the learning outcomes are equivalent, matching results from other studies showing that media and technologies are not the preeminent factors impacting instructional outcomes. In the corporate sector, the International

Data Corporation (2004) predicted a 30 percent increase in yearly corporate e-learning spending worldwide through 2008, with the market growing from $7 billion in 2005 to over $15 billion in 2008. As the study noted, the press focuses on the high profile failures, not the everyday successes.

Similarly, rather than focusing on whether online or classroom instruction is more effective, successful implementations have focused on *how* to make the most effective use of online technologies. Technologies have affordances, characteristics that can be exploited, to enhance teaching and learning, especially when used well and with adequate consideration (Ryder & Wilson, 1996). These affordances can support learning, allow connections to people and objects that are not in learners' immediate physical environment, and provide opportunities that are not easily available otherwise (Harasim, Hiltz, Teles, & Turnoff, 1996; Ryder & Wilson, 1996).

In corporate training, a Canadian report (corroborated by a private U.S. study) found that organizations have the most success with e-learning in certain subject areas, such as software and technical training (Bloom, 2003). e-Learning seems to be most successful— in terms of completions—with content that is either required or that is linked to an external incentive, such as certification.

Similarly, rather than replace the classroom, e-learning has supplemented the classroom in many learning environments. In schools, tools like electronic portfolios (Abrami & Barrett, 2005) have the potential to provide students with significantly higher levels of feedback on projects as well as help them learn how to accurately self-assess their learning and skills. Course management systems (CMS) have become *de rigeur* in most colleges and universities. Instructors use these systems to post syllabi, assignments, and lecture notes, as well as carry on discussions with students between class sessions. In the workplace, rather than designing learning programs that are exclusively online, many organizations have adopted a blended approach to learning, in which parts of the instruction occur online and the rest occurs in the classroom (Rossett, Douglis, & Frazee, 2003). Proving similarly popular are virtual classrooms, which provide for live instruction without the travel (Hoffmann, 2003).

# The Real News

e-Learning didn't replace classroom learning and does not seem poised to do so now. Lured by lower potential costs, executives in the workplace and administrators in universities and schools were not aware that e-learning takes, on average, 5.5 times the amount of development as classroom courses and, in university environments, requires more effort to teach because of the need for individual help, handling student frustrations, and assisting students with course technologies.

Despite satisfaction with online programs, students in online higher education courses are often uncomfortable using online learning communication tools such as discussion forums. Commonly reported problems include confusion about how to use the technologies and the learning curve imposed by them (Cartwright, 2000), reservations about putting their thoughts in print, and worry about perceptions by others and lack of visual cues (The Centre for Systems Science, 1994; Shank, 2002).

As a profession, we approached e-learning with much anticipation but too little analysis. Zemsky and Massy (2004) set out to find out how the reality of e-learning differed from the original assumptions about e-learning on higher education campuses and found that original assumptions were based on the mistaken notions of early adopters. Many institutions needed to make a commitment to improving educational quality and service when they invested in e-learning, but instead chose to invest solely in the software and hardware. The best outcomes from instruction, whether delivered online or not, come from good instructional practices and processes that support skills beyond the classroom.

As we see pockets of success—and strong success, like the use of course management systems in colleges and universities and blended learning in the workplace—we also see e-learning maturing from its youthful euphoria to a more reasoned discipline. Perhaps Gartner's (2005) Hype Cycle describes this trend. It explains how new technologies move from introduction to productivity phases, and provides a helpful way to think of the changes we are seeing in this field. When most technologies are introduced, they pass through a phase of inflated expectations, or hype. When expectations prove to be unfounded, an inevitable disillusionment follows. At the depths of this disappointment, the real possibilities for using the technology emerge. We've definitely passed through the hype stage into disillusionment. So perhaps, we can more easily and realistically consider the possibilities for e-learning, ones that can be sustained in a large number of environments.

That's the goal of this book—to initiate deep conversations about e-learning and propose real, do-able, and sustainable uses of e-learning that are valuable to all stakeholders.

Even without the hype, new technologies are adopted in stages. In the first, people use the new technology to do old things. In terms of e-learning, this meant automating record keeping and teaching rote courses. But people eventually realize that the new technology offers more promise than automating old tasks; they provide a new way of working. And we're starting to see that now. Online technologies let learners keep electronic portfolios that not only serve as an electronic archive, but as a source of feedback, and competency tracking and job-seeking tools. Learning management systems can track significant information about competencies and recommend career development strategies, assist with candidate selection, and perform similar tasks. In terms of teaching, online learning can blend with classroom learning in a variety of ways. We're also discovering informal learning—learning that challenges some of our very notions about objectives and evaluation (Driscoll & Carliner, 2005).

In other words, having moved past the hype, we can now really consider using e-learning in transformative ways. Doing so requires an honest assessment of what we have done and how it has fared, as well as realistic assessments of what we could do with e-learning, but have not yet done successfully.

Saul and I believe that the future of learning is inextricably tied to the use of technology for learning. We also believe that, rather than considering the use of technologies alone, we must consider their use within the broader context of learners, instructors (in whatever setting they find themselves), learning environments, and society. Technology is only important insofar as it supports these. And, in my opinion, we have not yet begun to harness the potential of online technologies for learning.

Our contributors share this belief, but each expresses it in his or her unique way, from his or her unique vantage. This book a conversation among these colleagues. So let's begin the conversation.

# References

Abrami, P., & Barrett, H. (2005). Directions for research and development on electronic portfolios. *Canadian Journal of Learning and Technology, 31*(3).

Bernard, R.M., Abrami, P.C., Lou, Y., Borokhovski, E., Wade, A., Wozney, L., Wallet, P.A., Fiset, M., & Huang, B. (2004). How does distance education compare with classroom instruction? A meta-analysis of the empirical literature. *Review of Educational Research, 74*(3), 379–439.

Bloom, M. (2003.) *e-Learning in Canada: Findings from a 2003 e-survey.* Ottawa, ON: Conference Board of Canada.

Carliner, S. (2003). Ethics and the marketing of technology for training and performance improvement: A commentary. *Performance Improvement Quarterly, 16*(4), 94–106.

Carliner, S., Groshens, J., Chapman, B., & Gery, G. (2005, May 23). Strategic trends: An analysis of 6 years of the *Training Director's Forum* survey. *Training Director's Forum.*

Cartwright, J. (2000). Lessons learned: Using asynchronous computer-mediated conferencing to facilitate group discussion. *Journal of Nursing Education, 39*(2), 87-90.

The Centre for Systems Science. (1994, September). Trouble in paradise. *Centre for Systems Science Update Newsletter, 6*(3). Simon Fraser University, Burnaby, BC.

Dolezalek, H. (2004). Industry report 2004. *Training, 39*(9), 21–36.

Driscoll, M., & Carliner, S. (2005.) *Advanced web-based training: Adapting real-world strategies in your online learning.* San Francisco, CA: Pfeiffer.

Gartner. (2005, August 5). *Gartner's hype cycle special report for 2005.* Retrieved from: www.gartner.com/DisplayDocument? ref= g_search&id=484424

Gery, G. (1991). *Electronic performance support systems.* Toland, MA: Gery Performance Press.

Harasim, L.M., Hiltz, S.R., Teles, L., & Turnoff, M. (1996). *Learning networks: A field guide to teaching and learning online.* Cambridge, MA: MIT Press.

Hoffman, J. (2003). *The synchronous trainer's survival guide.* San Francisco, CA: Jossey-Bass.

International Data Corporation (IDC). (2004, November). *Worldwide and U.S. corporate elearning 2004–2008 forecast: Behind the scenes with elearning, a business enabler.* Author.

Massey, J. (2002). *Quality and elearning in Europe.* Retrieved from: www.elearningage.co.uk/go1.htm

Parkin, G. (2005, March 18). *New paradigms for learning.* Retrieved from: http://parkinslot.blogspot.com/2005/03/new-paradigms-for-learning.html

Qayyum, A. (n.d.). Comparing apples and apple computers: Issues in costing e-learning and face-to-face teaching. Unpublished manuscript.

Rossett, A., Douglis, F., & Frazee, R.V. (2003). Strategies for building blended learning. *Learning Circuits, 4*(7).

Russell, T.L. (2005). *No significant difference.* www.nosignificant difference.org.

Ryder, M., & Wilson, B.G. (1996, February 14-18). *Affordances and constraints of the internet for learning and instruction.* Paper presented at Association for Educational Communications Technology (AECT).

Shank, P. (2002). Learning anew: An exploratory study about new online learners' perceptions of people interaction and learning to learn in an online course. In P. Barker & S. Rebelsky (Eds.), *Proceedings of educational multimedia, hypermedia & telecommunications (EDMEDIA)* (pp. 2167-2171). Charlottesville, VA: Association for the Advancement of Computing in Education (AACE).

Shank, P. (2004, December 6). An end-of-year-conversation with e-learning leaders. . . What's on their minds these days? *The eLearning Developers Journal.* Retrieved from: www.learningpeaks .com/pshank_Guild_endofyear2004.pdf

Sloan Consortium (Sloan-C). (2004). *Entering the mainstream: The quality and extent of online education in the United States, 2003 and 2004.* Retrieved from: www.sloan-c.org/resources/survey.asp

Sugrue, B., & Rivera, R. (2005). *2005 ASTD state of the industry report.* Alexandria, VA: American Society for Training and Development.

Van Buren, M.E., & Sloman, M. (2003). *e-Learning's learning curve: Will they come, will they learn?* American Society for Training and Development International Conference and Exposition. San Diego, California, May 18, 2003.

Zemsky, R., & Massy, W.F. (2004, June). *Thwarted innovation: What happened to e-learning and why.* Learning Alliance at the University of Pennsylvania. Retrieved from: www.irhe.upenn.edu/Docs/ Jun2004/ThwartedInnovation.pdf.

# Part II

# The Reality Versus the Hype of e-Learning

In this part of the book, we critically explore the e-learning that was proposed by the proponents of e-learning in its infancy in the late 1990s and the early part of the millennium and the reality that ultimately resulted. As contributor Margaret Driscoll notes, the difference between the initial hype and the current reality of e-learning is not as black and white as many people suppose. Chapters in this part include:

- Chapter 2, Hype Versus Reality in the Boardroom: Why e-Learning Hasn't Lived Up to Its Initial Projections for Penetrating the Corporate Environment by Margaret Driscoll, explores the challenges of making e-learning work in the corporate world. Specifically, this chapter contrasts the optimistic predictions of e-learning use and projections of e-learning growth with the reality experienced in the middle of the first decade of the millennium, identifies where e-learning has been successful, and places the reality of e-learning in the workplace in the broader context of long-term change.

- Chapter 3, Hype Versus Reality on Campus: Why e-Learning Isn't Likely to Replace a Professor Any Time Soon by Brent G. Wilson and Lee Christopher, provides a similar exploration of the challenges of making e-learning work in the academic world. Focusing on the role of the professor who is asked to teach online courses, the chapter explores some of the challenges that professors have encountered and, like the previous chapter, places the reality of e-learning on campus into the broader context of long-term change.

- Chapter 4, Knowledge Management: From the Graveyard of Good Ideas by William Horton, explores why one of the most promising forms of informal e-learning—knowledge management—has failed to achieve its potential by describing the challenges with technology and project management.

# Chapter 2

# Hype Versus Reality in the Boardroom

## Why e-Learning Hasn't Lived Up to Its Initial Projections for Penetrating the Corporate Environment

*Margaret Driscoll, IBM Global Services*

## About This Chapter

This chapter examines the question, "Why hasn't e-learning lived up to its initial projections for penetrating the corporate environment?" What might surprise you is that the answer is not as black and white as it might appear.

The literature provides an abundance of financial, organizational, and andragogical explanations for e-learning not developing as predicted but these explanations do not tell the whole story. A more insightful answer requires that we look at the original model that industry proposed for e-learning and what it promised; that we reconcile the optimistic forecasts for penetration of e-learning with actual usage; and finally that we examine how learning using the Internet is evolving. Without taking the long view and understanding the big picture, training

professionals are at risk of not seeing the dramatic changes
in the profession. And most important, training professionals
might just miss how the web and Internet are penetrating the
corporate environment.

# Introduction

During the dot-com boom, e-learning had something to offer
everyone and everyone needed to act to take advantage of this new
technology. The promise of e-learning was grand and thought leaders championed this vision everywhere from the COMDEX trade
show which, until the late 1990s, was the leading trade show in
the computer industry, to investment seminars. Countless articles
enumerated the advantages of this technology, and analyst reports
forecast double-digit year-over-year growth.

One needs to understand what was initially promised and projected for e-learning before answering the question, "Why hasn't
e-learning lived up to its initial projections for penetrating the corporate environment?" A review of the promises made in the late 1990s
seems laughable now, but at one time these promises served as the
data on which organizations made decisions to adopt e-learning
and on which well-known investors made optimistic predictions
(and investments). Time and experience have demonstrated that the
adoption of e-learning has been slower than forecast, and reviews
from learners have been less than enthusiastic (Islam, 2002).

This chapter specifically explores the question, "Why hasn't
e-learning lived up to its initial projections for penetrating the
corporate environment?" It first revisits the promises made about
e-learning during the dot-com era when broad-based business
audiences—including those outside of the learning function—
began taking notice of e-learning. It continues by describing the
bandwagon of corporate executives, industry analysts, and learning executives who promoted e-learning, and the irrational exuberance that ensued. Next, this chapter offers an initial explanation for
the failure of e-learning to achieve its intended promise, based on

an analysis of reports from the trade press. The chapter closes by offering another explanation, which suggests that perhaps the initial definitions and projections were flawed, and that, when we let go of our initial expectations, the state of e-learning now might be more encouraging than many believe.

# The Promise

In the late 1990s and early part of this decade, e-learning advocates lauded a number of benefits of the technology. Some focused on the business benefits, like Shelley Robbins. Writing slightly after the dot-com era, she offers an archetype description of what e-learning promised to deliver to organizations during what she calls the "fourth stage of evolution" (Robbins, 2002). She explains how the concept of e-learning evolved from simply putting a course online to using the Internet to orchestrate all learning with the adoption of a learning content management system (LCMS).

> These systems (LCMS) are designed to enable subject-matter experts, with little technology expertise, to design, create, deliver, and measure the results of e-learning courses rapidly. LCMS applications fundamentally change the value economics of e-learning content delivery by offering organizations a scalable platform to deliver proprietary knowledge to individual learners without bearing a prohibitive cost burden. (Robbins, 2002)

Under such a scenario, the primary beneficiaries were sponsoring organizations, who could achieve a competitive advantage through the creation and rapid delivery of proprietary knowledge. Organizations could reduce costs by eliminating class-related travel expenses as well as the costs of disseminating training materials. Under this scenario, e-learning would provide cost-effective, just-in-time, personalized learning at the desktop. Robbins was not alone; others including Hall (2000), Walker (2002), and Rochester (2002) were among the many promoting this view.

Rubenstein (2003) describes a different set of advantages, which primarily benefit learners:

> If you're well versed in e-learning, you can identify the three promises of e-learning or distance education (1) to deliver instructionally sound learning programs to mass audiences at a fraction of the cost of traditional learning systems; (2) to empower learners to take more control over their learning experiences; and (3) to provide learning opportunities for wider audiences who have varied learning styles and require more flexible schedules. (2003, p. 38)

With its promised potential to displace traditional classroom-based learning, John Chambers, then CEO of Cisco, declared e-learning as "the next killer application" for the Internet in the late 1990s and investors rushed to understand and invest in it. Reports from market analysts supported the assumption that e-learning would be rapidly adopted and widely used. International Data Corporation (IDC) provided the most widely quoted growth statistics, forecasting in 1999 that the global corporate e-learning market would grow from $US 3.4 billion in 2000, to $6.4 billion in 2001, and $US 23 billion by 2004—a compounded annual growth rate of 69 percent. Although the specific numbers differed, other analysts predicted similar meteoric growth. For example, investment firm Merrill Lynch estimated the e-learning market would grow from $US 3.5 billion in 2001 to "more than $25 billion in 2003" (Eklund, 2001). In the 2000 report, *The Emerging eLearning Industry,* SRI predicted that the corporate e-learning market would exceed $US 20 billion by 2005 (Trondsen, Edmonds, Teirgre, & Vickery, 2000).

Along with these predictions, experts predicted a similarly dramatic decline in the role of classroom learning in corporate training. In 2000, The Corporate University Xchange predicted that e-learning would account for 40 percent of corporate training by 2003, classroom learning filling most of the other 60 percent (W.R. Hambrecht + Co, 2000). The Gartner Group offered a more aggressive forecast, saying that "In 2003, traditional classroom training will represent less than 30 percent of all formal corporate training programs" (American Council on Education, n.d.).

Combine a persuasive, high-tech vision for learning and promises of exceptional cost savings with aggressive forecasts for market growth for e-learning and a similarly dramatic prediction of decline for classroom learning, and one can understand the irrational exuberance for e-learning at the height of the dot-com boom.

# The Bandwagon of Irrational Exuberance

Not surprisingly, then, when Cisco CEO John Chambers declared e-learning to be the next killer application on the Internet, he added, "It's so big, it's going to make e-mail look like a rounding error" (Friedman, 1999, A25). Believing that online training would become as commonplace as e-mail, forward-thinking training professionals rushed to pilot and adopt e-learning to avoid being left behind and computer-phobic classroom instructors feared for their jobs. They were supported by high-profile corporate executives, industry analysts, and executives in the field of learning.

Corporate executives were drawn to the promise of e-learning as a result of promises that "e-learning will prove to be an avenue for businesses to realize efficiencies needed to ultimately increase shareholder value" (Close, Humphreys, & Ruttenbur, 2000, p. 4). The value web, which posits that "as more and more products and services depend on the exchange of knowledge and information, knowledge and intangibles become mediums of exchange or currencies in their own right" (Allee, 2000, p. 41), started with the idea that an organization's greatest assets were its employees. In the knowledge economy, employees faced the rapid obsolesce of knowledge and the constant need for retraining. This problem was compounded by the "war for talent" (Michaels, Handfield-Jones, & Axelrod, 2001). HR professionals were challenged to deal with the shortage of skilled workers and the need to keep their current employees skilled. Pundits suggested that e-learning be considered as the weapon of choice in the talent war (Elkington, 2002; Ellis, 2002). Using e-learning, organizations could enhance the skills of their existing work forces rather than trying to hire new and expensive talent. Other options for addressing this skills shortage included Internet recruiting, stock options, and better recognition programs.

Corporate executives were not alone in their enthusiasm for e-learning. Hype and overstatement surrounding e-learning were characteristic of investment analysts, software vendors, service providers, and thought leaders during the dot-com boom. The seminal work that demonstrated over-stating the reach and potential of e-learning in all market segments was Michael T. Moe's, *The Web of Knowledge* (2000). This research report from Merrill-Lynch had something for everyone. Moe put institutions of higher education on notice that they would be competing for students with global corporations. These commercial institutions of higher education could leverage a market niche for learning. Moe explains, "The lack of convenient education options translates into an opportunity for innovative proprietary post secondary institutions that can provide a 'no nonsense,' 'customer-oriented,' efficient education model that is convenient, accessible, and relevant in today's world" (2000, p. 171).

Likewise, Moe put corporations on notice regarding the importance of e-learning:

> Where the resources of the physically based economy were coal, oil and steel, the resources of the new, knowledge-based economy are brainpower and effectively acquiring, delivering, and processing information. Those who are effectively educated and trained will be the ones who will be able to survive economically and thrive in our global, knowledge-based economy. Those who don't will be rendered economically obsolete. (Moe & Blodget, 2000, p. 35)

Everyone was getting in on the e-learning act. In addition to corporate thought leaders and investment analysts, training professionals were in the limelight. The covers and lead stories in glossy professional journals and business magazines featured training directors such as Tom Kelly of Cisco (Galagan, 2001) and Bill Wiggenhorn of Motorola (Wiggenhorn, 2000). Vendors used their advertising to make celebrities of those who adopted e-learning. One of the most notable campaigns was that of Centra Software, which featured full-page photos of training managers from well-known companies such as Wyndham hotels (Centra, 2001), AT&T (Centra, 2001), and Prudential Financial (Centra, 2001).

Practitioners too new in the field to remember, or otherwise not caught up in the e-learning hype at the time, are cautioned to put this phenomenon in context. e-Learning was a technology that promised to change the industry and it enjoyed broad support, as organizations were caught up in the broader web bubble. The Internet promised to transform every aspect of business, from supply chains to customer support, and from meetings to marketing and sales. Why not learning? Furthermore, the pundits of the day warned that organizations that ignored e-learning did so at their own peril.

Having this historic perspective on e-learning is essential because these assumptions, forecasts, and hype are often used as the yardstick against which success is measured. Given assumptions about e-learning replacing traditional classroom instruction and forecasts for widespread adoption, it is not surprising to find explanations that focus on obvious failures.

## An Initial Attempt to Explain Why the Promise Was Not Kept

Noticeably absent from all of the presentations of e-learning at this time are reports of failure. Re-reading white papers, re-scanning magazines, and re-analyzing tradeshow materials from the late 1990s and early 2000 provide ample examples of hype and promise. Noticeably absent at this time are stories about organizations that experienced failures, problems, and disappointments in implementing e-learning. There are no poster children for failures in e-learning. In contrast to success stories of early adopters and innovators, no publication showed pictures or told stories of the other—often more common—side of the story: the hundreds of e-learning courseware titles that went unused, the internal battles between IT and training, and the purchases of expensive learning management software that went un- or under-utilized.

Instead, the stories were shared privately, in informal conversations over coffee or lunch among colleagues in different divisions of the same organizations and different organizations.

The stories started being published as soon as the high-tech bubble burst. Ever emphasizing the positive, the trade press in the field couched failure in positive terms, using euphemisms such as "lessons learned," "pitfalls to avoid," "strategies for success," and "challenges." A review of the literature provides an amusing approach to cataloging failure; it appears that numbered lists are the preferred taxonomy, with catchy titles like "In eLearning No One Hears You Scream! 101 Pitfalls of eLearning" (Click2Learn, 2004), "8 Lessons About e-Learning from 5 Organizations" (Gold, 2003), and "Preventing e-Learning Failures: Ten Pitfalls and How to Avoid Them" (Weaver, 2002). The articles are based on anecdotal information, opinion pieces, and a few case studies in which names of the organizations affected have been withheld (presumably to avoid admitting failure in a field that only highlighted success).

In fact, if one reads the literature carefully, many failures are reported. In fact, twenty-one documents, including articles, white papers, and analyst reports written between 2000 and 2004, provided over two hundred pitfalls, lessons, and cautions. These articles offer no universal advice; the problems in each case seem to be unique, even though the people writing believe that the lessons apply more broadly than to a single organization. The diverse pieces of advice include "pay as you go" when investing in courseware libraries or "use a balanced scorecard to evaluate your program's success."

Although these reports of failure offer no common piece of advice, the advice that is offered falls into four key themes:

- Organizational barriers, in which an organization did not properly prepare for or support its e-learning effort

- Pedagogical problems, in which the e-learning programs did not achieve the intended results

- Technical problems, in which the technology selected did not address the real needs or resulted in some other unanticipated difficulty

- Financial problems, in which the e-learning project was under-funded and, therefore, could not produce the anticipated gains

The following paragraphs explore each of these themes in more detail.

*Organizational barriers* were the most frequently cited category of pitfalls. Five themes emerged from this category: (1) lack of cultural readiness; (2) failure to market the program; (3) poor alignment of goals; (4) absence of management support; and (5) failure to set expectations. The most frequently mentioned reasons for failure were related to the organization lacking the culture necessary to implement e-learning. Practitioners were advised to improve cultural fit by assessing learners' readiness and not assuming "build it and they will come." Failure to create market demand for e-learning programs was the second most frequently cited organizational problem. Failure to get management support for e-learning and the lack of alignment of e-learning programs to the primary business goals of the enterprise were a close third and fourth. The last organizational theme was a caution to set expectations, that is, not to oversell what e-learning could do.

*Pedagogical problems* were the second most frequently mentioned reason for failure. This category may have been larger if the analysis had included articles more narrowly focused on reasons for individual e-learning course failures. Two pedagogical themes emerged: (1) failure to focus on the learner and (2) the inadequacy of using e-learning as a stand-alone instructional methodology.

*Technology problems* were the third category of reasons that e-learning did not succeed as anticipated. The issues in this category seemed less rich than might be expected. Three themes emerged from the analysis: (1) get IT involved; (2) plan for integration; and

(3) the fixation on technology for technology's sake, rather than as a means of promoting and strengthening learning.

*Financial problems* was the last category of reasons that e-learning did not succeed as anticipated. It was the least mentioned category of issues. The only theme that emerged in this category was under-estimating the cost of e-learning programs. Although many organizations were drawn to e-learning to reduce learning costs, most did not realize that the savings in e-learning occurs in delivery with the elimination of class-related travel, but that development is significantly more time-consuming and, therefore, more costly than classroom courses covering the same content.

Probably the most positive way of approaching failure is to identify factors for increasing the likelihood of success of an e-learning implementation and the most comprehensive taxonomy of success factors for an e-learning implementation was compiled by SRI Business Consulting Intelligence (Edmonds, 2004). In a research report, SRI offers forty best practices in e-learning in four key areas: strategy, organization and process, content, and infrastructure. The report suggests that "companies need to have these right in order to create successful learning programs" (2004, p. 1).

## Another Explanation of the Situation

Given the growing body of literature that hints at and actively describes e-learning failures, as well as the general malaise of training professionals toward e-learning, one might conclude that e-learning has been a failure. Indeed, e-learning has been a failure if failure is defined by the current market size versus the market size projected earlier in the e-learning cycle. This section first explores some of the numbers associated with e-learning, including the mismatch between the projected and realized size of the market for e-learning and its market penetration, and the downward trend in spending on training since 2001. Then, it looks beyond the numbers to offer an alternate explanation of why e-learning today does not look like the situation that had been predicted in the late 1990s and first years of this decade.

## The Projected and Actual Size of the e-Learning Market

Consider the projected and actual size of the market in 2003. Merill Lynch had predicted that the market would reach $US 25 billion by 2003; a 1999 forecast by IDC predicted that e-learning would reach $US 23 billion by 2004. In contrast, an *Information Week* article in 2003 cited an IDC report estimating that the then-current size of the e-learning market was $US 6.5 billion (McGee, 2004).

Not only did e-learning fail to live up to its financial projections, but it did not live up to projections of its market share for total learning. Projections during the height of the dot-com era projected that e-learning would account for 40 to 70 percent of all formal training and traditional classroom training would account for just 30 to 60 percent. But classroom training has consistently remained at 70 percent of all training during this period. Table 2.1 shows the percentage of training that has been provided through different media between 1999 and 2004.

As the table shows, the classroom is as popular as ever in training. What appears to be changing is the use of other media, such as on-the-job training and self-study programs using books, manuals,

**Table 2.1. The Use of Different Media for Delivering Training, 1999–2004**

|  | Instructor-Led (Classroom) | Instructor-Led (from a Remote Location) | By Computer (No Instructor) | Other |
|---|---|---|---|---|
| 1999 | 73 | na | 14 | 13 |
| 2000 | 73 | 6 | 13 | 9 |
| 2001 | 77 | 5 | 11 | 7 |
| 2002 | 74 | 7 | 12 | 7 |
| 2003 | 69 | 10 | 16 | 5 |
| 2004 | 70 | 8 | 17 | 5 |

*Training* Magazine's Annual Industry Reports (1999–2004)

and videos. A Lifelong Learning Market Report from May of 2005 focusing on the role of e-learning places e-learning at less than 10 percent of the total corporate training market (Simba Information, 2005). This figure is higher than the average 3 to 4 percent reported in *Training* magazine's twenty-third annual industry report (Dolezalek, 2004). Similarly, training on the computer has not grown significantly during this time, although it accounted for a slightly larger percentage of total training expense in 2004 than it did in 1999.

Perhaps one reason that spending on e-learning and its market penetrations did not meet projections is that overall spending on training has dipped over for the past several years. Table 2.2 shows the overall spending on training in the United States since 1999. As shown in the table, since 2001, total spending has declined. In 2004, training organizations in the United States spent 10 percent less on formal training than they did in 2001, despite a rebounding economy. The decline in spending on formal training is worth noting because the investment level in training during 2004 was comparable to the investment levels in training during the mid-1990s. In other words, although classroom training still accounts for approximately 70 percent of all training, that 70 percent is a piece of a shrinking pie.

**Table 2.2. Total Dollars Budgeted for Formal Training**

| Year | Total Budget |
|------|--------------|
| 1999 | $54.0B |
| 2000 | $54.0B |
| 2001 | $56.8B |
| 2002 | $54.2B |
| 2003 | $51.3B |
| 2004 | $51.4B |

*Training* Magazine's Annual Industry Reports (1999–2004).

Keeping total spending down is a movement toward outsourcing and out-tasking, which are measures that organizations take to reduce total costs. Outsourcing is the process of shifting, delegating, and transferring an entire service or function normally done in-house to third-party service providers. Out-tasking is the process of taking isolated job activities that are not part of the core competencies of an organization and assigning them to contractors and third-party service providers. One particularly popular task to out-task is the management and support of learning technology. Meister (2003) notes that large corporations and government agencies have opted to outsource either their entire learning and education function or significant parts of it to third-party firms. Bersin (2005) found that "the area of huge growth is the outsourcing of training technology." In the study, 47 percent of companies surveyed use hosted LMS services, and 70 percent used hosted services for other learning technologies, such as virtual classroom, content management or collaboration.

## Looking Beyond the Numbers to Explain the Current State of e-Learning

In these numbers on overall spending on training and outsourcing lie alternate explanations for the failure of e-learning to live up to the initial projections than those suggested by the earlier review of the literature.

Rather than the organizational barriers, pedagogical problems, technical problems, and financial problems stated earlier, perhaps the failure of e-learning to live up to its initial projections can be explained by a confluence of three factors:

- A poor initial pedagogical model of e-learning

- Ambiguous distinctions between e-learning technology and productivity technology

- Increasingly blurred lines between learning and working

Although it is easy to identify these as distinct factors, they are all closely aligned and, therefore, should not be considered in isolation from one another. The next several paragraphs explore each of these factors in more detail.

Consider the poor initial pedagogical model of e-learning, based heavily on a behavioral paradigm in which online courses were little more than online workbooks. Their focus on tracking, scoring, and sequencing courses and reducing the number of learners who dropped out are all artifacts of formal learning. Course designers translated techniques and expectations of the brick and mortar classroom into e-learning functions. Even live virtual classroom programs relied on metaphors drawn from brick and mortar classrooms, such as hand-raising, giving learners permission to write on the white board, and sending learners to virtual breakout rooms.

Likewise, content was sold using the metaphor of a library. Content libraries promised the electronic equivalent of shelves full of books, available at the user's electronic fingertips. Although not particularly effective at using the medium or engaging learners, the features of this early pedagogical model were familiar and, therefore, useful when selling e-learning programs to managers who did not have educational backgrounds, were skeptical about learning online, and who needed to quickly understand the value proposition before approving a purchase order or project.

This pedagogical model quickly showed cracks. In a 2002 article on the shortcomings of e-learning, Forrester Research noted that "70 percent of those who start an e-learning course never complete it" (Islam, 2002, p. 23). Many of the courses that learners failed to complete were part of large libraries of courseware, which organizations licensed from major e-learning providers.

Unfortunately, many organizations purchased multi-year licenses for these libraries, and they were stuck. In these instances, an organization would purchase a license that assumed that most or all of their workers would take a large number of courses in a given year. Despite vendors' attempts to demonstrate that these libraries provided a return on investment, the numbers that vendors provided on actual usage told the real story: rather than large numbers of learners taking and completing a large number of courses, only a few learners started a limited number of courses, and only a small fraction of these learners completed those courses. A real comparison of the total cost of such a library on a per-user basis showed that the cost was actually much higher than the vendor promised. Vendors responded by changing the pricing model. Rather than a large licensing fee, organizations were charged only for what they used, called a pay-as-you-go system. But this new pricing model only fixed the cost issue, not the root cause: poorly designed courses that did not encourage people to take or complete them.

Proof of the weakness of the pedagogical model for e-learning model is demonstrated in *Training* magazine's 2004 annual industry survey. For ten categories of training, including topics such as communication skills, customer service, executive development, and technical skills, e-learning was a stand-alone delivery method for only 4 percent of the training. Organizations rely on traditional or blended learning for the majority of training in these areas.

A second, more technically messy alternative reason for the failure of e-learning arises from the definition of the term, e-learning. e-Learning has become a catch phrase that can mean different things to different people and, unfortunately, two people might use the term and mean different things. The challenge of categorizing different technologies and determining what constitutes e-learning can be seen in a survey by Ellis (2004), in which she tried to explain the contradictory definitions and a proliferation of technologies:

> Workplace learning professionals seem to be more clearly defining e-learning in relation to an actual learning experience. They're using such terms as *web conferencing, virtual classrooms, simulations, m-learning,* and so on—rather than infrastructure and authoring systems, such as LMSs and LMCSs, which were mentioned in previous years.

Similarly, in their Annual Industry and State of the Industry reports, *Training* magazine and ASTD, respectively, continually redefine their definitions of technology-based learning to keep pace with the latest technologies and terminology. Indeed, in the mid- to late-1990s, the problem was multiple terms for the e-learning concept—such as computer-based training, technology-based learning, computer-assisted instruction, and online learning—rather than one catch-all term that encompasses everything (Carliner, 2004).

In addition to not having clear definitions about what constitutes e-learning, the lines between applications intended for learning and other uses have eroded. In addition to using traditional e-learning applications like authoring tools, learning content management systems, and learning management systems, organizations are using more generally available communication media such as web conferences, instant messaging, mobile devices, video conferencing, blogs, online documents, application sharing, databases, knowledge management tools, and email for training. These technologies are used as stand-alone substitutes for traditional e-learning software, as well as to complement other training efforts. When users encounter technologies in e-learning that they encounter in any other use of their computer, they—and we—have difficulty defining the difference between learning and communication, as well as knowledge management, performance support, and reference use.

One practical implication of this technology overlap is that, when an organization deploys a technology like running web meetings, sharing sales data in knowledge bases, and tracking inventory on hand-held devices for regular business needs, the training group can tag along and extend the use of these technologies. A common example of this is the use of web-conferencing technology that is purchased for conducting e-meetings and is then commandeered and used for live virtual classrooms. In other cases mobile devices used to track sales or inventory are also being used to download and deliver training and performance support tools. As a result of this overlapping usage, organizations may be using e-learning or using the web and Internet to deliver training, but that content might not be viewed or tracked as formal learning. As the Internet has blurred the lines between working and other aspects of life, so it has blurred the lines between work and learning.

The idea of learning while one works is not new. A frequently cited study (Dobbs, 2000) substantiated what other studies found: 70 percent of what people know about their jobs, they learn informally from the people they work with.

This raises the third alternate explanation for why e-learning has not measured up to predications. Workplace technologies such as email, cell phones, databases, online reference works, application sharing, web conferencing, and instant messaging, to name just a few, are generating new ways to tap expertise and learn on the job, ways that the pundits did not anticipate when predicting the future of e-learning in 1998 to 2001.

One significant issue is that technology supports informal learning and that, in turn, is changing how people learn and how training professionals need to define learning. Informal learning refers to learning in which learners determine for themselves their own objectives, how they will be achieved, and when they have successfully achieved them (Driscoll & Carliner, 2005).

The use of technology to support informal learning was put forth in a manifesto on workflow learning by Cross and O'Driscoll (2005), where they describe a future scenario that may be closer than we think:

> We are . . . accustomed to production workers who have job descriptions and follow a script. Future workers will be value-driven because there is no script. Everything will be improvised. Learning will be fused into work, delivered in small fragments ("right size"), or whatever device tethers them to the Internet ("right device" and "right place") just when they need it ("right time"). In other words, we will have what we call workflow learning. (p. 32)

Recognition of informal Internet-based learning can also be seen in the definition of *learning on demand* (Vona & Granelli, 2005), which "shifts the [learning] experience from a single discrete event into a process that is embedded into the daily workflow" (p. 46). Vona and Granelli note that such learning often happens through a portal, a home page that provides users with access to all of the information they need about a particular topic, such as their jobs. They emphasize the role of portals in promoting informal learning, as well as applications such as chat rooms and message boards, immediate access to information (online reference or knowledge management) and access to mentors and experts (by email, instant messaging, and VoIP) in facilitating the learning experience. What distinguishes these views is that learning is embedded in the flow of everyday work tasks and that it is supported by both technology and people, rather than a solitary event, as promoted by the original pedagogical model of e-learning described earlier.

These three alternate explanations suggest not only the disappointing message that e-learning did not evolve as predicted, but the more affirming one that e-learning has, indeed, penetrated the corporate environment, but in ways that the pundits did not predict. Based on these, one might even conclude that the early models were badly flawed, but e-learning has been wildly successful.

Unfortunately, few studies indicate how much learning has shifted to informal "workflow learning" or "on-demand learning." But signposts exist. One of the best places to find them is the Pew Internet and American Life Project, which provides a longitudinal perspective. The 2001 report indicates that:

- 53 percent of adult Internet users have gone online to do research for school or job training.

- On any given day 8 percent of adult Internet users are online doing research for school or job training.

- 52 percent of adult Internet users have done job-related research online.

- On a typical day, 16 percent of Internet users are online doing job-related research. (Raines, 2005b)

More recent surveys show that informal learning through the Internet continues to grow:

> In 2004 Pew Internet and American Life surveys reveal that more than four in ten online Americans instant

message (IM). That reflects about fifty-three million American adults who use instant messaging programs. About eleven million of them IM at work and they are becoming fond of its capacity to encourage productivity and interoffice cooperation. (Lenhart, 2004)

Two surveys by the Pew Internet and American Life Project established new contours for the blogosphere: eight million American adults say they have created blogs; blog readership jumped 58 percent in 2004 and now stands at 27 percent of Internet users; 5 percent of Internet users say they use RSS aggregators or XML readers to get the news and other information delivered from blogs and content-rich websites as it is posted online; and 12 percent of Internet users have posted comments or other material on blogs. (Raines, 2005a)

The actual ways that organizations have used e-learning—both formally and informally—as contrasted with the ways predicted at the beginning of the e-learning boom in 1999 to 2001 should prove interesting to all e-learning professionals. On the most basic level, those who ignored e-learning altogether as a passing fad need to see the larger picture. Those who are skilled in developing formal e-learning programs based on a classic paradigm will find a shrinking niche for their skills. Similarly, those who followed the predictions without critically analyzing them and thinking about the practical reality of their implementation have also found themselves dealing with expensive miscalculations. The truth is, since the emergence of the current wave of e-learning in the late 1990s, spending on training has declined and e-learning has not gained traction in the ways predicted.

But it has gained traction in other ways, ways that are almost universally not tracked by the training industry and, often, implemented outside of our control. In other words, the real issue is not that e-learning did not live up to its initial projections but, rather, that e-learning has penetrated the corporate environment, but that it is not clear what role training professionals play in the actual implementations of e-learning.

# Concluding Thoughts

e-Learning did not have the 67 percent compound annual growth rate predicted by IDC in 1999, and it does not account for the 40 to 70 percent of formal workplace learning that was once predicted. Such hype and hard sell regarding what e-learning would look like, how it would be consumed, who would be producing it, and how learners would engage with it were all way off the mark.

The problem appears to be that the learning model that got our attention was flawed. And now, our profession is spending far too much time giving advice about how to fix the formal learning page-turner rather than focusing on informal learning, where the real growth and adoption of learning seem to be taking place.

Rather than trying to perfect formal e-learning skills or propping up formal e-learning with blending, simulators, or personalization, learning professionals' time might be better spent exploring and experimenting with informal and other types of learning at the intersection of the web, Internet, and mobile devices, where forms of knowledge management, performance support, and communication are developing.

The problem is that these areas have evolved with little or no involvement of learning professionals, so no well-defined role for trainers exists in them. It is tempting to want to hold onto the initial vision of e-learning with clear roles for training developers, managers, and facilitators. There is an effort to rein in these messy models by defining them as learning on demand; embedded learning; and workflow learning. The goal of defining and clarifying these fuzzy gray areas is to find a role for trainers. The issue may be that the model is not going to lend itself to high-value-added roles for training professionals.

The truth is, learning on demand and workflow learning may do to trainers what self-service elevators did to elevator operators—render us obsolete. Most implementations have been accomplished with little involvement of learning professionals. As David Merrill suggests in his chapter and Saul Carliner mentions in the closing chapter, rather than eliminate our roles, these new forms of learning might result in new roles for learning professionals, some of which are more challenging than those we currently have, others which place us in even more of a supportive role than we currently have.

One thing is certain: with declining spending on training and the increasing significance of learning materials developed without us, trainers need to revisit our role in these environments and, if we are to play a meaningful role in promoting workplace learning, need to follow learning in its new directions and seek opportunities closer to where the learning is taking place, such as in the line of business and in the development of applications and processes.

# References

Allee, V. (2000, July/August). Reconfiguring the value network. *Journal of Business Strategy, 21*(4), 36–41.

American Council on Education (n.d.). *For the record: Facts and figures in adult learning.* www.acenet.edu/AM/Template.cfm? [Retrieved March 13, 2007.]

Bersin, J, (2005). Business outsourcing: Pros & cons. *Chief Learning Officer, 4*(4), 34–45.

Carliner, S. (2004). *An overview of online learning* (2nd ed.) Amherst, MA: HRD Press.

Centra. (2001). Redefining learning and collaboration: Centra. *Training, 38*(12), 1.

Centra. (2001). Software the redefines eLearning and collaboration. *Training, 38*(5), 2.

Centra. (2001). We choose Centra. *Training, 38*(5), 2.

Click2Learn (2004). In *eLearning no one hears you scream! 101 pitfalls of e-learning.*www.elearningalliance.org/uploads/attachments/101_Pitfalls_of_eLearning.doc [Retrieved June 20, 2005.]

Close, R.C., Humphreys, R., & Ruttenbur, B.W. (2000, March). *e-Learning & knowledge technology: Technology & the internet are changing the way we learn.* Nashville, TN: SunTrust Equitable Securities Privatization Research Group.

Cross, J., & O'Driscoll, T. (2005). Workflow learning gets real. *Training, 42*(2), 30–35.

Dobbs, K. (2000). Simple moments of learning. *Training, 35*(1), 52–58.

Dolezalek, H. (2004). Industry report 2004. *Training, 39*(9), 21–36.

Driscoll, M., & Carliner, S. (2005). *Advanced web-based training: Adapting real world strategies in your online learning.* San Francisco, CA: Pfeiffer.

Edmonds, R. (2004). *Best practices in e-learning.* Menlo Park, CA: SRI Business Consulting Intelligence.

Elkington, J. (2002, November/December). Education and training through e-learning and the implications for defense. *Australian Defense Force Journal, 157,* 5–22.

Eklund, B. (2001, January 26). e-Learning takes off. *Red Herring.*www.cnnfn.com/2001/01/26/redherring/herring_elearning/. [Retrieved June 21, 2005.]

Ellis, J. (2002). *Engagement economy—part 1.* www.conspectus.com/2002/january/article15.asp. [Retrieved June 16, 2005.]

Ellis, R. (2004). *Learning Circuits'* e-learning trends 2004. *Learning Circuits, 4*(10). www.learningcircuits.org/2004/nov2004/LC_Trends_2004.htm [Retrieved November 9, 2004.]

Friedman, T.L. (1999, November 17). Next, it's education. *New York Times,* p. A25.

Galagan, P.A. (2001). The Cisco e-learning story. *Training & Development, 55*(2), 46.

Gold, M. (2003). 8 lessons about e-learning from 5 organizations. *Training & Development, 57*(8), 54–57.

Gomersal, C. (2004). Getting ahead of the learning curve. forum. nomi.med.navy.mil/wb/default.asp?action=12&BoardID=3&fid=32&read=448&Reply=676&...- 50k - Supplemental Result - [Retrieved March 13, 2007].

Hall, B. (2000). e-Learning building competitive advantage through people and technology. Online Forbes.com, Special

Advertising Section. www.forbes.com/specialsections/elearning/. [Retrieved May 29, 2005.]

International Data Corporation (1999). *Worldwide corporate e-learning market forecast and analysis 1999–2004.* Framingham, MA: International Data Corporation.

Islam, K. (2002, May). Is e-learning floundering? Identifying shortcomings and preparing for success. *Elearning Magazine, 3*(5), 23–26.

Lenhart, A. (2004). How Americans use instant messaging: Pew Internet and American Life Project. www.pewinternet.org/PPF/r/133/report_display.asp [Retrieved November 9, 2004.]

McGee, M.K. (2004, November 9). e-Learning predicted to recover—again. *Information Week.* Available online http://informationweek.com/story/showArticle.jhtml?articleID=52600125. [Retrieved November 9, 2004.]

Meister, J. (2003). Outsourcing enterprise learning. *Chief Learning Officer, 2*(9), 23–26.

Michaels, E., Handfield-Jones, H., & Axelrod B. (2001). *The war for talent.* Cambridge, MA: Harvard University Press.

Moe, M.T., Bailey, K., & Lau, R. (1999). *The book of knowledge: Investing in the growing education and training industry.* San Francisco, CA: Merrill Lynch, Global Securities Research and Economic Group and Global Fundamental Equity Research Department.

Raines, L. (2005a). The state of blogging. Pew Internet and American Life Project. www.pewinternet.org/PPF/r/144/report_display.asp [Retrieved March 13, 2007.]

Raines, L. (2005b). The internet and education: Findings of the Pew Internet and American Life Project. www.pewtrusts.com/pubs/pubs_item.cfm?content_item_id=729&content_type_id=8&page=p1 [Retrieved March 14, 2007.]

Robbins, S.R. (2002, April). *The evolution of the learning content management system.* www.learningcircuits.org/2002/apr2002/robbins.html [Retrieved September 2007.]

Rochester, J.B. (2002). e-Learning as a strategic corporate asset. *2002 Resource Guide, a supplement to the December issue of DM*

*Review.* www.dmreview.com/editorial/dmreview/print_action. cfm?articleId=4403 [Retrieved June 16, 2005.]

SIMBA Information. (2005). Leading e-learning vendors to generate $437.6M this year. *Lifelong Learning Market Report, 10*(10), 1–4.

Trondsen, E., Edmonds, R., Teirgre, G.Y., & Vickery, K. (2000). *The emerging eLearning industry.* Menlo Park, CA: SRI Consulting Business Intelligence.

Vona, M.K., & Granelli P. (2005). Portals: Enabling on-demand education. *Chief Learning Officer, 4*(4), 46–50.

Walker, L. (2002, March). e-Learning—Just-in-time. *The WriteEdge.* www.writeedge.com/articles/E-learning.asp. [Retrieved June 17, 2004.]

Weaver, P. (2002). Preventing e-learning failures: Ten pitfalls and how to avoid them. *Training & Development, 56*(8), 45–48.

WR Hambrecht + Co. (2000). *Corporate e-learning: Exploring a new frontier.* http://www.astd.org/NR/rdonlyres/E2CF5659-B67B-4D96-9D85-BFAC308D0E28/0/hambrecht.pdf [Retrieved March 13, 2007]

◆ ◆ ◆

## Summary of Main Points

Readers should take away the following main ideas from this chapter:

- During the dot-com era, corporate executives, industry analysts, and learning executives predicted the end of the classroom, that e-learning would become a $US 20-plus million business by 2003, and that e-learning would represent as much as 60 percent of all corporate learning. That did not happen.

- One explanation, based on a review of articles in the trade press, suggests that the problems were caused by:

    - Organizational barriers, in which an organization did not properly prepare for or support its e-learning effort

- Pedagogical problems, in which the e-learning programs did not achieve the intended results
- Technical problems, in which the technology selected did not address the real needs or resulted in some other unanticipated difficulty
- Financial problems, in which the e-learning project was under-funded and, therefore, could not produce the anticipated gains
- An alternate explanation is that:
  - e-Learning began with a poor initial pedagogical model of e-learning, based on a behaviorist and page-turning approach to learning. The reality is that e-learning is becoming integrated into portals and work flows, even though it is not necessarily labeled as e-learning.
  - Ambiguous distinctions between e-learning technology and productivity technology, and many technologies intended for general use in an organization—such as web conferencing, email, databases, and blogs—are actually used to promote learning.
  - The lines are increasingly blurred between learning and working, and many aspects of learning that occur online are not being measured as such.

◆ ◆ ◆

# Guiding Questions for Discussion

- Why did trainers believe that e-learning was going to become the dominant form of training by now? Why didn't that happen?
- Define the following terms and provide an example of each of them:
  - e-Learning
  - Learning on demand
  - Workflow learning

- Do you use the web for informal learning? How?

- What roles *do* trainers play in implementing informal learning in the workplace, such as workflow learning, embedded learning, and learning on demand? How does that contrast with the roles that trainers would like to play?

- What are the future skills needed by trainers?

- Is there a right balance among e-learning, workflow learning, and traditional classroom based learning?

- Where is learning using the web and Internet taking place in your organization? What lines of business sponsor that learning?

| Learn More About It | |
| --- | --- |
| Links | *Chief Learning Officer* magazine (www.clomedia.com/) |
| | Pew Internet and American Life Project (www.pewinternet.org/) |
| | First Monday (www.firstmonday.org/) |
| | Learning Circuits (www.learningcircuits.org/) |
| | e-Learning Centre (www.e-learningcentre.co.uk/) |
| Books, Papers, Reports, and Articles | Edmonds, R. (2004). *Best practices in e-learning.* Menlo Park: CA: SRI Business Consulting Intelligence. |
| | Cross, J., & O'Driscoll, T. (2005). Workflow learning gets real. *Training, 42*(2), 30–35. |

# Chapter 3

# Hype Versus Reality on Campus

Why e-Learning Isn't Likely to Replace a Professor Any Time Soon

*Brent G. Wilson, University of Colorado at Denver and Health Sciences Center, and Lee Christopher, Arapahoe Community College*

## About This Chapter

This chapter answers the question, "Why hasn't e-learning lived up to the initial anticipations for higher education?"

Perhaps one reason is that colleges and universities find themselves in the middle of a number of raging storms, from outcomes accountability to funding crises to academic freedom to encroaching commercial threats to academic independence. From a critical perspective, the middle of the storm is a tough place to judge the wind's ferocity and direction. From a practical perspective, the growth of online programs is not the most critical problem facing educators. All the same, e-learning continues to create headaches for administrators and anxious moments for faculty members (Kieman, 2005). In this chapter we survey the landscape of e-learning in higher education, noting many challenges and barriers that cumulatively lead many professors to resist the movement. It is that perspective of the professor that we highlight. As they commit to teaching online courses, faculty need assurances of concrete gains for their students, their programs, and their careers—in short, that their efforts will be rewarded. At the same time, the role of the instructor continues to be essential, particularly the need for a clearly projected sense of the teacher in online teaching environments. We conclude with a cautious optimism with no firm basis in fact or experience, but rather arising from the sense that challenges and problems have a way of becoming opportunities in the eyes of creative people—and that creative people is something that e-learning seems to attract in spades.

## Introduction

Imagine you are a new college student, signed up for a writing course required of all freshmen. You walk into the classroom and all you see on the blackboard is a list of assignments you must complete by the next class period with instructions to put the finished assignments in your teacher's mailbox at school. You leave the classroom, do the work, and leave it in your teacher's mailbox. You come back to class the following week and once again on the blackboard is a list of assignments to complete along with your grade for last week's work. This cycle continues throughout the semester. When completing the course evaluation, under what you "didn't like," no doubt you would respond, "The teacher wasn't ever there!"

This is one of the things that can happen in an online class—the teacher is never there. Or more commonly perhaps, this is a fear that many faculty members have—that they won't *be there* like they are for their regular classes. And that distance or invisibility takes away what teachers like about their jobs—being there with students, looking them in the eye, meeting their needs by presenting the best available intro to a subject, guiding their learning.

But faculty members have other fears about teaching online, particularly about the time and attention e-learning demands, both in developing courses and in teaching at all hours of the day. In this chapter we review some of the complications and obstacles that can arise as college faculty consider teaching online. These are not excuses for non-participation; rather, acknowledging and addressing these issues become important steps toward ensuring positive experiences teaching online and building successful e-learning programs. Specifically, this chapter first identifies faculty's concerns about the commitment to e-learning. Then it explores three of these concerns in-depth: (1) meeting students' core needs, (2) maintaining a sense of teaching presence, and (3) additional concerns affecting the implementation of e-learning in higher education. This chapter closes on an optimistic note with a discussion of ways faculty can make and sustain the commitment to e-learning.

## Faculty Concerns About the e-Learning Commitment

The public tends to see the work of faculty in higher education in terms of hours in the classroom. In contrast, the faculty themselves feel demands on their time coming from a variety of directions—research, teaching, administration, and service of various kinds. Increasingly, tenured faculty supervise the work of non-tenured and part-time faculty, ensuring quality teaching, student satisfaction, and expected learning outcomes (Berg, 2002). And just as today's faculty rely less on secretarial support than a previous generation of faculty, so also they take on more administrative types of work, such as curriculum planning, course and schedule planning, community liaison, recruiting, and promotion. Through these activities, rank-and-file faculty are routinely called on to keep programs strong and well-running.

Now add to this growing workload a new request, to develop and teach one or more courses for online delivery or, more substantially, supervise the development and implementation of a new online program (Beaudoin, 2002; Marcus, 2004). In the business of higher education, faculty members are entrepreneurial centers of activity, involved in activities such as running programs, competing for research grants and students, and managing outreach programs. Although those faculty in educational technology and similar programs have a natural interest in online courses and programs, faculty in other parts of the academy typically do not see the payoff. This payoff of e-learning needs to be apparent or it will be squeezed out of faculty priorities by other demands and opportunities (Dunlap, 2005).

Given this background, it's not surprising that time and resource concerns tend to be foremost on the minds of faculty when they consider teaching online (DiBiase, 2004). Lack of time, preparation, skills, resources—all the deficiencies we expect to confront—are legitimate concerns and potential obstacles to faculty participation (Lifter, Kruger, Okun, Tabol, Poklop, & Shismanian, 2005). A survey by the U.S. National Education Association (NEA), conducted in 2000, reported that the top concern among faculty about distance education is that they will do more work for the same amount of money (Howell, Williams, & Lindsay, 2003). While some schools compensate faculty for teaching online through release time, stipends, or both, many do not. Although time and resources top the list of concerns, a number of other barriers and obstacles exist, according to a lengthy list of concerns reported in a literature review by Maguire (2005). Two key obstacles include:

- Meeting students' core needs—things they expect and need from their higher-education experience

- Maintaining a sense of teaching presence and personal satisfaction from e-learning participation

Both of these obstacles relate to a professor's role with respect to distance education, in planning and design as well as in teaching the course. The next two sections explore these two obstacles. The section that follows identifies other issues that affect implementation of e-learning in higher education. See the section on Faculty Concerns with Distance Education at the end of this chapter for a full list of barriers and obstacles to faculty adoption of e-learning.

## Meeting Students' Core Needs

Online or face-to-face, students' needs remain fairly constant as they begin an undergraduate education:

- Hoop-jumping for academic and career credentials
- Developing a sense of belonging within the university by creating social connections with peers and instructors
- Receiving guidance, feedback, and support toward expertise
- Facing fair and thorough assessments
- Completing professional and practical induction into a community of practice

We faculty are prone to neglect some of these core needs and the activities that support them. For example, an evening class on campus may go for three hours with a fifteen-minute break in the middle. The *break time* can be more important than lecture time. And working in groups on projects can help students feel a part of an emerging community of practice, a relationship that may continue into their working careers. Many aspects of e-learning are intended to address student needs, such as distance education and online learning and course management systems. Its success in addressing core student needs, however, has varied.

Distance education in general, and online education in particular, arose in direct response to student needs for convenient access to programs (Larreamendy-Joerns & Leinhardt, 2006). In addition to providing convenience, online programs must address the core needs of undergraduate students, including developing academic and practical expertise and credentials and inducting them into new lives as productive workers. And whether face-to-face or online, students benefit from belonging to a peer group, from networking and mutual support within that group, as academic knowledge is developed and transferred into real-life working conditions outside of the school setting (Wilson, Ludwig-Hardman, Thornam, & Dunlap, 2004).

To aid in course development and administration, course management systems (CMSs) such as Blackboard, eCollege, and Moodle have arisen. These tools are popular, even for primarily residential courses, because they let instructors supplement classroom courses with electronic resources. An instructor can place a course syllabus online, along with visuals, assignments, and similar resources. In addition, instructors can administer tests online. And they can do so without learning HTML or how to use an authoring tool.

Many administrators falsely believe that a widely used course management system means that the institution is effectively using e-learning. It is not. As a resource for distance education, critics find course management systems to be seriously lacking. They are typically based on stereotyped notions of course needs and functions—units and lessons, assigned readings and discussions, exams and quizzes. The design of the software encourages instruction that is reading-intensive and for which the primary means of interaction is email and a discussion board. Some critics have called course management systems "e-learning lite" because their templated formats tend to mimic traditional instruction. Innovative pedagogy or imaginative learning activities that maximize online possibilities are not emphasized. Indeed, they are usually not feasible directly in the course management systems. Instead, course designers often must prepare innovative instruction sequences outside of the system (using tools like Dreamweaver and Flash) and link to them in these course management systems.

Instructors and course designers must draw on a variety of tools and strategies to meet students' core learning needs. Course management systems are helpful but need to be supplemented by external resources, both custom developed and publicly available on the web. Well-designed course materials, however, can lead to satisfactory levels of connection with the instructor and among students—a form of learning community achieved at the course level (Wilson, Ludwig-Hardman, Thornam, & Dunlap, 2004). We have found the best assurances for faculty are experiencing online courses for themselves. By trying them out, faculty can then see what's possible online and begin to work within the realm of the possible in meeting their students' needs.

## Maintaining a Sense of Teaching Presence

Instructors are essential to achieving students' core needs. Instructors are important, not strictly in terms of guidance and feedback, but also in terms of role identification and modeling. Not surprisingly, for many faculty members contemplating teaching online, establishing a continuing sense of presence and online connection with students is a concern. Here are some ways to cultivate a stronger sense of teacher presence for online environments (see also Farmer, 2004, for a discussion of open-learning resources):

- To introduce yourself to students, create a short two- to five-minute digital story. This provides students with a direct, personal sense of you as their instructor, including what motivates you and how you think about the content. An example of an instructor's use of a digital story is our colleague Joni Dunlap, who tells about her young daughter, her preparation for tenure, and how she acquired a passion for problem-based learning and related instructional strategies as an undergraduate business major (visit www .augustcouncil.com/~jdunlap/movie).

- Do personalized introductions all around, and ask students to include both photos and bios in their introductory material. Personal information and photos removes the anonymity that is typical of the online learning experience. Additional icebreakers add to the experience, such as asking students to post six truths and a lie and asking other students to guess the lie (see Iverson, 2005).

- Post a weekly announcement addressing the entire class. It might tell them what you have seen in their assignments or what's coming up this particular week. You might even ask students about some current event, like "Are you going to watch the SuperBowl this weekend and, if so, who are you pulling for?" This can be another chance to show some of your humor and humanity, and create a less anonymous learning experience.

- Create short audio files of announcements as an occasional alternative to text. Students can hear your voice, which reminds them that you're a real person.

- Send an email message to students that individually addresses their work in some way. Some e-learning instructors use a tickler system to send out individual notes to students on a regular basis. The ultimate goal is to interact with students in a way that recognizes them as individuals and makes them aware that you're aware of their learning.

- Selectively participate in the online discussions of your course in discussion boards, blogs, or wikis. Strategic insertion of posts into these online discussions reminds students that you are there and engaged in their conversation.

- Have real-time office hours using the chat tool or telephone. Alternatively, keep an office discussion area where students can post questions and get answers (from classmates as well as from you).

The key issue for ensuring the presence of the instructor is communication. In the traditional classroom, teachers talk to communicate. Online, teachers typically use the written word to communicate. Selective use of strategies like those above helps convey a level of human connection that deepens the sense of presence or felt connection between teacher and students leading, in turn, to greater possibilities for role identification, modeling, and learner engagement. And when teachers can offer a clear voice online, students are more likely to develop a voice of their own (de Montes, Oran, & Willis, 2002).

## Additional Concerns Affecting the Implementation of e-Learning in Higher Education

In addition to these core teaching concerns, many other issues affect whether instructors in higher education will embrace or resist e-learning in their teaching. One core set of issues pertains to ownership and control of course content.

The copyrights to e-learning developed by instructional designers and subject-matter experts are almost always owned by the organization that commissioned the work. These are called "works for hire."

Some universities may try to establish a work-for-hire relationship with instructors. More commonly, though, copyrights to courses developed by university instructors for use in academic settings are at least co-owned by the instructors who develop them. This is part of a larger academic concept called "academic freedom," which allows instructors to teach courses as their expertise suggests.

The challenge arises when university instructors develop e-courses. Because a university invests in the technology and often provides instructional designers to assist instructors in developing courses, the institution would like to own the copyrights to these courses. Yet, according to most agreements, the content itself belongs to the instructors. Complicating the matter further is the fact that some universities have set up their e-learning units as separate businesses, sometimes for-profit ones. Academic units are typically not-for-profit.

The bottom line is that universities often need to negotiate separate agreements with instructors on ownership of the copyrights to e-courses. Some universities have successfully negotiated such agreements; others have not. The existence of a satisfactory agreement, however, may affect whether instructors choose to teach e-courses and how much energy they put into their efforts.

# Making and Sustaining the e-Learning Commitment

We grant that not every professor is cut out to teach online. But a lot of faculty aren't all that effective in their classroom teaching, either, if we are to be honest. We do believe, however, that every faculty member can progress in his or her knowledge and competence relating to e-learning and find concrete ways to improve his or her effectiveness in leading, designing, and delivering online courses and programs. In other words, teaching online is a skill, as is teaching in any environment and, through feedback from students and peers and adjustment of teaching styles and practices, online instructors can become as effective as those in the classroom.

For those who make the commitment, many instructors think, "If I put the effort in (to committing to e-learning, developing really cool courses, and teaching online) . . ."

- Can I keep it—or will they fire me and keep the course materials?
- Will it last a while?
- Will I get tenure?
- Will I be seen as a team player in the dean's eyes?
- Will teaching be manageable, or will I be smothered and tethered forever?
- Are there resources to help me?
- Will it really help our students and our program?
- Will it really hold off the competition?
- Will I experience job satisfaction?

These are the kinds of concrete questions instructors in higher education ask as they review their many concerns and obligations. In the short term, the hierarchy in higher education will allow many tenured professors to avoid online classes in favor of other activities and assignments, but that period may be changing. Some students are required to take at least one course online. At this time, the requirement is experimental and does not affect everyone. But eventually, it might affect all instructors in higher education.

In the meantime, e-learning will continue to diffuse into higher education in the form of blended learning and supplemental online resources and assignments. The number of students served online will continue to grow and resources will steadily improve in quality, until the barriers and obstacles become less formidable. Over time e-learning is fast becoming integral to the culture of higher education, and e-learning work a more natural extension of faculty job descriptions.

# Concluding Thoughts

Professors aren't going away soon. In fact, rather than replace professors, e-learning *depends* on professors from top to bottom, from planning and design to management and delivery. Students still need strong and clear role models and guidance in their courses. They need a master-guide who can navigate them through new and challenging subject matter. At the same time, professors increasingly need e-learning as a tool for doing their jobs. Even campus classes require a level of e-learning access through flexible blended-learning resources. The mutual need—between professors and students—will lead to some adjustments over time in professors' roles. But they won't be replaced any time soon by learning technologies; rather, their effectiveness will be extended *through* those technologies.

In our rapidly changing world, the competition for higher-ed services is not just the college down the block—it is the proliferation of learning resources, on the job, self-directed, certificates, workshops—all the choices that adults have to further their learning, their credentialing, and their careers. Universities no longer enjoy a monopoly on knowledge and learning. It's out there, everywhere. We need to adjust our credentialing system and our outreach services to reflect the many paths toward expertise. Distance education programs are an increasingly important choice for many adults (Bates, 2000). As optimists, we believe that professors and the universities that hire them will respond, carefully, to the imperative for participation, finding ways to overcome the obstacles and concerns that presently confront them.

# References

Bates, T. (2000). Distance education in dual mode higher education institutions: Challenges and changes. Retrieved June 16, 2005, from http://bates.cstudies.ubc.ca/papers/challengesandchanges.html

Beaudoin, M. (2002). Distance education leadership: An essential role for the new century. *Journal of Leadership Studies, 8*(3), 131–135.

Berg, G.A. (2002). The role of adjunct faculty in distance learning. *International Journal on E-Learning, 1*(3), 7–9.

de Montes, L.E. Sujo, Oran, S.M., & Willis, E.M. (2002). Power, language, and identity: Voices from an online course. *Computers and Composition, 19*(3), 251–271.

DiBiase, D. (2004). The impact of increasing enrollment on faculty workload and student satisfaction over time. *Journal of Asynchronous Learning Networks, 8*(2). Retrieved June 16, 2005, from www.sloan-c.org/publications/jaln/v8n2/v8n2_dibiase.asp

Dunlap, J.C. (2005, May/June). Workload reduction in online courses: Getting some shuteye. *Performance Improvement, 44*(5), 18–25.

Farmer, J. (2004, October). Communication dynamics: Discussion boards, weblogs and the development of communities of inquiry in online learning environments. *Incorporated Subversion* [blog site]. Retrieved June 16, 2005, from http://incsub.org/blog/index.php?p=3

Garrison, D.R., & Anderson, T. (2003). *e-Learning in the 21st century: A framework for research and practice.* London: Routledge Falmer.

Howell, S.L., Williams, P.B., & Lindsay, N.K. (2003). Thirty-two trends affecting distance education: An informed foundation for strategic planning. *Online Journal of Distance Learning Administration, 6*(3). Retrieved June 16, 2005, from www.westga.edu/~distance/ojdla/fall63/howell63.html

Iverson, K.M. (2005). *e-Learning games: Interactive learning strategies for digital delivery.* Upper Saddle River NJ: Pearson/Prentice-Hall.

Kieman, V. (2005, February 18). Colleges' spending on technology will decline again this year, survey suggests. *Chronicle of Higher Education, 51*(24).

Larreamendy-Joerns, J., & Leinhardt, G. (2006). Going the distance with online education. *Review of Educational Research, 76*(4), 567–605.

Lifter, K., Kruger, L, Okun, B., Tabol, C., Poklop, L., & Shishmananian, E. (2005). Transformation to a web-based pre-service training program: A case study. *Topics in Early Childhood Special Education, 25*(1), 15–24.

Maguire, L.L. (2005, Spring). Literature review: Faculty participation in online distance education: Barriers and motivators. *Online Journal of Distance Learning Administration, 8*(1). www.westga.edu/~distance/ojdla/spring81/maguire81.htm

Marcus, S. (2004). Leadership in distance education: Is it a unique type of leadership—A literature review. *Online Journal of Distance Learning Administration, 7*(1). Retrieved June 16, 2005, from www.westga.edu/%7Edistance/ojdla/spring71/marcus71.html

Wilson, B.G., Ludwig-Hardman, S., Thornam, C., & Dunlap, J.C. (2004). Bounded community: Designing and facilitating learning communities in formal courses. *The International Review of Research in Open and Distance Learning, 5*(3), Retrieved June 16, 2005, from www.irrodl.org/content/v5.3/wilson.html

## Additional Resources

Allen, M.W. (2003). *Michael Allen's guide to e-learning: Building interactive, fun, and effective learning programs for any company.* Hoboken, NJ: John Wiley & Sons.

American Federation of Teachers. (2000). *Distance education: Guidelines for good practice* (pp. 1–25). Washington, DC: American Federation of Teachers—AFL/CIO. Retrieved July 22, 2004, from www.aft.org

Belanger, F., & Jordan, D.H. (2000). *Evaluation and implementation of distance learning: Technologies, tools and techniques.* Hershey, PA: Idea Group Publishing.

Burbules, N., & Callister, T.A. (2000). Universities in transition: The promise and the challenge of new technologies. *Teachers College Record, 102*(2), 271–293.

Compora, D.P. (2003). Current trends in distance education: An administrative model. *Online Journal of Distance Learning Administration, VI*(II). Retrieved February 24, 2005, from www.wetga.edu/~distance/ojdla/summer62/compora62.html

de Montes, L.E., Sujo Oran, S.M., & Willis, E.M. (2002). Power, language, and identity: Voices from an online course. *Computers and Composition, 19*(3), 251–271.

Duderstadt, J., Atkins, D., & Van Houweling, D. (2002). *Higher education in the digital age.* Westport, CT: American Council on Education.

Howell, S.L., Saba, F., Lindsay, N.K., & Williams, P.B. (2004). Seven strategies for enabling faculty success in distance education. *The Internet and Higher Education, 7,* 33–49.

Howell, S.L., Williams, P.B., & Lindsay, N.K. (2003). Thirty-two trends affecting distance education: An informed foundation for strategic planning. *Online Journal of Distance Learning Administration, 71*(3). Retrieved October 25, 2004, from www.westga.edu/~distance/ojdla/fall63/howell63.html

Joint Information Systems Committee (JISC). (2004). *Effective practice with e-learning: A good practice guide in designing for learning.* Retrieved March 1, 2005, from www.jisc.ac.uk/uploaded_documents/jisc%20effective%20practice3.pdf

Laughner, T. (2003). Program philosophy: Keeping sight of what's important. In D.G. Brown (Ed.), *Developing faculty to use technology.* Bolton, MA: Anker.

Lesko, P.D. (2004). Distance education is here to stay. *Adjunct Nation.* Retrieved October 22, 2004, from www.adjunctnation.com/magazine/article/print?id_article=387

Merrill, M.D., & Wilson, B.G. (2007). The future of instructional design. In R.A. Reiser & J.V. Dempsey (Eds.*), Trends and issues in instructional technology* (2nd ed.) (pp. 335–351). Upper Saddle River, NJ: Pearson/Prentice-Hall.

Moody, J., & Kindel, T. (2004). Successes, failures and future steps. *TechTrends, 48*(5).

Reeves, T.C. (2002). Keys to successful e-learning: Outcomes, assessment, and evaluation. *Educational Technology, 42*(6), 23–29.

Riffee, W.H. (2003). Putting a faculty face on distance education programs. *Campus Technology.* Retrieved October 18, 2004, from www.campus-technology.com/print.asp?ID=7233

Rubens, E. (2003). Innovative faculty development programs at IUPUI's center for teaching and learning. In D.G. Brown (Ed.), *Developing faculty to use technology* (pp. 215–218). Bolton, MA: Anker.

Sloan Report. (2004). *Entering the mainstream: The quality and extent of online education in the United States, 2003 and 2004.* Needham, MA: Alfred P. Sloan Foundation.

Sims, R., & Jones, D. (2002). Enhancing quality in online leaning: Scaffolding design and planning through proactive education. *Distance Education, 23*(2).

Sims, R., & Jones, D. (2003). Where practice informs theory: Reshaping instructional design for academic communities of practice. *Information Technology, Education and Society, 4*(1), 3–20.

Tarr, T., & McDaniel, R. (2005). IUPUI 'jump start' program for new faculty. *Distance Education Report, 8.*

Watson, G. (2003). Report from the trenches: Faculty development through a successful grassroots campaign. In D.G. Brown (Ed.), *Developing faculty to use technology* (pp. 228–232). Bolton, MA: Anker.

Wegerif, R. (2000, March 19). The social dimension of asynchronous learning networks. *Journal of Asynchronous Learning Networks, 2*(1).

◆ ◆ ◆

## Summary of Main Points

Readers should take away the following main ideas from this chapter:

- The fact that e-learning is just starting on university campuses affects our ability to provide perspective on its impact. We need to carefully observe impacts and trends over time.

- Faculty members have many concerns about e-learning, including constraints of time, resources, support from administration and faculty, and knowledge to teach online. They are concerned about course quality, student skills and needs, career impact, the available technology, ownership and control of the content, integrity, and privacy, as well as

the intellectual challenge, work flexibility, support and recognition for online teaching, and meeting student needs.

- Three primary concerns about teaching online are:

    - Integrating students into a community of learners, which
      includes ongoing and meaningful contact with peers and
      the instructor. Some people believe that course manage-
      ment systems support this need, but they are primarily
      designed to provide a place for classroom instructors to
      place a repository of classroom-related materials.

    - Maintaining a sense of teaching presence, which involves
      establishing the identity and presence of the instructor at
      the beginning of the course and ensuring that students
      are aware of the presence and availability of the instruc-
      tor throughout the course.

    - Resolving issues of copyrights and ownership of course
      materials, which differ from those of classroom courses in
      academia (which are owned by the instructor) and in
      industry (where the organization sponsoring the work
      owns the copyright).

For a number of reasons, higher education has been at the fore-
front of e-learning adoption. Critical to success, however, is the
faculty role in developing and delivering courses. Faculty must see
the personal and professional payoff for investing time and effort
online, and develop competence and confidence by doing the work
with appropriate support. Neither e-learning nor faculty are going
away any time soon; each depends on the other for success.

◆ ◆ ◆

# Guiding Questions for Discussion

- University professors are typically hired for their subject-
  matter expertise, not their ability to teach in the classroom,
  much less online. How can these experts be supported in
  their efforts to teach online and to create online programs?

- Online teaching in higher education involves a seemingly intractable tension between maintaining quality and controlling costs. What can individual professors do to teach worthwhile e-courses without killing themselves in the process?

- Universities often rely on part-time professors, who may rarely show up on campus to rub shoulders with full-time faculty, to develop and teach e-courses. How can part-time faculty convey the culture and values of a program—the intangibles—to students online, when they may be the least familiar with that culture?

- In what ways are issues and problems faced in higher education common to other settings of practice? Is higher education just another learning provider? If not, how does it differ?

- Good instructors are essential for e-learning, but expensive professors may be replaced eventually by more affordable part-time workers. How does e-learning affect differentiated workloads, where faculty negotiate customized work assignments (such as teaching classes and doing research)? Where does that leave e-learners?

## Learn More About It

Links       FacultyOnline.com, www.facultyonline.com

MIR Monument Information Resource—Index of top-selling textbooks with reviews and faculty using the textbooks

World Lecture Hall, www.utexas.edu/world/lecture. Online syllabi and links to Higher Education in the United States

Sloan Consortium, www.aln.org/alnweb/publications.htm

American Journal of Distance Education, www.ajde.com/

Educause, www.educause.edu/

European Journal of Open and Distance Learning, www.eurodl.org/

Journal of Asynchronous Learning Networks, www
.sloan-c.org/publications/jaln/index.asp

Journal of Excellence in College Teaching, http://ject.lib
.muohio.edu

Journal of Distance Education (Canadian Association of
Distance Education), http://cade.athabascau.ca/

Online Journal of Distance Learning Administration,
www.westga.edu/%7Edistance/jmain11.html

Tappedin.org, http://tappedin.org/tappedin/web/about.jsp.
Online technology, learning strategies, and support to
teach effectively online

| Books, | Allen, M.W. (2003). *Michael Allen's guide to* |
| Papers, | *e-learning: Building interactive, fun, and effective learning* |
| Reports, | *programs for any company.* Hoboken, NJ: John |
| and Articles | Wiley & Sons. |

Horton, W. (2006). *e-Learning by design.* Hoboken, NJ:
John Wiley & Sons.

Schank, R.C. (2002). *Designing world-class e-learning: How
IBM, GE, Harvard Business School and Columbia University
are succeeding at e-learning.* New York: McGraw-Hill.

# Appendix: Faculty Concerns with Distance Education

The following concerns are adapted from an initial set of categories
developed by Maguire (2005).

### Lack of Time

*Time drain.* Will e-learning require more time and investment
than preparing and teaching a classroom course?

*Equitable workload.* If I'm teaching online, will the extra work
be recognized?

### Lack of Resources

*Funding for design and development.* Who will do the work of developing e-learning courses, and how will these people be compensated?

*Stipends for extra work.* Will I be paid for the additional work involved in developing or teaching online courses?

*Media.* Who will pay for the additional media required for e-learning?

### Lack of Support

*Support from the administration.* Does the dean fully support e-learning? Is the university committed to e-learning success?

*Collegial communities of practice.* Where can I find other faculty engaged in e-learning? How can we find ways to interact and support each other's efforts?

*Technical support.* What help desk support is available to students and faculty? Is it available 24/7? If not, when is it available?

*Training.* What training is available to me as a faculty member to develop and hone my online teaching skills? Can I fit this training into my busy work schedule?

### Lack of Knowledge

*Technology skills.* Do I have the technical skills required to develop and teach e-learning courses?

*Instructional design.* How is teaching for e-learning different from traditional teaching? What do I have to do differently? Do I have the skills to design instruction for e-learning?

*Facilitation and management.* Am I prepared to facilitate and manage student interaction in an online environment?

### Concerns About Quality

*Lack of student interaction.* How can students enjoy high-quality interactions with me, with other students, and with the content?

*Teacher presence.* How can students benefit from me personally as an instructor and expert in the field? How can I
compensate for not being there physically?

*Equivalent learning experience.* Is e-learning proven to be an
equivalent learning experience to traditional instruction?
What can be done to make the two methods equivalent
in learning outcomes?

*Assessment methods.* How do I assess student learning? How
do I minimize cheating and fraud when students are
working from remote locations?

**Lack of Student Skills and Needs**

*Technology skills.* Do students have the tech skills required to
work online?

*Information-literacy skills.* Do my students know how to use
and evaluate information from the web?

*Teaching preferences.* What do I do when students are reluc-
tantly online and would rather take face-to-face classes?

*Self-directed learning skills.* Are my students mature enough
to take e-learning courses and complete the work
responsibly?

*Motivation.* Are students motivated to learn from a distance
and find the activities relevant and meaningful?

**Career Concerns**

*Job security.* How does my participation in e-learning affect
my job security?

*Diversion from research agenda.* Will my investment in e-learning
detract from my research agenda?

*Tenure and promotion.* Will e-learning help or hinder my
preparation for tenure and promotion?

*Institutional rewards.* What rewards and incentives
are available for e-learning participation—or
non-participation?

### Technology Base

*Poor infrastructure.* What kind of technology infrastructure does my institution have available?

*Technology access.* Do my students have good access to high-speed Internet connections and other required technology?

*Unreliable technology.* How reliable is the technology at my institution?

*Always-changing requirements.* How do I keep up with the always-changing requirements and standards related to learning technologies?

### Ownership and Control

*Copyright.* What claim can I establish over the e-learning resources I create and use?

*Sharing teaching and scholarly products.* How can I control distribution and dissemination of resources I create? What access do I have to resources created by others?

*Technology transfer.* How can I participate in the transfer of promising technologies into marketable products?

### Integrity, Privacy, and Human Issues

*Surveillance and privacy.* What control do I have over who enters and observes my e-classes?

*Security.* What threats to security must I deal with? How could these affect my work?

*Plagiarism.* How can I guard against plagiarism by students—and avoid it in my own development of course materials?

*Quality of life.* What effect on my life does e-learning have? How do I keep things manageable and sane, and avoid being controlled by the technology?

### Possible Incentives or Motivators for Faculty Participation

Intellectual Challenge

*Innovative work.* Am I prepared to do something innovative and pioneering with e-learning?

*Building enduring resources.* Can I leave a lasting legacy for others through my contributions in e-learning?

Work Flexibility

*Change of pace.* Will e-learning serve as a welcome alternative to my other work assignments? Will the e-learning provide a refreshing break from classroom teaching responsibilities?

*More flexible work schedule.* Will e-learning give me more flexibility in my work—staying at home, working at odd hours?

### Support and Recognition

*From colleagues.* Will colleagues notice and support my e-learning activity? Will I enjoy their respect and appreciation?

*From the dean.* Does e-learning fit into the dean's priorities? Will that support translate into tangible rewards?

*From the profession.* Is there a way I could leverage my e-learning work into a professional or research focus?

### Meeting Student Needs

*Student engagement with technology.* Can students do things online that they couldn't do in a classroom?

*Expanded access to markets.* Can we reach markets and types of students that we otherwise would not be able to reach?

# Chapter 4

# Knowledge Management

From the Graveyard of Good Ideas

*William Horton, William Horton Consulting, Inc.*

---

**About This Chapter**

This chapter answers the questions, "Why did a good idea like knowledge management fail, and can anything be done to resurrect the idea?"

Knowledge management includes all the techniques and technologies used to help a group make better decisions—individually and as a group. This is a worthwhile goal that has failed, largely because of vague notions and unmanageable means.

Typical knowledge management projects contain numerous difficulties that make them hard to implement and difficult to maintain. Many require manually entering information and continually updating it. Most only work if the whole company is involved and separate parts of the organization march in

---

Portions of this chapter came from *Knowledge Management: A Practical Evolutionary Approach* by William Horton and are used with his permission.

lockstep. Typical knowledge management projects are slow and unwieldy. They often involve infighting and politics. No wonder they have failed.

Despite typical problems, knowledge management is an important goal and can be implemented with fewer problems than have been typically seen. The basic processes of knowledge management are relatively simple and include: increase knowledge, capture knowledge, refine knowledge, share knowledge, and apply knowledge. Simple processes can be implemented to make these occur and thrive in any organization. What's needed is to rethink what we are trying to do and how we are trying to do it.

## Knowledge and Survival

The next time you see a bee buzzing around your petunias or roses, tip your hat to one of the most brilliant practitioners of knowledge management. And this knowledge management is done without technology, infighting, hassles, or bloated and unwieldy knowledge management infrastructure or processes. Each bee willingly does its part to capture, share, and apply knowledge.

Amazing?

No, survival.

Imagine being able to do the same thing inside an organization. And consider why it hasn't occurred already. Unlike bees, humans apparently like to make things complex and difficult. They get mired in fiefdoms, one-upmanship, and making things harder than they need to be. They attempt to herd cats instead of putting out food and allowing the cats to do what comes naturally—eat.

Knowledge management is a great idea that has, up to now, failed. This chapter explores why. It first explains why good ideas, including knowledge management, sometimes don't take off. Then it explores one of the reasons why: the tribulations of mistaking information for knowledge. Next, it reviews the typical problems organizations have faced when trying to implement knowledge management and suggests practical ways to implement rational knowledge management processes in any organization.

# Knowledge Management, a Good Idea That Didn't Take Off

Hot technologies often cool down. As Margaret Driscoll noted in Chapter 2, the e-learning industry fell for a hyped-up vision of the economic and instructional impact of the technology that never took hold.

In our defense, falling for hype is endemic to the entire field of technology. Consider what has happened in the broader field of technology. *Spectrum*, the magazine of the Institute for Electrical and Electronics Engineers, 'fessed up to over-enthusiasm about some technologies. In a November 2004 article titled "Write or Wrong," Cherry and Guizzo note some of the magazine's own false predictions:

- *Artificial intelligence*. For three and a half decades, starting in the 1950s, *Spectrum* ran many articles on artificial intelligence and, in June 1984, predicted that "expert systems that mimic human experts' abilities to make decisions—would replace air-traffic controllers by the year 2000." President Reagan did replace many air-traffic controllers, but that was a labor dispute, not a technological breakthrough. And in 2007, as of the writing of this book, humans still run the air-traffic control system.

- *Breeder nuclear reactors*. In March 1969, *Spectrum* told us that "Breeder reactors are expected to play an increasingly important part in the overall energy generation picture in the United States, particularly after the mid-1980s." In truth, experimental breeder reactors proved expensive and unreliable. Today only one such reactor is in service in Russia, and it is scheduled to be replaced in three years.

- *Hydroponics*. In 1997, *Spectrum* told readers about GE's Geniponics division's use of hydroponics, the process of growing plants indoors in nutrient-rich water (rather than soil) to produce tomato crops of 200 kilograms per square meter, over thirty times the yield of conventional farming. "The profits and social benefits of these engineered plants and vegetables seem enormous," gushed *Spectrum*. However, the cost of electricity to grow the plants was so costly that GE sold the unit to Control Data, which shut down the operation a few years later.

- *Electrical generation.* In July 1978, *Spectrum* told readers, "There is a good chance that, by the year 2000, the term blackout (societal definition) will be considered to be a term out of the Dark Ages." An August 1994 article called the earlier article "prescient." Prescient or not, in August 2003, a massive blackout hit the northeast United States and the Canadian province of Ontario. No one was especially surprised.

And who can forget Bill Gates' gushing writing in the foreword to the *OS/2 Programmer's Guide*: "I believe OS/2 is destined to be the most important operating system, and possibly program, of all time."

If you do not know what OS/2 was, thank you, because you just made my point.

Good ideas all, they nevertheless failed to live up to their hype or to achieve the potential they offered.

## Ditto Knowledge Management

Another good idea that has yet to achieve its promise or potential is knowledge management (KM). Knowledge management was the darling of the business press in the mid-1990s. The inspiring claims of business results were no doubt true—but about as typical as the claims for diet plans and hair-restoration tonics.

For example, to prove the value of its new CasePoint knowledge management system in diagnosing problems with customer equipment, Xerox conducted a contest to identify which customer-support technicians were most effective at diagnosing problems, fully expecting the results to correlate with use of the knowledge-management system. The top two winners were people who hardly ever used the system. The top-ranking user of the system scored only one-third as many points as the winner, who almost never used the system (Stewart, 2001).

Many adopters of knowledge management have regretted their haste in trying to implement it. Ernst & Young admits that their initial investment of $100 million in IT-based knowledge management was wasted (Sveiby, 2001). Companies like Coca-Cola and Morgan Stanley have hired and then fired chief knowledge officers (Stewart, 2001). Pillsbury Research and Development built an online forum for exchange of ideas. Six months later, not one single person had even logged on to that system, much less exchanged an idea (Barth, 2000).

The darling then became the despised. Bain and Company found that, out of twenty-two categories of electronic management tools, knowledge management ranked dead last in terms of user satisfaction (Barth, 2000). According to Stowe Boyd, president of Running Light, a Washington, DC-based consulting firm, "The high-flying and aggressively proselytizing advocates of knowledge management (KM) that formerly graced the podiums of now-defunct KM conferences are finding that their staffs are being cut, their projects go unfunded, and their CKO-ships are liable to be reorganized out of existence" (Barth, 2000). Researchers now acknowledge a 50 percent failure rate for knowledge management projects. Daniel Morehead, director of organizational research for British Telecommunications of Reston, Virginia, pegged the rate at nearly 70 percent (Ambrosio, 2000).

## Defining Knowledge Management

So what exactly is this failure known as knowledge management? What is its nature? Does it even exist? Or is it just another vaporous management fad? We have no shortage of definitions for the term knowledge management. Unfortunately, most definitions are quite abstract, relying on lots of other undefined terms and a stratospheric level of vagueness. A quick Google search turned up these definitions:

> Knowledge management is the practice of harnessing and exploiting intellectual capital to gain competitive

advantage and customer commitment through efficiency, innovation and faster and more effective decision-making. (Barth, 2000)

Knowledge management is the strategy and processes to enable the creation and flow of relevant knowledge throughout the business to create organizational, customer and consumer value. David Smith, Unilever (Knowledge Nurture, 2005)

Succinctly put, KM is the process through which organizations generate value from their intellectual and knowledge-based assets. (Santosus & Surmacz, 2005)

An effort to capture or tap an organization's collective experience and wisdom—including the tacit know-how that exists in people's heads—and to make it accessible and useful to everyone in the enterprise. (Gordon, 1998)

Real knowledge management is much more than managing the flow of information. It means nothing less than setting knowledge free to find its own paths. It means fueling the creative fire of self-questioning in organizations. (Allee, 1997)

Steve Barth nailed it when he called knowledge management a "metaphor gone wrong" (2000). We can no more manage knowledge than we can institutionalize wisdom, bottle creativity, or herd cats. The problem with vague, abstract, grandiloquent definitions of knowledge management is that they naturally lead to vague or unworthy goals for projects. Often KM projects espouse lofty goals, such as "become a learning organization" or focus tightly on a single short-term problem such as reducing employee turnover. This vagueness of goals is what DestinationCRM terms "Ready-Fire-Aim" (Shekawat, 2002).

Let me give you my definition of knowledge management. I define knowledge management as *how groups of people make themselves collectively smarter*. Knowledge management deals with groups of people. Training educates individuals; knowledge management educates entire organizations and populations. The group of people may be the employees of Royal Widgit Limited. Or it may be the faculty of Lightspeed University. Or the customers and potential customers of BlottoBlaster Software, Inc.

Central to the concept of knowledge management is the concept of knowledge. Probably the best definition of knowledge comes from Karl-Erik Sveiby: "Knowledge = A Capacity to Act" (2001). I can't add anything to that.

In knowledge management, the group makes itself smarter. Corporate or government executives don't inject their wisdom into their staff and laborers. Consultants, no matter how brilliant, don't transfer wisdom to clients. Knowledge management does not involve forcing knowledge on a group from outside. Knowledge management works best when the group needing the knowledge pulls in the ideas and insights it needs at the time.

Knowledge management has the potential to make a group collectively smarter. Knowledge management includes all the techniques and technologies used to help the group make better decisions—individually and as a group. We can encourage, we can enable, and we can empower knowledge growth and flow, but we cannot force it to happen.

# Mistaking Information for Knowledge

Philosophers have debated the concept of knowledge for millennia. And just when you thought you knew what it meant, along comes knowledge management to throw in a couple of new ideas of what we mean by knowledge. The following sections first explore what knowledge really is and its hierarchy, then explore two phenomena that are often mistaken for creating or managing knowledge: overloading people with information and managing documents.

## The Knowledge Hierarchy

In knowledge management, knowledge is more than "knowledge." When we talk about knowledge, we mean more than a strict definition of the term knowledge might imply. Figure 4.1 shows the

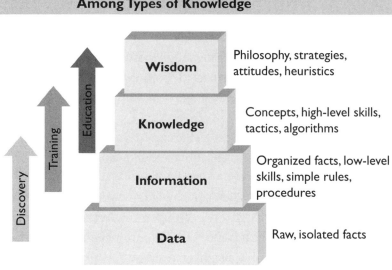

**Figure 4.1. The Pyramid of Knowledge, Which Differentiates Among Types of Knowledge**

pyramid of knowledge, which demonstrates the hierarchy among different types of knowledge.

At the bottom of the pyramid is *data*. Data consists of raw, isolated facts. Think of tables of temperature and humidity recorded by an automated weather station. Those numbers are just data.

The next tier of the pyramid is *information*. Information consists of organized facts, low-level skills, simple rules, and basic procedures. A chart of changing temperatures would be information, as would a simple step-by-step procedure for changing the batteries in the automated weather station.

*Knowledge*, in its strictest meaning, builds on information. It includes concepts, high-level skills, tactics, and algorithms. The relationship between daily temperature fluctuations and yearly fluctuations would be an example of knowledge, as would a statistical technique for detecting variations from historical trends of temperature and humidity.

At the top of the pyramid is a block called *wisdom*. Wisdom is the hardest to define and equally hard to achieve. It consists of philosophies, strategies, attitudes, and heuristics, which transfer knowledge from one context to another. Wisdom allows one meteorologist to predict weather more accurately than other meteorologists.

Knowledge management includes all the processes that increase the amount of material at the upper levels of the hierarchy. Unfortunately, we do not have good names for the process of ascending the levels of the pyramid. The term "discovery" is often used, especially in the sciences, to refer to the process of inferring information or knowledge from data. In industry, the terms "training" and "learning" refer to efforts to help people transform information they already possess into knowledge they can apply. In academic circles, people use the term "education" to refer to processes that refine knowledge into wisdom.

## Information Overload Is a Problem, Not a Solution

Business workers are flooded with data and drowning in information. The advance of information technology has, if anything, made the problem worse. The volume of business and technical literature is overwhelming. To read the material published on chemistry in just one year would take seven hundred years. Reading one year of material published on biomedicine would take 2,200 years. Every year the Institute for Electrical and Electronic Engineers (IEEE), just one professional association, publishes more than 330,000 pages of new technical articles and papers.

Just increasing the amount of information does not make for more knowledge because information overload just adds noise— content that ultimately distracts people from the effort of turning information into knowledge and knowledge into wisdom. The build-up of information collapses into something worse than raw data. The effects of information overload are an economic and psychological burden. A 1996 study by Reuters, titled *Dying for Information* (Waddington, 1996) provided telling statistics:

- Half of managers say they cannot cope with all the information they receive.

- Two-thirds said they needed high levels of information to do their jobs but believed that information was underutilized.

- 47 percent felt that acquiring information distracted from their main job responsibilities.

- Two-thirds said information overload lessened job satisfaction and created tension with co-workers.

- 42 percent blamed information overload for ill health.

- 60 percent said they missed social engagements and were often too tired for leisure activities because of information overload.

And Reuters should know. Reuters spews forth 27,000 pages of information each second.

We need *knowledge*, not more data and information. The solution to information overload is not more information—even information about information overload just adds to the problem you are experiencing first-hand about now. What is needed is an ability to turn raw data and information into productive knowledge and wise decisions. If knowledge management is to prove anything more than a passing fad, it must provide the conceptual enzymes to digest the enormous meal of facts and figures put before us.

## Document Management Is Not Knowledge Management

Many organizations have mistaken a more efficient handling of documents as a comprehensive form of knowledge management. Content management systems (CMS) do a great job at automating much of the process of generating complex manuals, websites, specifications, reports, brochures, help files, and other paper and electronic documents (Rockley, Kostur, & Manning, 2003; Sutton, 1996). However, generating and using knowledge involves a lot more than what is found in documents.

One common mistake is "building the grand database in the sky to house all your company's knowledge" (Ambrosio, 2000). Databases and search engines do not respond well to poorly phrased requests. Often, by the time something is in a document, it is stale, and by the time the document is in the database, it is obsolete.

Many projects aim to make existing knowledge resources more readily available. The centerpieces of such projects are content management systems and other document management software. This "supply-side quicksand"(Shekawat, 2002) provides what the organization has, rather than what employees and customers need. As a result, usage is often limited and impact is rare.

# Typical Problems, Difficult Solutions

Knowledge management projects pose a variety of problems, some practical, some political. This section explores them. It first explores the types of practical problems that hinder a knowledge management project. Then it presents two more serious problems faced in knowledge management projects—both pertaining to the challenges posed by people: The Borgs vs. the Flower Children and the Knowledge Hoarders.

## Practical Problems Affecting Knowledge Management Projects

Typical knowledge management projects contain numerous difficulties that make them hard to implement and difficult to maintain. Knowledge management often requires labor-intensive activities, such as entering information and metadata (descriptive information about the information, such as its author, a brief description, and cataloging information, like index entries) and continually revising the system (including updating changed information and pruning outdated information), tasks of which people quickly tire, and so they cease doing them.

Many KM projects aren't scalable (that is, usable outside of a small, well-defined context). They only work if the whole company or entire product line is on the system. They often require many separate organizations that follow substantially different processes to march in lockstep. Such projects shackle together hardware engineering, software development, training, documentation, product support—and all their consultants, contractors, and vendors—to single schedules, budgets, and operating procedures. There is a reason convicts were shackled together—and it was not to improve their speed and agility.

With KM efforts shackling organizations, KM rarely provided the speed or agility that its proponents promised (Shekawat, 2002). Often projects took so long to implement that, by the time they were up and running, the organization had replaced its CEO, rewritten its mission statement, discontinued part of its product line, entered three new markets, and turned over 30 percent of its workforce. Nobody could remember why the KM system was built in the first place. In addition, these projects were plagued with two common people problems, explored in the next two sections.

## People Problem 1: Borgs vs. Flower Children

*Problem:* Knowledge management is highly political. Two groups, or political parties, dominate. They differ in approach and outlook. Unfortunately, there is not too much overlap or interchange between these two groups.

Consider the "Borg" and the "Flower Child" shown in Figure 4.2. On the right is the "Borg." It takes a technical approach, recommending applications of technology to bridge knowledge gaps.

**Figure 4.2. The Flower Child and the Borg**

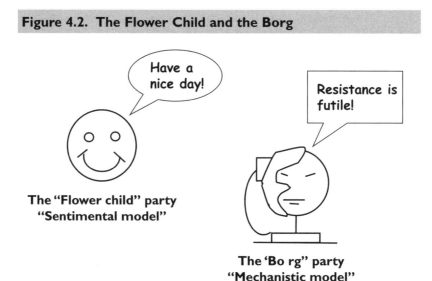

The "Flower child" party
"Sentimental model"

The 'Bo rg" party
"Mechanistic model"

Borgians typically hang out in the information technology department. They believe in giving everybody powerful networked computers and forcing them to use them for every possible activity. Borgians love electronic performance support systems (Gery, 1991) and content management systems (Rockley, Kostur, & Manning, 2003; Sutton, 1996).

Members of the opposite party dismiss "Borg" members as nerds and soul-less technicians. Tom Stewart of *Fortune* magazine calls the ways Borgians think the "mechanistic model" (2001). The shortcomings of their great contribution, the "big database in the sky," have already been pointed out.

On the left is the "Flower Child." It prefers a soft organizational approach to knowledge management. The Flower Child typically has a background in psychology, philosophy, or organizational theory. The Flower Child's solutions often involve reorganizing and retraining individuals. Stewart (2001) refers to this as the "sentimental model."

Borgians refer to members of the "Flower Child" party as "fluffmuffins." The term "flower children" is not too far off as some consultants literally adorn their web pages with floral images (www .margaretwheatley.com). Flower Child solutions rely on huge amounts of collaboration. Unfortunately, collaboration is not a panacea. Consider that:

> Collaboration is great, but we act only one person at a time. Teams don't act. (And team meetings are notorious black holes for productivity.) Only individuals act. (Knowledge Management Connection, 2004)

There appears to be little dialogue between the two groups. Indeed, they seem engaged in a cold war. Some conferences feature one group while other conferences feature the other. The different groups read different professional magazines and journals and visit different websites. If either mentions the other group, it is usually to dismiss their ideas as not worthy of serious consideration. Although both groups use many of the same terms, they often mean quite different things by those terms.

*Solution:* Combine efforts. Intramural warfare seldom leads to effective knowledge management. Defensive barriers tend to wall in pockets of knowledge and divide up precious budgets. Rather than trying to encompass all knowledge management efforts yourself, consider forming partnerships and joint ventures with these other efforts and the departments that sponsor them. The U.S. Postal Service succeeded only after it bridged the gap between IT and HR, both of which had competing knowledge management initiatives underway (Ambrosio, 2000). (Marc Rosenberg and Steve Foreman explore this issue in more detail in Chapter 9 of this book.)

## People Problem 2: The Knowledge Hoarders

*Problem:* Although dogma and inertia may be among the most intractable barriers facing knowledge management, implementing knowledge management may require that people overcome another barrier: changing "the way we do things here." As a result, some people inevitably lose power. Often knowledge management projects must begin without grassroots support, sometimes in the face of active resistance by the grassroots.

One reason for this resistance is the tendency among people to hoard information, which is a common practice in many corporate cultures. Unique knowledge confers power to the individual hoarding it. Competition for promotions discourages sharing knowledge. The results are informational "priesthoods" that hold knowledge close and do not share it with others who need to know.

Corporations encourage such hoarding with "need-to-know" policies and cultures, in which only those who have a need to know have access to certain information. Being placed on a need-to-know list confers a sense of importance to the individual that's similar to knowledge hoarding. The "need-to-know" culture discourages sharing knowledge. Security concerns often encourage excessive secrecy.

*Solution:* Provide a compelling reason to change. Corporate cultures do not change in response to slogans and catch phrases printed on posters, coffee mugs, pencils, and mouse pads. Even young employees have seen management fads come and go.

If you want employees or customers to change their behaviors, give them reasons to change. Show them the clear, immediate benefits of acquiring and sharing knowledge. Make the benefit financial. Pay for sharing rather than hoarding. Revise performance appraisal procedures to reward cooperative ventures, long-term improvements, and group-wide progress.

Leadership for change needs to come from the top. Early in a project, obtain executive support for your efforts. If you cannot gain support, go underground. Do small, effective projects until you develop support at the staff level. Then you will have undeniable proof that will appeal to high-level executives.

# Rational (Simple) Knowledge Management Processes

Knowledge management is just a metaphor. We cannot "manage" knowledge. What we can do is to improve the processes and ways that organizations store and track content and use that content to make better and better decisions.

Knowledge management systems are so shrouded in management mythology and technobabble that it is easy to lose sight of how simple they can be. The simplest example is quite simple indeed. It is the beehive. Every spring day, hundreds of bees sortie forth in quest of nectar. Once one of the emissaries locates a promising patch of pansies or petunias, he flies back to the hive, where he does a unique figure-eight dance. The angle of the figure eight informs other bees of the angle of the patch of flowers relative to the angle of the sun. And the frenzy of the dance specifies how far to fly in that direction.

By this simple process, bees perform the basic functions of all effective knowledge management systems: they increase, capture, refine, share, and apply knowledge—all without management consultants or intranets. They increase knowledge each time a bee discovers a source of nectar. The knowledge is encoded or captured in the form of a dance. Successive bees reporting on the location serve to refine the directions for finding the nectar. The dance shares that knowledge, and the steady flow of bees to and from the flowers helps apply that knowledge to the benefit of the hive.

The basic processes of knowledge management are relatively simple and often do not require the purchase of new technology. Organizations get smarter by five complementary processes: increase knowledge, capture knowledge, refine knowledge, share knowledge, and apply knowledge. Each of the following sections explores one of these.

## 1. Increase Knowledge

Effective organizations continually increase knowledge. On the non-technical side, the most direct way to increase knowledge is through old-fashioned classroom training. As Margaret Driscoll noted in Chapter 2, classroom training continues to thrive in the day of e-learning. No surprise; it's still one of the most effective ways to increase knowledge. Reading is another, especially from a well-stocked and well-indexed library. Discovery and invention activities can guide the learner to discover principles.

Technological tools also contribute to increasing knowledge. Online documents and courses make learning available across a network twenty-four hours a day. An electronic course catalog can make it easier for people to find the online or classroom course they need. Likewise, a library database or search facility can help them find the book, magazine, website, or other knowledge resource they need.

## 2. Capture Knowledge

Capturing knowledge puts it into a permanent and easily shared format. We take knowledge locked in a single human brain and make it sharable. Capturing knowledge used to mean writing it down on paper. Today capturing knowledge usually involves recording it in electronic form. Increasingly, we record information in computer files and databases. Some organizations, faced with either high turnover or, more significantly, those that have faced low turnover in the past but are anticipating a large number of retirements as their workers reach retirement age, are concerned that failing to capture knowledge can cause dire problems, such as the loss of valuable contact lists and information on the way that tasks are performed (Stewart, 2001).

Capturing knowledge in a manner that enables sharing does not require writing formal white papers or reports. A tip posted to a bulletin board is more sharable than one in the back of the mind. A Post-it® Note is more sharable than an unspoken idea (assuming it's legible). An idea that someone can explain is more sharable than one that cannot be articulated.

Think of how knowledge capture can be a routine part of the way you do business. For example, Dell's build-your-own-computer web pages not only entice customers, they capture up-to-the-moment marketing information about what each segment of their market wants and is willing to pay for (Stewart, 2001).

Although organizations recognize that capturing knowledge is important and is often easily accomplished with the available resources, many organizations make it a low-priority task and therefore don't do it. But not only is capturing knowledge important, it's not really that tough to do. Consider the following ways to get started capturing knowledge:

- Debrief employees—before they leave a job, when they complete a project, and as they accomplish a difficult objective.

- Conduct an "after action review." Follow the practice common in the U.S. military after a combat mission: ask how results differed from expectations, why the difference occurred, and what can be done better next time (Stewart, 2001).

- Give employees incentives to document their best practices and insights. Target the people who passionately love a subject to do this (Denning, 2000).

- Make the entry of the content easy:
  - Conduct classes in typing, so capturing knowledge in an electronic form is not so painful.

- Provide scanners so people can capture drawings, sketches, and other simple ideas.

- Use handwriting recognition programs to convert scribbled notes to editable text.

- Use voice-recognition programs so those who are better talkers than typists can contribute.

- Encourage people to use digital cameras to record every bright idea they spot. Ask them to write just a sentence or two explaining the picture.

- Create a clip-art library of the industry-specific symbols and images people need to create drawings and diagrams to record their ideas.

- Document processes, procedures, and best practices. The very process of developing material of any type requires interviewing experts and making sense of their ideas.

- Save transcripts of collaborative activities such as online discussions and chat sessions.

- Walk around the work areas of people and note their notes. What have they thumb-tacked to a bulletin board? What have they taped to the wall? What notes sprout like petals around their computer monitors? Such observations capture useful information and identify priorities for categories that should be captured more formally. Encourage these workers to share their personal tips with others, and provide them with an easy way to do so.

Some of the most effective efforts at sharing knowledge come from having employees post their best practices—or just good ideas—to an easily accessible location on the organization's intranet or network.

The key to success in such efforts is to make sharing as quick and simple as possible. One solution is to provide an online form to fill in. The contents of the form are automatically posted to a discussion forum or entered into a database.

As an alternative, you can provide a word-processing template for people to enter and format their ideas before manually submitting them. The cost for software could be less than a thousand dollars, and often can be implemented in less than a day.

## 3. Refine Knowledge

Merely capturing knowledge is not sufficient. At one point, Pricewaterhouse Coopers had 120,000 databases, approximately one per employee (Sveiby, 2001) (information overload to say the least).

Refining knowledge means making it more useful by verifying facts, correcting mistakes, updating ideas, augmenting ideas, clarifying expressions, and generalizing conclusions.

We refine knowledge when we make it more complete, more concise, more precise, more accurate, more up-to-date, more useful, and more understandable. Or put more simply, we refine knowledge to put it in context.

Consider this example. The government passes new tax regulations. A tax firm not only reads the regulations, but then prepares a booklet for its clients that explain how the new regulations specifically affect clients and how they should change their information-gathering activities and withholdings to reflect the new regulations.

Refining knowledge is not complex. For example, the common process of boiling ideas down into a concise document or course often requires correcting errors, filling in gaps, expressing ideas more succinctly, and organizing them logically.

Simple ways to refine knowledge include:

- Delete or archive out-of-date or obsolete documents.

- Edit and update recorded information.

- Summarize information to make it more concise, generalizing it to make it apply to more situations, abstracting it to make it simpler (for people who do not need details), and suggesting how people might use the information in their everyday activities.

- Index information so that people can find it easily.

- Organize and format information so that internal relationships are clear.

- Use analysis software to spot trends and infer principles.

- Investigate data-mining and extraction software to pluck nuggets of knowledge from the gigabytes of recorded data.

## 4. Share Knowledge

Knowledge is multiplied when it is shared. We share knowledge when we present it to others, when we publish and distribute it, and when we discuss it with others. Sharing knowledge secures it against loss. Discussions among those possessing knowledge can lead to new insights and applications which, in turn, leads to better knowledge. People who share knowledge support each other. Training is sharing knowledge. Every time someone creates an effective course module and someone else takes it, knowledge is shared.

Consider the instance of open-source software, where many volunteer software developers work as a team to develop and enhance products like Linux and Moodle.

Sharing multiplies individual knowledge. What was in one brain is now in many. Earlier, I mentioned a failure of a system by Xerox. Let me balance the picture with a success story of knowledge sharing. Xerox's Eureka database of tips from copier repairmen was used by 15,000 people on over 250,000 repair calls a year, saving Xerox $11 million (Brown, 1991).

The next several sections explore ways to share knowledge. The first provides a number of general suggestions for sharing knowledge. The subsequent sections explore specific suggestions for sharing knowledge: first general suggestions, then suggestions for making knowledge accessible, small, and reusable.

### General Suggestions for Sharing Knowledge

- Schedule informal presentations and brief training sessions.

- Publish simple frequently asked questions, executive summaries, and "cheat sheets."

- Rotate job assignments and send people on training assignments.

- Provide training in techniques for sharing knowledge, such as public speaking.

- Implement discussion groups, newsgroups, bulletin board systems, and electronic forums and make them widely available and easy to use.

- Create a help desk where people can ask questions of an expert.

- Establish standards for file formats, fonts, and colors so documents produced by one group can readily be used by another.

- Provide templates to make sharing content easier. Not only do templates simplify the entry of data for the contributors, but they also help readers by providing information in consistent locations.

- Set up conference rooms, complete with equipment for conference calls, computer screen projection, videoconferencing, and white boarding capabilities.

People are often more than willing to share knowledge. Consider the fads (or are they established trends?) of blogging and podcasting. In contrast, coerced sharing is inherently problematic. Managers in IBM's Global Knowledge Management Consulting and Solutions group tied compensation and bonuses to workers' contributions to an intellectual capital management system. "Everyone submitted," says Scott Smith, managing principal of the group, "but we are on a calendar year, so 90 percent of the submissions came in between December 15th and 31st" (Barth, 2000). (Admittedly, the process needs refinement. With no process of quality control, Smith noted that entries were "incredibly long and unintelligible.")

## Making Knowledge Accessible

One critical part of sharing knowledge is to make it accessible. If users can quickly find an individual explanation, fact, or procedure when they need it—without having to take the entire course or read the entire document—a knowledge product provides just-in-time training.

Making information findable on a website is no easy task. There are a variety of practical tools that can be used to make information findable. First, include a table of contents or system of menus so that people can drill down to the topic they need. Another simple, but radical, suggestion is to add an alphabetical index. That way, people unfamiliar with the structure of your material can find the individual topic or module they want. If an index is too much work, consider adding a full-text search facility.

Specific navigation aids can help too. For example, browse buttons can lead people in a logical sequence through related modules. By defining unfamiliar terms, a glossary can help people take modules of an e-course out of sequence without becoming confused. A map can help consumers understand how the knowledge is organized and lead them to form a clear mental model that will guide them in navigating it.

## Keeping Knowledge Chunks Small

Many people do not have time to take a long course, read a large book, or navigate a large website. Many cannot predict their needs for knowledge far enough in advance to schedule the required time. Others have very specific needs and are loath to sit through a week-long course to get the half-hour of instruction that meets their needs. So miniaturize content (that is, keep the size of content chunks, like a page or lesson, small) and modularize content (that is, make information into chunks that can stand alone).

Figure 4.3 shows a structure that miniaturizes and modularizes a body of the content of a course or document. Divide it into a linked collection of mini-modules, each focused on a specific, useful subset of the total subject. Each might correspond to a chapter or lesson from the original. Further divide the material into micro-modules taking say half an hour to consume. Then create nano-modules that take just a few minutes to go through.

### Figure 4.3. A Structure for a Body of Content

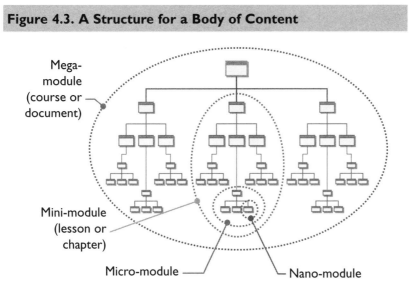

The more you can match your offerings to the specific, immediate needs of individuals, the more effective you will be in increasing knowledge.

### Reusing Knowledge

Consider publishing your courses, documents, and their supporting materials in multiple formats so that more people can make use of them. Not everyone can take an electronic course or read an electronic document, especially ones designed for high-speed connections. Nor can everyone take a classroom course.

One way to address this challenge is designing content for use in many different formats, known in some circles as *single sourcing*, in which a single source file is used to produce the material in different formats, in many cases, that might not be possible. A more realistic approach is engineering content for a variety of formats.

Figure 4.4 shows an example of the extent to which content can be engineered to serve multiple purposes. In Figure 4.4, a presentation about tools and technologies for e-learning is used for a variety of presentations. Over time, it grows a bit long and, in response, we added a menu so people could choose different categories of

**Figure 4.4. Re-Engineered Content**

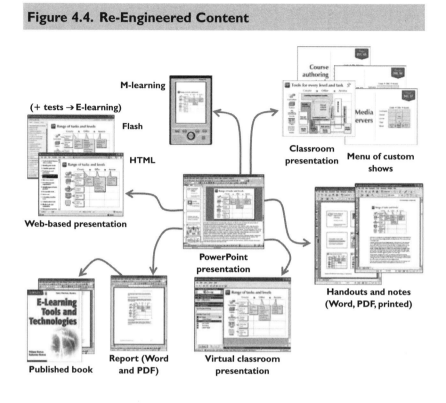

tools to learn about when viewing the presentation on their own. People asked for handouts, and these could be exported from PowerPoint to Word, published in Adobe Acrobat PDF, and printed on paper. The same presentation could be used in virtual-classroom presentations using online meeting systems. The presentation can also be exported to Word and formatted as a formal report. And that report could evolve into the manuscript for a book. The presentation can be saved for the web to create an online presentation in HTML. It can also be converted to Flash with Articulate. Tests could be added to turn it into a piece of stand-alone e-learning. Finally, just for grins, the content can be converted to a form that plays on a Pocket PC to create mobile learning.

Note how one simple PowerPoint file led to dozens of face-to-face and online presentations, handouts, reports, and a book. Think what you can do with your content.

## 5. Apply Knowledge

Unless knowledge is applied, it is of no use. Applying knowledge involves planning, deciding approaches to take, designing objects, building them, and solving problems that occur along the way. Applying knowledge is the payoff of knowledge management. By applying knowledge, it is put into action to make a profit, improve someone's life, or to save the world. Without application, the other processes are just a silly academic exercise.

When Lou Gerstner took over leadership of a stagnant, foundering IBM, he looked at how IBM managed its knowledge. Gerstner pointed out that IBM did a superb job of the first four processes: increase knowledge, capture knowledge, refine knowledge, and share knowledge. Its labs made breakthrough discoveries with regularity and continually added to earlier discoveries. It recorded and published its discoveries better than any other company in the industry.

However, IBM failed to exploit its own knowledge and was in danger of becoming like the Xerox Palo Alto Research Center, which in the 1970s created most of the innovations that fueled the success of companies like Apple Computer, Sun Microsystems, and Microsoft, but that never appeared in mainline Xerox products.

Far too many documents and courses fail to emphasize application of the knowledge they convey. Without application, knowledge is inert and impotent. We can correct that oversight.

Simple activities to promote application of knowledge include:

- Study, evaluate, and improve the decision-making process within an organization.

- Remind people to consider the consequences of actions before taking them.

- Embed knowledge into work processes so that people do not have to consciously remember to apply the knowledge.

- Embed knowledge into tools, such as the computer programs people use to perform their work.

- Publish catalogs and repositories in which workers can easily find the knowledge they need just when they need it.

- Create directories of electronically accessible experts, on call, ready to help.

- Use collaboration mechanisms to follow up with learners after training to ensure that they are applying what they learned.

- Use discussion forums to help workers share tips, success stories, and solutions to difficult problems they encounter when applying knowledge.

## Concluding Thoughts

Good ideas often hibernate through a winter of discontent. They may marry and produce brilliant offspring. They may blend in and work successfully behind the scenes. They may languish patiently for better technology or a more educated public.

Pen computing became a footnote until tablet computers premiered . . . fifteen years later. Apple's Newton hand-held computer failed, but the concept lives on in the Palm and Pocket PC units, which sag the business suits of executives worldwide. The car phone, which was once an expensive novelty, is now the ubiquitous mobile phone.

Voice recognition comes back every few years . . . and each time it is more capable. High-definition television (HDTV) was late but finally pulled into the station. "High-definition television, with a much sharper picture than is currently available, is expected to be in retail stores before the decade is out" (Cherry & Guizzo, 2004). The decade mentioned was the 1980s. High-definition television hit retail stores in 2003. With the United States announcing the end of analog broadcasts in early 2009, HDTV will quickly become commonplace.

The same will be true of knowledge management. With our help, that is.

## References

Allee, V. (1997). *The knowledge evolution: Expanding organizational intelligence.* Boston, MA: Butterworth-Heinemann.

Ambrosio, J. (2005). Knowledge management mistakes: Experts reveal five pitfalls to avoid when starting down the knowledge management path. *Computerworld* 2000. www.computerworld.com/printthis/2000/0,4814,46693,00.html. [Retrieved January 23, 2005.]

Barth, S. (2000). *Defining knowledge management* DestinationCRM .com. www.destinationcrm.com/articles/default .asp?ArticleID=1400. [Retrieved April 30, 2005.]

Barth, S. (2000.) *KM horror stories*. DestinationKM. www.destinationkm.com/print/default.asp?ArticleID=923. [Retrieved January 23, 2005.]

Brown, J.S. (1991). Research that reinvents the corporation. *Harvard Business Review*, pp. 102–111.

Cherry, S., & Guizzo, E. (2004, November). Write and wrong. *Spectrum*, pp. 74–80.

Denning, S. (2000). *The springboard: How storytelling ignites action in knowledge era organizations*. Boston, MA: Butterworth-Heinemann.

Gery, G.J. (1991). *Electronic performance support systems*. Tolland, MA: Gery Performance Press.

Gordon, J. (1999). *The whole enchilada: Intellectual capital and you*. *Training* magazine 1998 [cited September 13, 1999]. Available: www.trainingsupersite.com/publications/magazines/training/909cover.htm.

Knowledge Management Connection. (2005). *10 (different) myths of knowledge management*. The Knowledge Management Connection 2004. Available: www.kmconnection.com/KM_myths.htm. [Retrieved January 23, 2005.]

Knowledge Nurrure. (2005). *Starter kit for knowledge management*. Available: www.knowledge-nurture.com/web/bulabsty.nsf/pages/starter+kit?opendocument.[Retrieved April 30, 2005].

Rockley, A., Kostur, P.,& Manning, S. (2003). *Managing enterprise content: A unified content strategy*. Indianapolis, IN: New Riders Press.

Santosus, M., & Surmacz, J. (2005). *The ABCs of knowledge management*. Knowledge Management Research Center, 2005.

Available: www.cio.com/research/knowledge/edit/kmabcs.html. [Retrieved April 30, 2005].

Shekawat, U. (2002, July 24). *The KM kiss of death.* Available: www.destinationcrm.com/articles/default.asp?articleid=2418.

Stewart, T.A. (2001). *The wealth of knowledge.* New York: Currency.

Sutton, M. (1996). *Document management for the enterprise: Principles, techniques, and applications.* Hoboken, NJ: John Wiley & Sons.

Sveiby, K.-E. (2005). *Knowledge management—Lessons from the pioneers.* Sveiby Knowledge Associates, 2001. Available: www.sveiby.com/KM-lessons.doc. [Retrieved April 23, 2005].

Waddington, P. (1996, January 19). *Dying for information? A report on the effects of information overload in the UK and worldwide.* Available: www.reuters.com. [Retrieved June 24, 1999.]

◆ ◆ ◆

## Summary of Main Points

Readers should take away the following main ideas from this chapter:

- Many technologies, including artificial intelligence, breeder nuclear reactors, hydroponics, electrical generation, and knowledge management, have not lived up to their initial hype.

- Definitions of key terms related to knowledge management:

    ▪ Knowledge = A Capacity to Act (Sveiby, 2001).

    ▪ Knowledge management is "how groups of people make themselves collectively smarter" and increase the amount of material at the top of the *knowledge hierarchy.*

    ▪ An organization uses knowledge management to make itself smarter.

- Many people mistake information for knowledge.

    ▪ The knowledge hierarchy consists of data (raw, iso-lated facts), information (organized facts, low-level skills, simple rules, and basic procedures), knowledge (which builds on information and includes concepts, high-level skills, tactics, and algorithms), and wisdom (philosophies, strategies, attitudes, and heuristics that transfer knowledge from one context to another).

- Information overload refers to the flood of information crowding business and personal environments as a result of improved information processing. Overloading information does not increase the flow of knowledge, it slows it down.

- Managing documents with systems like content management systems improves the storage of documents, but rarely improves the flow of knowledge, or even the ease of finding information.

• Successful knowledge management, therefore, faces significant obstacles to success.

• They are labor-intensive and are not scaleable. But the most significant obstacles are interpersonal, related to the differences between the technical staffs (the Borgians) and the learning staffs (the Flower Children) and organizational cultures that encourage knowledge hoarding and limiting access to information.

• Making knowledge management happen involves a number of simple, practical steps, many of which do not involve the purchase of new technology. These include:

- Increasing knowledge by making it more accessible to people

- Capturing knowledge by making it easier for people to record what they know

- Refining knowledge so it is expressed in a way that's useful to others

- Sharing knowledge, which involves making knowledge accessible, keeping knowledge chunks small (and easy to find and quick to use), and reusing knowledge

- Applying knowledge—that is, acting on the messages in the content

- Knowledge management may not be a good idea gone bad but, more like other technology innovations, a concept ahead of its time, like the Apple Newton (which lives on in the Palm and Pocket PCs) and high-definition television.

◆ ◆ ◆

## Guiding Questions for Discussion

- Given all the early knowledge management problems, why should organizations attempt knowledge management now?

- How can typical problems be avoided in future knowledge management efforts?

- Which of the ideas for simple knowledge management make the most sense in your organization?

- What other simple ideas can be added to these lists?

- How can we share these ideas with others?

- What can be done to persuade information hoarders and the "need to know" culture to take a more open approach to knowledge?

---

**Learn More About It**

Links                CIO's Knowledge Management Research Center, www.cio.com/research/knowledge/

Centre for Advanced Learning Technologies Knowledge Management and Workflow,

www.insead.fr/CALT/Encyclopedia/ ComputerSciences/Groupware/Workflow/

|  | Sveiby Knowledge Associates Library, www.sveiby.com/library.html |
|---|---|
|  | Information Research, http://informationr.net/ir/index.html |
|  | Education Network Australia Knowledge Management Community Area, www.edna.edu.au/edna/page2092.html |
| Books, Papers, Reports, and Articles | Rosenberg, M. (2006). *Beyond e-learning: Approaches and technologies to enhance organizational knowledge, learning, and performance.* San Francisco, CA: Pfeiffer. |

# Part III

# Technology Issues

This part explores some of the technical challenges that have affected the growth of e-learning in academic and corporate environments. Chapters in this part include:

- Chapter 5, Infrastructure for Learning: Options for Today or Screw-Ups for Tomorrow, by Patti Shank, L. Wayne Precht, Harvey Singh, Jim Everidge, and Jane Bozarth, addresses the challenges of preparing an infrastructure for e-learning in organizations. This chapter addresses specifically questions like: How do needs vary with different phases in the use of e-learning in an organization? What infrastructure is essential? What's nice to have? What challenges should people be aware of, like obsolete file formats? Is technology for learning likely to merge with similar technologies in other fields, such as a merger of learning content management systems with more widely available content management systems? Last, this chapter considers why technology is so complicated that the industry has had to spawn a sub-industry of people who advise others on how to choose and implement the infrastructure.

- Chapter 6, e-Learning Standards: A Framework for Enabling the Creation and Distribution of High-Quality, Cost-Effective, Web-Delivered Instruction by Pat Brogan, critically examines standards efforts. After a quick survey of the standards, this chapter explores issues such as the ongoing problems with interoperability—even after products conform to standards the IMS bit off more than it could chew with the terminology issue and what a realistic prognosis is for learning objects. This chapter also addresses issues such as whether these standards protect current e-learning developers from the problems of obsolete file formats that existed before and whether standards really matter to smaller organizations, which aren't developing or purchasing large libraries of e-learning.

- Chapter 7, Learning with Objects by Patrick Parrish, explores the challenges of reusable learning objects. After describing what learning objects are (so that readers have a common definition of the concept, as definitions are a challenge in this area), this chapter presents two paradigms for exploring learning objects. From each perspective, the assumptions underlying and ignored by the paradigm and resulting effect on how learning objects affect work and everyday life. The chapter closes with a brief description of a promising effort to employ learning objects in a professional development context.

- Chapter 8, Web 2.0 and Beyond: The Changing Needs of Learners, New Tools, and Ways to Learn by co-editor Patti Shank, explores Web 2.0, the emerging generation of software driving the web in general and e-learning in particular. After defining Web 2.0, this chapter explores the changing nature of information and learning, then considers the changing nature of learners (especially those who have grown up with the Internet). Next, it explores the response to these changes by providing an inventory of the software tools that characterize Web 2.0, such as blogs, wikis, "google jockeying," and "mashups." Then the chapter considers how Web 2.0 is creating new ways to learn and closes by considering these changes within the broader context of e-learning.

- Chapter 9, Locked Out: Bridging the Divide Between Training and Information Technology by Marc J. Rosenberg and Steve Foreman, addresses personnel challenges associated with learning technology: Are training organizations capable of managing new learning technologies in ways that are consistent with corporate Information Technology (IT) requirements? and Are IT organizations capable of responding to the unique requirements that new learning technologies present? Some of the challenges result from the learning staff's limited understanding of the technology; some of the challenges result from the IT organization's lack of understanding of the changing role of the learning staff. This chapter explores these problems and suggests ways to address them.

# Chapter 5

# Infrastructure for Learning

Options for Today or Screw-Ups for Tomorrow

*Patti Shank, Learning Peaks, Inc.;*
*L. Wayne Precht, University of Maryland*
*University College; Harvey Singh, Instancy, Inc.;*
*Jim Everidge, Rapid Learning Deployment; and*
*Jane Bozarth, State of North Carolina*

## About This Chapter

Learning infrastructure—that is, the hardware, software, delivery mechanisms, and processes that deliver and manage learning programs—can be crucial to the success of an e-learning effort. A strong infrastructure provides access to instructional content and helps stakeholders, such as instructional designers, faculty, department heads, and corporate executives, track usage, completion rates, assessment scores, and other outcomes of interest. The term "learning management system" (LMS) is often used synonymously with learning infrastructure, but an LMS by itself is usually only part of a learning infrastructure.

Infrastructure can deliver and track learning, but it can also block e-learning—literally. For example, if a course is available to supervisors and a specific supervisory job code has been incorrectly input into the human resources information system that talks to the learning management system, learners with that job code will not have immediate access to the course—a hassle. If an e-learning program involves streaming audio or video, and the organization's network doesn't have the bandwidth needed to run these programs or otherwise limits access to these types of files, these media will take forever to load or perhaps not run at all—more than a hassle. Some infrastructure may be incompatible with other company applications and network infrastructure. And information technology (IT) folks aren't always that happy to help with these and other learning infrastructure problems if they were not part of the learning infrastructure selection process.

This chapter answers the questions: "Why is learning infrastructure important?" "Why is learning infrastructure such a challenge?" and "What are some common mistakes that learning infrastructure purchasers make?" We start with a discussion of why learning infrastructure is such a complex issue. Next, we differentiate among learning infrastructures in corporate and academic settings. Last, we critically explore learning infrastructure challenges, by describing some of the most typical mistakes e-learning specialists have made when purchasing infrastructure components.

## Introduction

Imagine a group of architects, builders, and planners designing a large office building in the business area closest to where you live. They spend hours considering the merits of fountains versus sculptures and considering novel interior spaces where people can work. After the building construction has begun, someone realizes that no one has included parking spaces, elevators, electrical wiring, network wiring, or plumbing. A few members of the group suggest looking at the much larger building next door and retrofitting their own building with the exact same things—no thinking needed. But the building next door is a medical office building and was designed for tenants with very specialized needs. Does the big office building under construction really need a biohazard waste storage room?

Laughable? Perhaps. But organizations regularly approach planning their infrastructures for organizational growth and performance, and specifically for learning, in a similar manner. They too often ask others what they purchased (and assume they have the same needs), are wowed by bells and whistles (and pay for things they'll likely never use), and end up locked into processes that aren't sustainable; in other words, they don't perform due diligence.

The moral of the story is that the infrastructure, facilities, services, and processes that support day-to-day activities, are crucial to all endeavors. In a building, infrastructure includes the foundation, framing, wiring, plumbing, and ductwork that makes the building habitable, and services and processes, such as replacing light bulbs, monitoring security, and making repairs to the building, so people who work in the building can do their work and not think about building infrastructure at all.

Learning infrastructure typically includes the hardware, software, delivery mechanisms, and processes that deliver and manage learning programs. This includes hardware such as servers and workers' desktop computers, software such as learning management systems and authoring applications, delivery mechanisms such as routers and network wiring, and services and processes such as systems maintenance and the help desk.

Learning infrastructure has an effect on other network resources, and that's why it's a good idea to work in concert with, not in opposition to, the people who maintain the general technology infrastructure for an organization. For example, although an instructional designer might consider a video sequence essential to learning, an organizational technology infrastructure specialist may consider it a "bandwidth hog." And guess what happens when the learning designers ask for help getting the "hog" to learners' desks?

This chapter explores issues associated with learning infrastructure. It starts with a discussion of why learning infrastructure is such a complex issue. Next, it differentiates among infrastructures in corporate and academic settings. Last, this chapter critically explores infrastructure challenges by describing some of the most typical mistakes made when purchasing infrastructure components.

## What Makes Learning Infrastructure Such a Complex Issue?

Consider the following situations. In the early days of computer-based training, one instructional designer who knew a lot about the design of online learning—but little about its technology components—purchased a minicomputer (which, by today's standards, is the size of a super computer). Not realizing that minicomputers had special environmental requirements, he placed the computer in an empty office. Unfortunately, to dissipate the heat generated by the system unit, the computer required a specially air-conditioned room (more than typical requirements). Eventually, the circuitry of the computer fried from the heat. More recently, the information technology (IT) department of a large government agency halted the purchase of e-learning management applications because no one had conducted an assessment of the impact of these applications on the agency's network. The IT department had difficulty making sure that the network could meet response time targets and, with the addition of a bandwidth-intensive applications, that challenge would become more difficult. In a university, students who were trying to use an online video-based lecture from an outside organization could not do so. The IT department prevented video files from coming through the network during regular working hours because, in the past, files brought the network to a standstill.

Little of the learning literature explores the impact of e-learning infrastructure on existing technology frameworks. This may be because analyzing infrastructure needs and constraints is not in a typical training director's or department head's skill set. During the early days of computer-based training (CBT), infrastructure wasn't an issue because CBT ran on computers that were not connected to a network and, in many cases, were solely dedicated to CBT. But now, most e-learning typically runs on an intranet (an internal network within an organization), on the Internet, or on computers that are used for a variety of purposes, including learning.

The next section expands on the description of learning infrastructure provided earlier in this chapter. Then, it describes key parts of a learning infrastructure. It closes by identifying the key components of a learning infrastructure.

## What Is Infrastructure?

When used as an information technology term, infrastructure refers to the underlying technical components and processes (generally hardware, software, and delivery mechanisms) that are used to deliver information technology services. When used for learning, the term infrastructure primarily refers to applications that create, deliver, manage, personalize, and evaluate learning programs. The hardware, delivery mechanisms, and processes are usually in place and part of the organization's existing technology infrastructure. Although hardware may already be in place, it needs to be analyzed again for learning purposes, because existing technology infrastructure components, such as PC operating systems, available media players (such as Flash or Windows Media Player), and bandwidth (how much data can be transmitted at a time), become constraints on the e-learning that the organization can support and, ultimately, its strategy for providing learning online.

Table 5.1 shows some of the key factors contributing to the complexity of learning infrastructures.

In addition to these complexities, the requirements of different stakeholders within a single organization may vary, necessitating the addition of infrastructure components to meet different (and sometimes mutually exclusive) business needs. These stakeholders include trainers, designers, developers, faculty, instructors, administrators, and learners.

Organizations that get their infrastructure needs right often do so by first identifying and addressing the needs of their constituencies. Most do so by creating committees and advisory groups with

| **Table 5.1. Factors Contributing to the Complexity of the Infrastructure for Learning** | |
|---|---|
| **Factor** | **How It Contributes to the Complexity of the Infrastructure for Learning** |
| Technology Dependencies | Successful implementation of an infrastructure for learning almost always requires the full support and expertise of the IT department, which will usually have primary responsibility for installing, maintaining, and upgrading the infrastructure. Making sure that the chosen applications run efficiently and effectively on the network involves assessing how the proposed technology interacts with the existing technology infrastructure within the organization, including hardware devices, client workstations, computer networks, servers, disk space, and band-width support. For example, a learning group might be interested in implementing video-based learning, but if the IT department has limited or prevented access to video files, this will be difficult. Similarly, the organization might be interested in implementing a particular learning management system (LMS), but it might require use of related applications that the organization does not have. |
| | In other words, when making decisions about learning infrastructure applications, the organization needs to consult with the IT group to determine whether the applications are compatible with the organization's technology infrastructure and, if they are, to assess the impact of the applications on the technology infrastructure. |
| Customization | Off-the-shelf, the applications used in an e-learning infrastructure rarely work together as desired, nor do they exactly match the technology requirements of the organization purchasing them. In many cases, the organization needs to customize the reports generated by learning infrastructure applications. In other cases, programming changes are needed. For example, consider the organization that wanted to purchase an LMS to track learners and learning assessments for a certification program. Although the LMS could generate randomized multiple-choice questions, it could not randomize questions by objective, reducing the validity of the test. So the testing module of the LMS needed to be modified to match the organization's testing needs. |

| | |
|---|---|
| **Table 5.1. Factors Contributing to the Complexity of the Infrastructure for Learning, (Continued)** | |
| **Factor** | **How It Contributes to the Complexity of the Infrastructure for Learning** |
| | When considering applications to be used in learning infrastructure applications, match the needs of the organization with functions and features of applications that best meet those needs. Also determine how much the "extras," such as additional programming and function, will cost to get a total picture of functionalities and cost. |
| Integration Challenges | If e-learning in corporate environments is going to be truly integrated into the work environment, as many experts advocate, then it must also be integrated with other applications used in the enterprise, including human resource information systems (HRIS), customer relationship management (CRM) systems, financial systems, enterprise content management systems (ECMS), and existing web portals. Similarly, in academic environments, e-learning must be integrated with systems like student information systems (SIS), existing web portals, and financial systems. In addition, if an organization purchases several learning infrastructure components, these must be integrated with one another. Despite the existence of standards for exchanging data (called *interoperability*), when the different applications come from different vendors, each of whom uses a different underlying technology, such as Enterprise Java, Microsoft.NET, and various database technologies, integration is often difficult. |
| | Analyze integration needs, including the technology underlying the components that are supposed to be integrated and assess the ease of integrating content and information among these systems. Add integration costs to additional costs for programming and function. |
| Standards | One of the purposes of standards for e-learning is to increase the likelihood of interoperability among platforms. But e-learning standards work better on paper than in reality. Key for promoting interoperability among e-learning applications (especially LMSs and learning content management systems (LCMS)) is the Sharable Content Object Reference Model (SCORM) and Package Exchange Notification Services (PENS). Although great strides |

| Table 5.1. Factors Contributing to the Complexity of the Infrastructure for Learning, (Continued) | |
|---|---|
| **Factor** | **How It Contributes to the Complexity of the Infrastructure for Learning** |
|  | have been made with standards, interoperability challenges persist. In the next chapter in this book, Pat Brogan provides an in-depth exploration of standards issues. When implementing e-learning standards, plan for that fact that integration won't be a slam dunk. |
| Vendors | Because few organizations design their own systems for creating and managing e-learning, the majority depend on vendors to provide these applications and related services. In many instances, vendors also host the resulting e-learning. |
|  | But the large number of vendors in this field (at one point, industry analyst Bryan Chapman counted 128 different learning management systems, although the number in early 2008 is closer to sixty-five), as well as their varying levels of size and maturity create a number of problems. To lock in customers, many vendors of e-learning applications have tried to create a proprietary aspect to their applications that makes migration to competing applications difficult. (This has been an ongoing practice in learning applications, predating the current e-learning wave.) In other instances, to create demand for their class of product in general—and their own products in particular—vendors have misrepresented their products to naïve consumers (Carliner, 2003). In other instances, vendors are financially weak and may go out of business, leaving an organization without support for a product on which it has become dependent. |
|  | Before an organization makes learning infrastructure purchases, it needs to perform due diligence on its vendors, verifying both the claims that they make, as well as their financial health. |
| Consumers | Many decision makers and influencers involved in teaching and learning have limited experience using technology, much less making technology purchases. Yet the complexity of the technology, the interrelationships among the different technology components of a learning infrastructure, and the arrangements for related services demand that decision makers and influencers |

| Table 5.1. Factors Contributing to the Complexity of the Infrastructure for Learning, (Continued) | |
| --- | --- |
| **Factor** | **How It Contributes to the Complexity of the Infrastructure for Learning** |
| | have a minimum level of knowledge. But too many don't know what they need, provide vendors with incomplete or incorrect information, and cannot critically develop adequate requests for information from vendors or analyze vendors' responses. As a result, many consumers make weak decisions, sometimes because a vendor took advantage of their naiveté, but more often because they were too uninformed to make good decisions. For example, one vendor complains that potential clients too frequently use standard requests for proposals (RFPs) from well-known industry analysts, which often identify requirements that these potential client organizations do not really have. As a result, the vendor prepares a proposal that meets the stated requirements but not the actual needs. |

representatives from each stakeholder unit to define requirements, business needs, learning processes, standards, guidelines, and selection criteria, and vendor evaluation checklists. When such organizations feel overwhelmed, they often hire experts who have no stake in the resulting choice to assist them through the process of defining requirements and selecting components of the e-learning infrastructure.

## Key Issues to Address in a Learning Infrastructure

A learning infrastructure needs to address several key issues. The first is the underlying learning strategy, which describes how learning will support business needs and strategies.

Although a critical part of the learning infrastructure, strategy is often given far less thought than required. As a result, the organization might purchase technology for its learning infrastructure that doesn't provide the support or data needed or ties their hands in building the types of learning that can be provided. For example, without a strategy, a university might choose the least expensive course management system (CMS), which would be more difficult to use or have fewer needed features than a seemingly more costly CMS. As a result, usage of the CMS falls way below expectations, resulting in an expense that appears to be unjustified. As Van Buren and Sloman (2003) note, organizations that prepare a strategy for e-learning are more likely to be satisfied with the results.

The second key issue that learning infrastructure must address is the technology components and related support elements needed to help the organization realize the underlying strategy. The technology components of a learning infrastructure typically include:

- Hardware, including not only the physical network hardware, such as the servers and routers, but also the performance of that hardware, including the target uptime and reliability of the network, as well as provisions for backing up network resources

- Applications, including operating systems, learning management systems, learning content management systems, enterprise content management systems, course management systems, and databases, as well as related issues, such as security

- Processes, including provisions for training end users, faculty, trainers, and others on how to use the technology, as well as provisions for technical support, requesting changes to the network, and similar operational issues

The range of technologies that address these needs can be classified broadly into three categories:

- Those that support teaching and learning, such as learning management systems (LMS) and learning content management systems (LCMS)

- Those that can be used to *support* teaching and learning, such as peer-to-peer (P2P) applications, blogs, wikis, workflow management applications, and performance support and help tools

- Those that are needed to support the teaching and learning technologies named in the first two bullet points, such as networks, servers, firewalls, and Internet protocols

Broadly speaking, learning infrastructure requirements and models tend to vary dramatically between the following two environments:

- Corporate training (public, private, and military), including workforce development, training new employees, job-task-related training, and product or service training for internal and external customers and partners

- Academic, including colleges and universities and similar educational institutions, and online programs, including support for online and hybrid courses for degree and non-degree programs

The differences between the requirements for these two environments or markets are significant enough that most infrastructure vendors have chosen to focus on one or the other. Although some started by focusing on one market and tried to expand into the other, few have been successful in penetrating both, although the infrastructure needs of these two markets differ, the broader needs do not. The next major section of this chapter specifically explores the different learning infrastructures needed for these two markets. More immediately, the next sub-section explores terminology associated with technology infrastructures.

## Descriptions of the Key Components of a Learning Infrastructure

Before considering the key components of the learning infrastructure, one should first familiarize oneself with the most common terms used to describe a learning infrastructure. Following are these terms and some concise definitions, as they are being used in this chapter.

*Interoperability* is the capacity of content and systems to work with other content and systems. For learning content, this commonly means that content developed to work in one vendor's learning infrastructure component, such as an LMS, is expected to also work in a similar learning infrastructure component sold by another vendor.

*Learning standards*, when applied to learning infrastructure, typically means adherence to technical standards that are intended to assure that learning content will be run on similar "standards compliant" infrastructure components and might be interoperable.

A *learning management system* (LMS) is an application that handles learning-related administrative tasks such as creating course catalogs, registering users, providing access to online courses or course components, tracking users within courses, recording data about learners (such as test scores and pages visited), and providing reports about usage and outcomes to stakeholders.

A *learning content management system* (LCMS) is an application that manages aggregation (putting together) of learning content, typically called learning objects, allows administrators or designers to search for desired content, convert content format, and sequence learning objects into courses. Some LCMSs integrate authoring capabilities.

*Learning objects* are digital media elements (such as text, graphics, audio, video, and animations) that can be aggregated to form lessons, modules, or courses and are intended to be granular enough to be usable in a variety of courses. For example, an online new-hire orientation might include a module on policies, pictures of corporate officers, and a scavenger hunt game in which learners search the company intranet to figure out where different corporate functions are housed. Each of these digital media elements may be used in other courses.

With these definitions in mind, one can now consider which hardware, software, delivery mechanisms, and processes an organization should consider assembling to create a learning infrastructure. Table 5.2 identifies the major ones. Note that not all components are used by all organizations or available from all vendors. Organizations may implement some or all of these components at once or they may be implemented in a phased approach.

Although these components are discussed here as separate components, vendors who design and sell learning infrastructure are increasingly designing systems that integrate multiple components. For example, although content authoring and content management are separate components, they are often provided in the same application. Some vendors package multiple components to make things easier for clients, ensure that components work together, and, dare we say, make it harder for organizations to change vendors.

**Table 5.2. The Hardware, Software, Delivery Mechanisms, and Processes an Organization Should Consider Assembling to Create a Learning Infrastructure**

| | |
|---|---|
| Content Authoring | Tools that let designers, instructors, and faculty design and develop learning content. May include some or all of these features: |

- Multiple outputs, such as printed materials, CDs, and DVDs, Internet-based content, and print. An advantage of the ability to produce material in multiple formats is the ability to share content across media and reuse and re-purpose content to meet the unique requirements of different users, groups, and organizations.

- Collaborative content development, which partner on the design, writing, and editing of content. Such applications often include function that facilitate reviews, acceptance of review comments, and approval of material before publishing.

- Multiple types of content, which may include academic and job-related material that uses text, graphics, audio, video, and multimedia.

- Templates, which let designers, SMEs, and others enter content into "forms," ensure consistency in terminology and the appearance of screens among different contributors, and reduce the programming and maintenance needed to publish and maintain the content.

| | |
|---|---|
| Content Management | Facilitates creation, storage indexing, searching, and categorizing of source content. Specifically, content management helps designers and developers find and link related content, aggregate content, create new content from existing content, and update existing content everywhere it is used in courses and other instructional materials. Content management often includes these features: |

- Protection, which provides backup and redundant storage.

- Security, which limits access so that only authorized people can add, update, and publish content.

**Table 5.2. The Hardware, Software, Delivery Mechanisms, and Processes an Organization Should Consider Assembling to Create a Learning Infrastructure, (Continued)**

| | |
|---|---|
| | • Version control, which monitors and tracks versions to make sure that people are working with the correct version. |
| | • Indexing, to help content developers find content that they need. Most content management systems provide the ability to "tag" content with relevant key words and identify significant characteristics (such as a test question or a photograph), increasing the likelihood that searches will produce meaningful results. |
| | • Reporting, which provides information about the use and characteristics of the content, such as completion rates and recent updates. |
| Learning Management | Tracks learners and their progress through courses. Learning management functions often include:<br><br>• User management, which let administrators enroll groups and subgroups, manage information about users (such as updating email addresses or job category), and provide reports on users.<br><br>• Training management, which tracks the use of training resources, such as course schedules, classroom use, and registrations and class lists.<br><br>• Development planning, which provides both learners and managers with tools to determine training needs, link these needs to courses, resources, coaching, or other learning opportunities, and track training plans for individual workers and progress against plans. |
| Assessments and Evaluations | Tracks learners' scores on assessments and evaluations of courses and other learning events. Specifically, tracking capabilities often include:<br><br>• Reports on student progress through courses, performance on graded assignments, and completions. |

**Table 5.2. The Hardware, Software, Delivery Mechanisms, and Processes an Organization Should Consider Assembling to Create a Learning Infrastructure, (Continued)**

|  |  |
|---|---|
|  | • Analytical and data-mining capabilities to report on broader trends on the use of learning activities, such as the impact of learning on the organization. |
| Knowledge Management | Captures, compiles, organizes, and indexes the knowledge and skills acquired by people and groups in an organization. Ideally, this happens while people perform their work. As this body of captured knowledge grows, an organization can use it to assist other workers and teams. An analysis of this captured knowledge can lead to evolution of best practices. |
|  | For example, if a project is successfully completed by a team in one division of a company, their proposals, work plans, correspondence, and other documents are available to other teams in other divisions, as well as any lessons learned that the original team members might have recorded. Knowledge management can also be used for training or in support of the learning environment. For example, the University of Maryland University College refers students and support people to their extensive knowledge base as the first source of answers for questions about their WebTycho course management system. |
| Performance Support | Provides assistance while performing a job task. This assistance could involve access to system resources and records and instructions or guidance on how a job function is to be performed. Workers might receive performance support upon request, or it might run in the background, monitor work-related activities, and automatically provide assistance as anticipated. An example of performance support is the applications commonly used by customer service staff, which prompt service representatives to ask particular questions and provides pre-scripted answers plus links to related information. |
| Competency Management | At the individual level, helps a person identify the competencies needed for success in his or her current |

**Table 5.2.  The Hardware, Software, Delivery Mechanisms, and Processes an Organization Should Consider Assembling to Create a Learning Infrastructure, (Continued)**

position, provides information about the competencies needed for other positions, and describes training and other developmental activities that can address a gap between the competencies needed and the competencies an individual currently has. Also allows updates to an individual's competencies to reflect competencies acquired in training programs and elsewhere.

At the organizational level, tracks the skills of all workers in the organization and can be used to identify who has a specific competency needed elsewhere in the organization.

| | |
|---|---|
| Workflow Management | To successfully plan and deliver learning programs, an organization needs to manage a large number of related activities. The specific activities vary depending on the type of learning involved (such as formal or informal learning), mode of delivery involved (such as online or classroom), and various other factors.<br><br>Workflow management helps managers and project managers choose the most relevant activities and sequence them for best results. Organizations can use workflow management for creating, reviewing, and publishing learning content, especially e-learning content. |
| Integration | For maximum effectiveness, the interlocking learning infrastructure components must be linked together. For example, information created using authoring components can be organized using content management components and delivered using learning management components. To really happen, however, these must work together. Furthermore, these must often interact with other systems. For example, universities cannot let students enroll unless they have paid tuition, information which comes from a financial or student information system. Corporations may track courses taken by a single employee and update this information in a human resource information system. |

An example of integrated components can be found in Wayne's organization, where its enterprise resource planning (ERP)/ enterprise resource management (ERM) system, PeopleSoft, has been integrated with its LMS, WebTycho. As a result, financial and administrative functions are handled by PeopleSoft, which exchanges the information with WebTycho for use in enrollment and course management, and, as Wayne notes, an even tighter integration is needed. For example, reporting and tracking features need to be added to help with assessment outcomes initiatives. A tight integration results in stronger performance of the entire learning infrastructure.

Ultimately, infrastructure is about tradeoffs. Most learning projects don't have endless funding and open deadlines, so stakeholders must make decisions about which components their learning infrastructure needs and what type of infrastructure makes sense and cents.

# Infrastructures for Learning in Corporate and Academic Settings

Some organizations think they need a sophisticated infrastructure for learning because LMS and LCMS vendors have made them seem like must-haves. But unless an organization has many learners, needs to track learners or courses, or has lots of content to be repurposed in a number of ways, this expenditure may not be needed (or not *yet* needed). Some needs may be met with small home-grown applications, rather than enterprise-level ones. Furthermore, different types and sizes of organizations need different types of learning infrastructure. Building on the general issues and components of a learning infrastructure described in the previous section, this section attempts to describe the specific types of learning infrastructures typically needed in corporate and academic settings.

## Learning Infrastructures in Corporate Settings

A corporate learning infrastructure is intended to support individual and corporate learning. Generally, this involves reporting on learner enrollments, showing training compliance, managing and reporting on learning and learning outcomes, and assessing the return on its investment.

The type of infrastructure needed in a corporate setting depends on four factors: business needs, the size of the organization, a decision to build or buy, and the use of commercial or open source applications.

Let's start with business needs. Organizations need to mitigate risk (that is, provide evidence of training completion, typically on compliance and high-litigation-potential content) or influence workplace skills. A learning infrastructure supports these needs differently.

- *Mitigate risk*. A management reporting system may be the top priority. The organization can use LMS data to provide evidence of meeting training compliance and an affirmative defense in case of litigation.

- *Influence workplace skills*. The ability to catalog and deliver content (often with an LCMS) becomes important as more content is developed and reuse of content becomes a strategy for achieving cost savings in influencing workplace skills. In addition, some LMSs provide competency tracking, which can assist with the task of monitoring skills.

What about the size of organization? Jim feels corporate organizations need around 2,500 learners (such as employees, customers, or suppliers) to provide a reasonable return on the cost of a learning infrastructure. He explains, "If a company is not in the 'Top 5' of their market segment, they probably shouldn't purchase their infrastructure." He believes Top 5 organizations should buy from one of the top vendors because they have the bulk of the market and need to support many different types of industries and customers. "If you buy from a vendor who is not in the top 5," he explains, "you may be stuck with an application that goes in a direction you won't like (for example, you are a financial services company and your vendor's top clients are utility companies, so the vendor's product becomes more and more geared toward tracking ISO standards and engineering compliance—issues of no value to you)."

Wayne looks at this from a university perspective, noting that organizations that are top 5 in their segment and have just 2,500 learners are often small potatoes to a vendor who provides infrastructure components to higher education instructions, which often have tens of thousands of learners. He recommends selecting infrastructure based on the needs of your organization, rather than the vendor's market share.

Small to medium-sized organizations should consider leasing learning infrastructure. Application service providers (ASP) or fully hosted learning infrastructure (also referred to sometimes as a "managed services" solution) may be a good option for organizations that do not have their own internal IT teams supporting installation and rollout of learning infrastructure. In an ASP arrangement, organizations lease applications and often pay for use by number of concurrent users. Such arrangements work well if the number of learners starts out small and is likely to grow over time, because the pricing is typically flexible. Hosting is usually a flat fee-for-service paid annually, and that lets an organization track a designated number of learners.

With leasing arrangements, Jim cautions organizations to examine contractual periods and not get locked into a long-term deal (more than two years) because needs are likely to change. But organizations need to cautiously approach short-term contracts, too, because costs can escalate and, once the use of the application gains momentum, an organization is usually reluctant to move to another system.

Jim also advises organizations without strong applications development capabilities to avoid using open source applications. Although tempted by the low cost of these applications (essentially freely available), they usually require a little to a lot of additional custom development to make them fit an organization's needs and integrate with other applications. Many organizations do not have the capacity to provide this extra development effort and should instead consider hosted infrastructure. Many organizations naïvely assume that open-source applications require no extra development and maintenance, and learn, after spending much time and money, this isn't the case. But Wayne offers some hope, noting that, if an organization selects mature open source applications whose capabilities closely match an organization's needs, the need for extensive customization and maintenance is relatively small. The Apache web server is an excellent example because it is a stable and mature open source product that drives more than half of the Internet's websites.

## Learning Infrastructure in Academic Settings

In contrast, learning infrastructure in an academic setting is intended to support the education of part- and full-time students and the course development and teaching activities of instructors. This typically involves managing enrollments, degree requirements, and transcripts for individual learners and tracking tuition payments, as well as hosting course elements and tracking student use and assessments. In addition, the infrastructure supports classroom learning by providing online access to course materials.

Given the heavy use of the learning infrastructure in higher education, one of the key issues is adapting to the large number of users and ensuring that the infrastructure is always available (called *uptime*). When an educational institution has more than a few thousand students, which is equivalent to two hundred to five hundred simultaneous users, it requires an extensive hardware and software structure, called an *enterprise class infrastructure.* Before this point, an LMS on a single server may work just fine.

Consider WebTycho, the infrastructure used on the systems of the University of Maryland University College (UMUC). When UMUC's distance learning enrollments hit the few thousand mark, the school had to rapidly expand a single system to a cluster of four machines and redesign distance learning applications to work in that new environment.

Faculty and students expect higher education learning systems to be available whenever they want to do their work, which essentially means twenty-four hours a day, seven days a week, 365 days a year (called *24 × 7 × 365 uptime*). Users notice and complain about the difference between 97 percent and 99.999 percent uptime.

In addition to the number of users and uptime, other issues that need to be considered when designing infrastructure for an academic environment include:

- *Redundant Internet service provider (ISPs) connections.* Wayne explained how his organization once lost its Internet connection while a new building was being built. As a result, he now has that connection and a separate fiber connection to a disaster recovery site about a mile away. That site has its own Internet connection through a separate ISP, and Wayne's organization has the ability to quickly cut over almost seamlessly.

- *Backup power.* Wayne explained how frequent and severe thunderstorms convinced his group members that they needed a reliable backup system. His backup power system can provide as much as thirty minutes of battery power for the whole data center.

- *Hardware firewalls.* Many higher education institutions left their networks open in the early days of the Internet, but loose security resulted in viruses and students hacking into private data. Academic technology specialists have started taking security as seriously as their counterparts in industry. One way that academic technology specialists can secure their networks is by establishing labs, isolated from the main network, in which students can work on projects and avoid damaging data elsewhere on the network.

Although technology functions needed to support corporate and academic learning environments are similar, the applications used are different, optimized for the intended environments.

Specific features that affect the choice of specific components of *any* learning infrastructure include the following:

- *The purpose of the content.* Some organizations purchase course management systems (CMSs) like Blackboard and

Moodle to support classroom courses by providing space for course documents (such as the syllabus and lecture notes) and managing online discussions. Others need to deliver courses that are taken entirely online.

- *Mode of delivery.* Depending on whether courses are delivered synchronously or asynchronously, different infrastructure applications may be needed. Most CMSs let instructors teach asynchronously, but virtual classroom applications, like Adobe Connect or WebEx, are needed to teach synchronously.

- *The volume of learners.* Different applications can handle different numbers of learners. For example, Citrix Online's Go to Meeting application allows instructors to teach synchronously to a small group of learners but its Go to Webinar application allows presenters to present to larger audiences.

- *Skill level of content designers.* If individual instructors are developing their own instructional materials, the learning infrastructure should ideally simplify the task of creating and posting materials without lots of training and support. If experienced instructional designers and developers are developing instructional materials, more complex tools may be used.

Most online learners are task-oriented. Online learners are often fitting online courses into an already busy life and want to know what is required of them to succeed in a given task and how to perform that task most effectively and efficiently. They are not savvy enough to isolate network, server, and application issues that impact successful completion of learning. In fact, these issues should ideally be invisible to users.

So that these issues are invisible to users, academic technology specialists must pay special attention to choices that affect system performance. Academic learning infrastructures can be built on commercial or open source applications. With a strong eye to controlling costs, academic institutions are now more likely to consider open source applications, but higher education institutions sometimes find that scaling is the biggest problem with open source applications. Most open source applications are script based, run against a single database, and run on a single server. But once usage grows beyond a certain level and the organization exceeds the capacity of its current learning infrastructure, the only choice for most organizations using an open source application is to move the open source application to faster and larger machines. These applications do not run on clusters of servers (the arrangement described earlier for UMUC). The open source application, Sakai, does run on clusters, but technical and hardware resources are beyond the capabilities of many organizations.

But many institutions of higher education choose open source applications because many commercial products for the academic environment seem to have lost touch with the main purpose of their product. These course management systems typically have little-used features that crowd the interface and don't include features that instructors and learners most want, such as making it easy to save specific discussion threads and collaborative writing tools.

# Critically Exploring Infrastructure Challenges

As mentioned at the beginning of this chapter, the complexity of learning infrastructure makes it difficult to understand, plan, price, and purchase. Vendors who make these decisions seem easier than they really are and purchasers who are happy to let vendors make decisions seem easy only exacerbate this problem. Together, the complexity and human challenges create a host of problems, not the least of which is purchasing an infrastructure that will remain unused or underused because it doesn't meet the organization's needs. This section explores the eight most common mistakes organizations make as they begin to consider and implement learning infrastructure.

## Mistake 1: Not Determining Requirements Before Choosing Learning Infrastructure Components

Jane was asked to consult on the purchase of an LMS, whose purchase price would exceed US $1 million. When she arrived with her list of criteria, one of the key decision makers said, "Well, we're not going to ask them to prove whether the LMS does every single thing we want." Spend that much without careful consideration? Crazy but not unusual.

The truth is, most purchasers of learning infrastructure do not adequately prepare for the decisions they need to make. Many feel overwhelmed and are easy prey for any pitch that makes the process seem less daunting.

The right approach to designing and implementing learning infrastructure is to start by compiling a detailed list of business requirements for learning in general and e-learning specifically. That is, the first step in preparing for the learning infrastructure is to prepare a strategic plan for the learning group. Although it acknowledges e-learning, a strategic plan for the learning group is much broader and identifies key business needs and matching learning initiatives for the strategic period. (Because each organization operates differently, the strategic periods in different organizations vary, but typically range from two to four years.) At the least, develop a training plan that identifies which material will be presented in the classroom, which through technology, and how technology can support other aspects of the training operation. Optimally, the plan should estimate timetables for addressing these components of the training plan so that an organization can analzye how a learning infrastructure can best help deliver the results promised in the plan. This advance planning is important for a variety of reasons. As mentioned earlier in this chapter, organizations that have a strategic plan for learning are significantly more likely to be satisfied with their results. In addition, a current analysis of LMSs used in industry (Bersin, 2005) shows that most organizations only stay with an LMS for four years before changing and need to be prepared for the change.

After developing a strategic plan for learning, then develop a strategic plan for learning technology. Patti often implores organizations to build a long-range training plan, then develop a plan for the learning infrastructure, before contacting LMS vendors. Instead, she finds that most organizations still insist on selecting an LMS first, almost always without adequate data. A year or two later, however, these organizations often tell her that their LMS implementation has been a nightmare, sometimes including the elimination of people who obligated the company to a small fortune without knowing what was needed. Some have made the best of a bad situation by forcing content developers to tailor their training to the LMS. Had they started with business requirements, these organizations would be tailoring their LMSs to learning needs, not vice versa. Others scrap their existing systems and start the entire process again, this time beginning with business requirements (which is where they should have started in the first place).

When developing these requirements, organizations must first interview key stakeholders about their needs and analyze those needs before speaking with vendors, especially, the capabilities that learning technology must support. The result of this effort should be a list of capabilities needed by an organization's learning infrastructure. An example of a requirements document for an LMS is provided at the end of this chapter.

The next step, after determining requirements, is to create scenarios of work processes that describe common and important uses of the infrastructure components (for example, a scenario describing a recertification process, from notifying a manager and employee of recertification needs, to enrollment of staff in recertification courses, through tracking test and performance assessment results, and notifying the manager and employee of recertification results and next steps. A typical scenario might describe six or more work processes. The importance of each of these key work processes should then be ranked. These provide specific processes that vendors will need to demonstrate when trying to sell their systems to you. That is, rather than letting the vendor demonstrate its application, ask the vendor to demonstrate how the application performs the tasks identified in your scenarios. This lets you see how each vendor's application handles scenarios that are important to your organization. Because no system perfectly matches needs, consider scoring the choices for their performance on each task, weight the score by the relative importance of each task, and calculate an overall score to determine which system will *best* meet the organization's needs. Also assess the system on its price (including support and maintenance costs) and its "fit" with the existing technology infrastructure of the organization (an issue that is described later). Last, ask the vendor for contact information for the last five to ten installations of the product so that you can check references. (Don't just ask for "references" because these will likely be prescreened. Asking for the last five or more installations may get you more honest appraisals of the product.)

Although this is a sensible approach, some organizations, unfortunately, are doomed to avoid it. Consider a situation that Patti had with one of her clients. The client didn't like the LMS they had spent a small fortune on a few years earlier and convinced the company CFO that the company needed to buy another. When Patti asked what the training department needed to do differently, the manager wasn't sure because her group hadn't really used the old LMS much. Her staff just had a vague feeling that it was inadequate. Patti had pushed them to develop a list of requirements, but they thought that process would be too time-consuming, especially when they could get approval so easily. A couple years later, however, they are unsatisfied with the second LMS and haven't started making any real progress in using technology to meet their ever-expanding learning needs.

## Mistake 2: Not Analyzing Whether You Really Need an LMS

Jane notes that one of the most expensive mistakes organizations make is thinking they need to have a LMS or LCMS before they can *do* e-learning. "Many organizations think they need an LMS to track completions and test scores," she says. "But many don't have the need for the capabilities of a full-scale LMS, like tracking competencies [and] matching training to career paths." Unless organizations have these needs, an LMS is an expensive waste of resources.

As an example, she shares this story about a training department for an auto-parts retail chain. The stores in the chain only had Internet access on the store managers' computers. Furthermore, the company wasn't oriented toward the use of online resources for other aspects of its operations. Despite this limited access to the Internet and lack of computer use, the training manager insisted that e-learning development begin with the purchase of an LMS. "The last I heard," explains Jane, "they bought a very expensive product from a big LMS vendor and even the vendor thought they weren't ready for it." The vendor is worried that the client will blame the LMS (and the vendor's company) when nothing is accomplished.

As this story demonstrates, rather than purchasing an LMS, many organizations can initially make do with more readily available and less expensive alternatives. Table 5.3, which is adapted

**Table 5.3. Inexpensive Solutions for Learning Management Needs**

| Question | Non-LMS Solution |
|---|---|
| How many people accessed this page? | Free hit counter |
| Who accessed this page? | Free survey ("registration form") |
| Who reached the last page? | Printable completion form |
|  | Free survey on last page ("completion form") |
|  | Send an email note upon completion (and copy someone in the training department) |
| What score did Bill get on the test? | Give Bill a paper-and-pencil test. |
|  | Email Bill the test with a time limit for taking it; have him email it back to you for scoring. |
|  | Use a quiz engine |

Adapted from J. Bozarth. (2005). *e-Learning Solutions on a Shoestring: Help for the Chronically Underfunded Trainer.* San Francisco, CA: Pfeiffer.

from Jane Bozarth's *e-Learning Solutions on a Shoestring: Help for the Chronically Underfunded Trainer* (2005), shows how simple solutions can often provide simpler tracking without an expensive LMS.

## Mistake 3: Allowing Vendors to Control the Process

Too many organizations invite vendors to come in and demonstrate their products before they are ready to see them. Vendors typically demo features and scenarios they know work well. They often have pre-set scenarios that are guaranteed to work smoothly as the vendor provides a rehearsed commentary about how intuitive and easy the product is to use. (You've likely seen this approach from vendors on the expo floor at training conferences.) The demos also feature "cool and useful" features that customers add to their limited lists of requirements. Jim says this process often results in what he calls a "Frankenstein list" of requirements. A more common term is "feature creep," in which an organization requests an increasing number of features (whether they need them or not), which come at great cost to the organization in the form of extra licensing and implementation costs.

As consumers of automobiles have learned that they must become knowledgeable of what they want and what they're willing to spend before entering an automobile showroom, so consumers of learning infrastructure must learn that they need to become knowledgeable of what they want and what they're willing to spend (or can get approval to spend) before speaking with vendors. One of the best resources for doing so is the plan mentioned earlier. As noted in the description, not only do the lists of business requirements help sharpen the selection process, but the related scenarios provide a more reasoned means of demonstrating the product. The scenarios describe everyday uses of the learning infrastructure, and the demo can focus on how the products handle your tasks.

In other words, rather than letting the vendor determine what to show, provide the vendor with a list of tasks to demonstrate. Focus on tasks rather than features. Features merely state what the capabilities of the system are, whether or not those capabilities reflect your needs. Because many consumers compare products by the features they offer, many vendors include them, but the features might not be needed or, worse, they might be needed, but might not operate as expected under everyday conditions.

In contrast, tasks represent processes that must be performed every day. Ultimately, the test of everyday use determines whether the learning infrastructure successfully meets these requirements. Certain features might demonstrate well, but might not be reflective of everyday use. For example, if the demonstrator has to fiddle through multiple screens and steps to perform what should be a simple task, that task is likely to be even more challenging for the end user, who isn't nearly as familiar with the system. Note, too, that vendors often try to evade work flow scenarios that don't show their product in the best light; evading a demonstration of one of your key work processes indicates that the product is not likely to meet your needs. Also, if no vendor can easily accommodate your everyday needs, you might conclude that your expectations for the application are unrealistic.

## Mistake 4: Not Considering Other Factors When Choosing Learning Infrastructure Components

Demonstrations should not be the only basis for choosing learning infrastructure components. They are just one factor and should be weighted with several others. Table 5.4 indicates other key factors to consider in decisions about infrastructure purchases.

Using these issues—as well as others that may be important to your organization—create a decision matrix that compares vendors side-by-side on each of the issues. This gives decision makers a complete picture of each vendor, not just a feature match. It is often useful to rank order vendors after demonstrations. You can then do a more thorough evaluation on the highest-ranked vendors. An example of a vendor decision matrix for an LMS is provided at the end of this chapter.

**Table 5.4. Additional Factors to Consider When Purchasing Learning Infrastructure Components**

| | |
|---|---|
| Technical Assessment of the Underlying Technologies | Analyze the underlying technologies. This review should address long-term support for, and viability of, the underlying technologies. Determine the following: |
| | • Whether the technology is built using an industry standard programming language or is proprietary. Propriatory systems add risk if the organization wants to change vendors, if the vendor is purchased by another vendor (common in the industry) or goes out of business. |
| | • Whether the product conforms to desired learning standards (see the next chapter for more details). |
| | Both for expertise as well as internal politics, invite the IT staff to help you conduct this analysis. If they are not available, hire a consultant and keep the IT department in the loop. To avoid potential conflicts of interest, have the consultant sign a statement that he or she has no business dealings with, or ownership stake in, any vendor whose applications are under consideration. |
| Assessment of the Compatibility of the Proposed Learning Technology with the Organization's Technology Infrastructure | In addition to an assessment of the underlying technology in general, also assess its compatibility with the existing technology infrastructure of the organization. Determine the impact of adding the learning infrastructure on overall system performance. Ideally, use the same people who assisted with the overall technology assessment to perform this assessment, too. |
| Assessment of the Application Development Process | Review the process by which the vendor develops applications to assess: |
| | • To what degree is development influenced by customer needs? Does the vendor have a customer advisory group to provide input? How big is it? How long has it existed? How often do they meet? |

| Table 5.4. Additional Factors to Consider When Purchasing Learning Infrastructure Components, (Continued) | |
|---|---|
| | • How much and what type of support is available during and after implementation of the application? Is support provided by full-time support staff or by developers who are reluctantly performing this responsibility as an add-on task? |
| Business Fundamentals (Also Called Due Diligence) | Verify the viability and reliability of the vendor. To assess viability, assess the financial viability and credit worthiness through SEC filings (if they are a public company), or consult an industry analyst if the vendor is private. (You may need to purchase a report or pay for consulting services to obtain this information, but a few thousand dollars up-front might save hundreds of thousands of dollars or more later on.) |
| References | Find out how customers really feel about the product. At least contact the references provided by the vendor. You might also check satisfaction surveys. Note, however, that companies supply the names of their customers to the services evaluating satisfaction, so the sample might not necessarily be a representative one. |
| | This also raises a more significant issue: the most honest references are ones *not* provided by the vendor. So do some private networking and sleuthing to find other customers. Check marketing documents, case studies, and quarterly and annual SEC filings that refer to customer implementations for companies. Also ask the vendor to provide a list of customer implementations in the prior twelve to eighteen months and randomly call customers from this list. Also attend conferences in the industry to find and talk to customers. |
| Cost Analysis | On a financial basis, determine whether to lease or purchase the application. Request quotes for both options from the vendor, and ask the estimate to cover a two- to three-year period. Make sure that the purchase price covers support and maintenance. In general, the annual lease |

| | |
|---|---|
| **Table 5.4. Additional Factors to Consider When Purchasing Learning Infrastructure Components, (Continued)** | |
| | cost usually is 30 to 40 percent of the purchase price, but includes basic technical support and maintenance. |
| | In addition, plan for the purchase of additional assistance to train administrators and users, unplanned changes (but budgeted all the same), and to support internal users. |
| Exit Strategy | Specifically, consider how to exit the purchase if, after a period of implementation, the product does not work as expected. Similarly, if negotiating a lease, provide a clause that allows an exit at one year if performance is unsatisfactory. |

## Mistake 5: Forgetting About Maintenance of the Learning Infrastructure

Maintaining the learning infrastructure goes far beyond registering users and keeping the system running. Maintenance involves two key tasks: maintaining the learning application itself and maintaining the infrastructure on which it runs.

Maintaining the application may involve some or all of the following:

- Archiving old data and instructional materials

- Removing lapsed users from the list of authorized users

- Training and adding new instructors (for instructor-led courses)

- Updating the learning infrastructure components with the latest patches or releases and

- Testing updates and changes to make sure they work as expected and don't cause problems with other learning infrastructure components or the overall technology infrastructure

- Training users and administrators on new components, patches, or releases

- Adding enhancements to the application such as customizing the interface to reflect branding and to take advantage of customized features

Maintaining the infrastructure on which the learning technology runs may involve some or all of the following (many of these tasks are similar to those for maintaining individual applications):

- Installing patches and new releases for the server operating system

- Testing updates and changes to make sure they work as expected and don't cause problems with other components or the overall technology infrastructure

- Analyzing user and resource loads to determine when hardware needs to be upgraded or replaced

- Monitoring bandwidth utilization and modeling projected growth to determine when bandwidth needs to be augmented

As the use of technology for learning grows, it often makes sense to add a separate system (or cluster of systems) for testing upgrades before rolling them out to the live, production servers.

One other maintenance challenge pertains to product migrations—that is, moving from one product to another (or an entirely new version of a system). A product migration usually requires not only reinstallation of an entire system but may also require partial or complete conversion of the data used with the system. Complicating migration is the fact that vendors often sell them to customers as upgrades to existing products, rather than as what they really are: a product migration that involves actual changes to the application. The "upgrade" moniker implies less work, but moving from an old application to a new one is substantial work. In some cases, it is essentially like purchasing a new product. Therefore, the decision to purchase the "upgrade" should be approached with the same diligence as buying and implementing a new application.

## Mistake 6: Not Planning for Learning Infrastructure Support

Don't underestimate the amount of technical support and training required for people who use the learning infrastructure. You might not think that learners, course designers, and instructors, especially tech-savvy adult learners, would have all that much trouble with what is essentially a website. But they do, and if you are not ready for it, you will face serious problems because, if learners cannot easily access and use online materials, they'll be highly frustrated, a state that interferes with learning.

Customers often receive an agreement from their vendors to provide this support, but the agreement is often too vague to be meaningful. They do not state specifically what types of support will be provided and the charges for that support. For example, will the vendor provide training? Online or in the classroom? If online, synchronously or asynchronously? If in the classroom, at the customer's facilities or the vendor's?

Similarly, customers often purchase products from vendors who are later merged with, or purchased by, another company. When that happens, questions arise about what happens to the original agreements regarding support. Does the vendor guarantee the same level of support as the product changes? Or will the customer eventually have to move over to the acquiring company's products?

Customers may mistakenly believe that leased learning infrastructure reduces their support needs. In fact, the high level of coordination between the customer and the vendor often requires as much effort as if the technology were hosted internally. The real advantage in leased learning infrastructure is that these systems can be implemented in half the time as purchased systems.

In higher education, an additional success factor is the support of faculty, which often makes or breaks the success of the entire distance learning strategy. Supporting faculty often means providing information on topics such as benefits and limitations of the learning systems, how to use and troubleshoot them, how to use these systems to design and teach courses. This support must be available to the faculty who will use it months before these courses go live. It's hard to overestimate the significance of training stakeholders. In his role supporting a learning infrastructure in a university, Wayne observes that the chief complaints are the faculty's lack of skills with the technology and teaching online.

## Mistake 7: Not Figuring *All* of the Costs

Jane explains that the price of the infrastructure components is just the tip of the iceberg. Here are some other costs you may need to factor in, according to Jane and Patti.

- Consulting fees for analyzing needs and other beneficial up-front tasks such as composing a training plan
- Licenses
- Delivery
- Installation
- Consulting fees for implementation
- Consulting fees for integration
- Training infrastructure users and retraining as components are added, upgraded, or changed
- Programming fees for customization
- Maintenance fees
- Service fees
- Fees for technical support
- Staffing for operating and maintaining the infrastructure
- Upgrades
- Adding additional users

## Mistake 8: Forgetting About Users' Infrastructure

The organization's technology and learning infrastructure aren't the only infrastructure that should be considered. Wayne explains that his organization tried to add voice capabilities to the real-time chat application on the WebTycho system used at his university. The addition was delayed because the average user did not have the bandwidth for voice. When the university first thought about adding voice to its real-time chat application, about 80 percent of the users had dial-up connections. Voice chat generated 1.5 times more data traffic than the connection could handle. In other words, when designing an infrastructure for learning, one must consider not only organizational infrastructure, but also the infrastructure of users such as learners and instructors.

## Concluding Thoughts

The purpose of this chapter is to discuss the complexities of learning infrastructure and share lessons learned through numerous learning infrastructure implementations in corporate and academic environments. One important lesson is that purchasing learning infrastructure components is not a one-deal shot, because whatever learning infrastructure components are purchased will eventually need to be replaced. Some of that results from changes in technology, but the need to upgrade the infrastructure often results, too, from the success of an organization's learning initiatives. If the learning initiatives supported by the learning infrastructure are successful, new content will be added and the number of users registered and the number of hours they spend learning will likely surpass the demands of the existing learning infrastructure, so upgrades will be needed to keep up with this increased demand. The related costs and complexity of upgrades are the cost of doing well.

In organizations that remain on top of their technology, this often happens gradually, through upgrading a part of the network and changing parts of it as the need arises. In organizations that try to live with the technology purchased today for as long as they can—as well as when a major technology shift occurs—the upgrade happens in its entirety. Consider the evolution in learning infrastructure at Wayne's university. The school used the commercial mainframe-based LMS, PLATO, from about 1985 to 1992.

UMUC then built its own client-server-based LMS, called Tycho, which the organization used from 1992 to 1999. A new web-based version of Tycho, called WebTycho, was built in 1997. It was phased out in 2007, when a new highly scalable, J2EE version of Tycho was introduced.

Some institutions move even more quickly than UMUC. For example, Wayne knows of a university that moved over a period of six years from WebCT to Prometheus to WebTycho. For institutions that lease applications, the up-front investment is lower, so the mobility among systems can be higher. All of the transitions can be complicated when data cannot be easily exchanged among them. Learning objects that comply with standards simplify some of this transition, but not all. The next chapter explores the issue of standards in-depth.

If you're feeling overwhelmed by all the options and opportunities, you're not alone. Complexity is the nature of information technology projects.

It's not the options that create all the problems—so does the failure of learning specialists to understand the options, how the different options support different types of learning, and how the technology must link to the larger technology infrastructure of the organization to facilitate easy access to learning. Taking the time to research these issues, with the help of your IT department and learning infrastructure consultants, if needed, and reach well-reasoned conclusions admittedly has a cost but, as we hope the opening scenario demonstrates, failure to research and consider infrastructure issues has a much higher cost.

The highest cost, however, might not be dollars and cents but the impact of the learning strategy that the learning infrastructure supports. Our experiences with technology implementations have suggested that some much needed outcomes are more likely to be realized with the technology infrastructure to support them. The changes we hope to see include:

- Learning that is not only available on-demand, but *fused* with work. By fusing, we mean that the job tasks people must perform and the learning needed to support those tasks are tightly interconnected. Learning would be embedded within business processes and work flows rather than as a separate, and often disconnected, activity (which relegates "learning" to "events" that require special circumstances, rather than the day-to-day upgrading of skills and performance with the help of smart tools).

- Blending of formal and informal learning (which is believed to be the primary means for most learning) that takes into consideration both individual and social learning paradigms. (Patti explores this issue in Chapter 8.)

- More blending of classroom and technology-based learning to take advantage of the unique characteristics of each.

More than being about technology, learning infrastructure is intended to support learning, that fundamental human activity that cuts across all human barriers—methods, ages, backgrounds, economic circumstances, industries, and countries. Using technology to support this process offers benefits and challenges. The key in considering technology is not to try to guess the future but to make excellent decisions that prepare you to capitalize on it, even when that future cannot be fully known.

# References

Bersin, J. (2005, April 1). Evaluating LMSs? Buyer beware. *Training, 42*(2), 26–31.

Blackboard Inc. (2005). *Blackboard Inc. reports third quarter 2005 results.*www.blackboard.com/company/press/release.aspx?id=776679

Bozarth, J. (2005). *e-Learning solutions on a shoestring: Help for the chronically under-funded trainer.* San Francisco, CA: Pfeiffer.

Carliner, S. (2003). Ethics and the marketing of technology for training and performance improvement: A commentary. *Performance Improvement Quarterly, 16*(4), 94–106.

Van Buren, M.E., & Sloman, M. (2003, May 18). *e-Learning's learning curve: Will they come, will they learn?* American Society for Training and Development International Conference and Exposition. San Diego, California.

◆ ◆ ◆

## Summary of Main Points

Readers should take away the following main ideas from this chapter:

- When used as an information technology term, infrastructure refers to the underlying technical components and processes (generally hardware, software, and delivery mechanisms) that are used to deliver information technology services. When used for learning, the term infrastructure primarily refers to applications that create, deliver, manage, personalize, and evaluate learning programs.

- The term learning management system (LMS) is often used synonymously with learning infrastructure, but an LMS by itself is not a learning infrastructure. An LMS may just be one of the key components of an overall learning infrastructure.

- Key factors contributing to the complexity of the technology infrastructure include:

  - Technology dependencies (one technical component that depends on aspects of another)

  - Customization

  - Integration challenges

  - Standards

  - Vendors

  - Consumers

- Different stakeholders within an organization may have different requirements for learning infrastructure. Key stakeholders need to be involved in the process of selecting and implementing learning infrastructure.

- An infrastructure for e-learning needs to address several key issues:

  - An underlying strategy, which explains how learning supports the needs of the organization in which the infrastructure will be installed

  - The technology components and related support that help realize the underlying strategy as well as the range of technologies that support the type of teaching and learning that the organization wants to implement

  - The technology component of the infrastructure, which addresses hardware, software, and delivery mechanisms

- Technologies fall into three categories:

  - Those developed to support teaching and learning such as learning management systems (LMS) and learning content management systems (LCMS)

  - Those that can be used to support teaching and learning, such as peer-to-peer (P2P) applications, blogs, wikis, workflow management applications, and performance support and help tools

  - Those needed to support the teaching and learning technologies named in the first two bullet points, such as networks, servers, firewalls, and Internet protocols

- Learning infrastructure requirements and models tend to vary dramatically between corporate and academic environments.

- Components of an infrastructure for learning should address some or all of the following:

  - Content authoring, tools that let designers, instructors, and faculty design and develop learning content

  - Content management, tools that facilitate creation, storage, indexing, searching, and categorizing of source content

- Learning management, tools that track learners and their progress through courses, as well as related tracking of training department resources

- Assessment and evaluation, which tracks the individual performance of learners on assessments as well as evaluations of courses and other learning events

- Knowledge management, tools that capture, compile, organize, and index the knowledge and skills acquired by people and groups in an organization

- Competency management, tools that help an individual identify competencies for current and desired positions and suggest training and other activities to bridge any gaps in competencies. At the organizational level, these tools track workforce skills and can be used to identify individuals with certain competencies

- Workflow management, tools that help to successfully plan and deliver learning programs and related activities

- Integration, which ensures that the interlocking components of a learning infrastructure work well together

- Services, which help organizations manage part or all of the learning infrastructure

• Issues to consider in establishing learning infrastructure in *corporate* environments include:

  - Business needs

  - Organizational size

  - Internal capabilities to support a learning infrastructure

  - Business arrangements with infrastructure vendors

• Issues to consider in establishing learning infrastructures in *academic* environments include:

  - Supporting the education of part- and full-time students

  - Supporting the number of users

- Purpose of providing material online, teaching directly online or supporting classroom learning

- Synchronous or asynchronous delivery

- Volume of learners

- Source of materials

- Making the infrastructure invisible to learners

- Choosing commercial or open-source applications

- Several critical issues arise when considering the technology infrastructure for learning. These include:

  - Choosing components of the learning infrastructure based on business requirements, which many organizations do not adequately identify before beginning their shopping for technology

  - Comparing business requirements to the components of the learning infrastructure the vendor can offer

  - Choosing technology based on ability to meet organizational needs, not because of "cool" features

  - Performing due diligence on vendors and components

  - Considering issues that might not be readily visible in a product demonstration when choosing technology. These include:

    - Technical assessment of the underlying technology

    - Assessment of the compatibility of the proposed learning technology with the organization's technology infrastructure

    - Assessment of the applications development process used by the vendor

    - Business fundamentals (also called due diligence)

    - References

- Cost analysis

- Lease exit strategy

- Planning for maintenance of the infrastructure

- Planning for support of the infrastructure

- Considering the broader impact of the technology infrastructure on the organization

◆ ◆ ◆

# Guiding Questions for Discussion

- How should organizations determine their *real* infrastructure requirements?

- What planning is needed in order to adapt to typical changes in the market, technologies, and business needs?

- What next steps should be taken to not become one of the myriad companies and higher education institutions that are unhappy with their learning infrastructure purchase?

## Learn More About It

Links    These following resources are primarily for a higher-education audience. Reports and comparisons are also available for a training audience through (fairly expensive) reports by industry analysts.

- Wikipedia article on learning management systems: http://en.wikipedia.org/wiki/Learning_Management_System

- Evaluations of higher education LMSs: http://dir.wolfram.org/learning_management_systems.html

- Jay Cross' Internet time blog, www.internettime.com/blog/

- Stephen Downes' website: www.downes.ca/

- Edutools: www.edutools.info/
- Virtual learning environments comparison: www.atutor.ca/atutor/files/VLE_comparison.pdf

Less pricey reports are available through:

- Training Media Review (www.tmreview.com/)
- eLearning Guild (www.elearningguild.com)
- PENS LMS Testing (http://pens.lmstesting.com/)
- EIfEL (European Institute for E-Learning) (www.eife-l.org/)

| Books, Papers, Reports, and Articles | The following resources are primers on the various technologies for e-learning. If you are unsure about a certain type of technology or its use in e-learning, one of these books is likely to help you. |
|---|---|

Carliner, S. (2004). *An overview of online learning.* (See Chapter 3). Amherst, MA: HRD Press.

Shank, S., & Sitze, A. (2004.) *Making sense of online learning.* San Francisco, CA: Pfeiffer.

Horton, W. (2004). *e-Learning tools and technologies.* Hoboken, NJ: John Wiley & Sons.

## Acknowledgments

This chapter was primarily written by Patti Shank and Wayne Precht, with input and insights from Harvey Singh, Jim Everidge, and Jane Bozarth. Because this is a complex topic with multiple stakeholders and technologies and wrong decisions are extremely costly, we wanted more than one point of view. We decided to do this by hearing from multiple people who are involved on different levels. Patti compiled the final chapter with their input, but not all of the comments reflect all contributors' opinions.

◆ ◆ ◆

# Example of a Requirements Document for an LMS*

## ABC Corporation Business Requirements for a Learning Management System

The Learning & Development organization needs to implement a results-oriented approach to training employees across the organization. A survey of training and performance processes across ABC's business units reveals a diverse mix of approaches and tools for training. The purpose of this project is to provide a common infrastructure for employee training consistent with strategic and operational objectives.

## Current Situation

ABC Corporation training must adhere to EPA regulations, ethics codes, and documentation of Standard Operating Procedures (SOPs). Each business unit is responsible for its own employee training activities. Although training is decentralized, many training needs are similar from one business unit to another. Risks caused by lack of consistency among business units include the following:

- SOPs—ABC Corporation employees must follow a variety of SOPs. Managing employee training on SOPs and notifying affected employees of changes to SOPs is critical, but not consistently implemented.

- Compliance—Regulatory training is critical but implemented differently in different business units.

- Training records—There is no central repository of training records. Training systems in different business units do not communicate with each other. Data is housed in different applications, and consolidated reports for training and compliance aren't possible without a great deal of manual effort.

---

*Adapted from documentation by Jim Everidge.

- Metrics—Success metrics are different from one business unit to another.

## Business Needs

ABC Corporation wants to centralize learning infrastructure so content can be reused, common metrics can be implemented for assessing individual skills and competencies, training and certification paths are similar across business units, compliance needs are efficiently met, progress of each employee is consistently monitored, central reporting capabilities can be leveraged, business process workflow is better supported, and redundant systems are consolidated. Although infrastructure will be centralized, business units will control training that is delivered to their employees.

The following capabilities are required:

- Central learning infrastructure across business units

- Common architecture

- Centralized compliance tracking

- Centralized SOP distribution and tracking and changes quickly implemented in affected units

- Central reporting against external (compliance) and internal (development) needs

- Consolidated reporting

- Enterprise enrollment and registration

- Easier reuse of content across the organization

- Collaboration to enhance communication among business unit training organizations

- Access to subject-matter expertise across the organization

- Ability to implement company-wide training programs

- Synchronous training via the Internet to a global audience

- Competency development and tracking

## Additional System Requirements

These include:

- Course registration approval/manager approval
- Email notifications
- Attendance tracking
- Launching/tracking of AICC/SCORM-compliant content
- Enrollment/cancellation tracking
- Curriculum management
- Blended curriculum management
- Certification management
- Assessment/evaluation
- Job codes, job descriptions, roles assignments
- Classroom management

## Use Case Scenarios to Test Vendor Applications

1. Standard Operating Procedures
2. New Hire Training
3. Classroom Training Management
4. Online Training Content
5. Competency Management

# Costs

We will determine the following costs for each application:

- Enterprise LMS
- Change/Transition Management
- Integration
- Customization/Configuration
- Testing

- Training

- Validation

- Licensing (eighteen months)/year

- Hosting (eighteen months)/year

- Eighteen-Month Total Cost

## Value Assessment

Following are the benefits desired from a centralized infrastructure:

| Benefit | Value |
|---------|-------|
| Better compliance tracking | • Accuracy—All compliance training data in one place<br>• Access—More complete reports in case of audits<br>• Cost avoidance for audit penalties<br>• Cost savings on insurance premiums |
| Efficient SOP distribution and tracking | • Accountability—Applying SOPs to job<br>• Time savings—Reduction in manual tracking<br>• Faster dissemination and implementation of new processes |
| Flexible training | • Timely distribution of new information<br>• Self-paced learning activities, available any time<br>• Measure effectiveness of training and make adjustments |

| | |
|---|---|
| Reuse of content | • Efficiencies in content development |
| | • Reduced time needed for maintenance of content |
| | • Consistency and accuracy of content and message |
| | • Shorter modules that are easier to fit in learning |
| | • Just-in-time training |
| | • Training specific to roles |
| Competency modeling | • Map competencies to training content |
| | • Reveal development gaps objectively |
| | • Targeted individual development plans mapped to competencies |
| Improved metrics and reporting | • Consistency of reporting |
| | • Manageable audit trails and compliance reports |
| | • Improved understanding of the value of training dollars |
| Shared common architecture | • Time and cost savings from shared administration, fewer manual processes, avoidance of redundant systems |
| Enterprise enrollment and registration | • Shared training opportunities |
| | • Self-service/one-stop-shopping |

## List of Capabilities for a Learning Management System

Manage records for the certification of our field personnel. Certification involves the following:

- Showing proof of liability insurance

- Demonstrating mastery of conceptual skills (that will be taught through a series of asynchronous e-learning modules)

- Demonstrating mastery of skills involved in making our product, as observed by a certified specialist

- Successful completion of several supervised product assemblies

- Successful completion of several unsupervised product assemblies

- Remind users that certification is going to expire (which will occur between twelve and twenty-four months after initial certification; we are still in the process of deciding this)

- Let managers in regional and head office locations see reports on who is certified and the progress of learners going through certification

We anticipate approximately 150 to 200 certifications in year 1, and 200 to 300 certifications in years 2 through 3. We want the system to manage our learning programs in the following ways:

- Manage enrollments in classroom courses, as well as records of performance on tests, observations, and completions of courses

- Manage e-courses, including enrollments, pre-tests, giving credit to learners who pass pre-tests, recommending modules to take to learners who do not successfully complete the pre-test, "serving up" recommended modules to learners, administering a post-test, and recording scores of the post-test. e-Courses will probably be produced in Adobe Flash, Dreamweaver, or Authorware.

- Manage testing of learners, including creating and administering tests with objective questions and tracking scores and reporting them, as well as recording, tracking, and reporting results of test questions performed off-line

- Manage enrollments in possible live virtual classes (we have not selected software)

- Provide the opportunity to charge nominal fees to implementers for enrollment in courses

We may also choose to make courses available to learners who are outside of the certification program and manage auxiliary records for our certification by:

- Keeping records on the re-certification process, which involves (1) showing again proof of liability insurance, (2) completion of a set number of implementations (the records will be kept elsewhere, but once verified, the information will be recorded), (3) refresher training (some of which will be online, the rest will be in the classroom), and (4) additional monitored assemblers

- Keeping records on related certifications, including certifications for monitors (people who supervise the assemblies immediately after the courses) and train-the-trainers

And provide additional services:

- Generate automatic email notices for purposes such as (but not limited to) the following: verifying enrollment in courses (both e-courses and classroom courses), notifying people that their certifications are going to expire, and keeping in touch with learners

- Generate custom reports about certified implementers and implementers in training

- Support several languages. At first, the system should support French and English, but should be able to handle the following additional languages: Chinese (Mandarin), Dutch, German, and Spanish

- A customizable module on how to use the LMS that we could provide to our end-users
- Interchange data with other systems, including human resources information systems and other learning management systems

We would like to see information regarding the following:

- How your system will help us address these needs
- The tasks that we would need to perform to install, customize, launch, and support the system in *hosted* mode (although software support would be provided by you, we want your estimate of the additional labor we would need to support learning in our organization)
- The tasks that we would have to perform to install, customize, launch, and support the system if we install the system ourselves (including both technical and learning support)

◆ ◆ ◆

# Example of a Decision Matrix for a Software Purchase

|  | Vendor 1 | Vendor 2 | Vendor 3 |
| --- | --- | --- | --- |
| Manage records for the certification of our field personnel. (1 = difficult, 5 = easy) | 3 | 4 | 4 |
| Manage our learning programs (1 = difficult, 5 = easy) | 3 | 5 | 4 |

| | Vendor 1 | Vendor 2 | Vendor 3 |
|---|---|---|---|
| Ability to make courses available to learners who are outside of the certification program (1 = difficult, 5 = easy) | 2 | 5 | 5 |
| Provide additional support (1 = useless support, 5 = useful support options) | 2 | 4 | 4 |
| Technical assessment of the underlying technology (1 = old, inflexible technology, 5 = current, flexible technology) | 1 | 4 | 4 |
| Assessment of the compatibility of the proposed learning technology with the organization's technology infrastructure (1 = completely incompatible, 5 = compatible) | 3 | 4 | 4 |

|  | Vendor 1 | Vendor 2 | Vendor 3 |
|---|---|---|---|
| Assessment of the software development process (1 = programmer-driven, 5 = customer-driven) | 3 | 5 | 4 |
| Business funda-mentals (also called due diligence) (1 = major concerns, 5 = viable organization) | 3 | 5 | 2 |
| References (1 = poor, 5 = excellent endorsement) | 3 | 4 | 5 |
| Cost analysis (1 = not affordable on our budget, 5 = affordable on our budget) | 1 | 3 | 4 |
| Lease exit strategy analysis (1 = locked in, 5 = can get out of) | 1 | 3 | 4 |

# Chapter 6

# e-Learning Standards

## A Framework for Enabling the Creation and Distribution of High-Quality, Cost-Effective Web-Delivered Instruction

*Pat Brogan, Anystream*

**About This Chapter**

One of the major topics in the discussion of e-learning is standards. Some are technical standards that are intended to ensure that e-learning programs are inter-operable (that is, run on many different platforms without difficulty) and that content can be re-purposed with a minimum of work. Others focus on content—providing a common means of cataloging content so people can easily find it and making content accessible to persons with disabilities. Although standards are intended to make e-learning easier to develop, exchange, and use, the standards themselves have, at times, been anything but easy.

This chapter answers the question, "Why?" In this chapter, I first provide a rationale for unique standards for e-learning, above and beyond those needed for the web. Next, I describe the key standards developed for e-learning. Last, I consider whether or not standards have benefited e-learning. In appendixes to this chapter, I review relevant standards and specifications for e-learning.

# Standards and the Current Wave of e-Learning

Although the Internet has provided a cost-effective and far-reaching infrastructure facilitating the delivery of instruction, as Margaret Driscoll notes earlier in this book, the reality is that the benefits realized fell short of market expectations in the late 1990s and early 2000s, the initial years of the e-learning market revolution.

Some first-generation e-learning products simply disappointed on impact. These basic web pages looked like any of the other amateur web pages appearing with alarming frequency at the time and failed to engage learners on a visual level, much less through interaction.

Other first-generation e-learning products had the potential to engage learners visually and intellectually, but they tried users' patience as users waited for them to load because the pages frequently were not optimized for the web. For example, the authoring tool, Authorware, and the presentation graphics tool, Director, were designed to run on stand-alone personal computers. Although materials created in these tools could be distributed through the web, they could not be distributed in their original form. The materials needed to be "re-packaged" by the system using a program called Shockwave and returned to their original format for viewing. As a result of the conversion process, as well as the additional information that needed to be transmitted with material produced with this software, performance slowed. (The publisher of these authoring tools—Macromedia—quickly developed more efficient replacement tools that did not require the "shocking" process, including add-ons to Dreamweaver to develop e-learning and Flash to develop animations.)

If the appearance and performance of early e-learning efforts disappointed, so did its failure to achieve its promise of providing just-in-time, just-in place training, which would provide learners with just the learning they needed, at the time and place they needed it. Instead, organizations invested in converting existing classroom and workbook content for distribution on the web. The quality of the content often fell short of even meeting quality expectations of the previous generation of computer-based training (CBT), which made extensive use of multimedia.

To be honest, however, e-learning veterans of the CBT era were used to such disappointments, having seen it several times before, including the limited success of the earliest programmed-instruction approaches to computer-based training in the 1960s, the failure of the laser disk in the 1980s, and the limited take-up of multimedia in the early and mid-1990s.

Despite the disappointments of the e-learning market revolution in the late 1990s and the early years of this decade, this e-learning revolution seemed to have the potential to last, for e-learning to finally gain some traction within various learning environments and become more widely used.

Despite the then-current crop of disappointing courses, e-learning specialists also observed other trends that bode well for the wide adoption of e-learning this time, even if the first results seemed to betray the promise. Previous eras were characterized by proprietary authoring and presentation tools, which forbade the interchange of learning content. That is, courses developed in a particular authoring tool required that learners have a special viewer for looking at material created in that tool installed on their computers. Materials developed in another authoring tool could not be viewed with that viewer (at a cost of approximately $50 per computer, this cost created another barrier to the adoption of computer-based training), nor could the authoring tool associated with that viewer be used to revise materials developed in the other authoring tool. Finding e-learning content was also nearly impossible electronically; people needed to scour the packaging accompanying the diskettes, laser disks, and CDs on which they were provided. In addition, many companies adopted standard configurations for computers and disallowed the use of plug-ins.

One catalyst for this collaboration was the emergence of industry-wide standards for creating and viewing content. The emergence of HTML as the primary tool for creating web-based content (and related web software, like XML, PHP, and Java) ensured the easy interchange and interoperability of content (that is, content developed on one computer could be easily viewed on others, regardless of the hardware and operating system of that other computer). Browsers replaced the viewing software. Because browsers are available ubiquitously and at no cost to users (indeed, they usually came installed on most personal computers), people could easily view e-learning content. As a result, organizations could create and easily exchange learning content. At first, this spurred the interest in e-learning in general, but this also spurred interest in sharing content, whether organizations would share entire courses or parts of them. But the more these initial standards spurred interest in e-learning, the more e-learning developers realized their limitations.

This chapter explores what happened next. It first provides a rationale for unique standards for e-learning, above and beyond those needed for the web. Next, it describes the key standards developed for e-learning. Last, the chapter considers whether or not standards have benefited e-learning. Appendices to this chapter review relevant standards and specifications for e-learning.

# A Rationale for Unique Standards for e-Learning

If standards already guide the development of content for the World Wide Web, a logical question is why an additional set of standards is needed for e-learning. Several issues drive this need. First are the general goals for effective standards. Next are the specific e-learning activities that standards are supposed to address. But to illustrate why standards are needed to address unique aspects of e-learning that would not be covered by other software and web standards, I present a case of the challenges faced by one e-learning publisher that demonstrates the practical need for standards.

## Two Cases Demonstrating the Need for Standards

Consider first the case of Academic Systems (subsequently acquired by Lightspan Inc. and then Plato Learning), an educational software publisher that developed and marketed high-quality math and English-writing instruction. In some ways, Academic Systems sounded like a success story. The company raised and spent over $50 million in venture capital. Over 200,000 students used the software, and research showed that its instruction was not only effective, but in many cases, superior to traditional textbook-based approaches.

But the company did not succeed on an economic level. Development costs and maintenance exceeded industry averages, many of which could be directly attributed to a lack of standards. All of the content was custom-developed, taking twelve to eighteen months to develop a course. During that time, course authors typically created content using proprietary authoring tools like Authorware™ or Director™. Authors would create a storyboard of a lesson, next mock up screens to show scope and sequence of instructional interactions, and then program the logic, record audio and video, and, last, construct a database to track the progress of learners through the course. The output was a set of forty CD-ROMs, which contained the course, but also required connection to a network and a sizeable Oracle database with records of learners' progress. In addition, because no standard viewer existed, Academic Software also needed to purchase licenses for learners to see the learning material. Two versions of each course were needed: one for the Mac platform, the others for the Windows platform, although, in the end, given the overwhelmingly Windows usage by the target population, maintaining the Mac platform was not economically feasible.

Standards could have reduced costs throughout this process. Had standards permitting organizations to easily find existing content and reuse it—perhaps content that might have been purchased from another organization—many development costs might have been avoided. Had standards for interchanging information about student performance been in place, the need for an extensive database could be reduced or eliminated. Had standards existed for viewing, the need to maintain materials for several platforms would have been avoided. Admittedly, the use of browsers, which were initially facilitated by the HTML standard established in the early 1990s, addresses the last issue. But the other issues are problems posed uniquely by e-learning, and existing standards for the exchange of content on the web do not fully address the challenges of reusing content—especially content produced by different organizations—and the exchange of student information. Only standards specifically developed for e-learning can do that.

As standards could have benefited organizations developing learning content for sale, they also could benefit nonprofit learning institutions, such as universities. Consider the case of mythical State University, which entered the distance education business early. Like any university, State University needed to track student grades and time and usage of selected content, and to document this progress before providing academic credit. Because no external programs could provide this for early academically focused courses offered online, distance and mediated learning environments into the late 1990s needed to have these feedback mechanisms built in.

Building in these tracking and reporting functions caused distance learning applications to be more complex than they needed to be, requiring more extensive programming assistance for distance education than should be necessary. Learning specialists had to decide which information to track, and then programmers were needed to not only program in the tracking of that information, but pass it between the learning software and either an academic management system or university database.

Because the programming was linked to the proprietary instructional content and to specific academic management systems or customized databases, it could not be reused. If State University adopted several different instructional libraries, the university would be forced to acquire a separate course management system for each course. Because the data in each of these separate course management systems was unique, integrating student data across management systems and databases or extracting the information to be uploaded and consolidated into another database was difficult. Standards could specify which data would be tracked and how it could be stored and exchanged among different types of programs.

## Goals for Effective Standards

As described in The Masie Center document, *Making Sense of Learning Specification and Standards: A Decision Maker's Guide to Their Adoption*, "Standards help to ensure e-learning effectiveness and resource investments by promoting the following goals: *interoperability, reusability, manageability, accessibility,* and *durability*." I am substituting *adaptability* for manageability, as one of the long-term benefits of using standards.

*Interoperability* refers to the process of preparing content on one system and using it on another, where the content performs consistently, regardless of operating system, browser brand, or device type. In other words, a course could be developed on a Mac running under Mac OS and run under Safari. A learner could use that course on a Windows system and run the course under Explorer, and the course would operate as intended. This type of interoperability reduces the challenge of implementing projects, because they can trust the content will operate everywhere.

*Reusability* refers to the ability to use content again for a different purpose, a process called the *repurposing of content*. Take, for example, a statistics lesson on computing the median of a table of figures. This lesson could be appropriately used in math classes, statistics classes, social and physical sciences, and in the corporate world, in finance or marketing and development curricula. In a traditionally designed online learning unit, the lesson would be embedded in a much larger course. Reusing that lesson requires extensive manual work, requiring that the developer copy the lesson, strip out all of the unrelated material, and insert it into the second course. In a reusable course, the lesson would be stored as a separate file, which could ideally be used "as is" in the second course. The primary benefit of reusing content is financial. An initial investment in the development of instruction can be recovered when the content is reused. When using the content within an organization, the organization avoids a cost for developing the content a second time. When selling the content externally, the organization usually receives a royalty fee.

Reusability of material encompasses two technical functions. The first is *interoperability*, which is also a broader goal for standards and discussed just before reusability. The second is *findability*. That is, the standards need to permit people to easily find information developed by other sources that might be reused. Although this sounds like a simple task, the practical reality is that many computer users have only a passing understanding of their own filing systems and have difficulty finding materials on their own computers, much less finding that of strangers. Therefore, standards had to provide a means of commonly identifying content so others can easily find it.

*Adaptable* content can be leveraged in different contexts. Consider again the statistics lesson. If it were constructed as a reusable learning object (RLO), the lesson could be repurposed in support of various instructional scenarios, with examples or practice problems specific to the context. What would happen is that the system would gather information about the student and the learning context, next choose exercises, practice problems appropriate to that situation, then present the adapted RLO to the learner. Ideally, content can be adapted in a variety of ways, including different sequencing of content and supporting different learning styles.

The last goal guiding the development of standards is *accessibility*. In the context of web-delivered content, accessibility refers to efforts to make the web usable for people with visual, auditory, and other physical disabilities, including cognitive processing disabilities and visually impaired elderly web users. On the one hand, early web applications typically ignored these users, so many users were left out of the web applications. On the other hand, the estimated 750 million-plus people with disabilities worldwide (and growing each year)—including people with limited visual, auditory, physical, and cognitive abilities—are increasingly turning to the Internet as an invaluable resource for information and communication.

Users with disabilities require different levels of support in order to access the web and the rich media content on it. This support ranges from relatively simple accommodations like enlarging the font size on a browser to more complex accommodations, such as using a text-only browser that reads the content aloud. Graphics and animation require additional effort to ensure that they are accessible to learners with visual impairments. To be accessible to these users, designers must provide text descriptions of animations, controls, and navigational features. Standards identify the situations in which support is needed and suggest how to address it.

But accessibility standards are not just limited to users of web content, they also address designers of web content. Accessibility standards are also needed to ensure that people with disabilities have the ability to create content, so a second area of concern for accessibility standards pertains to the design of authoring tools. Making authoring accessible is a means of ensuring that persons who are otherwise capable, but have physical disabilities, are able to realize their full employment potential. For example, although someone might not have the ability to hear, that person might still have the ability to design visually attractive screens for e-learning. Or a person who has a severe visual impairment might be able to compose a clear explanation of a statistical formula. They can perform these tasks if the authoring tools permit them to do so. Most people with disabilities who create websites and other web content largely rely on the accessibility features of their operating systems to support their work. Many of these features are the same as those available to learners and include magnification of fonts, change of display colors to high contrast, converting text to speech, and providing short-cut keys.

In terms of *durability*, standards need to support the longevity of learning content. In the early days of online learning, each major hardware or software upgrade immediately made the learning content obsolete because it could not be run on the new system. As a result, the content had a relatively short shelf life. In addition, the cost of converting e-learning to the new environment hindered investment in online learning.

## e-Learning Activities That Standards Are Supposed to Address

e-Learning standards are supposed to address a number of issues. First, standards are intended for learning and course management systems. LMSs and similar learning management software capture and retain information about a learner's location in a course, so the learner could resume a course at the place left off.

A second issue that standards are supposed to address is the tracking of student activities and scores, and providing these results so that teachers, human resource specialists, and instructors could measure student progress and usage and track the time spent in learning activities (as some industries mandate).

A third issue that standards are supposed to address is the facilitation of the assembly of learning content from different sources into a single course. Specifically, standards are supposed to let learners control the sequencing of content and let the system adapt content in response to learners' input. For example, a system might adjust the delivery of content in response to a learner expressing a preference for a particular learning style. The assembly of content in response to learner input, especially the adaptation of content in response to learners' input, is a response to early research on artificial intelligence, when theorists envisioned that systems like these—called *adaptive learning systems*—would be easy to build.

# The Key Standards for e-Learning

In response to the specific needs identified and in keeping with the spirit of the goals, several organizations have attempted to develop standards for e-learning. This section explores them. First, it describes the evolution of standards for e-learning. Then it identifies the specific standards used to drive the design, development, and delivery of e-learning.

## But First, a Quick Discussion of Terminology

Although this chapter almost exclusively uses the term "standards," the term, as used in this chapter, is broader than its meaning in the standards community. In reality, a standard is just one of a series of interrelated concepts that attempt to address interactions among software and hardware over the Internet.

A standard actually represents the last phase in a series of milestones intended to take an idea for coordinating interactions among software and devices. The first phase results after someone or a group of people recognizes a situation in which some coordination of efforts will result in more efficient or economical interactions among programs or some similar benefit to users. In many ways, this idea is similar to that proposed by Rummler and Brache (1995) for human performance technology. They note that efficiencies and improvements are often achieved by examining and re-engineering the interactions among groups within and across organizations.

If the issue is a non-technical one, it is usually proposed as a guideline. Guidelines often address design and editorial issues, with the intention of ensuring consistency among the many designers and developers of related e-learning materials. For example, each module in an e-course might be written by different course authors, but because users perceive the course as a single unit, it must appear as such to users. Guidelines would ensure that the screen design is consistent, that headings and text are formatted consistently, and that terminology is used consistently, among other issues.

Although guidelines are regularly revised and sometimes their intentions are captured as templates to minimize the likelihood that individual course authors might stray from the guidelines, once a guideline is proposed it usually remains a guideline.

If the issue is a technical one, the individual or group proposing the idea prepares a specification, which identifies the need to be addressed and the manner in which it will be addressed. For example, a specification might indicate how student records might be exchanged among systems.

In some cases, a specification might be preceded by a reference model or some similar working paper, which proposes an idea that needs to be refined.

Once a specification has been in use for a while and proven its utility, it can become a standard. Wikipedia (2006) defines "standard" as follows:

> A specification for which significant implementation and successful operational experience have been obtained may be elevated to the *Internet standard* level. An Internet standard, which may simply be referred to as a *standard*, is characterized by a high degree of technical maturity and by a generally held belief that the specified protocol or service provides significant benefit to the Internet community.

Standards are also distinguished by who can issue them: only a limited number of organizations have the authority to do so. Although most organizations can propose guidelines and specifications, only official standards bodies have the authority to issue a standard. Usually these are organizations that are international and whose authority is recognized by a number of governmental and nongovernmental organizations. In terms of the Internet and related software and hardware usage, the primary bodies that have the authority to issue standards are the International Standards Organization (ISO), the World Wide Web Consortium (W3C), and the Institute of Electrical and Electronics Engineers (IEEE).

No organization focused solely on e-learning or learning-related issues has the authority to issue standards.

## How Standards for e-Learning Evolved

If the standards for learning and accessibility are complex, that is because they represent a complex interaction of private corporations, government agencies, nonprofit industry alliances, and standards bodies.

Standards can develop in several ways. Some are mandated by legislation, as in Section 508 of the Federal Rehabilitation Act. These mandates are called *de jure* standards, a phrase derived from Latin meaning "of the law." Others emerge in a *de facto* way through the power of the market, such as the victory of the VHS format for video over Betamax in the 1980s, and the current battle over formats for high-definition DVDs.

Other standards emerge through a purposeful effort of interested parties, such as efforts since the 1980s by the Aviation Industry CBT Committee (AICC) to enable high-quality computer-based training (CBT). Because of requirements by oversight bodies like the U.S. Federal Aviation Administration (FAA) and International Civil Aviation Organization (ICAO) that employees of airlines and similar aviation-related businesses receive certain minimum hours (and types) of formal training each year and that the training be formally tracked, the AICC had a strong incentive, at first, to focus on tracking of student activities, facilitating the reporting of these activities, and tracking the results of formalized training. But efforts went further and, as a result of this, a series of guidelines for computer-based training evolved that have served as the prototype of guidelines and standards used today for much e-learning. One special focus of AICC efforts is the specification for computer-managed instruction (CMI), which provides specifics for communicating information about learners and their progress among learning systems. First-generation learning management systems often marketed themselves as being "AICC-compliant," which means that these systems exchange information with other systems in a way specified by the guidelines. As a result of these standards, AICC-compliant systems facilitated the tracking and reporting of learner progress, as required by these overseeing bodies.

Although the AICC was initially motivated by external requirements to develop its standards, other organizations were motivated by an interest in making the most effective use of learning technology and the World Wide Web in their efforts to develop standards, like the U.S.-based Instructional Management Systems (IMS) Global Learning Consortium, an organization of primarily higher-education-focused members, which also began in the 1980s. The organization has developed resources that allow organizations to easily find information published on the web through its metadata specification, exchange content through the content packaging specification, and exchange information about student performance on tests through its question test interchange (QTI) specification. The primary means for exchanging this information would be within learning management systems (LMSs) and learning content management systems (LCMSs).

Sometimes, rather than mandating standards, governments try to act as a catalyst for developing and adopting standards, as the Advanced Distributed Learning (ADL) Lab of the U.S. Department of Defense has done. Established by former President Clinton, the agency has a mission to promote the adoption of e-learning technologies across the public and private sectors. One particular area of interest for the ADL has been promoting the adoption of LMSs and LCMSs, and reusable learning objects (RLOs). To promote the use of reusable learning objects (which are discussed in more detail by Patrick Parrish in Chapter 7 of this book), the ADL developed and promoted its shareable content object reference model (SCORM). Ideally, organizations that follow SCORM when designing RLOs and use SCORM-compliant LMSs and LCMSs should be able to easily exchange objects. Two published versions of the model have emerged. In addition to developing SCORM, the ADL also developed specifications for conducting tests of systems to ensure that they are compliant with the standards and sample applications that comply with the reference model. Most U.S. federal agencies require that the e-learning authoring and management tools and courseware they purchase conform to the SCORM. The ADL hoped that this would provide a critical mass of purchasers that would move SCORM from a government standard to one that would be used industry-wide. To support this goal, the ADL established centers where vendors and consumers could test their e-learning content, LMSs, and LCMSs for conformance against specifications and standards.

SCORM also served as the foundation of a specification for a learning object model (LOM), which the Institute of Electrical and Electronics Engineers (IEEE), a professional association of engineers that also acts as a worldwide standards body, ratified in 2001. The IEEE has a committee focused on learning technologies, the Learning Technology Standards Committee (LTSC).

A last group of standards were developed by the American Society for Training and Development (ASTD). In response to suggestions from its members, who were wondering how they could recognize an effective e-learning course, ASTD developed a list of observable and measurable criteria for effective e-learning. Organizations could then submit their e-learning courses to an ASTD service that would assess the extent to which the courses conformed to the criteria. If they conformed sufficiently, the e-courses would be "certified" and bear a seal, much like the Good Housekeeping Seal of Approval. This seal would provide a quality indicator that potential consumers could consider in a purchasing decision.

## Scope of Standards and Specifications

As standards and specifications relevant to e-learning have evolved, the range of issues that they address has similarly evolved. e-Learning standards and specifications now address the following issues:

- The communications interface
- The packaging of content

- Metadata that provides contextual information about content

- Guidelines for assessment to facilitate testing

- Accessibility of content

- Sequencing and presentation of content

The next several sections describe the applicable standards and specifications.

## The Communications Interface

This standard refers to the way that online resources exchange information among one another. These resources include content (text, graphics, and lessons), learning management systems, and databases with information about learning content or learners. In programming terms, this communications framework is like an application program interface (API).

## The Packaging of Content

This standard explains how pieces of online instructional content are labeled, so that a system can reassemble the content according to the context. Within e-learning, the primary use of packaging specifications is in conjunction with eXtensible Markup Language (XML) to identify information about the nature of the content, such as whether it is a table of contents or metadata.

This standard also provides information about test questions. Having this information lets learning specialists best assess a student's mastery with the available questions in a question library, because it can help the specialist choose the most appropriate questions. For example, within a subject area that has fairly specific instructional goals, a question library may be constructed from which information may be pulled, depending on level of knowledge, specific subject area, or audience appropriateness.

## Metadata That Provides Contextual Information About Content

This standard is used with the packaging function just described to provide a framework for developing online learning content as separate objects that can be logically combined into other objects to create a cohesive unit. Based on identification information in the metadata, a system or a learning specialist can identify objects to use in a learning program as well as the order in which those objects should appear.

## Guidelines for Assessment to Facilitate Testing

Although such content may be packaged by the system at the time of use, it can also encompass one key learning function: assessment. In order to assess knowledge, testing is frequently embedded in instruction. To enable learning specialists to use questions and answers online in a modular way and for the recording and managing of answers—just as the previous standard facilitates the use of content in a modular way—another specification was needed.

That specification is the IMS Question and Test Interoperability (QTI) specification. QTI describes a means by which the data about questions and tests can be represented in software so that the data can be easily exchanged among programs tracking testing data. QTI also provides a means of representing learners' test results so that data, too, can be exchanged among programs.

In practical terms, when test information, test questions, and student results are represented according to QTI standards, results for a test taken by J.Q. Learner in a course created in Authoring tool can be transferred to J.Q.'s permanent student record in an unrelated learning management system. Another practical implication of this specification is that learning specialists can create tests from questions in several different test-item databanks.

## Accessibility of Content

This standard refers to the presentation of information on a web-delivered page so that any user, regardless of physical or other usage limitations, can understand the information and navigate through a page or application. This standard results from legislation by the U.S. Congress: Section 508 of the Federal Rehabilitation Act. Its intent was to expand upon the provisions for accessibility in work and access to public environments that was afforded by the Americans with Disabilities Act. Although the law is a U.S. law and compliance is only required for online resources developed for the U.S. federal government, it has become a de facto standard followed by governments, corporations, and other groups developing online resources throughout the world.

Achieving the goal of accessibility is often accomplished through the use of various assistive technologies, such as screen readers for those with limited vision, text of narrations for persons with limited or no hearing abilities, assistive devices for those with physical limitations, and other ways of helping people with limitations use applications and websites.

Appendix A provides a list of specific ways to make web content accessible.

### Sequencing and Presentation of Content

This standard provides a means of assembling RLOs in a way that best supports users' needs. Specifically, achieving this standard involves pulling content from a database or repository based on information known about users and presenting content from different sources into a common look and feel.

## How Different Standards and Specifications Work Together

Although a number of individual standards and specifications exist, they work together to facilitate efforts such as the exchange of data about learners and learning content and the assembly of learning programs at the time of need by sequencing together several RLOs.

One possible framework of how e-learning content can be developed as components and, later, assembled with other components (RLOs) and delivered as complete learning programs is illustrated by a hierarchy. At the lowest level of the hierarchy are content assets, or learning objects. At the next level up, these learning objects are assembled into collections. These collections are then "packaged" by the system and presented to learners, following an appropriate logic. To assemble the objects, the system must know what each asset is, and this information is generally contained in metadata (data about data). The specific types of information contained in the metadata is described in the IMS specification and the IEEE.

Once the learning objects are developed, they are assembled into a cohesive learning program by either an LMS, LCMS, or similar content delivery system. Figure 6.1 shows the typical functions of an LMS.

Until now, this discussion has only considered RLOs from the perspectives of the system and the people providing and developing learning content. Figure 6.2 shows this entire learning system from the perspective of the learning. This system, which is admittedly idealized, is a feedback-driven system as depicted, in which the learner is presented personally contextualized content that is delivered through an LMS or LCMS. Examples of personalization include adjusting the type of content to the learner's context, the sequencing of instruction and assessment based on the learner's needs, adjusting the types of media presented, and providing the use of audio, if the learner learns better in a multi-sensory environment.

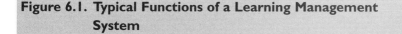

**Figure 6.1. Typical Functions of a Learning Management System**

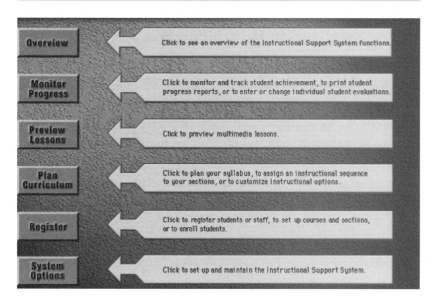

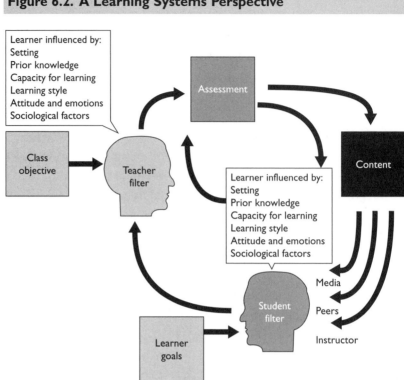

**Figure 6.2. A Learning Systems Perspective**

Learner influenced by:
Setting
Prior knowledge
Capacity for learning
Learning style
Attitude and emotions
Sociological factors

Assessment

Class objective

Teacher filter

Content

Learner influenced by:
Setting
Prior knowledge
Capacity for learning
Learning style
Attitude and emotions
Sociological factors

Student filter

Media

Peers

Instructor

Learner goals

# Have Standards Benefited e-Learning?

The two cases presented at the beginning of this chapter either directly suggested or implied that standards could offer a number of benefits to e-learning. In the case of Academic Systems, standards for the development and use of content could help reduce both development times and costs by facilitating the reuse of content, ideally across different authoring systems. Standards could have also reduced implementation and support expenses for Academic Systems. Cross-platform browsers would eliminate the need to support materials on separate platforms and standards for tracking and reporting learners' progress would reduce the need for custom databases and reports, a problem encountered by State University. The lack of standards forced State University to unnecessarily invest in separate course management systems for different e-learning programs.

The next logical concern, then, is whether the standards in which parts of the e-learning community have so extensively invested themselves over the past few years have had the intended effects. That is, have standards, at the least, facilitated the easy exchange of learning objects and student data and, at the most, reduced unnecessary expenses for organizations?

One framework for considering this issue is the Masie Center's goals for effective standards for e-learning presented earlier in this chapter: *interoperability, reusability, adaptability* (which I substituted for manageability), *accessibility,* and *durability*. Although, to the best of my knowledge, no study has specifically explored whether standards have benefited e-learning, perhaps anecdotal evidence can provide some useful insights.

In terms of interoperability, standards, for a time, created more problems than they solved. One of the ultimate goals of interoperability was to make it possible for people to use content developed on one authoring platform on any platform. Under ideal circumstances, a learner could do so using only industry-standard software, like a browser.

Although courses developed solely for use under a browser can be easily interchanged, much data about them cannot be interchanged without using learning management software, especially LMSs. The SCORM model was supposed to facilitate the interchange of content among LMSs, but SCORM is actually a model, rather than a standard. Courses could conform to a particular SCORM model and not be interchanged among systems. In the past year or two, that problem has been cleared up, and users can more easily interchange learning content when it conforms to the SCORM model.

In terms of reusability, standards have facilitated the reuse of content, but probably not in the way that was originally envisioned by some of the most visionary thinkers in e-learning. When the concept of reusability was popularized in about 2001, it was in conjunction with reusable learning objects. The concept proposed that learning material could be stored in small units and assembled on the fly according to users' needs.

While academically challenging, that concept of reusability had many practical flaws. It lacked a clear definition of object, and that confused many people: Was an object a sentence? Photograph? Screen? Video clip? Entire module? The definition encompassed all of them but, in the vernacular, primarily came to mean a unit of instruction.

The other practical flaws had to do with assembling content on the fly. Some proposed that this could be done based on the learners' learning style, but practical implementations assumed that the difference between a visual learner and verbal learner is that the visual learner wants the pictures first and the verbal learner wants the text first. In reality, they require separate development efforts. But more fundamentally, according to some experts in learning theory, research has not shown that adjusting content to learning styles makes a significant difference in outcomes.

Other implementations proposed that learning could be adjusted based on learners' performance. Some simple implementations of this concept had been in use since the earliest days of CBT: learners would begin a course with a pre-test and the system would only require the learner to complete units whose test questions he or she did not pass on a pre-test. But more recent versions of the concept involved systems providing tailored learning sequences based on feedback to exercises. The reality is that most instruction that appears to be adaptive is actually developed using prescribed instructional paths with the application logic being programmed in manually. Eventually, researchers hope to be able to assemble content from several sources and present it in a uniform way with sequencing that makes sense to the learner and isn't too complex for the management or delivery system. But both the practical design issues, as well as the standards for making this happen, are still in development.

In a less specialized approach to popularizing the concept of learning objects, some organizations—usually backed with large amounts of government research money—developed repositories of learning objects that others could use, usually free of charge. But usage of these repositories disappointed their developers, some attracting more researchers interested in who was using the repositories than actual end-users. As a practical matter, then, the use of standards to promote usage of RLOs has not yet proven viable in a practical sense.

But another set of standards, originally intended to support the development of RLOs, has proven effective in supporting a more practical side to reuse. One of the major problems in large organizations with several locations and divisions is that they have several courses that teach the same content, each buried in the catalog of a different training department. The use of metadata stored with e-courses, however, can help organizations better track their inventory of courses so they can find materials when needed and avoid either purchasing or, more expensively, redeveloping, courses they already own.

Similarly, organizations are finding that they can avoid costly development efforts for graphics and other visual sequences by combining metadata for finding content, along with other procedures, to avoid re-creating material that already exists. For example, one organization that produces medical training and has invested in the design of costly medical illustrations requires its course developers to demonstrate that a requested illustration does not yet exist before authorizing development of a new medical illustration.

In addition, organizations often need to reuse content, but not necessarily within the context of learning. Consider a product description. The one used in a marketing brochure should be similar to the one used in a user's guide, which should match the description on the corporate website, which should match the description in courses. Only one of these four situations pertains to learning, yet standards only intend to facilitate the exchange of content in learning contexts; they do not facilitate the exchange of information in non-learning contexts. In fact, people who would like to exchange information in these contexts use an entirely different class of software. Rather than using a learning content management system (LCMS), they use a content management system (CMS).

In terms of adaptability, a number of the challenges in terms of RLOs have already been mentioned. But some organizations are finding ways to address this challenge. For example, SAP uses RLOs but, recognizing that some aspects of learning are dependent on the context, includes a particular type of learning object called the glue object, a unique object for a particular learning context (and that might not be reused) and that glues together the content in the other learning objects.

In terms of accessibility, strong efforts have been made to make learning content accessible to learners, with the understanding that accessible pertains to accessible by persons with disabilities. Although evidence is only anecdotal, awareness of these needs among the designers and developers of e-learning seems to be high.

In terms of durability, standards have definitely contributed to the longevity of learning content. Although hardware and software have significantly evolved since the rise of e-learning in the late 1990s, courses that were developed then can run on the equipment now, usually with no modifications. That is, when someone installs a new operating system on a computer (for example, moving from Windows 2000 to Windows XP), the learning content is still usable without modification.

Further contributing to the durability of learning content has been the emergence of broader web standards. For example, the rise of Flash (and its file formats, .swf or .swv for Flash video) as a de facto standard has solved the problem of plug-ins (special software that "plugs into" a browser at the time of use to run multimedia materials), which usually required a feared download and often dreaded unintended consequences at the user's end.

Although Masie's goals are useful for considering standards, they do not seem to address the challenge of transferring information about students, which has been the subject of extensive work in the area of standards. The resulting standards have facilitated a significant automation of record-keeping in most learning groups, from corporate training departments to schools. As this book is being written, a large number of organizations have already transferred their learning records to online systems. Others are following, as the costs and complexities of implementing these learning management systems (LMSs) are reduced. Ideally, this move to automated record-keeping should result in fewer errors and increased efficiencies, especially in terms of reduced numbers of staff members required to manage learning records. Although no study has specifically explored the impact of learning management on the size of administrative staffs in learning groups, the automation of record-keeping does not seem to have resulted in any major staffing changes. However, a sharp rise in productivity levels—as measured by the number of courses for which a training staff member has responsibility—was reported by the American Society for Training and Development in its 2004 *State of the Industry Report*. Perhaps the increased use of learning management software lets a single person have responsibility for more courses.

In addition, Masie's goals do not address other issues in which standardization is helpful: the preparation of world-ready content. World-ready content pertains to learning materials that can be easily and efficiently translated into other languages and, similarly, easily localized—that is, have the content communicated in locally appropriate ways. Sometimes, localizing content simply involves a change of spelling. For example, the spelling "localization" used in this book is American; in the United Kingdom, the term would be spelled "localisation." In other instances, localizing content involves more substantial changes to content, such as changing mentions of retirement programs from 401(k) plans in the United States to retirement savings plans (RSPs) in Canada and superannuation schemes in Hong Kong. This is especially important for e-learning used in large, multinational organizations, as well as e-learning sold in the open market.

One last issue that Masie's goals overlook is the simplicity of standards. In an ideal world, standards should be invisible to end-users of e-learning. Except for those standards that pertain to content, standards should primarily be of interest to programmers and others responsible for creating an e-learning system. People who are administrators of e-learning inside an organization or creating e-learning content should not need an in-depth understanding of standards. Unfortunately, e-learning standards have not proved simple. Indeed, even end-users of e-learning sometimes feel that they must learn about SCORM and similar types of standards.

In summary, standards have addressed some of the challenges of developing online learning materials and learning online. But they have not necessarily done so quietly or simply and, as a result, might have ultimately created as many problems with e-learning projects as they hoped to avoid.

## References

Rummler, G., & Brache, A.P. (1995). *Improving performance: How to manage the white space on the organization chart.* San Francisco, CA: Jossey-Bass.

Sugrue, B., & Rivera, R. (2004). *2004 ASTD state of the industry report.* Alexandria, VA: American Society for Training and Development.

Wikipedia. (2006). Entry on standards. http://en.wikipedia.org/wiki/Internet_standard. [Retrieved February 23, 2006.]

## Trademarks

Authorware and Director are trademarks of Adobe Corporation. Windows, Windows 2000, and Windows XP are all registered trademarks of Microsoft Corporation.

◆ ◆ ◆

## Summary of Main Points

Readers should take away the following main ideas from this chapter:

- Standards already guide the development of content for the World Wide Web.

- e-Learning standards were originally intended to address earlier challenges posed by computer-based training: the limited interoperability of content (that is, content developed on one computer could be easily viewed on others, regardless of the hardware and operating system of that other computer) and the difficulty of finding content.

- Standards could have helped develop the market for e-learning by:

  - Making content developed for sale more interoperable and, therefore, usable on the systems of more organizations. Standards also could have reduced costs by permitting organizations to easily find existing content and reuse it

  - Making it easier to track student progress and share the records with other systems, and making content developed for one university easier to use in others

- Effective standards should achieve these goals:

  - Interoperability, which refers to the process of preparing content on one system and using it on another, where the content performs consistently, regardless of operating system, browser brand, or device type

  - Reusability, which refers to the ability to use content again for a different purpose, a process called the *repurposing of content*. Reusability of material encompasses two technical functions: interoperability and findability (permit people to easily find information developed by other sources that might be reused)

  - Adaptability, which means that the content can be leveraged in different contexts

  - Accessibility, which refers to efforts to make the web usable for people with visual, auditory, and other physical disabilities, including cognitive processing disabilities and visually impaired elderly web users

  - Durability, which refers to the need to support the longevity of learning content

- Standards are specifically intended to address these issues:

  - Help LMSs and similar learning management software capture and retain information about a learner's location in a course, so the learner could resume a course at the place left off

  - Track student activities and scores and provide the results so that teachers, HR specialists, and instructors could measure student progress and usage and track the time spent in learning activities (as some industries mandate)

  - Facilitate the assembly of learning content from different sources into a single course

- Standards, guidelines, specifications, and reference models have been proposed to address these issues. Each has a distinct meaning—a standard actually represents the last phase in a series of milestones intended to take an idea for coordinating interactions among software and devices:

  - Recognition that a situation in which some coordination of efforts will result in more efficient or economical interactions among programs, or some similar benefit to users

  - One of the following occurs:

    For non-technical issues, a guideline is proposed. Guidelines often address design and editorial issues, with the intention of ensuring consistency among the many designers and developers of related e-learning materials.

    For technical issues, a specification, which identifies the need to be addressed and the manner in which it will be addressed. In some cases, a specification might be preceded by a reference model or some similar working paper that proposes an idea that needs to be refined.

- Once a specification has been in use for a while and proven its utility, it can become a standard.

- Standards are also distinguished by the International Standards Organization (ISO), the World Wide Web

Consortium (W3C), and the Institute of Electrical and Electronics Engineers (IEEE). No organization focused solely on e-learning or learning-related issues has the authority to issue standards.

- If the standards for learning and accessibility are complex, that is because they represent a complex interaction of private corporations, government agencies, nonprofit industry alliances, and standards bodies.

- Standards can develop in several ways. Some are mandated by legislation, as in Section 508 of the Federal Rehabilitation Act. Other standards emerge through a purposeful effort of interested parties, such as efforts since the 1980s by the Aviation Industry CBT Committee (AICC) to enable high-quality computer-based training (CBT). Sometimes, rather than mandating standards, governments try to act as a catalyst for developing and adopting standards, as the Advanced Distributed Learning (ADL) Lab of the U.S. Department of Defense has done with the development of SCORM.

- e-Learning guidelines, specifications, reference models, and specifications address the following issues:

  - Communications interface—the way that online resources used e-learning exchange information among one another

  - Packaging of content—how pieces of online instructional content are labeled so that a system can reassemble the content according to the context

  - Metadata—the contextual information about the content

  - Facilitation of testing and sharing of results

  - Accessibility of content to people with disabilities

  - Sequencing and presentation of content

- Standards work together in a hierarchy, starting at the content level, with a level of activity at the course level and at the administration level.

- Evidence is still being collected about whether standards have benefited e-learning. In terms of achieving the Masie Center's goals for effective standards:

  - For interoperability, after some initial problems, the standards are starting to show benefits, although work still needs to continue.

  - In terms of reusability, organizations are finding ways to reuse existing content, although in more modest ways than people initially anticipated with the concept of reusable learning objects, which has not yet proven feasible on a practical level.

  - In terms of adaptability, standards seem to have had an impact.

  - In terms of accessibility, the standards have, at the least, raised awareness among designers and, at the most, made content more accessible.

  - In terms of durability, standards have definitely contributed to the longevity of learning content.

- Standards have also facilitated the automation of record-keeping in learning groups.

- Standards have not facilitated the world-readiness of content—that is, the ability to use content developed in one place in different countries and cultures.

- Standards are not simple, and are not easy for end-users of them (in this case, administrators and creators of e-learning).

◆ ◆ ◆

## Guiding Questions for Discussion

The following questions apply:

- Why do standards matter?

- Who should care about standards?

- How do you know whether content or management systems are compliant?

- When should I adopt a standard versus a specification?

- How much real support for standards is taking place in content development today?

- What is involved in maintaining support for standards in content libraries?

- How much critical mass support is needed before we reap the benefits from supporting learning standards?

- Where does the end-user benefit?

## Learn More About It

Links        U.S. e-Learning Organizations and Websites

- Advanced Distributed Learning, www.adlnet.org

- Adobe e-Learning and Accessibility Center, www.adobe.com (Note that this is a commercial site)

- Airline Industry CBT Consortium, www.aicc.org

- Instructional Management Systems, www.imsproject.org

- The Inclusive Learning Exchange (TILE), www.inclusivelearning.ca/tile/index.html

- Learnativity, www.learnativity.com

- Masie Center, www.masie.com (Note that this is a commercial site)

- New Media Center, www.newmediacenters.org/e-Learning

Organizations Outside of the United States

- ARIADNE, www.ariadne-eu.org (Europe)

- CANCORE, www.cancore.ca/en/ (Canada-English) and www.cancore.ca/fr/ (Canada-French)

- CENORM, www.cenorm.be/isss (Central Europe)

- CETIS, www.cetis.ac.uk (U.K.)

- Dublin Core, http://dublincore.org/ (U.K. and Europe)

- EDNA, www.edna.edu.au/edna/page1.html (Australia)

*(Continued)*

- International Standards Organization, www.iso.org (worldwide, 150 country partners)
- Joint Information Systems Committee, www.jisc. ac.uk (U.K., higher ed)

## Accessibility-Focused Organizations

- World Wide Web Consortium (W3C), www.w3.org
- W3C Web Content Accessibility Guidelines, www. w3.org/TR/WCAG10/
- W3C Web Content Accessibility Guidelines Curriculum, www.w3.org/WAI/wcag-curric/
- Adaptive Computer Technology Training Centre (Canada), www.ec.gc.ca/act/
- European Accessibility, http://europa.eu.int/information_society/policy/accessibility/index_en.htm
- Guidelines for U.K. Government Web Sites, www. e-envoy.gov.uk/Webguidelines.htm
- IEEE, http://standards.ieee.org
- Introduction to Web Accessibility, www.Webaim. org/info/intro
- U.S. Government Accessibility, www.section508.gov

## Accessibility Resources

- Bobby, now known as Watchfire, http://webxact. watchfire.com/ (Offers a free service provided by CAST to help web-page authors identify and repair significant barriers to access by individuals with disabilities)
- CEN-ISSS Learning Technologies Workshop Accessibility Properties for Learning Resources, www.cen-aplr.org
- The eAccessibility target of eEuropa Action Plan, http://europa.eu.int/information_society/eeurope/2002/action_plan/eaccess/index_en.htm and http://europa.eu.int/information_society/eeurope/2005/all_about/action_plan/index_en.htm

- IMS ACCPRF (Accessibility Profile) specification, www.imsglobal.org/accessibility/

- RevealWeb, www.revealweb.org.uk/ (Offers a range of resources that are available in Braille, moon, audio, and digital talking books, large print and contact details of organizations that hold titles in accessible formats in the Register of Suppliers)

- TechDis Metadata Specification—Version 1.2, www. techdis.ac.uk/metadata/spec.html.

- W3C's Checklist of Checkpoints for Web Content Accessibility Guidelines 1.0, www.w3.org/TR/WCAG10/full-checklist.html

- W3C's Core Techniques for Web Content Accessibility Guidelines 1.0, www. 3.org/TR/WCAG10-CORE-TECHS/

| | |
|---|---|
| Books, Papers, Reports, and Articles | (Note that all of these are available online.) Hodgins, W. (2002). *Learning objects and learning standards: Everything you ever wanted to know but were afraid to ask.* |

www.newmediacenters.org/projects/lo/sap_stand_wayne.shtml. [Retrieved March 7, 2007]

Center for Educational Technology and Information Systems (CETIS). (2004). *Learning technology standards: An overview.* www.cetis.ac.uk/static/standards.html. [Retrieved March 6, 2007]

The IMS Accessibility Profile (ACCPRF). Waltham, MA: IMS. www.imsglobal.org/accessibility/. [Retrieved March 6, 2007] Meta-data specification.

www.techdis.ac.uk/metadata/spec.html. [Retrieved March 6, 2007]

SCORM_2004_conformance requirements document.

www.adlnet.org/screens/shares/dsp_displayfile.cfm?fileid=1108 [Retrieved March 6, 2007]

Masie Center. (2003). *Making sense of learning specification and standards: A decision maker's guide to their adoption.* Saratoga, NY: The Masie Center. www.masie.com/standards/s3_2nd_edition.pdf [Retrieved March 6, 2007]

IEEE 14.84.12.1—2002 Standard for Learning Object Metadata. http://ltsc.ieee.org [Retrieved March 6, 2007]

# Appendix A. Four Ways to Make Web Content Accessible

The benefits of making web content accessible to persons with visual, hearing, and other disabilities are several. At the least, those doing work for governments and other organizations requiring it can comply with the legislation. (See "Learn More About It" elsewhere in this chapter for a list of national and regional policies on accessibility.)

In addition, making web content accessible makes it usable by the largest number of people. But complying with accessibility guidelines is also a moral imperative, because it ensures that users are not excluded on the basis of physical ability. This moral imperative is especially important to people working in the field of learning. One of the primary goals of our work is opening horizons for our learners. How can we do so if physical barriers prevent learners from participating in the learning?

But how can we make web content accessible? Consider these suggestions:

1. *When designing elements of the interface,* make sure that they are organized in a way that can be easily understood and manipulated. For example, a layout for which navigation is difficult or, worse, inconsistent among screens, creates problems for users, even ones who do not have disabilities.

2. *To make content accessible to people who are visually impaired,* make sure that images, image maps, and the graphical elements of the interface are all documented with descriptions that can be displayed through rollover text. A voice reader can convey what's in the graphic image for people who cannot see it.

Similarly, note that content in tables, forms, and frames may not be presented logically by software that reads screens to visually impaired users.

3. *To make content accessible to people who are hearing impaired*, make sure that all narrated content or spoken dialogue is available for display in a text form, so people who cannot hear this material can read it. This problem specifically arises when using audio-based multimedia segments, visual cues in learning materials, and interfaces that rely primarily or exclusively on voice cues.

4. *To make content accessible to users with other disabilities*, consider the following:

   - Dyslexics have difficulty with screens and views that are visually "busy," as do older adults.

   - Many sites have poor color contrast, which reduces readability for people with color deficits and low vision and for older adults.

   - Although learning specialists like to suggest the use of kiosks, they are usually not accessible to the physically challenged, such as people in wheelchairs.

   - Many e-learning applications require a keyboard or a mouse, yet not all users can manipulate these, nor do all environments—especially pubic environments—come equipped with the required input/output devices.

# Appendix B. Technical Specifications and Standards for e-Learning

The following standards and specifications are those relevant to the developers in the industry at the time this book was written. Note, however, that standards for e-learning are always evolving. To ensure that you are using the latest information, it is recommended that you consult the websites named in this chapter to determine what changes or enhancements have been made since publication. Because specificity and accuracy are critical when working with standards, the information on these specifications is taken directly from the sources, and not restated.

The key learning standards and specifications being considered for adoption today include:

- Sharable Content Sharable Content Object Reference Model—SCORM
- Metadata
    - IMS Metadata
    - ISO 15836 standard—Dublin Core Metadata Element Set
- IEEE LOM
- QTI Specification
- Accessibility
- World Wide Web Consortium (W3C) Checkpoints (which is not discussed in this book)

## Sharable Content Object Reference Model (SCORM)

The Sharable Content Object Reference Model (SCORM) is a product of the Advanced Distributed Learning (ADL) association, developed collaboratively with other standards bodies, government entities, and learning-focused organizations around the world.

SCORM was developed to enable the creation of reusable learning content as "instructional objects" within a common technical framework for computer and web-based instruction. SCORM describes a technical framework by providing a cohesive set of guidelines, specifications, and standards. The ADL developed a model for creating and deploying e-learning content. From the SCORM website:

> At its simplest, it is a model that references a set of interrelated technical specifications and guidelines designed to meet high-level requirements for learning content and systems. SCORM describes a "Content Aggregation Model (CAM)" and "Run-Time Environment (RTE)" for learning objects to support adaptive presentation of content based on criteria such as learner objectives, preferences, and performance. SCORM targets the web as a primary medium for delivering instruction. It does so

under the assumption that anything that can be delivered by the web can be easily used in other instructional settings that make fewer demands on accessibility and network communications. This strategy eliminates much of the development work once needed to adapt to the latest technology platform because the web itself is becoming a universal delivery medium. By building upon existing web standards and infrastructures, SCORM frees developers to focus on effective learning strategies.

SCORM is a collection of specifications and standards that can be viewed as separate "books" gathered together into a growing library. Nearly all of the specifications and guidelines have been created or developed by other organizations. These technical "books" are presently grouped under three main topics: Content Aggregation Model (CAM), Run-Time Environment (RTE), and Sequencing and Navigation (SN) (introduced in SCORM 2004). Additional specifications are anticipated in future SCORM releases. SCORM currently provides an application programming interface (API) for communicating information about a learner's interaction with content objects, a defined data model for representing this information, a content packaging specification that enables interoperability of learning content, a standard set of metadata elements that can be used to describe learning content, and a set of standard sequencing rules that can be applied to the organization of the learning content.

SCORM 2004 is the current specification. A specification and content example is available that describes the SCORM 2004 Run-Time Environment Version 1.3.1 Data Model and models the usage of several data model elements. The purpose of the content example is to provide information and examples for organizations and individuals to assist them in implementing the SCORM 2004 model. The Data Model Content Example Version 1.0 is a SCORM 2004 Conformant Content Aggregation Package.zip file. The content package can be imported into any SCORM 2004 conformant LMS and used as an example or a reference model.

In addition to creating the SCORM specifications and examples, the ADL Initiative funded a network of four ADL co-laboratories to support testing and certification by interested parties—developers, buyers, vendors, and educational institutions. Today, over 155 companies are registered developers with some level of certification. To find the locations of these ADL facilities, visit www.adlnet.org/index.cfm?fuseaction=colabovr. The ADL Initiative established an ADL Partnership Lab in the United Kingdom and in Canada. The ADL also sponsors events and "plugfests" where vendors and members can come and test their content for SCORM compliance.

## Metadata

Metadata, or information about data, is important in facilitating the reuse of data. Information that is typically captured includes author, content type, file size, intended audience, and frequently, discipline subject area.

### IMS Metadata

In IMBs, this information is described in the information model. How descriptive information becomes associated with the content is described in the XML binding, and the XML schema is the machine readable method of structuring the XML. Best practices include supporting implementation materials and advice. The most recent specification for metadata was released by IMS in July 2004 and includes the following:

- Information Model
- XML Binding
- XML Schema Definition
- Best Practices and Implementation Guidelines

*The Information Model:* The Information Model describes the information that is considered important for the specification. It shows the relationship between the various pieces of information involved in the model. It is a human-readable document that specifies what must be encoded in the machine-readable documents to conform to this specification. The information model describes the core aspects of the specification and contains parts that are normative for any binding claiming to conform to this specification.

It contains details of semantics, structure, data types, value spaces, multiplicity, and obligation (that is, whether mandatory or optional).

*XML Binding:* The XML binding is a formal document describing the information model and its binding to an XML schema. It is normative for any XML instance document that claims to employ this specification, whether by reference or by declaration of the namespace reserved for this specification. When data is missing or incomplete or inaccurate, the information model takes precedence. The XML binding is released with an XML schema definition file. Conformance issues are addressed in the binding document, as the binding document will be used judge conformance.

*XML Schema Definition:* The XML schema definition defines, in a machine-readable format, the required syntax and structure of valid XML instance documents conforming to this specification. The XML schema should be used in system implementations.

*Best Practice and Implementation Guide:* The best practice and implementation guide provides guidance in implementing the specifications and contains responses to common questions expected from developers, including examples of the accessibility metadata AccessForAll LIP specification, whose goal is to support accessible content creation.

## ISO 15836 Standard—Dublin Core Metadata Element Set

The Dublin Core Metadata Element Set is the ISO 15836 standard for core metadata. There is also a Qualified Dublin Core Metadata Element Set with additional terms and extensions. Dublin Core metadata is not domain-specific. An encoding of the AccessForAll metadata specification will be suitable for use in a Dublin Core Application Profile for accessibility of resources.

# IEEE LOM

The IEEE LOM (Institute of Electrical and Electronics Engineers' Learning Object Metadata) consists of a profile for learning object metadata. It contains a description of semantics, vocabulary, and extensions.

This standard specifies a high-level architecture for information-technology-supported learning, education and training systems that describes the high-level system design and the components of these systems. This standard covers a wide range of systems, commonly known as learning technology, education and training technology, computer-based training, computer-assisted instruction, intelligent tutoring, metadata, etc. This standard is pedagogically neutral, content-neutral, culturally neutral, and platform-neutral. This standard (1) provides a framework for understanding existing and future systems, (2) promotes interoperability and portability by identifying critical system interfaces, and (3) incorporates a technical horizon (applicability) of at least five to ten years while remaining adaptable to new technologies and learning technology systems. This standard is neither prescriptive nor exclusive.

The purpose of developing system architectures is to discover high-level frameworks for understanding certain kinds of systems and their interactions with other related systems. By exposing the shared components of different systems at the right level of generality, the learning systems architecture promotes the design and implementation of reusable learning objects or components.

The architectural framework developed in this standard is independent of the specific details of implementation technologies (for example, programming languages, authoring tools, or operating systems) necessary to create the system components or the content or learning management systems necessary to manage learning objects.

## QTI Specification

To address the needs of assessment consistency and test item interoperability, IMS has developed the IMS Question and Test Interoperability (QTI) specification, currently available in its v2.0 Final Specification. The QTI spec was developed with the following objectives:

- Provide a well-documented content format for storing items independent of the authoring tool used to create them

- Support the deployment of items and item banks from diverse sources in a single learning or assessment delivery system

- Provide systems with the ability to report test results in a consistent manner

## IEEE LOM-LTSC Specification 1484.12.1-.4

The IEEE Learning Technology Standards Committee (LTSC) has been providing for the development and maintenance of the learning object metadata (LOM) standard. This process is an international effort with the active participation on the LOM Working Group committee representing more than fifteen countries. Most recently, June 12, 2002, this resulted in the first IEEE accredited standard to be completed by LTSC, the 1484.12.1 LOM data model standard. This is the first of a multi-part standard for learning object metadata, which LTSC LOM is responsible for maintaining, developing, and evolving. The scope of efforts addressed by this working group includes the following standard for information technology—education and training systems—learning objects and metadata:

- 1484.12.1: IEEE Standard for Learning Object Metadata

- 1484.12.2: Standard for ISO/IEC 11404 Binding for Learning Object Metadata Data Model

- 1484.12.3: Standard for Learning Technology-Extensible Markup Language (XML) Schema Definition Language Binding for Learning Object Metadata

- 1484.12.4: Standard for Resource Description Framework (RDF) Binding for Learning Object Metadata Data Model

This standard specifies the syntax and semantics of learning object metadata, defined as the attributes required to fully describe a learning object. Per the LOM interpretation, learning objects are defined in the specification as, "Any entity, digital or non-digital, which can be used, reused, or referenced during technology supported learning." Examples of technology supported learning include computer-based training systems, interactive learning environments, intelligent computer-aided instruction systems, distance learning systems, and collaborative learning environments. Examples of learning objects include multimedia content, instructional content, learning objectives, instructional software and software tools, and persons, organizations, or events referenced during technology supported learning.

The learning object metadata standards focus on defining the minimal set of attributes needed to allow these learning objects to be managed, located, and evaluated. The standards support extending the basic fields and entity types, and the fields can have a status of obligatory (must be present) or optional (may be absent). Relevant attributes of learning objects to be described include type of object, author, owner, terms of distribution, and format. Where applicable, learning object metadata may also include pedagogical attributes such as teaching or interaction style, grade level, mastery level, and prerequisites. It is possible for any given learning object to have more than one set of learning object metadata. The standard will support security, privacy, commerce, and evaluation, but if metadata fields are provided for specifying descriptive tokens related to these areas, the standard does not address how these features are implemented.

# Appendix C. Accessibility Guidelines and Standards

Accessibility guidelines and standards attempt to create a level playing field in providing access to web-delivered content for people with disabilities. Guidelines and standards have been developed to promote and, in some cases, mandate, compliance so that all can access content as equally as possible. The key initiatives include:

- W3C Web Accessibility Initiative
- Section 508 Standards
- Individuals with Disabilities Education Act
- Americans with Disabilities Act

By way of background, the World Wide Web Consortium (W3C), the international organization that sets standards for the web, has made accessibility a major initiative with its committee, the Web Accessibility Initiative (WAI). The WAI leads several working groups that have developed checkpoints and guidelines for accessibility that have been referenced and adopted by governments and organizations around the world. The most widely adopted of all of these guidelines and standards are the Web Content Accessibility Guidelines. Consisting of fourteen guidelines and sixty-four checkpoints, this document serves as the basis of almost every major standard around the world.

Governments and organizations have elected to support different levels of compliance, both mandated and recommended, with priority-two checkpoints being the basis of policy in Europe and Japan. On August 7, 1998, the President of the United States signed the Workforce Reinvestment Act of 1998, which includes the Rehabilitation Act Amendments of 1998. Section 508 of the Rehabilitation Act, as amended by the Workforce Reinvestment Act of 1998, requires that U.S. federal agencies develop, procure, maintain, or use electronic and information technology that lets federal employees with disabilities have access to, and use of, information and data in a comparable fashion to those without disabilities. The only exception is when an undue burden would be imposed on the agency. This legislation is commonly referred to as Section 508.

Section 508 guidelines were informed by and reference WAI guidelines, but they are not identical. Section 508 guidelines are most similar to priority-one guidelines of the WAI, but the U.S. federal guidelines modified some of the language. Canada, Australia, and the United Kingdom adopted similar, and in some cases more stringent, guidelines from the WAI's priority-one and priority-two guidelines. The current standards in Japan, as reflected in Japanese Industrial Standards X8341–3, are based on priority-one and -two checkpoints, with some priority-three and some new checkpoints unique to this document.

The initial focus of accessibility projects was on making websites offering services accessible. In the e-learning content area, accessibility is a major architectural consideration. Any dynamic website or application poses challenges to creating accessible content, given that the content is generated by programming logic.

Current metadata specifications have not provided adequate support for authoring accessible delivery of educational resources. As a result, it has been difficult for current systems to ensure conformance of accessibility requirements. IMS released a specification IMS Learner Information Package Accessibility for LIP (ACCLIP), which is a model for describing and recording user preferences regarding content, display, and control of learning resources. The AccessForAll Metadata specification (ACCMD) defines accessibility metadata that is able to express a resource's ability to match the needs and preferences of a user's ACCLIP profile. As a result, systems are able to select the appropriate resource for each user, providing user experiences that adapt to individual needs. Because these specifications offer a modular approach to accessibility, defining each aspect of the user preference or resource characteristic separately, systems can determine to whom each resource is accessible and under what circumstances. More recently, The Inclusive Learning Exchange (TILE), a learning object repository that supports complete customization of the learning content to the individual needs of each learner, has built upon these efforts.

## Key Section 508 Accessibility Checkpoints for Web Page Design

Separate from the IMS guidelines are the guidelines published by the World Wide Web Consortium, the W3C, under the Web Accessibility Initiative working group's guidance. This organization has published guidelines from which legislation in several countries has been adopted. A summary of the key checkpoints is shown in Exhibit 6.1.

**Exhibit 6.1. Key Checkpoints**

- A text equivalent for every non-text element shall be provided (e.g., via "alt," "longdesc," or in element content).

### WAI Checkpoint 1.1

- Redundant text links shall be provided for each active region of a server-side image map.

### WAI Checkpoint 1.2

- Equivalent alternatives for any multimedia presentation shall be synchronized with the presentation.

### WAI Checkpoint 1.4

- Web pages shall be designed so that all information conveyed with color is also available without color, for example from context or markup.

### WAI Checkpoint 2.1

- Row and column headers shall be identified for data tables.

### WAI Checkpoint 5.1

- Documents shall be organized so they are readable without requiring an associated style sheet.

### WAI Checkpoint 6.1

- Pages shall be designed to avoid causing the screen to flicker with a frequency greater than 2 Hz and lower than 55 Hz.

### WAI Checkpoint 7.1

- Client-side image maps shall be provided instead of server-side image maps, except where the regions cannot be defined with an available geometric shape.

### WAI Checkpoint 9.1

- A text-only page, with equivalent information or functionality, shall be provided to make a website comply with the provisions of this part, when compliance cannot be accomplished in any other way.

The content of the text-only page shall be updated whenever the primary page changes.

**WAI Checkpoint 11.4**

- When pages utilize scripting languages to display content or to create interface elements, the information provided by the script shall be identified with functional text that can be read by assistive technology.

- When a web page requires that an applet, plug-in, or other application be present on the client system to interpret page content, the page must provide a link to a plug-in or applet that complies with the standard.

- When electronic forms are designed to be completed online, the form shall allow people using assistive technology to access the information, field elements, and functionality required for completion and submission of the form, including all directions and cues.

- When a timed response is required, the user shall be alerted and given sufficient time to indicate more time is required. A method shall be provided that permits users to skip repetitive navigation links.

*Source:* The W3C's Checklist of Checkpoints for Web Content Accessibility Guidelines 1.0, www.w3.org/TR/WCAG10/full-checklist.html.

## Accessibility Implementation Considerations

Building compliant web pages should be an organizational process, the result of an organization-wide policy. Organizations are encouraged to develop accessibility guidelines. Many websites have a policy link on their home page. A good example can be found at http://aol.com/accessibility. It is far easier to design compliant web pages at the time of authoring, rather than retrofitting content. Tools to promote compliance are built into current versions of popular authoring tools like Macromedia's Dreamweaver™ and Flash™.

Accessibility expert Mike Paciello suggests the following simple design guidelines:

- Always provide alternative text for images (ALT = "text").
- Use short, functional text descriptions for images and text links.
- Use ALT text for bullets, horizontal rules, or thumbnail links.
- Consider using a text "anchor" page for tables.
- Keep layouts simple and straightforward.
- Avoid side-by-side (columnar) presentation of text.
- If using graphics to provide organization or structure to the document, attach ALT text to images that supply the same changes in context that the visual cues provide.
- Buttons that perform the same function on different pages (for example, "return to home page") should be in a consistent location on the page.
- All image maps should be client side and use ALT text for each link.
- Provide text transcripts of audio and video events.
- Test your pages for color contrast.
- Do not use blinking text or marquees.
- Use relative font sizes; do not use absolute font sizes.
- Provide e-mail versions of forms (downloadable).
- Do not use browser-specific tags; stick with standard HTML.
- Always test your pages with a variety of browsers.

Diagnostic tools and services that help content developers determine whether their web pages are in compliance with the guidelines and standards are available at no charge or for a minimal fee. For more information, visit the Accessibility Resource Center at www.adobe.com/accessibility.

One of the more popular testing tools, formerly known as Bobby, now called WebXACT, is available from Watchfire at www.watchfire.com/products/webxm/accessibilityxm.aspx. Watchfire's accessibility module scans a website for over 170 comprehensive web-accessibility checks and generates reports on where the site may not be complying with the following legislation:

- US Section 508

- UK Disability Discrimination Act

- W3C's Web Content Accessibility Guidelines (WCAG)

- France's AccessiWeb guidelines

- Canadian Common Look and Feel

- eEurope Plan

Watchfire does so for websites regardless of their size or complexity.

# Appendix D. Standards Acronym Decoder

| | |
|---|---|
| ACCLIP | IMS Learner Information Package Accessibility for LIP |
| ACCMD | IMS AccessForAll Meta-Data (this specification) |
| AICC | Airline Industry CBT Committee |
| CP | IMS Content Packaging Specification |
| DCMES | DCMI Dublin Core Metadata Element Set |
| DCMI | Dublin Core Metadata Initiative |
| DRI | IMS Digital Repositories Interoperability Specification |
| EARL | W3C Evaluation and Report Language |
| IEEE | Institute of Electrical and Electronics Engineers |
| LOM | Learning Object Metadata (usually used in IEEE LOM) |
| MIME | Multipurpose Internet Mail Extensions |
| RDF | Resource Description Framework |
| SCORM | Sharable Content Object Reference Model |
| TILE | The Inclusive Learning Exchange |
| W3C | World Wide Web Consortium |

# Chapter 7

# Learning with Objects

*Patrick Parrish,*
*The COMET® Program*

## About This Chapter

People often embrace new instructional technologies with such optimism that we fail to recognize their limitations, a phenomenon that was definitely observed with learning objects. Like standards, learning objects (short instructional components that can be reused) have been a major topic of discussion in e-learning over the past several years. But much of the conversation has focused on how to implement learning objects, rather than on the more fundamental issues of their potential as educational tools.

In response, this chapter explores the question, "What are the different implications of learning objects to learning and instruction?" After critically examining technological optimism in general, I turn my attention to learning objects. First I briefly describe them. Next, I look at two paradigms of instructional practice, control and open systems, and determine which assumptions each paradigm makes and ignores about knowledge and learning, from the perspective of each, ask what is gained and given up with learning objects—that is, how might learning objects change how a person works and learns? I close the chapter by briefly describing a promising effort to employ learning objects in a professional development context.

# Whither Learning Objects?

New technologies dazzle us with their promise. Fascinating us with their unfathomable workings and ever-growing capacity (more memory storage, more pixels, more operations per second, more horsepower, more speed), new technologies often generate such optimism that we believe they are the solution to even our largest challenges.

Listening to the opening keynote speech by Rodney Brooks, robotics expert and director of MIT's Computer Science and AI Lab, at a recent annual conference of the Association for Education and Communications (AECT), I noted how quickly the audience, myself included, became enthralled with his descriptions of advancing computer technologies and promises that they will change our futures more than we can currently imagine possible. The implications of even his more down-to-earth projections were difficult to fully grasp. If advances in digital memory storage capacity in general, and iPod technology in particular continue at their current trajectory, iPods will be able to hold the contents of all the text in the U.S. Library of Congress, and what is more, by the year 2024, iPods will also be able to hold every film ever made. After shaking off fanciful thoughts of never being at a loss for the perfect film to watch, I eventually realized that somewhere in between these two years, iPods will be able to hold every e-learning resource ever created. In other words, in the foreseeable future we will be able to have every online document, training tutorial, animation, simulation, game, webcast, podcast, or whatever other forms *learning objects* might take, conveniently stored in our pockets or purses. These would cover every topic taught anywhere and would be ready to use whenever the urge for learning strikes. The problem is, I couldn't tell whether my exuberant response to this nearly infinite access was based on liberation or on greed.

The enthusiasm Brooks inspired is a perfect example of what Kant (2001) calls *the sublime*, in which a rational appreciation of something that is incomprehensible to the senses (like the number of stars in the universe or *pedabytes* of information) instills in us an enjoyable feeling of reason's superiority over imagination and nature. I believe that this concept of the sublime explains our often indiscriminant optimism toward new technologies. Like most of us, I share in enjoying the continual wonders of technological and scientific advancement and every day I gratefully reap their benefits. But I also worry about the tacit but pervasive belief, especially among e-learning advocates, that more technology is better and that technology is the first place to look to meet society's challenges. And I am concerned with what Rose (2003) sees as a pervasive assumption of the inevitability of a technology-driven future, the assumption by technology proponents like Brooks that people should be willing to trust and go along for the ride while technologists create the new world, just because they can. I have this concern about technology in general, but it particularly concerns me when I see it expressed in the teaching and learning enterprise. The concept of learning objects that has been frequently promoted in our community is a primary example of this belief in technology.

On a personal level, I think flights of reason are much more dangerous than flights of fancy, and I would ultimately trust imagination and nature over reason any day. So when I find myself caught up in the sublime and lusting over the latest technology, as I did during Brooks' presentation, I try to step back and imagine what life with such technologies might *really* be like, beyond the optimistic hyperbole that inevitably accompanies their introduction. I ask:

- What assumptions are being made by the technology proponent, and what facts does he or she ignore about human nature?

- What might I have to give up if I adopt the new technology in order to accept the apparent benefit it offers? In more practical terms, what might change about the way I work, learn, and interact with others if I freely admit the technology described by the proponent into my life?

These are not easy questions to answer because technologies have become so entwined in everyday life that people find it difficult to see the effects of technology as something separate from other influencing factors that, in turn, make answering the questions even more urgent. Given that the momentum to adopt technology often overshadows such questions, the questions might also appear to be merely academic. The more pressing concern may be to find a way to adopt the technology or operate outside of general society. But authors like Rose (2003) suggest that we can value our technologies and, at the same time, hold onto our own volition and assume responsibility for the ways technologies are adopted. As instructional technologists, we should never be blind adopters. Our roles should include assessing new technologies, imagining new instructional uses for them, considering their potential abuses, and recommending only appropriate applications.

There are more systematic ways to consider the impacts of technology (for example, McLuhan & McLuhan, 1988), but a fun, and perhaps in the end equally effective, way to ponder them is to pretend you're preparing a standup comedy routine about them. Comedians have a way of bypassing hyperbole to quickly uncover the assumptions we make and point out our foibles and short-sightedness in ways that make us laugh at and appreciate human nature. We might even consider comedy as a form of social inquiry, with the ability to produce laughter as its measure of validity. So what if Rodney Brooks had been replaced by Jerry Seinfeld riffing on the same projections of our future? I offer as a few imagined passages from a routine I'm sure Jerry would never perform on stage:

I don't know about you, but my 20 gigabyte iPod began to intimidate me a long time ago. And they say it's only a few years before an iPod can hold a terabyte of data—that's almost two years of music! Think about it. It's going to be a burden to carry around two years' worth of music, because if make the investment, I know I'll somehow feel obligated to find the time to listen to all of it. I'll probably begin driving out of my way just to fit in few more songs—"just a hundred more miles and I can check off ABBA and finally move on to John Abercrombie." And you know, it's not just the heavy obligation. I'm solidly middle-aged now, and it's a little depressing to be able to measure my mortality in relation to my iPod capacity.

Once they reach 10 terabytes or so, in less than ten years, iPods will be able to hold the entire contents of the Library of Congress, which is something of a mixed blessing if you think about it. I've wanted to have a copy of the Library of Congress for some time now, but I've always assumed that the extensive home renovations I'd need to do to hold it all would be way too inconvenient. Now—well pretty soon anyway—I can have the entire library in my pocket! This may sound great, but think of the responsibility. And I'm not just talking about having to re-shelve the periodicals. It's like the teacher telling you the dictionary solves all your spelling problems. When someone asks you a question, you can't just say, "I don't know" anymore, because they'll just tell you, "You have the Library of Congress in your iPod. Look it up, dummy." I think I'd rather have an excuse to be ignorant about some things.

And I'm sure you've seen the new video iPods. Well, they tell us that in less than twenty years an iPod will be able to hold every movie ever made. I can just imagine my wife and I trying to agree on which of every movie ever made we want to watch tonight.

After an hour of fruitless debate, I suspect we'll end up
preferring to sit through "Dharma and Greg" reruns
rather than continue arguing.

These imagined jokes point out at least three objections to the
unbridled optimism about ever-increasing digital memory capacity. First, people become frustrated consumers when they possess
more information than they can use. Attempting to use the excess
information only interferes with more productive uses of time.
Second, even though that overwhelming amount of information
is readily available, people are left to their own devices to navigate and assimilate it, rather than being guided to new discoveries by someone more knowledgeable, like a teacher (or radio disc
jockey). Third, being left to find and interpret information on their
own, people might not have a meaningful place to begin and,
rather than experiencing the freedom to explore a subject in its
entirety, are likely to become paralyzed by overwhelming choices,
a phenomenon that Richard Saul Wurman (1989) calls *information
anxiety.*

One could raise these objections to many e-learning technologies, including reusable learning objects. Yet many e-learning advocates hold such optimism that these objections are not considered.
This optimism frequently takes two forms, following two competing
paradigms in education (also reflected in Wiley, 2003; Wilson, 2001).
One paradigm proposes that the primary role of education and
training is to transmit a standard canon of the accumulated knowledge of a set of recognized experts. This paradigm assumes the
need for control and consistency, for automation, predictability, and
standards. The second paradigm assumes that open systems are a
better guide. It calls for open and self-organizing learning communities and accepts open-endedness and variability in outcomes as natural and desirable for allowing individuals and groups to construct
relevant knowledge.

This chapter explores the phenomenon of learning objects in the
context of these two paradigms. First, I briefly describe learning
objects. Next, I look at these two paradigms—control and open

system—and, from each perspective, determine which assumptions the paradigms make and ignores about knowledge and learning. For each paradigm, I ask what is gained and what is given up with the use of learning objects—that is, how might a broad implementation of learning objects change how a person works and learns? I close the chapter by briefly describing a promising effort to employ learning objects in a professional development context.

# About Learning Objects

Learning objects are short instructional components that are products of a design strategy and software techniques whose goal is to facilitate their discovery by learners and reuse by course developers. That may sound straightforward enough, but the definition of the term *learning object* has been long debated (Friesen, 2003; Parrish, 2004; Schatz, 2005; Wiley, 2002). One reason for the debate is that instructional technologists seem bent on declaring what a learning object is versus understanding what a learning object is meant to achieve.

In the broadest definition, a learning object can be any learning resource. It can be a small piece of a learning program, like an illustration or a description of a concept, an entire unit of instruction or an entire course. Others would like to narrow this definition so that you can know a learning object when you see it, but, I think this is a dubious goal. I have proposed that rather than define a learning object as a particular form, it should be defined by its use (Parrish, 2004). In other words, a learning object is any online learning resource offered for reuse in creating learning experiences.

The concept of learning objects is inspired by the software engineering paradigm of object-oriented programming. In object-oriented programming, software developers reuse blocks of code, called objects, in many different contexts and, because code can be used many times, the strategy reduces the time and cost needed to develop programs. Examples are the routines needed for cutting, pasting, and copying text. The basic properties of the routines are the same, so developers write the instructions once and call these instructions from many places within a program and use them again in other programs.

But can instructional content be reused in the same way as programming code? Because programming is considered an engineering discipline that deals with creating tools and instructional technology is considered a design discipline that deals with creating knowledge, many wonder whether the concept transfers. In fact, the comparison may only promote confusion and create false expectations. One way that some people have distanced the concept of learning objects from object-oriented programming is by calling learning objects *online learning resources* (Littlejohn, 2003), which also better demonstrates what is not so new about learning objects. Learning resources have always been reused, even if they weren't always found online (Wiley, 2005). Furthermore, the term "online learning resources" avoids the negative connotations of the word "object" because knowledge is dynamic and open-ended, not fixed or constrained by predefined attributes (Parrish, 2004). The concept of learning objects is ultimately about their use, not their internal properties.

Even though the fundamental concept of learning objects is not really new, designing learning resources so they can be effectively reused involves some new design approaches. These include:

- Dividing instructional content and activities into discrete, coherent units

- Embedding or linking to "metadata" that accurately describes the characteristics of those learning resources to increase the likelihood that intended users will discover them

- Using a relatively context-free design that facilitates adaptation of the resource to fit multiple instructional contexts (such as reducing visual, conceptual, and functional constraints)

The only one of these new design approaches that is an essential quality of learning objects is the first—dividing instructional content and activities into discrete, coherent units. However, in theory, the other two design approaches should extend the utility of the learning resources and are what generate the excitement with learning objects. They believe that the increased utility of objects should increase their use, thus it generates reducing costs, facilitating instructional development, and increasing access to learning content.

Despite intense conversation about learning objects that perhaps peaked with David Wiley's 2001 online book. *The Instructional Use of Learning Objects* the long-term influence of learning objects on the everyday practice of e-learning remains to be seen as of the writing of this book. This lack of substantial influence may result from the extremes in which people have proposed using them. One is to provide exceptional control over learning. A second is to provide exceptional openness in learning. But perhaps the potential for impact lies somewhere in the middle. The next three sections explore these different approaches. The next considers the control paradigm, the following considers the open systems paradigm, and the third looks at more practical approach to learning objects that represents something between the two.

# Using Learning Objects to Achieve Increased Control Over Learning and Instructional Design

The hope that technology will provide control over chaotic, sometimes seemingly uncontrollable, aspects of instructional design is as old as the discipline. Long before instructional technologists were even thinking in terms of learning objects, they were trying to automate the processes of instructional systems design (Spector, Polson, & Muraida, 1993) and delivery (such as Merrill, 1999) by reducing content to digestible sizes. Just as the goal of automation in manufacturing is to avoid human error and inefficiencies, so the goal of automating instructional systems design and delivery is to make those processes more efficient and teacher- or designer-proof, as well as make learning outcomes more predictable. Automated instructional design systems work by having learning content broken into small units and then helping instructional designers sequence them according to prescribed algorithms. The most ambitious approaches to automating instructional systems design—also similar to the most ambitious approaches to learning objects—are aimed at creating intelligent tutoring systems that make decisions on-the-fly during student use. Such systems are achieved by dividing instruction into discrete units designed to help learners achieve specific, incremental learning outcomes prescribed by measures of learner performance and readiness. Because they provide readily available chunks of instructional content, learning object systems strongly support the goals of automated instructional systems design and delivery (Merrill, 2002).

In fact, all instructional systems design (ISD) models are, in a sense, about increasing control over the complexities of learning systems by reducing and classifying content. Nearly all describe a range of methods to be selected based on a given set of learning conditions, such as the nature of what is to be learned, the desired learning outcomes, and the characteristics of learners and the learning environment (Reigeluth, 1999).

Even ISD approaches that are much less ambitious than automation, such as efforts to define competencies and create standardized evaluations, focus on decomposing content to address the needs of individual learners at some diagnosed stage of learning. All approaches to ISD, from defining competencies to automating the process, are daunting tasks. So it's no wonder that some instructional technologists optimistically embrace the creation of reusable learning object libraries and the adoption of the learning content management systems proposed to deliver them.

Such approaches follow a particular control-based model of education, and is rooted in a series of assumptions. Several of these are worth exploring. The most significant is that learning occurs in predictable patterns that can be modeled using algorithms. The control paradigm assumes that human learning is like physical phenomena for which predictable relationships can be uncovered, verified, represented with algorithms, much like one of Newton's equations, and modeled on a computer. Because the relationships among content, learners, and presentation are assumed to be predictable, the resulting learning materials are designed with these relationships in mind and assumed to be foolproof. A related assumption is that knowledge is composed of predetermined contents like equations—that its qualities and contents are fixed, can be operationalized in observable and measurable terms, and can be categorized by predictable relationships that lead to learning. A final assumption, one deeply rooted in the market economy, is that efficiency in the learning enterprise is a primary goal—that we must do all we can to control the instructional design and learning processes so that both can occur as rapidly as possible to reduce their costs.

But each of these assumptions has its flaws. The assumptions that learning and knowledge can be represented by predictable, fixed relationships are challenged by current mainstream learning theory. In the more widely held view, learning cannot be fully described by metaphors of transmission or computation, and is more productively viewed as participation in social systems (Jonassen & Land, 2000). Under this social constructivist paradigm, not only is learning impossible to model in predictable detail, but knowledge itself is never fixed. Rather, knowledge is socially constructed in an ongoing process of negotiation within a community of practice (Lemke, 1997). Although the control paradigm in education has roots in the laudable goal of individualizing the learning experience, it is a dubious form of individualization that only offers self-pacing within mechanized delivery of standardized content (Rose, 2004).

The third assumption, that efficiency is a primary goal, is difficult to challenge because the drive for efficiency is so deeply rooted in our society. However, any consideration of efficiency is always value-laden; societies tend to more frequently recognize inefficiency in those activities that they value less, because they want to invest as little time, energy, and thought in them as possible. Despite many public statements to the contrary, organizations and societies often fall short in their investments in education and training. Many fail to see education and training as an investment—they view them as a cost. But it could be otherwise if they valued developing people with capacities to learn and create, and not merely perform skills that have been taught.

What do learners give up with learning objects designed under the control paradigm? In the extreme case, learners may never be exposed to artfully designed learning materials and never have spontaneous personal interactions with a trusted teacher and a cadre of fellow students, and instead have to settle for predictable learning on their own with objects. Although their acquisition of prescribed skills and knowledge may happen more efficiently (given good object-oriented instructional design), learners may lose out on the less tangible benefits that come with less controlled approaches. For example, learning in an environment in which knowledge is measured by the objects acquired, learners may never recognize their own value as individuals or develop their own capacities as knowledge generators. In other words, automated learning experiences may be efficient in achieving narrowly defined objectives but, in the long run, may be ineffective in developing people who can contribute to a growing organization, profession, or society.

What does an instructional technologist give up in using learning objects designed according to a control paradigm? If the instructional design process proceeds in the direction of automation, and instructional design becomes more a matter of populating object templates and sequencing objects, little actual design is required, and the results are likely to be uninspiring. Design automation does not carry the promise of other types of automation—that is, automating the menial tasks to free workers for the more intellectually challenging and emotionally rewarding ones—it does the opposite. It eliminates those opportunities to make learning experiences fun, memorable, and inspiring.

# Using Learning Objects to Achieve Open Learning Systems

In contrast to the control paradigm of education is the open learning systems paradigm. This paradigm arises from the belief that technology can create an open society of equal opportunity and with free exchange of ideas. Technologies, especially information technologies, are seen as great equalizers and catalysts for societal change. For example, it may be assumed that with the introduction of the Internet and free online repositories of shared learning objects, affordable quality education is freely available because all learners have access to the same information and learning opportunities. Open discussion boards, blogs, and rating systems may even provide equal access to the breadth of possible interpretations of these learning objects. In this paradigm, technology is assumed able to create a society in which no user is privileged over another. One merely has to log in. This belief is consistent with, and supportive of, the democratic goals of education. Not surprisingly, this openness conflicts with control and automation.

Although the values underlying the open systems paradigm are in keeping with the mainstream of the educational community, and its goals are consistent with those of any democratic society, its assumptions should be assessed all the same. It is rooted in the belief that knowledge is socially negotiated in communities and that advancements in information technologies broaden those communities and increase their resources. The Internet has the potential to make the world a classroom, and free Internet communication tools make other Internet users fellow learners. Teachers are no longer isolated practitioners struggling to create or find funds to purchase learning resources to engage their students, as online resources are freely available, and teachers merely have to gather them or guide students to them.

But this assumes that technology provides equal access. Even with rapidly declining costs for computers (as of this writing, a $US100 desktop computer has been developed), wide access does not necessarily result. Technical, practical, and cultural barriers continue to prevent many people from adopting technology and prevent others from making effective use of it (Burbules & Callister, 2000). A second assumption is that large numbers of quality materials will be shared online and that metatags will facilitate their cataloging for easy searching. Although digital repositories of educational resources are making great strides, such as the National Science

Digital Library (NSDL) (www.nsdl.org) and the Multimedia Educational Resource for Learning and Online Teaching (MERLOT) (www.merlot.org), real limitations exist. On the one hand, there is a problem of volume—the sheer number of resources to sort through using metadata that may not match the criteria or needs of all users. On the other hand, is the effort necessary to catalogue what are often very small resources? Some valuable resources don't make it into repositories. Metadata also causes costs to contribute to and manage libraries to increase.

Intellectual property considerations also limit sharing. Sharing is more likely to happen in environments in which learning materials are developed for open use, such as universities and schools. But in environments where people develop learning materials to generate a profit, such as textbook publishers and online learning companies, free sharing is unlikely to happen. In fact, many content providers, especially private ones in need of generating stronger revenue streams, are increasing their charges for online content, thus limiting access, rather than expanding it.

A third assumption underlying the open systems paradigm is that making reusable learning objects is easy, but this ignores the matter of context. Content developers may be reluctant to share materials if it means forgoing the contextual information that helps materials fit well within their original instructional system. The widely accepted theory of situated learning, which holds that learning and cognition are always unique to a particular context, suggests that to separate content and context is misguided (Lemke, 1997). For borrowers also, removing inappropriate context or maneuvering around it might be more difficult than simply creating new materials. For learners, attempting to integrate diverse learning objects may complicate learning, rather than facilitate it.

A final assumption that should be challenged is that substantial borrowing of content is something desirable. Arguments for borrowing are typically made on an economic basis. But if learning is more than merely acquiring information and, rather, a social activity, it is likely so because it requires close observation and participation in knowledge construction activities. Although learning communities should be open to outside influences, they also benefit from a degree of boundary (Wilson, Ludwig-Hardman, Thornam, & Dunlap, 2004) and limited size, both of which support developing trust and shared meanings and goals (Wenger, 1998). Although instructional technologies like learning object repositories certainly extend the size of learning communities, and the multiple perspectives these additional resources bring may foster more resilient knowledge than being exposed to a single instructor, textbook, or online learning module, these additional resources will always be remote "objects," rather than products of living and breathing members of a collaborative community.

What is given up in an open learning environment supported by learning objects? Although there may be much to gain by leaving behind an isolated classroom, the loss of the intimate connections that can develop in a shared, guided learning experience cannot be replaced by learning with borrowed objects. If a substantial implementation learning objects sacrifices the development of personal knowledge in collaboration with instructors and other learners, the cost may be too high. If the use of inexpensive learning objects replaces the creation of well-integrated experiences carefully crafted by dedicated instructional designers, meaningful learning may be at stake.

# Practical Implementation of Learning Objects

No paradigm is inherently good or bad, and neither is any technology. But applying a technology without examining the limitations of the assumptions underlying it can lead to unintended and undesirable outcomes. Radical optimism for technology may do more harm than good if it ignores other possible solutions and marches forward without a wary eye for negative repercussions.

Taken to its extremes, any technology ends up reversing its original benefits, warn McLuhan and McLuhan (1988). In other words, indiscriminate use of technologies like learning objects could end up stifling learning, rather than enhancing it. The proposals made by many proponents of learning objects have certainly been extreme, such as claims that they would require a redefinition of arts and humanities courses for the sake of student "consumers" (Downes, 2000) and lead to a ten-fold increase in the productivity of instructional technologists (Hodgins, 2002). Fortunately, the claims have become more modest, and more interesting, in recent years (Schatz, 2005; van Merriënboer & Boot, 2005; Wiley, 2005). Perhaps it takes extreme claims to allow an instructional technology to take hold in the imagination of users, but eventually we see more moderate, realistic expectations and projects then reflect these new expectations.

At the Cooperative Program for Operational Meteorology, Education, and Training (The COMET® Program), the organization where I work, we have initiated a series of object-oriented projects within a curriculum to train forecasters about winter weather events. For this curriculum, we are developing a series of case-based learning modules that use learning objects as supporting topics, which develop the background knowledge that can help learners make good decisions in the case exercises (Parrish & Muller, 2003). (The project can be found at http://meted.ucar .edu/norlat/snow/index.htm.) In this way, the learning objects are designed to support meaningful knowledge construction as learners engage in authentic activities. Because the mechanisms for different types of winter weather overlap, the learning objects created for one case are suitable to support other cases as well. As more cases are developed, some objects may be reused many times. In addition, the learning objects are made available in collections that group related topics to support learners more interested in reviewing the conceptual material than engaging in the longer instructional case studies. The objects are easily accessed individually as well as for use by other trainers or university faculty.

The implementation of learning objects just described represents a modest approach to adoption. On a technical level, the objects described here are primarily created as Flash applets, some with audio narration, which employ a wide variety of design approaches appropriate for the content they treat. In terms of content, these materials do not rely on a strict definition of what comprises a learning object—some contain evaluation and practice, some merely present concepts or procedures. They are not yet cataloged with metadata because they are intended for use only within a small community, and those interested are likely to find them. However, if the creation of a larger library of learning objects becomes a priority, metadata can be added easily. Most significantly, the learning objects we have designed do not sacrifice context because they are intended to be used as is. We assume that instructors incorporating the objects will supply their own appropriate context and use the objects as supplementary resources without bothering to customize them. Finally, no single paradigm is embraced in this implementation. The cases with their supporting topics are carefully designed to address predetermined learning objectives, but the cases also share the subjective knowledge of a community of experts and only loosely comprise a predetermined curriculum.

# Concluding Thoughts

As Emerson (1957) observed, "The machine unmakes the man." In the extreme, learning objects and similar instructional technologies used for capturing and disseminating information and training have the potential to separate learners from the act of creating knowledge. They may also separate instructional designers from the creative enterprise of designing experiences that help learners develop in unique ways. But this doesn't have to be the case if they are used wisely.

As Rodney Brooks continued in the keynote presentation that I described at the start of this chapter, the coming availability of neural interfaces for computer technologies will allow people to directly interact with computers and computer-driven utilities through their thoughts. He reminded participants in the audience that this capability will be coming in the near future—it is not some distant prophecy currently in the realm of science fiction. His group and others like it are already considering the associated problems that neural interfaces pose.

Unlike most technological innovations, which seem, by comparison, to merely be small extensions of existing capabilities, I feel that neural interfaces have the potential to be truly revolutionary. And the thought of neural interfaces is just as frightening as it is exhilarating. What new capabilities might become possible once people are free of such clunky devices as keyboards and computer mice? What new creative applications will evolve for computers—and for that matter, people—once they become intimately joined? What new forms of art and communication might become possible? What improvements to design and engineering processes might result?

My exhilaration, however, is tempered by the thought that cognitive scientists often view human thought processes as something akin to computer processing. Will neural interfaces merely make such theories self-fulfilling when the interfaces are designed according to them? Will what could potentially be an expansion to human capabilities become something quite predictable, or even limiting? What qualities of our human nature could be forgotten and tossed aside for the sake of computer efficiency? I'll be more comfortable with the coming introduction of neural interfaces when I know that, in addition to cognitive scientists, computer scientists, and software engineers, the development team includes artists, philosophers, and stand-up comedians.

# References

Burbules, N.C., & Callister, J.T.A. (2000). *Watch it: The risks and promises of information technologies for education.* Boulder, CO: Westview Press.

Downes, S. (2000). *Learning objects* [Essay]. Retrieved July, 2002, from www.atl.ualberta.ca/downes/naweb/Learning_Objects.htm

Emerson, R.W. (1957). Works and days. In S.E. Whicher (Ed.), *Selections from Ralph Waldo Emerson* (pp. 365–374). Boston, MA: Houghton Mifflin.

Friesen, N. (2003). *Three objections to learning objects* [HTML document]. Retrieved July 21, 2003, from http://phenom.educ .ualberta.ca/~nfriesen/

Hodgins, H.W. (2002). The future of learning objects. In D.A. Wiley (Ed.), *The instructional use of learning objects.* Bloomington, IN: Association for Educational Communications and Technology. Available online at http://reusability.org/read/.

Jonassen, D.H., & Land, S.M. (Eds.). (2000). *Theoretical foundations of learning environments.* Mahwah, NJ: Lawrence Erlbaum Associates.

Kant, I. (2001). The critique of judgment. In R. Kearney & D. Rasmussen (Eds.), *Continental aesthetics: Romanticism to postmodernism* (pp. 5–42). Malden, MA: Blackwell.

Lemke, J.L. (1997). Cognition, context, and learning: A social semiotic perspective. In D. Kirshner & J.A. Whitson (Eds.), *Situated cognition: Social, semiotic, and psychological perspectives* (pp. 37–55). Mahwah, NJ: Lawrence Erlbaum Associates.

Littlejohn, A. (Ed.). (2003). *Reusing online resources: A sustainable approach to e-learning.* London: Kogan Page.

McLuhan, M., & McLuhan, E. (1988). *Laws of media: The new science.* Toronto: University of Toronto Press.

Merrill, M.D. (1999). Instructional transaction theory (ITT): Instructional design based on knowledge objects. In C.M. Reigeluth (Ed.), *Instructional-design theories and models: A new paradigm of instructional theory* (pp. 397–424). Mahwah, NJ: Lawrence Erlbaum Associates.

Merrill, M.D. (2002). Knowledge objects and mental-models. In D.A. Wiley (Ed.), *The instructional use of learning objects.* Bloomington, IN: AECT.

Parrish, P.E. (2004). The trouble with learning objects. *Educational Technology Research & Development, 52*(1), 49–67.

Parrish, P.E., & Muller, B. (2003). *Making a case for object-oriented instructional design: A case-based learning system on winter weather forecasting.* Paper presented at the AECT Annual Convention, Anaheim, California.

Reigeluth, C.M. (1999). What is instructional-design theory and how is it changing. In C.M. Reigeluth (Ed.), *Instructional-design theories and models: A new paradigm of instructional theory* (pp. 5–29). Mahwah, NJ: Lawrence Erlbaum Associates.

Rose, E. (2003). *User error.* Toronto: Between the Lines.

Rose, E. (2004). Is there a class with this content?: WebCT and the limits of individualization. *Journal of Educational Thought, 38*(1), 43–65.

Schatz, S.C. (2005). Unique metadata schemas: A model for user-centric design of a performance support system. *Educational Technology Research & Development, 53*(4), 69–84.

Spector, J.M., Polson, M.C., & Muraida, D.J. (Eds.). (1993). *Automating instructional design: Concepts and issues.* Englewood Cliffs, NJ: Educational Technology Publications.

van Merriënboer, J.J.G., & Boot, E. (2005). A holistic pedagogical view of learning objects: Future directions for reuse. In J.M. Spector, C. Ohrazda, A. Van Schaack, & D.A. Wiley (Eds.), *Innovations in instructional technology* (pp. 43–64). Mahwah, NJ: Lawrence Erlbaum Associates.

Wenger, E.C. (1998). *Communities of practice: Learning, meaning, and identity.* Cambridge, UK: Cambridge University Press.

Wiley, D.A. (2002). Connecting learning objects to instructional design theory: A definition, a metaphor, and a taxonomy. In D.A. Wiley (Ed.), *The instructional use of learning objects.* Bloomington, IN: Agency for Instructional Technology and Association for Educational Communications and Technology. Available online at http://reusability.org/read/.

Wiley, D.A. (2003). The coming collision between automated instruction and social constructivism. In C.M. Gynn & S.R. Acker (Eds.), *Learning objects: Contexts and connections* (pp. 17–28). Columbus, OH: The Ohio State University. Available online at http://morty.uts.ohio-state.edu/learning_objects/documents/TELR-LO7screen.pdf

Wiley, D.A. (2005). Learning objects in public and higher education. In J.M. Spector, C. Ohrazda, A. Van Schaack, & D.A. Wiley

(Eds.), *Innovations in instructional technology* (pp. 1–9). Mahwah, NJ: Lawrence Erlbaum Associates.

Wilson, B.G. (2001). Trends and futures of education: Implications for distance education. *Quarterly Review of Distance Education, 3*(1), 65–77.

Wilson, B.G., Ludwig-Hardman, S., Thornam, C.L., & Dunlap, J.C. (2004). Bounded community: Designing and facilitating learning communities in formal courses. Paper presented at the Annual Meeting of the American Educational Research Association, San Diego, California. Available online at http://carbon.cudenver.edu/~bwilson/BLCs.html.

Wurman, R.S. (1989.) *Information anxiety: What to do when information doesn't tell you what you need to know.* New York: Doubleday.

◆ ◆ ◆

# Summary of Main Points

Readers should take away the following main ideas from this chapter:

- Learning objects are short instructional components that are products of a design strategy and software techniques whose goal is to facilitate their discovery and reuse.

  - There is still much ambiguity about what a learning object is. In the broadest definition, a learning object can be any learning resource. It can be a small piece of a learning program, like an illustration or a description of a concept, a unit of instruction, or an entire course. Although intended to provide flexibility, the broad definitions have created more confusion than clarity.

  - The concept of learning objects is inspired by the software engineering paradigm of object-oriented programming. In object-oriented programming, software developers reuse blocks of code, called objects, in many different contexts and, because code can be used many times, the strategy reduces the time and cost needed to develop programs.

- Designing learning resources so they can be effectively reused involves several new design approaches. These include:

  - Dividing instructional content and activities into discrete, coherent units

  - Embedding or linking to "metadata" that accurately describes the characteristics of those learning resources to increase the likelihood that intended users will discover them

  - Using a relatively context-free design that facilitates adaptation of the resource to fit multiple instructional contexts

- Two competing paradigms characterize the goal of learning objects:

  - Control paradigm, which is based on the belief that automating instructional systems design and delivery will make those processes more efficient and teacher- or designer-proof, as well as make learning outcomes more predictable.

  - Open systems paradigm, which is based on the belief that technology can create an open society of equal opportunity and with free exchange of ideas. Access to the Internet and learning objects provides equal access to learning content.

  Table 7.1 contrasts the key components of the two paradigms.

- A practical approach to implementing learning objects is demonstrated by a series of case-based learning modules that use learning objects as supporting topics, which help learners make good decisions about severe winter weather events (http://meted.ucar.edu/norlat/snow/index.htm)

| Table 7.1. Comparison of the Control and Open Systems Paradigms of Learning Objects | | |
|---|---|---|
| | **Control Paradigm** | **Open Systems Paradigm** |
| General goals for instructional technologies | Efficiency, predictability, control over chaos, preservation of culture | Equal opportunity, free and open exchange, cultural evolution |
| Assumptions about learning | People learn best within well-structured environments | People learn best as participants in open learning communities |
| Attitude toward complexity | Complexity is to be controlled and minimized through application of technology and automation | Complexity is to be embraced as a source of innovation and growth |
| Desired applications for technology | Well-defined classification schemes and standards, automated systems that require little human intervention or decision making | Applications that facilitate communication, sharing of resources, and collaboration |
| Use of standards | To create predictability, allow automation, to set predefined goals for learning | To increase interoperability, to foster resource sharing |

| Table 7.1. Comparison of the Control and Open Systems Paradigms of Learning Objects, (*Continued*) | | |
|---|---|---|
| | **Control Paradigm** | **Open Systems Paradigm** |
| Shared beliefs | Technologies create economies of scale, make more efficient use of limited resources | |
| Challenges to their assumptions | There can be no algorithms for learning. Knowledge is not fixed and transferable; it is individually and socially negotiated. Automated instruction may inhibit creatively problem solving and generate new knowledge. | Access to technology is limited. Borrowing and reintegrating is not easy. Knowledge development is fostered in bounded communities, not highly open ones. Integrated experiences are difficult to create from disparate materials. |

◆ ◆ ◆

# Guiding Questions for Discussion

Some questions from this chapter include:

- What additional objections or support for using learning objects can you think of? (Perhaps these objections and supporting arguments might come from paradigms not discussed here.)

- McLuhan and McLuhan's *Laws of Media* (1988), which I reference several times in this chapter, offers a more complete set of questions for analyzing the effects of new technologies. Answer the questions below regarding learning objects and other instructional technologies, including the Internet. (A few possible answers are provided as examples, using the technology of the car.)

  - What human capabilities are enhanced? That is, which aspects of experience and modes of thinking are emphasized over others? (For example, cars enhance the ability to travel and transport things, emphasizing mobility over stability.)

  - Which capabilities, aspects of experience, or modes of thinking are not valued or pushed aside? (For example, if they drive everywhere, people seem to have less appreciation and knowledge of their immediate environs and get less exercise.)

  - What older mode of activity is being recalled or retrieved from obsolescence? (Considering cars again, they provide access to natural environments when urban areas grow too large to quickly escape otherwise. Individual transportation allows people to lead more private lives, as is possible in non-urban environments.)

  - If pushed to its extreme, how might the new technology reverse its benefits? (Too much use of cars creates traffic jams, which reduces the efficiency of travel. Also, people become physically slower through lack of exercise.)

- Imagine you are writing a standup comedy routine about education and training from the viewpoints of an instructional designer and a learner. Come up with a few jokes offering observations about learning and teaching with learning objects. Also come up with a few jokes with observations about potential experiences using neural computer interfaces.

| **Learn More About It** | |
|---|---|
| Links | www.reusability.org, the site where David Wiley originally published his book on reusable learning objects and where he publishes updates and additional commentary |
| Books, Papers, Reports, and Articles | Books with substantial treatment of learning objects and related topics <br><br> • Gynn, C.M., & Acker, S.R. (Eds.). (2003). *Learning objects: Context and connections.* Columbus, OH: The Ohio State University. Available online at http://morty.uts.ohio-state.edu/learning_objects/documents/TELR-LO7screen.pdf <br><br> • Littlejohn, A. (Ed.). (2003). *Reusing online resources: A sustainable approach to e-learning.* London: Kogan Page. <br><br> • Spector, J.M., Ohrazda, C., Van Schaack, A., & Wiley, D.A. (Eds.). (2005). *Innovations in instructional technology.* Mahwah, NJ: Lawrence Erlbaum Associates. <br><br> Books offering a critical analysis of technological innovations <br><br> • Burbules, N.C., & Callister, J.T.A. (2000). *Watch it: The risks and promises of information technologies for education.* Boulder, CO: Westview Press. <br><br> • McLuhan, M., & McLuhan, E. (1988). *Laws of media: The new science.* Toronto: University of Toronto Press. <br><br> • Rose, E. (2003). *User error.* Toronto: Between the Lines. |

# Chapter 8

# Web 2.0 and Beyond: The Changing Needs of Learners, New Tools, and Ways to Learn

*Patti Shank,*
*Learning Peaks, Inc.,*

## About This Chapter

The Internet has changed lives in ways that could not have been imagined only ten or fifteen years before the writing of this book. The Internet itself is undergoing subtle but important changes that are changing how we gain and use information and, most relevant to this book, learn.

The increasing adoption and ubiquity of the Internet and the growth of user-contributed content through easy-to-use tools is being called "Web 2.0" by Internet analysts and has important implications for learning. This chapter answers the questions, "What is Web 2.0 and what does it mean for learning?" In it, I first explore the changes in the nature of work, then consider how learners themselves are changing (especially those who have grown up with the Internet). Next, this chapter presents an inventory of social application tools that characterize Web 2.0, such as blogs, wikis, "google jockeying," and "mashups." Then I explore how Web 2.0 is creating new ways to learn and close by considering these changes within the broader context of e-learning.

# Introduction

Consider the following "wired" situations. Katya, a travel consultant, is instant messaging (IM) a friend to make dinner plans while reviewing a travel blog (www.gadling.com) for information to help a client. Kami, the sales manager for an electronics store, is using a social bookmarking site to find resources on high-definition television (HDTV) (http://del.icio.us/search/?all=HDTV) and finds a link to news about an upcoming product launch that may affect her store. Khalid, an information systems intern from the nearby university, is helping the company review the usefulness of new technologies for its website. He finds good AJAX (a programming technique that loads updated data onto open web pages without the user needing to refresh—such as when *The New York Times* home page is automatically updated with the latest news every fifteen minutes) resources from web developers around the globe on a number of online programming forums. He regularly reads the Professional PHP Developers blog (www.phpdeveloper.org/) to keep on top of new developments and insights and participates in discussion forums about new approaches for building interactive web applications.

This is not a view into the future; it is a description of everyday life in 2007, when this chapter was written. More to the point, the Internet has changed how we live and work, and has done so in ways we couldn't have imagined even ten or fifteen years ago. And the Internet itself is undergoing subtle but important changes in the ways that people receive and use information.

The Internet is not only increasingly ubiquitous, it is also increasingly vital to functioning in everyday life. For example, when you have an appointment and need directions, how do you get them? Ten years ago, I asked for directions. Now I go to Google Maps. How do you research new cars? Ten years ago I read *Consumer Reports* and hoped the cars I was interested in were reviewed recently enough to be useful. Now I use *Consumer Reports'* car-buying web application to search for cars that match my specifications. You can probably think of many things you do differently because of the Internet. And while you and I remember how we did things before the Internet, many of our children grew up with computers and Internet access.

Research by the Pew Internet and American Life Project (May 2006 and April 2006) highlights how connected Americans have become. More than 70 percent of respondents (more than 140 million adults) are Internet users. Forty-two percent have broadband Internet connections in their homes, up 40 percent from a year earlier. Although much of the growth in home broadband connections has come from middle income households, and adults with lower incomes are less likely than adults with higher incomes to be online and have home access, still more than half of the adults living in households with an annual income of less than $30,000 are online. Internet usage in the United States is high, but U.S. usage is exceeded in other countries, such as Canada, Finland, and South Korea.

The Pew survey also provides insights into the ways that people use the Internet. Respondents report that the Internet helps them to do their jobs and gain information about hobbies, purchases, and health care. Almost fifty million say they have personally posted content online. When the Pew Internet and American Life Project first asked about posting online content in 2002, only a handful of early adopters responded affirmatively. In early 2006, more than half of the home broadband users under the age of thirty said they had posted online content, as have more than one-third of home broadband users over thirty.

The increasing adoption and ubiquity of the Internet and the growth of user-contributed content have important implications for learning. Tools for delivering content have become far easier to use. Just a few years back, understanding HTML and FTP and using complex authoring tools to post online content was necessary. Technical knowledge is far less an impediment to posting content today. For example, Blogger.com (www.blogger.com) lets users post content by filling in forms. del.icio.us (del.icio.us/) provides tools to easily share bookmarks with others. And Flickr (www .flickr.com/) provides easy tools for uploading and sharing pictures. Not only is sharing content using these three tools easy, many of these kinds of tools are free, removing another barrier to use. People are increasingly sharing information, getting help, finding people with similar interests, and learning from each other. This shift from a one-way to a two-way medium is much closer to Tim Berners-Lee's (widely considered to be the founder of the Web) original notions of how the Web should work.

Web technologies are changing old patterns of learning and enabling new ones in three key ways. First, when people want to learn about a topic, they increasingly look online for information, articles, webcasts, book reviews, and courses. In addition to formal approaches to learning, such as courses and tutorials, informal approaches are also growing, the second way in which patterns of learning are changing. With so many information sources available online, many people search for information that makes sense in terms of their own needs. People are increasingly looking online to find experts to consult, using online social applications like LinkedIn. People reach these contacts through email and instant messaging, or check their online diaries, called blogs (short for weblogs). The third way in which patterns of learning are changing is that, thanks to easier-to-use tools for sharing content online, people are not only assuming the role of learner, they're increasingly assuming the role of instructor as well.

The web applications that facilitate these new, easier uses of the Internet are part of a movement that some call Web 2.0. Rather than a formal set of standards, Web 2.0 represents a re-envisioning of the World Wide Web as a two-way medium. Wikipedia, the Web 2.0-enabled collaborative online encyclopedia, provides a good description of this shift:

> Web 2.0, a phrase coined by O'Reilly Media in 2003, and popularized by the first Web 2.0 conference in

2004, refers to a perceived second generation of web-based communities and hosted services—such as social-networking sites, wikis and folksonomies—which facilitate collaboration and sharing between users. This phrase has since become widely adopted.

This chapter explores what is commonly referred to as Web 2.0, or the growth of the read-write web and online social applications, and its impact on learning. Specifically, it first explores how work has changed and what is needed to support these changes. It then considers how younger learners (especially those who have grown up with the Internet) use the Internet and learn. This chapter then presents an inventory of the software tools that characterize Web 2.0, such as blogs, wikis, "google jockeying," and "mashups." Next this chapter explores how these online applications facilitate new ways to learn and closes by considering these changes within the broader context of e-learning.

# The Changing Nature of Learning

Along with the expanding role of the Internet, the nature of work, information, and learning have also changed dramatically in the past thirty years. Sociologists, management experts, learning theorists, and others have commented extensively on the transition from industrial-era to information-age work during this period. Industrial era jobs were primarily focused on manufacturing products, and the typical job was routinized, with predictable tasks and outcomes. To prepare people to work in such environments, education and training practices were developed and pervaded the lifelong education system, from kindergartens to corporate training rooms.

Information age jobs are primarily focused on delivering services to people, developing intellectual property of value to others, and helping people make more effective use of the information available to them. Although some aspects of those jobs are predictable and can be routinized, the defining characteristic of information age jobs is their problem-solving nature. Problem solving involves unpredictable and non-routine tasks and the ability to prioritize competing demands, using multiple, often conflicting information sources and keeping up with changing needs, all to solve complex problems with constantly changing information. The information demands on the job are mirrored in daily life. For example, as consumer products move from being mass-manufactured to mass-customized (in which organizations tailor their products and services to meet the needs of a well-defined market niche, rather than whomever chooses to buy them (mass-market)) and as people must take increasing responsibility for managing complex issues such as retirement investments, managing their credit ratings in an era of increasing fraud, and securing second opinions on medical diagnoses, they increasingly rely on the Internet for up-to-date information and access to expertise and support.

This section explores these changes and their impact on learning. Although some of these issues are addressed elsewhere in this book, I review some of the key issues to provide a context in which to consider how Web 2.0 technologies respond to these changes. This section starts by explaining how learning needs to change from being event-driven, utilized if and when offered, to on-demand, utilized as needed. Next, it explores how learning has moved from rote repetition of facts to the collaborative construction of knowledge. Then this section explores how content has expanded from a finite body of facts to an endless array of interconnected and constantly changing knowledge. This section concludes by exploring how the publication of content has transformed from authoritative and verified material to content on which users must conduct their own due diligence.

## From Take-It-When-It's-Offered to On-Demand Service

As a result of a more flexible approach to work and a growing body of available information, traditional, scheduled courses fail to meet a number of learning needs. Most take-it-when-offered course-based learning is inherently subject to time limitations. Content "covered" is limited to what can be covered in the allotted time. And, in most cases, time constraints make it difficult or impossible for learners to customize what is learned to their own situation, reducing the likelihood of transfer to the real world.

Traditional courses are scheduled to be taught at particular times and places, and learners who might have a need for the content at a time other than a scheduled class time face serious problems. For example, a new worker might need a training course before he or she can begin certain types of work, but because the course is not scheduled for weeks after the person starts work, he or she either works without critical information or is forced to be less productive until the course is completed. This is wasteful (in terms of time and money) and is also potentially risky.

Waiting for needed training is inconsistent with environments that increasingly offer instant access to people through email and telephones and twenty-four-hour access to services like shopping, restaurants, and information. Workers and organizations are increasingly expecting needed training and performance support to be available as needed, too. And why not?

In addition to demanding learning programs when needed, learners are increasingly seeking the flexibility to tailor learning content and environments to suit their needs. This may involve building custom "courses" or "tracks" from among a selection of granular lessons that best meet the need of the performer and the job. One of my clients is using this approach in order to meet the needs of various jobs and levels, and another client is training groups in the organization to customize content rather than putting out generic courses that may not be valuable. This customization is happening in higher education, too. Some undergraduate and graduate students are creating an entire major by restructuring courses from other programs for their own needs. As other products and services become mass-customized to meet the needs of unique people and groups, there is an increasing demand that instruction be mass-customized to meet individual and group needs as well.

## From Rote Repetition to Collaborative Construction of Knowledge

In response to changing work and social realities, governments have launched efforts to reform school systems in Canada, China, the United States, and other places. And some workplace training organizations are redefining their roles from developers of take-it-when-it's-offered courses to promoters of support and training (and other interventions) that meet the changing realities of the workplace.

Typical lock-step take-it-when-it's-offered courses are often too simplistic and don't match the complexities of the real world. This kind of instruction, whether academic or corporate training, is too often an event to be endured so a checkmark can be entered next to each learner's name, a waste of resources that could be better utilized to meet the learning needs of individuals and organizations.

Many widely followed instructional design practices assume that the purpose of instruction is to automate behavior, primarily through memorization, drill, and practice. Because many jobs no longer consist of mainly routinized tasks, this makes no sense.

Recently, more expansive views about instruction and desired outcomes have begun to take hold. Designers are increasingly interested in interactive activities that allow learners to discover principles and apply them in particular contexts ways (rather than telling learners what to think). Some designers are providing opportunities for learners to interact with one another and subject-matter experts to better understand the complexities involved in real-world work and to be conscious of multiple perspectives. As a result, the one-way communication typical of early self-paced online instruction is moving slowly toward more interactive and more meaningful learning activities.

Because job performance relies heavily on current and relevant streams of information, and with information increasing in amount and complexity, people are forming information networks (both social and technical) to access generalized knowledge within a domain and find people and resources within those networks for access to specialized knowledge. Groups of people with shared interests are forming ad hoc and more formal networks that meet mainly in cyberspace, using discussion forums, mailing lists, and a host of other network-enabled communication technologies. These networks allow people in complex fields to learn from one another, share resources, and competently deal with a body of knowledge that is always expanding and is, in any case, larger than the capabilities of any one person in the network, no matter how expert they are.

This need for a network of expertise is certainly true in my field. Certain email lists help me stay abreast of the diverse skills needed to handle complex learning and performance problems. These networks help me keep up-to-date with my own field and other fields that impact mine, such as graphic design, usability, information architecture, accessibility, and so on. By skimming postings, saving those that interest me, searching archives for discussions on a specific topic, and posting questions to the group, I am able to handle more of the complex interdisciplinary issues that arise in my work. I can send private emails to people on the list who are more expert in areas I am less expert in and answer emails from others who need to borrow some of my expertise.

In the domains of informal and lifelong learning, these networks help people address the knowledge needed to remain current in a chosen field and the knowledge contained in tangential fields. Stephen Downes (2005) a prolific blogger and presenter on instructional technology issues, asserts that knowledge networks need to be:

- Decentralized so that flow increases and risk of network failure is reduced

- Distributed so that knowledge is created and enhanced by all and divergent views are maintained

- Disintermediated (that is, no moderator) to facilitate direct access to people and content

- Dynamic to afford new information, people, and ways of operating

- Desegregated so that learning and work are mixed, allowing learning as the need arises

People who are adept at using technology to get up-to-date information are bypassing traditional courses to build their own learning infrastructure because this mode seems to provide faster and better information. Consider an example from my own work life. I recently needed specific information while I was at a client's workplace and used my web-enabled cell phone and Verizon's EVDO broadband WWAN network to find the information I needed on the spot. I then used my cell phone to ask someone else's opinion. While speaking to me, she sent an instant message to a co-worker in another country and received an authoritative answer, and her co-worker text messaged me with some URLs to guide further learning. And when I attended a learning sciences conference recently, I answered emails from clients and vendors using the conference center's wireless access while taking notes in each presentation. I sent parts of my notes to a co-worker while the presentation was in progress.

This way of working is becoming increasingly commonplace. I don't have to know it all as long as I can call on my network and the vast amounts of information available at my fingertips. Because of this, ubiquitous Internet access is becoming an expectation. Rather than wait for a course or depend on predigested information, I find information, evaluate its veracity, ask questions, make sense of it, and use it.

## From a Finite Body of Facts to an Endless Pit of Content

The amount of information people have to deal with and the complexity of job demands are growing all the time. For instance, consider the growing complexity of one job: instructional designer. In the 1980s, the primary job of an instructional designer was to design and develop courses. Nearly all of those courses were intended for face-to-face delivery, although a few might have been intended for other media, such as print, slide shows, and perhaps audiotape or videotape. Now instructional designers are expected to positively impact individual and organizational performance and build not only courses, but also non-instructional interventions like job aids (also known as performance support tools). They're also involved in redesigning workplace processes. Instructional designers are expected to positively impact projects linked to strategic initiatives and be expert on selecting and using a wide range of media and learning infrastructure. They're often expected to make a business case for their recommended solutions and demonstrate the return on investment of the resulting product. Experts are increasingly advising instructional designers to make evidence-based decisions—that is, evidence rooted in recent research, which require instructional designers to make more of an effort to read and interpret academic literature, especially research journals. In addition to these expanded job expectations, employers also expect instructional designers to develop expertise in the subject areas in which they design materials, such as finance, security, health care, pharmaceuticals, or manufacturing.

Take a look at the International Board of Standards for Training, Performance, and Instruction's (2000) list of competencies for instructional designers and you'll see a list of skills that encompass many domains. This expansion of the job scope of the instructional designer is occurring at a time when spending on training has declined or remained flat (as reported in *Training* magazine's annual industry surveys from 2001 through 2005).

Increasing job scope and complexity is not limited to instructional designers, of course. The expanded scope of many jobs requires workers to be familiar with an expanded domain that is constantly changing. For example, my accountant says that changes in tax law each year make continual learning part of the job.

Although work scope is increasing for many jobs, less time is available to learn and master new information. In other words, workers cannot possibly make sense of all of the incoming information in their own domains, much less in tangential domains. Furthermore, with job responsibilities in an ongoing state of change even within a given domain, workers must constantly renew their knowledge and skills to remain employed and employable.

Although no one can accurately predict what people will need to learn to keep current in their fields or gain competence in another field in ten or twenty years, it's critical that workers develop general strategies for maintaining their knowledge and skills as a field changes. This includes taking advantage of formal resources, such as courses, journals, and websites, as well as informal resources like networking. Workers also need strategies for assessing the completeness and accuracy of content they use, including unfamiliar websites and the people in their technology-enabled networks. Most significantly, workers must learn how to discern among important, relevant, and actionable information (that is, information they should do something about) and information that can be ignored. With some studies anecdotally reporting that as much as 40 percent of a professional's time is spent looking for relevant information, these researching skills are vital.

## From Authoritative, Verified Content to "Buyer Beware"

Much of the debate regarding the quality of online instructional content focuses on which *type* of instruction is best: classroom or online, synchronous or asynchronous e-learning. This argument is ridiculous. Study after study has shown them to be equally effective (for example, see Bernard, Abrami, Lou, Borokhovski, Wade, Wozney, Wallet, Fiset, & Huang, 2004; Sitzmann & Wisher, 2005), assuming that they're well-designed in the first place (a significant assumption, to be sure). The more significant issue is whether these resources offer credible information on which users can reliably base decisions.

When work is complex and information is constantly changing, it's almost never enough to know just what you know, even if you know a lot. There's simply too much to know. When working in complex, dynamic domains, even experts feel a need to consult the expertise of others to make sound decisions. In addition to the philosophical reasons provided earlier, this practical need to seek the best knowledge drives the increasingly collaborative nature of learning.

As textbooks are increasingly regarded as out-of-date the moment they are published (and besides, getting them often requires a visit to a book store or library), people turn, instead, to information in websites, blogs, online journals, and the like. One study comparing the quality of the content in the time-honored *Encyclopedia Brittanica* with that in the community-prepared Wikipedia found that the Wikipedia was about as reliable as the traditional source. But Wikipedia also has a strong process for generating, reviewing, and verifying the accuracy of the content, as well as protecting it from sabotage. Most other sources do not.

In fact, the Internet is full of questionable information. Some is obvious, such as the spam messages that try to lure unsuspecting users to counterfeit websites to divulge sensitive financial information. But much of it is not obvious, such as a practicing professional's self-published blog filled with context-sensitive assertions that are not generalizable to other contexts. If someone uses this professional's assertions as the basis of learning materials, then hundreds or thousands of learners may learn incorrect information.

Because the volume of domain and general information has grown beyond the ability of any person to master and it keeps growing faster than anyone can keep up with, learners should focus on developing the skills needed to find resources (including people) and discerning the credibility and applicability of information learned to current problems.

# The Changing Nature of Learners

As the nature of learning has changed, so has the nature of learners themselves. Consider this. The Pew Internet and American Life Project (2002) observed that current college students were born around the time PCs were introduced and, by the time these students were in high school, computers were in wide use. Almost all of these students regularly use computers and more than 80 percent have easy access to the Internet (probably more since the study was conducted). They use the Internet and other networked technologies (like cell phones and Blackberries) to connect to people and information for all aspects of their lives. They cannot imagine any other way of being.

These findings have two practical implications about the nature of learners in the digital age. First, many propose that substantial and identifiable differences exist between those who were raised with digital technologies (net-gens) and those who were not. The other issue has to do with comfort with learning informally.

## Differences in Learning Between Net-Gens and Other Generations

A Kaiser Family Foundation study (2003) found that at ever earlier ages, children are developing digital literacy. Although access to computers and the Internet is not equal across all populations, many without home access comment that they use computers and the Internet in schools and libraries and, even without home access, consider the Internet to be critical to their lives.

Using social networking websites like MySpace and FaceBook, video sharing websites like YouTube, instant messaging tools like AOL Instant Messenger and Yahoo Messenger, young people use the Internet as a one-stop shop for information, sharing, communicating, networking, fun, and so on. They gather and attend to input from multiple sources, and are often comfortable shifting their attention rapidly and piecing together the seemingly disparate pieces of content from all of these different sources. In the process of attending to all of these multiple sources of input, these young people finish homework assignments, share tips and advice, and participate in activities that can ultimately be defined as learning. As a result of these experiences, some hypothesize that people raised using computers and the Internet think in a less linear manner (Brown, 2002), have better visual-spatial skills, learn better through discovery methods, and are more visually literate (Oblinger & Oblinger, 2005).

It's not just that these "net-gens" and "digital natives" are comfortable dealing with, and learning from, multiple sources of information. They feel empowered to connect to anyone, learn about anything, at any time, and favor direct relationships and connections, not predigested information. As might be expected, these learners thrive on connected and dynamic learning environments far different from the static learning environments that their teachers encountered and now provide. They increasingly expect much more open and collaborative learning environments.

John Seely Brown (2002) calls the World Wide Web "a transformative medium, as important as electricity." While most media "push their content at us," he explains, the web allows users to be receivers and senders of content. Brown explains how younger people are able to do numerous things concurrently, like listening to music while sending instant messages to friends and doing their homework. Although older folks (perhaps you, and definitely me) think that this type of multiprocessing lacks focus and can't possibly facilitate understanding, he found that the attention spans of the teens he studied were similar to executives, who are capable of switching focus very quickly. So we could assume that the multiprocessing skills these young people are perfecting will benefit them in the workplace, especially a workplace where they face constant interruptions and conflicting priorities.

## Comfort with Informal Learning

As a result of all of this multi-tasking, many researchers and theorists have observed that much learning occurs online, even if it seems to be off-task from a well-identified learning activity, such as homework. Such incidental learning is called "informal" learning. Informal learning can be defined as the lifelong process by which individuals acquire and learn to apply knowledge and skills from ongoing life experiences and activities—at home, work, and play, and from friends, family members, co-workers, books, articles, television, radio, films, travel, conversations, and all the people and things an individual comes into contact with. These tend to be non-course-based activities, including (but certainly not limited to) discussions, help, presentations, information sharing, recommendations, and resources provided in response to expressed interests and needs by people who share a common interest or domain (McGiveney, 1999).

Informal learning often takes advantage of the social and technical networks described earlier. Consider these experiences.

My college-aged son regularly sends me links to Wikipedia articles (www.wikipedia.org/). He finds this editable, online encyclopedia a good jumping off place for his inquiries. Recently, while we were watching *60 Minutes*, a current-events television show, he logged onto his laptop using a wireless connection and reviewed a Wikipedia article on the program's current topic. During the commercial break, he showed it to his dad and me to support his claim that the topic was being presented in a biased manner.

Consider too these examples. A programmer friend regularly posts and answers questions at Slashdot (slashdot.org), a place for computer-oriented folks to exchange information and support. My daughter found a great deal of help planning her wedding with resources and discussion forums on The Knot (www.theknot.com).

Informal learning is gaining interest and respect among educators because it's increasingly accepted that this is how people learn *most* of what they know and can do. This is especially true in workplace learning; some research suggests that people learn as much as 70 percent or more of their job skills informally (Driscoll & Carliner, 2005). Practicality dictates that training departments simply cannot scale up to handle the need for this quantity of training.

In practical terms, that means that the most likely way for Khalid, the intern we met at the beginning of this chapter, to learn about the latest AJAX programming developments is informally. In this case, he could go online to del.icio.us and evaluate resources that are tagged "AJAX." He might notice that Bob recommends great web programming resources and adds Bob to his network so he can easily find the new resources Bob posts. Then Khalid might also talk with Frank, the programmer in the next cubicle. Frank could IM one of his crackerjack programmer buddies to see if it would be okay for Khalid to IM him with questions.

Good learning opportunities? You betcha. Would it be better for Khalid to wait until he's back in school next semester to ask his programming professor? Or find a class given in a distant city in two months? Those options may help him develop the skills formally, but not now—and, in the meantime, he would be less productive. An informal, self-directed learning approach helps learners take responsibility for their job skills and develop skills when and where they're needed.

Informal learning that takes advantage of networks and the Internet uses technologies such as email, instant messaging, voice over Internet protocol (VoIP) telephony, and social applications. Learning stops being an event; it is embedded in daily work and life activities.

Although informal learning makes sense from both a practical and a technological perspective, its acceptance is by no means universal. Many people, especially baby boomers and older generations, are used to being told when, how, and what to learn. They are comfortable with receiving predigested information provided by a person in authority (such as a teacher, instructor, trainer, or boss). Often, these people are both uncomfortable and unlikely to learn on their own. Indeed, they believe that updating their knowledge and skills is someone else's responsibility. These workers may refuse to search out or pay for their own training opportunities, even if the training could lead to better job opportunities. In the workplace, the concept of taking ownership for one's own learning and employability—that is, identifying skill needs and ensuring that they're addressed, regardless of who pays or how those skills are acquired—began during the economic restructuring of the early 1990s. It was called, at the time, the "new employment contract." What it meant was that learners had to be responsible for their own skills and employability. This did not sit well with people who expected to stay in one job or at least one company forever.

Letting learners be responsible for when, what, and how to learn has upsides for organizations, but can also be daunting. Despite the fact that K-12 teachers, university instructors, and management in corporations all support, in theory, learners taking responsibility for their own learning, the reality is that people in positions of authority like to maintain control over how people are informed and who knows what. When people can obtain information on their own, the balance of power shifts.

Even in instances in which informal learning is accepted, one key challenge is helping learners integrate what they've learned. Although they may learn on their own, many learners still need guidance in the learning process and in determining what to do with that learning. They may need help finding learning resources and, once found, assessing their credibility. They may need help transferring the knowledge to their own circumstances. They may need opportunities to practice using new skills and extended support to make sure that the skills transfer to the real world. This changes the nature of teaching from that of imparting knowledge to supporting and coaching learners.

# An Inventory of Web 2.0 Tools for Learning

In response to the changing nature of learning and learners, new technologies have evolved. In this section, I provide an inventory of several of the most promising and individually describe them. These technologies include blogs, wikis, social bookmarking, collaborative writing, voice-over Internet protocol (VoIP), podcasting, instant messaging (IM), google jockeying, and mashups (make your own web portal). But first, I describe some general principles on which these technologies are based.

## General Principles on Which Web 2.0 Technologies Are Based

Tim O'Reilly (2005) described the burst of the dot-com bubble in the early 2000s as expected because shakeouts are a common characteristic of large-scale technology revolutions. In fact, he says, shakeouts are an indication that the technology is beginning to reach the point at which wide adoption is occurring. Certainly that was the case in the growth of the web. Between 1993 (when the first browsers appeared) and early 2000, the web went from something that only a few computer geeks knew about to something that was becoming central to work and personal lives.

In terms of technology, O'Reilly coined the term "Web 2.0" to describe trends in successful web implementations. Three trends appear to describe what is happening with the web—the read/write web, the web as a platform, and microcontent.

The read/write web implies that the new web is increasingly a two-way medium, where people can be both users of existing content as well as providers of content. What makes this possible are tools that let people create content extremely easily, tools like blogs and wikis.

The web-as-platform trend explains how software applications are seamlessly knitted into websites, such as embedding MapQuest or Google maps in the middle of travel-related applications (so people can see exactly where they're supposed to go). Such applications are increasing. The primary catalyst for these applications are Internet-based application programming interfaces, or APIs, which allow communication between applications.

Microcontent, the third trend of Web 2.0, breaks away from the notion of web as "pages" and "sites" to focus on smaller web elements that can be aggregated or disaggregated and recombined. Examples of microcontent include blog entries, wiki revisions, podcasts, API elements (like maps), and AJAX-enabled pages that load changing content (called dynamic content), such as yesterday's sales, pulled into the page from a database, without the need to reload the page. Microcontent elements are combined using syndication technologies like RSS to form new content.

In the next nine sections, I'll describe some of the tools that are emerging and provide examples of each in use. Later, in the resources section, I identify ways to learn about and try out these tools for yourself.

## Blogs

A *blog* (shorthand for weblog) is typically a series of chronologically arranged (most recent at the top) online journal entries that is frequently updated by its author, often called a *blogger*. A blog can be created and updated using easy-to-use applications that allow the blogger to post new articles without any programming knowledge. Many blogs also allow readers to easily post comments.

Blogs are an increasingly popular means of sharing personal opinions and commentary on any number of topics. Bloggers on the same topic commonly cross-quote each other. In fact, bloggers on a specific topic often read each other's blogs, reference and link to them in their own blogs, and post comments on each other's blogs. "Trackback" and "ping" capabilities allow a blogger to know when other bloggers have referenced or written about one of his or her posts.

Blogging has become one of the fastest-growing trends on the web because blogging is an incredibly easy and inexpensive way to post content. (Indeed, some of the tools are free to use.) Examples of blogs include the Educause blogs (http://connect.educause .edu/blog) and the thesocialsoftwareweblog (http://socialsoftware .weblogsinc.com/).

## Wikis

Like blogs, *wikis* are easy-to-use web publishing tools. The term is adapted from the Hawaiian word for fast. Wikis are web applications that allow a group of users to collaboratively add and edit web content without any programming knowledge. The best-known example of a wiki is Wikipedia (http://en.wikipedia.org/wiki/ Main_Page, for the English version), which I've already mentioned several times in this chapter.

Because anyone who is given permission to change content can edit a wiki's content, most wikis contain edit tracking and page history so that changes can be traced and reversed, if needed. Wikipedia was built using MediaWiki (www.mediawiki.org/wiki/MediaWiki), an open source wiki application. There are numerous free and paid wiki applications, including Socialtext (www.socialtext.com/), which is widely used for enterprise wikis. Wikis are especially useful for collaboratively edited knowledge bases.

An example of a wiki used specifically for learning is the Romantic Audience project (http://ssad.bowdoin.edu:8668/space/snipsnap-index), a collaborative learning project by students enrolled in Bowdin College's English 242 course.

## Social Bookmarking

Social bookmarking applications allow users to easily save and categorize collections of their bookmarks of web pages using keywords called *tags* and to share the bookmarks with others. Users can effortlessly save others' bookmarks into their own collections and subscribe to bookmark lists of others or specific tags so they can see what their favorite bookmark posters have added or when new links for a given tag are added. An example of a social bookmarking application is del.icio.us (http://del.icio.us).

For example, enter "AJAX" into the del.icio.us search form and you'll see a list of popular resources on the topic. You can similarly search for resources on almost any topic and can see how valuable others have found each resource by reviewing the number of users who saved any given resource to their own bookmark collections.

Reviewing others' bookmarks is useful because it can make finding useful resources faster and easier. In theory, a Google search would also yield a list of pages, but a user would have to sift though dozens of sites, many of which would be marginal. Checking the bookmarks of others can shortcut the search process dramatically. This approach also helps users keep the list up-to-date with minimal effort because users can subscribe to any tag (the keywords people use to describe their bookmarks) to obtain information about new resources that have been posted on the topic.

Social bookmarking has important implications for learning. Providing a central place to store links can help groups of learners (such as classes, teams, and researchers) who might otherwise lose these links across email messages, course management systems, and documents. A social bookmarking site on a specific topic may create the means for finding others with similar interests who can provide additional resources, perspectives, and opportunities for collaboration. The practice of tagging can help learners reflect on the resource and the domain being studied and see new perspectives as they view others' tags for the same or similar items.

An example of social bookmarking used for learning is the del.icio.us site set up for the Social Software Affordances course at the Teachers College, Columbia University (http://del.icio.us/tag/ccte/). This course is about social applications and uses social applications like the previously mentioned social bookmarking site, a blog (http://ssa05.blogspot.com/), and a wiki (www.annenberg.edu/ssaw/pmwiki/socialsoftware).

## Collaborative Writing

Tools for collaborative writing let users easily create documents and collaboratively add to and edit them. These services are similar to wikis but they provide a familiar editing interface that is more like word processing than wiki editing (which feels geeky to some). Examples include Writeboard (http://writeboard.com), Writely (www.writely.com), and JotSpotLive (www.jotlive.com).

Web-based collaborative writing tools are useful for a variety of learning applications, including collaborative learning projects and team documentation. Team-based projects, in which students collaboratively create a project such as a report or a creative project, are a staple of learning. One challenge that most teams experience—especially in higher education or in workplace learning situations—is getting the team together. Busy schedules make meeting and sharing work difficult. Collaborative writing tools provide a technology tool to bridge that barrier.

Other uses for collaborative writing tools exist, too. For example, one conference hired Dean Shareski, a curriculum consultant with the Prairie South School Division in Moose Jaw, Saskatchewan, Canada, to facilitate collaborative note-taking so participants could keep up with the conversations happening in the sessions they could not attend.

## Voice Over Internet Protocol (VoIP)

Voice over Internet protocol (VoIP) refers to a group of technologies that facilitate transmission of voice conversations over a data network, usually the Internet. An advantage of these telephone calls is that they generally do not incur a charge beyond what the user is paying for Internet access and the VoIP service. Examples of services offering telephone calls over the net are Skype (www.skype.com) and Vonage (www.vonage.com). In fact, numerous friends tell me they have switched their primary home telephone system to VoIP telephone providers. The major advantage these friends cite is the low cost. A disadvantage is that if the power or your broadband Internet connection is down, access is gone. Because many people also have cell phones, this may not be too much of a problem.

The line between VoIP and instant messaging (another Web 2.0 technology that I'll describe soon) appears to be blurring as well. Skype also facilitates text chats and sharing files and can be used by people running systems under the Linux, Windows, and Mac operating systems. A work group in which I participate has members located in cities around the world and has started using Skype for team conference calls.

An example of Skype in higher education is the Mixxer language exchange project (www.language-exchanges.org). This project helps language learners locate language partners who are studying each other's native languages. Language partners use VoIP to help each other practice and learn a foreign language.

But VoIP has many applications other than telephony. One especially useful application of VoIP in learning is in virtual classroom software, such as Adobe Connect, WebEx, GoToMeeting®, and Elluminate. They allow speakers to present to participants who are logged. When presenting, speakers use slides, polls, and chats, in addition to voice. Although weak at first, the quality of these connections is dramatically improving. The online synchronous presentations I have given in the last year have all used VoIP, with good results.

## Podcasting

Podcasting is a methodology for publishing multimedia files. Podcasting was initially associated with audio files, but video files are also being distributed this way. It offers audio and video content on niche topics and distributes it to people who are interested in that content. Users either download the files individually or subscribe to an ongoing podcast (one that is regularly updated) and automatically receive updates.

At their most basic, audio podcasts are an updated version of audiotape recordings, which were a popular form of training in the 1980s and 1990s. However, more sophisticated uses of podcasts are emerging. Some are combined with blogs and are used to provide course content to learners. Others use podcasting to integrate audio and video into class assignments or course assessments. One example is the student podcasting project at Morse Elementary School in Tarrytown, New York (http://blog.tufsdbuilds.org). Additional learning-focused podcasts can be found on the Education Podcast Network (http://epnweb.org).

## Instant Messaging

Instant messaging (IM) is a tool for real-time, synchronous communication and collaboration between two or more people who are logged onto a network or the Internet. This is different from email, which affords asynchronous communication and generally involves a delay between sending of a message at one end and receiving it at the other. Instant messaging requires an IM client program on each person's computer that facilitates two-way communication. The communication can occur using text messages (usually short ones) and voice and video messages. Most IM applications indicate whether the people on the user's contact list are currently online. Although there are dozens of IM applications, some of the most common IM applications include AOL Instant Messenger, Yahoo Messenger, Google Talk, and ICQ. These IM applications are free.

Because one of its best-known uses is teens talking to other teens in the late afternoon and evening, many dismiss instant messaging as the domain of young people. Pew (2004) surveys indicate that more than fifty-three million Americans who are online use an IM program. For example, instant messaging is actually widely used in corporate environments to ask questions and get assistance internally (Hook, 2006) and as an alternative to telephone-based help lines externally. One of my clients has an expert available on an internal IM system to answer questions phoned in on the company's customer service lines. And just the day I wrote this chapter, I used a web IM application to ask a product specialist some questions about a product I am thinking of purchasing.

Admittedly, in many organizations, adoption of IM occurs without the blessing of management and company IT departments, who understandably are fearful of the potential for network security problems. Some organizations have banned IM usage, but enterprising employees are finding ways around these dictums. Hook (2006) says that, rather than banning IM and forcing employees to go underground with tools they find useful, companies should adopt secure enterprise instant messaging applications.

## Google Jockeying

Google jockeying occurs when a participant in a presentation or class openly surfs the Internet, during the presentation or class, for terms or websites that the presenter or instructor mentions or that are related to the topic being presented. For example, the participant might search for definitions, examples, and graphics or multimedia that expand on or illustrate concepts being presented. Typically, the presenter or instructor uses one screen to show his or her slides and another screen to show the result of the web searches. Other search engines may be used and the person doing the searching may also be navigating directly to sites provided by the presenter or instructor.

According to Educause (2006), this started with a professor at the Annenberg School for Communication at the University of Southern California and has since been incorporated into other courses. Some conferences and workshops have adopted the practice and it seems to be spreading. This practice may help learners stay engaged and focused. It makes back-channel conversations about the topic explicit and can model means for finding diverse resources and evaluating online information. However some people aren't comfortable multitasking in this way and the process can be very distracting. I used this strategy during an online presentation recently and some participants loved it (probably fellow ADDers) while others felt it was too distracting.

Stephen Downes (2006) finds this idea fascinating: "You know, I'm beginning to think I should ask for multiple screens and projectors at my talks—a screen for the Google jockey, a screen for the audience live conference chat (aka, the backchannel), a screen for the photo montage, and more. The problem with lectures (for me, at least) is that they are one-channel—the information bandwidth is tiny. But more channels could add a lot of texture and depth to the experience."

## Mashups or Make Your Own Web Portal

Mashups pull together content from more than one source to create completely new online services. They also allow users to build personalized web portals that combine the web applications they most use. Internet-based application programming interfaces (APIs)—programming building blocks—have made mashups relatively easy to build. APIs make it easier to develop applications by putting the building blocks together. Much as blogging tools put web publishing into the hands of lots and lots of non-technical people, Internet-based APIs lower the barrier to developing web applications. An example of a mashup is Frappr (www.frappr.com). It combines data from Google Maps with data from social networking sites like MySpace to create a map of where the user's contacts live. For an example of an Internet-based API for creating mashups and the mashups that exist as a result of them, check out www.mashupfeed.com.

I personally have found one mashup to be particularly useful. Google's personalized web page (www.google.com/ig) allows users to pull together chosen web content in one location. My own personalized Google portal has the following elements: weather in Denver and Columbia, Maryland (where I used to live), the time in locations where our contractors live, my daily horoscope, my to-do list, my Google search history, Google's chat application, movie show times for my zip code, and news headlines.

## The Impact of New Technologies on Course and Learning Management Systems

Inexpensive and free web applications for creating communications like blogs, wikis, and mashups or for communicating by voice or text lower or eliminate the barrier to developing and sharing content on the web. As a result, some thought leaders are saying the days of the current generation of course management systems (CMSs), such as WebCT, Blackboard, and Moodle, and learning management systems (LMSs), such as SumTotal, Plateau, and Saba, are numbered, because neither can easily facilitate or track the type of informal learning engendered by Web 2.0 applications.

# New Ways of Learning Promoted by Social Learning Applications

Many of the tools described in the last section are variations on existing, well-known tools. For example, as mentioned earlier, podcasting is an Internet incarnation of presentations through cassette tape or audio or video broadcast. IM has similarities to leaving brief notes for others. Blogs are akin to topical newsletters with lists of resources to learn more. Collaborative writing has been accomplished by sending word process or documents back and forth through email. Sharing resources among friends, family, co-workers, and others has been going on for ages. VoIP replaces one technology (phone service over phone line channels) for real-time audio communication with another (phone service over Internet channels).

What *is* different is the speed, efficiency, and scale of information dissemination and collaboration, which has critical implications for learning. Along with speed, efficiency, and increased scale, these tools can provide an abundance of potentially valuable information. They also have the potential to provide too much of this information, and much of it might not be so valuable and, as a result, can cause stress and anxiety from excessive choice and content. Many other tools are emerging for which the uses are not particularly clear and it's hard to say what will happen with them over time. Dozens of Web 2.0 applications are emerging and, as a result of past experience, I expect a shake-out. But one early indication is clear: these tools are providing a foundation for new ways of sharing and managing individual and group knowledge.

One other issue is clear. Although the concept has been around for well over a decade, the issue of knowledge management—that is, managing knowledge as a resource—is more often talk than action. Many discussions of knowledge management focus on the issue conceptually, rather than practically. The types of applications described in this chapter are creating an alternate type of knowledge management, one that users are finding to be far more useful than the top-down corporate knowledge management applications that are difficult to use and, ultimately, don't make knowledge easier to manage. Blogs, wikis, social bookmarking, IM, and mashups are increasingly used by individuals, whether sanctioned by their organizations or not, because they facilitate the quick finding and managing of information when it is needed.

Ultimately, Web 2.0 applications and those who use them facilitate the just-in-time, just-when-needed, just-enough approach to learning that thought leaders have advocated for nearly two decades, under the names electronic performance support systems (EPSSs) (Gery, 1991), workflow-based learning (Adkins, 2003), and informal learning. For learning to thrive in such environments, people must have the ability to:

- Determine personal and organizational learning needs

- Find good resources and people (who can help) to meet those needs

- Evaluate what others share and quickly draw distinctions between important and unimportant, on-target and off-target

- Make sense of dynamic and conflicting information, and have the flexibility to deal with it

- Integrate learning into everyday life

- Read in English, because so much of the content is in English

When organizations first deal with Web 2.0 applications, they often try to impose centralized control, like the organizational ban on instant messaging. The result is mega-tools like knowledge management systems in corporate environments and integrated course management systems in higher education environments. But these mega-tools often go unused or under-used because users find tools that work for them, for their purposes, rather than adhere to organizational dictates.

# Concluding Thoughts

Networks and the Internet have fundamentally changed how people find information, collaborate, keep in touch, express themselves in text and through media, and determine which sources to trust. Expectations about access to and speed of information have drastically changed as well. Even though people are often deluged with information, most Internet users cannot imagine how they lived without it. (Certainly the editors of this book can't.)

Many of the technologies discussed here are emerging, merging, and changing as we speak. Clearly, it is too early to say how the tools will impact learning in the long run, but it isn't too early to try them and consider their uses. Similarly, many critical questions raised by these technologies are unanswered, including ownership of collaboratively authorized content, how these types of tools will be supported by IT departments and others, how content experts such as faculty and corporate experts will be supported in using these tools, what enterprise-level incarnations of these tools are needed, and what business models will emerge to support the continued development and existence of these tools.

But some things are already clear. It is far easier to post micro-content (such as a blog posting or a comment) than to develop web pages. It is easier to use a social bookmarking site to collaboratively create a list of bookmarks on a given topic than to email multiple people for their favorite websites and then find and use these emails. Blog postings are increasingly mined for emerging trends and issues, but this used to be the domain of formal media such as magazines and radio. Applications are evolving that allow for personalized portals, allowing individuals to control what content they wish to be connected to and how they wish to learn. Are these tools beneficial? We don't have many answers yet, and there are certainly kinks to be worked out. But these tools lower the barriers to publishing and exchanging content, and that has powerful implications for learning and the publishing of learning content.

The easy exchange of content turns copyright on its ears, and plagiarism has become a serious concern on campuses. But the Internet has had a significant impact on students' expectations. Institutions of higher education are having a hard time dealing with younger learners who expect 24/7 access to people and help. But it's not just the younger learners who expect this. Although we did not grow up with the technology and do not necessarily use the Internet for social interaction and connectedness, baby boomers like Saul and me have come to expect on-demand customer service and, as a result, also expect 24/7 access to people and help.

The need for current and future workers' to continually update their knowledge and skills may drive education and training organizations to use fewer resources to build static content and more resources to support learners' search for applicable resources and to help them find and use these resources. A related and larger challenge is transforming most learning materials (whether classroom courses, webcasts, online tutorials, or workbooks) from one-way presentations of content to two-way interactions that facilitate application and critical thinking. Although needed, these are often missing from workplace learning programs. To fill this void, many workers have found their own ways to reflect critically through their own informal learning networks. This trend is likely to accelerate as people learn to use the tools described in this chapter, which let them publish online content without programming or authoring skills. Rather than fight this, smart organizations will find ways to harness informal networks to promote more learning and sharing of knowledge.

Whether in the education system or the workplace, technologies for learning change and are changed by those who use them. Networks and the Internet are continually providing new ways of teaching and learning that go beyond the traditional constraints of time and place. When discussing them, however, the focus should be less about technology and more about methods to share, support, and collaborate. Because these technologies are new and changing, people should not only use them, but also critically think about them. Watch them emerge and how people creatively use them. Track the uses that catch on and the ones that don't. Follow the eventual consolidation. Share these understandings with others (perhaps using a blog or wiki), and consider how to help learners and other stakeholders live with the inevitable changes wrought by these technologies.

Even as organizations work to adopt these ways of working and learning (an effort that will continue for the next several years), researchers are already busy working on the Web 3.0. The goal is to provide a practical implementation of the semantic web. According to the Wikipedia (2006), "The semantic web is a vision of web pages that are understandable by computers, so that they can search websites and perform actions in a standardized way." Or, as Markoff (2006) observes, its "goal is to add a layer of meaning on top of the existing web that would make it less of a catalog and more of a guide—and even provide the foundation for systems that can reason in a human fashion. That level of artificial intelligence, with machines doing the thinking instead of simply following commands, has eluded researchers for more than half a century." An example of a Web 3.0 technology would be one that could scour the web and provide responses to requests like, "Suggest trips that both my parents and children would enjoy to the Caribbean, and provide a list of possible trips, complete with airfare, hotels, rental cars, and sightseeing packages."

The bottom line? As the often quoted phrase says: "May you live in interesting times."

## Acknowledgments

I would like to thank Kirsti Aho and Mark Nichoson of Adobe Systems Inc. for their assistance in preparing this chapter.

# References

Adkins, S. (2003). Workflow-based e-learning: Next-generation enterprise learning technology. *Learning Circuits, 4*(8).

Anas, L. (2006, May 28). Lecture, inquire, Google. Boulder, CO: *Daily Camera*. Available: www.dailycamera.com/bdc/buffzone_news/article/0,1713,BDC_2448_4733634,00.html.

Berlind, D. (2006, January 27). Mashup ecosystem poised to explode. ZDNET blogs. Available: http://blogs.zdnet .com/BTL/?p=2484.

Bernard, R.M., Abrami, P.C., Lou, Y., Borokhovski, E., Wade, A., Wozney, L., Wallet, P.A., Fiset, M., & Huang, B. (2004). How does distance education compare to classroom instruction? A meta-analysis of the empirical literature. *Review of Educational Research, 74* (3), 379–439.

Brown, J.S. (2002, February). Growing up digital. How the web changes work, education, and the ways people learn. *USDLA Journal, 16*(2). Available: www.usdla.org/html/journal/FEB02_Issue/article01.html

Bryant, T. (2006). Social software in academia. *Educause Quarterly, 29*(2). Available: www.educause.edu/apps/eq/eqm06/eqm0627.asp

Downes, S. (2005, March 9). Learning networks: Theory and practice. Available: www.downes.ca/files/palermo.ppt.

Downes, S. (2006, May 17). OL daily. Available: www.downes.ca/archive/06/05_17_news_OLDaily.htm

Downes, S. (n.d.). e-Learning 2.0. Association for Computing Machinery, Inc. Available: www.elearnmag.org/subpage .cfm?section=articles&article=29-1

Driscoll, M., & Carliner, S. (2005). *Advanced web-based training: Adapting real-world strategies in your online learning.* San Francisco, CA: Pfeiffer.

Educause. (2006). 7 things you should know about Google jockeying. Available: www.educause.edu/ir/library/pdf/ELI7014.pdf

Freedman, T. (Ed.) (2006). Coming of age: An introduction to the new world wide web. Available: http://fullmeasure.co.uk/Coming_of_age_v1-2.pdf

Gery, G. (1991). *Electronic performance support systems*. Tolland, MA: Gery Performance Group.

Gotta, M. (2006). *Trends in social software*. Midvale, UT: Burton Group.

Hindle, T. (2006, January 19). The new organization. *The Economist.* Available: www.economist.com/surveys/displaystory .cfm?story_id=5380483

Hook, B. (2006, January 6). Instant messaging creates headaches for IT professionals. *e-Commerce Times.* Available: www.ecommer-cetimes.com/story/39295.html International Board of Standards for Training, Performance and Instruction. (2000). Instructional design competencies. Available: www.ibstpi.org/Competencies/ instruct_design_competencies_2000.htm

Kaiser Family Foundation. (2003, October 28). New study finds children age zero to six spend as much time with TV, computers and video games as playing outside. Available: www.kff.org/ entmedia/entmedia102803nr.cfm.

Markoff, J. (2006, November 12). Entrepreneurs see a web guided by common sense. *New York Times*. Available: http://select .nytimes.com/search/restricted/article?res=FA0C12FC3D5A0C718 DDDA80994DE404482

McGiveney, V. (1999). *Informal learning in the community. A trigger for change and development.* Leicester, UK: NIACE.

Oblinger, D.G., & Oblinger, J.L. (Eds.). (2005). Educating the net generation. Available: www.educause.edu/ir/library/pdf/ PUB7101.pdf

O'Reilly, T. (2005, September 30). What is Web 2.0? Available: www.oreillynet.com/pub/a/oreilly/tim/news/ 2005/09/30/what-is-web-20.html

Pate, W. (2005, June 6). How do we define Web 2.0? What's Web 2.0 website. Available: www.whatsweb20.com/will-pate/ how-do-we-define-web-2-0

Pew Internet & American Life Project. (2002, September 15). The Internet goes to college: How students are living in the future with today's technology. Available: www.pewinternet.org/pdfs/PIP_College_Report.pdf

Pew Internet & American Life Project. (2004, September 1). How Americans use instant messaging. Available: www.pewinternet.org/pdfs/PIP_Instantmessage_Report.pdf

Pew Internet & American Life Project. (2006, April 26). Internet penetration and impact. Available: www.pewinternet.org/pdfs/PIP_Internet_Impact.pdf

Pew Internet & American Life Project. (2006, May 28). Home broadband adoption. Available: www.pewinternet.org/pdfs/PIP_Broadband_trends2006.pdf

Shareski, D. (2006, April 13). Open space consultant's conference. Available: http://ideasandthoughts.org/2006/04/13/open-space-consultants-conference/

Surowiecki, J. (2005). *The wisdom of crowds.* New York: Anchor Books.

Sitzmann, T.M., & Wisher, R. (2005). The effectiveness of web-based training compared to classroom instruction: A meta-analysis. In S. Carliner & B. Sugrue (Eds.), *Proceedings of the 2005 ASTD research-to-practice conference-within-a-conference* (pp. 196–202). Alexandria, VA: ASTD Press.

Wikipedia. (n.d.). Web 2.0. Available: http://en.wikipedia.org/wiki/Web_2.0

◆ ◆ ◆

## Summary of Main Points

Readers should take away the following main ideas from this chapter:

- Rather than a formal set of standards, Web 2.0 represents a re-envisioning of the World Wide Web as a two-way medium.
- Web 2.0 applications address the changing nature of learning. Characteristics of this changed nature of learning include:

- An on-demand and as-needed service rather than something that is taken when it's offered

- From predigested content to collaborative construction of knowledge

- From a finite body of facts to an endless array of knowledge

- From authoritative and verified material to content on which users must conduct their own due diligence

- Web 2.0 applications also address the changing nature of learners, including learners who have grown up with the technology and, as a result, easily multi-task.

- The new Web 2.0 applications are based on three core principles:

  - A read/write web, in which the web is a two-way medium, where people can easily be users of existing content as well as providers of content

  - The web-as-platform, in which web applications are seamlessly knitted into websites, such as embedding MapQuest or Google maps in the middle of travel-related applications

  - Microcontent, in which people no longer think of the web as "pages" and "sites" and, instead, focus on smaller web elements of content that can be aggregated or disaggregated and recombined

- Web 2.0 technologies include:

  - Blogs, which are dated online journals that are frequently updated by their authors, who are often called *bloggers*

  - Wikis, which, like blogs, are easy-to-use web publishing tools and are web applications that allow a group of users to collaboratively add and edit web content without any programming knowledge

  - Social bookmarking applications, which allow users to easily save and categorize collections of their bookmarks of web pages using keywords called *tags* and to share the bookmarks with others

- Tools for collaborative writing that let users easily create documents collaboratively and add to and edit them. These services are similar to wikis, but they provide a familiar editing interface that is more like word processing than wiki editing (which feels geeky to some).

- Voice over Internet protocol (VoIP), a group of technologies that facilitate transmission of voice conversations over a data network, usually the Internet, such as Internet telephony and voice-over narration of online webcasts.

- Podcasting, a methodology for publishing multimedia files. Podcasting was initially associated with audio files, but video files are also being distributed this way. It offers audio and video content on niche topics and distributes it to people who are interested in that content. Users either download the files individually or subscribe to an ongoing podcast (one that is regularly updated) and automatically receive updates.

- Instant messaging (IM), a tool for real-time, synchronous communication and collaboration between two or more people who are logged onto a network or the Internet. This is different from email, which affords asynchronous communication and generally involves a delay between sending of a message at one end and receiving a message at the other.

- Google jockeying, which occurs when a participant in a presentation or class openly surfs the Internet during the presentation or class for terms or websites that the presenter or instructor mentions or that are related to the topic being presented, in order to provide additional resources and insights to be used by all participants.

- Mashups, which pull together content from more than one source to create completely new online services.

They also allow users to build personalized web portals that combine the web applications they most use. Internet-based application programming interfaces (APIs)—programming building blocks—have made mashups relatively easy to build. APIs make it easier to develop applications by putting the building blocks together.

- Inexpensive and free web applications for creating communications, like blogs, wikis, and mashups, or for communicating by voice or text lower or eliminate the barrier to developing and sharing content on the web.

- Although some Web 2.0 technologies are similar to existing ones, they:

  - Increase the speed, efficiency, and scale of information dissemination and collaboration

  - Create anxiety from dealing with an abundance of choice and content

  - Change the top-down and formal approach that has dominated learning to more flexible ones and ones focused on the learner

  - Challenge all learning environments to promote greater interaction and more critical thinking

◆ ◆ ◆

# Guiding Questions for Discussion

Some questions that come from the material presented here include:

- Are these new tools a fad or do they represent an underlying need that should be filled?

- How might each of these tools be used to support your learning? Your organization's learning?

- What are the downsides to using these tools? Can the downsides be mitigated?

- Are these approaches and tools likely to replace more traditional approaches to teaching and learning?

| **Learn More About It** |
| --- |

Links What is Web 2.0?, www.oreillynet.com/pub/a/oreilly/tim/ news/2005/09/30/what-is-web-20.html

Try these tools for free:

- Blog: www.blogger.com
- Wiki: www.wikispaces.com
- Social bookmarking: http://del.icio.us/
- Collaborative writing: http://writeboard.com
- VoIP: www.skype.com
- Podcasting: www.podomatic.com/
- Instant messaging: www.ceruleanstudios.com/
- Mashup/personalized web portal: www.pageflakes. com/

# Chapter 9

# Locked Out

Bridging the Divide Between Training
and Information Technology

*Marc J. Rosenberg,*
*Marc Rosenberg and Associates, and*
*Steve Foreman, InfoMedia Designs*

## About This Chapter

Previous chapters in this section explored the technical issues
raised by e-learning technology. But implementing and operating these technologies also creates a variety of management and
interpersonal problems. This chapter answers the question, "What
people problems does technology create, especially for the
information technology (IT) group (the group that, in most organizations, is responsible for planning, implementing, and supporting hardware and software, including support for e-learning)?"
Specifically, in this chapter, we explore the often divergent needs
and perspectives of the training and IT functions, and why communication and collaboration among the two groups has often
been difficult. We identify the major consequences and risks that
can result when training and IT fail to work together and identify
the benefits of a tighter working relationship between the two.
We continue by presenting specific actions that each organization
can take to create a more collaborative environment and close
by examining how a stronger partnership between training and IT
can serve as a model for how training can work successfully with
other groups in an organization.

# Introduction

Alarmed by a growing number of companies whose executives have been charged with accounting fraud and other crimes, the CEO of a company in the United States asked his corporate university to create a course that would provide training on compliance with the country's Sarbanes-Oxley law, which "establishes new or enhanced standards for all U.S. public company boards, management, and public accounting firms" (Wikipedia, 2006) and related issues, and to deliver the training to all 20,000 global executives and managers as soon as possible. Of course, the CEO knew that the solution to the perceived problem required more than training, but he also knew that training would be a significant part of how the business ensured its compliance with this new U.S. law and related international laws and regulations. To meet the tight deadline as well as the heavy record-keeping requirements, the training organization turned to e-learning and started building a highly interactive, media-rich program that, in pilot testing, appeared to deliver the necessary skills and knowledge in an efficient, engaging, and effective manner. The e-learning program even included a video address by the CEO stressing the importance of the training.

Now came time to deploy the program. The training department approached the IT group about delivering the course on the company's computer network. Although the chief information officer (CIO) was well aware of the CEO's concerns about accounting, she had never been briefed about the training program that the CEO commissioned to address it. When her group heard about the training program, which, at this point, was well under development, several concerns arose. The group managing the servers was alarmed by the video in the course. The IT group did not support servers for streaming video. The group responsible for networking had similar concerns. The networking staff was shocked by the number of large video files that needed to be delivered to desktop browsers through the corporate intranet.

In short, the IT staff had strong reservations about delivering the course to managers and executives working in the corporate headquarters, let alone the sixty-plus locations around the world. The IT group needed time to prepare for release of the course, including several weeks to install the course on staging servers, where new or changed software applications are tested before they are made live, and run a series of tests of the performance of the network running the video. Furthermore, the IT group didn't know that the leader of the corporate university had sent an email to all managers in the corporation telling them that the course would be available in a few days, adding that they should take the course as soon as possible. Feeling boxed into a corner and pressured by the CEO, the CIO pulled valuable resources off from other critical projects to calculate the impact of the course on the corporate network. Her staff projected that the maximum number of simultaneous users who could access the course without negative impact to other mission critical applications was just twenty people. Because this was unacceptable, course deployment was delayed.

The next day, the CEO called the CIO and the chief learning officer (CLO) into his office to explain what happened. The CIO stated that the course did not conform to IT standards and would bring the corporate network to a crawl. Training would have to redesign the course, remove the rich media components—including several executive videos—and deliver the course in a format that used simple graphics and text. The CLO was embarrassed and could only state that he would look into how much time it would take to redesign the course.

In other words, somewhere on the path to implement e-learning in an organization, practical IT considerations can derail plans if learning specialists completely overlook these issues. The purpose of this chapter is to explain why situations like this can happen (perhaps do happen all too often) and what training and IT professionals can do to avoid them. Specifically, in this chapter, we explore the often divergent needs and perspectives of the training and IT functions and why communication and collaboration among the two groups has often been difficult. We identify the major consequences and risks that can result when training and IT fail to work together and identify the benefits of a tighter working relationship between the two. We continue by presenting specific actions that each organization can take to create a more collaborative environment and close by examining how a stronger partnership between training and IT can serve as a model for how training can work successfully with other groups in an organization.

## The Inherent Tensions Between Training and IT

Little dispute exists that learning is essential for organizational success and that traditional classroom training cannot, by itself, support all the learning needs of an organization. To augment traditional training strategies, the use of e-learning has become more of a priority in all types of organizations and, to realize true economies and efficiencies, e-learning ultimately must have an enterprise-wide scope.

Little dispute exists, too, that the technology investment for e-learning is significant and that, to receive the most value from it, e-learning must integrate with the existing enterprise IT to avoid duplicate spending, while at the same time making content conveniently available to learners on their desktops. Gone are the days when training organizations could go their own way with regard to learning technology; it has become too complex and expensive. Training applications require sophisticated networks, reliable servers, and 24/7 support to deliver learning to everyone who needs it, when and where they need it.

Customers demand more convenience and flexibility, less disruption in how training is delivered, and faster and better access. The nature of the work demands more frequent updates to training content. Both training and IT have a vested interest in meeting these demands.

The next two subsections explore how training became more dependent on IT and the specific types of tensions that exist in the relationship.

## How Training Became Dependent on IT

Training organizations have been experimenting with technology for the last forty years. Most of the experiments have been short-lived. From "green screen" computer-based training to full-motion interactive videodisc, many seemingly high-potential innovations lasted but a few short years, only to be replaced by the next big thing. From the information technology perspective, this was fine, as long as activity was limited to training centers and on work stations specifically intended for use with training applications.

But as organizations established computer networks and most workers had one or more PCs dedicated to their own use, training professionals have sought to distribute e-learning through these corporate intranets, extranets, and the Internet, rather than on dedicated work stations in a learning center. Further advancing these trends are enterprise applications such as learning management systems (LMS), learning content management systems (LCMS), virtual learning systems (VLS), and knowledge management systems (KMS), which use the Internet to deliver training and information to users at their own desks, rather than in a learning center. Training organizations have tried a number of approaches to implement these applications; some training organizations have outsourced these applications, others have created their own technology groups, and still others have relied on the corporate IT function to support these applications. Some training organizations have experimented with several or all of these models. Figure 9.1 shows the different approaches; it emerges from research on LMSs conducted by the eLearning Guild, a worldwide community of practice for e-learning professionals (www.elearningguild.com).

The findings are consistent with what we have been hearing: that corporate IT departments are becoming increasingly involved with e-learning. What has changed in recent years is that many training organizations have faced increased pressure to abandon their own solutions and outsourcing and, instead, use the services of corporate IT. Doing so is intended to ensure security and conformance with corporate technology standards and policies, lower

**Figure 9.1.  Who Manages the Technical Operations of LMSs?**

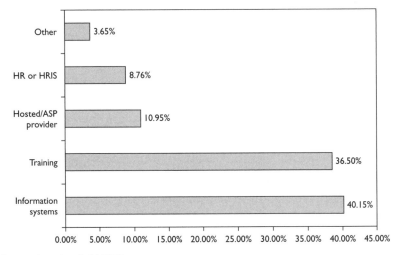

Source: eLearning Guild, 2005a.

corporate spending through consolidation of servers and data centers, and increase the reliability of systems.

## The Tensions Resulting from Increased Dependence

Another eLearning Guild study shows that conflict exists in the relationships between training and their IT departments. Figure 9.2 shows the results of this study, which suggest that many training organizations view reliance on IT as more of an obstacle than an enabler. Training professionals, who have previously been free to experiment with some of the most leading-edge technologies, often feel constrained by the rules and restrictions imposed by IT. Many training groups have found that the vendors to whom they have outsourced their technology were responsive and customer-focused, whereas the experience of working with their organization's IT group, in contrast, feels more like that of a hostage. And, while training professionals generally understand how much time it takes to design, develop, and deliver an e-learning solution, they are often confounded by the additional time IT "tacks on" to a project before it can actually be deployed.

**Figure 9.2. The Relationship Between Training and IT**

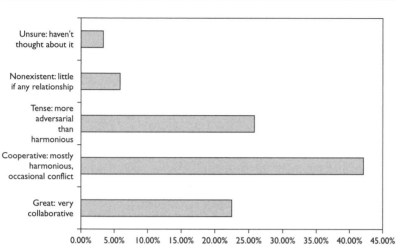

*Source:* eLearning Guild, 2005b.

The key areas of tension seem to be the following:

- Are training organizations capable of managing new learning technologies in ways that are consistent with corporate IT requirements?

- Are IT organizations capable of responding to the unique requirements that new learning technologies present?

- Are internal networks designed to meet the needs of e-learning applications and technologies?

Despite their differences, the two groups ultimately have the best interests of the organization in mind and can only succeed when bridges are built between them.

## Two Different World Views

Before we can talk about building bridges, however, we must understand the essential differences in how training and IT groups approach their work.

IT organizations often see e-learning in the same way as they see other enterprise applications (that is, applications that affect, and are used by, a majority of people in an organization) in terms of technology—servers, applications, networks, and data. From this perspective, efficiency, reliability, and security are the critical goals to achieve. This happens through:

- Standardization (that is, using the same types of hardware and software as much as possible throughout the organization, because the lack of variation simplifies support)

- Resource consolidation (sharing servers and administration between multiple applications to make sure that the IT group is able to effectively manage activity on the network and everything that can affect its performance)

- Careful planning (to make sure that new applications work with the standard setup and do not adversely affect performance of other pieces of the network), usually done several months, if not well over a year in advance

- Rigorous process management (to effectively manage work load and customer expectations)

One of the better-known challenges of an IT group is a network problem. When a program disrupts the network, others in the organization usually blame the IT department. Of course, this is the same department responsible for handling the calls to the help desk and for troubleshooting and resolving the problem. Therefore, technology planning is approached carefully, methodically, and as thoroughly as possible.

The view of e-learning is quite different among trainers. Among them, technology is an enabler for learning: a tool to be used, manipulated, and adjusted as the need arises. For example, while the planning horizon in IT is several months or a year, planning happens on a shorter time frame in training. Once identified, learning and human performance problems must be addressed rapidly, before they affect organizational performance. Besides, many training groups are often brought in at the last minute to solve a human performance problem, and internal clients expect a quick solution, usually in a matter of weeks—or a few months at most.

From a training perspective, many new opportunities are offered by technology. These opportunities include:

- The ability to introduce content published by outside vendors, such as libraries of software technical, or soft-skills training. By linking to this "off-the-shelf" content, trainers are free to focus on training issues that require their unique knowledge of the organization.

- The ability to provide solutions in a shorter time frame. Technology speeds up the deployment of new and updated training programs to large target audiences.

- The ability to apply approaches to learning that are less like one-size-fits-all classroom and better reflect the more individualized and just-in-time approaches that characterize current thinking in adult learning theory, instructional systems, and industrial psychology. Doing so requires experimenting with applications of technology to address human performance problems and, if the experiments show promise, putting them into place quickly.

In the process, however, these new and innovative solutions might not have been vetted in ways that the IT organization likes. The issues of compliance and control with technology standards, so central to the management of IT, are seen as obstacles that slow or stifle dissemination of learning throughout the organization.

This culture clash discourages cooperation and, quite often, promotes conflict.

On one side, there is the IT staff, who find that learning technology is "all over the place," unwieldy and unmanaged, too costly and unreliable. The training organization has too much "unauthorized" technology that does not conform to corporate standards, and training people are not team players. Rather, they are undisciplined and "out of control." Their technology involves too many variations, too many vendors, and too much customization; it needs to be simplified and standardized. Worst of all, many IT professionals feel that trainers like to use the most complex technology available, such as streaming media, webcasting, application sharing, web conferencing, instant messaging, mobile computing, and other applications that put undue stress on the network. At the end of the day, from a traditional IT perspective, training can be seen as non-conforming and rebellious—a skunk works that needs to be brought in line. In short, they'd say, "Unless training plays by our rules, they put us in a position to fail." Their concern is that training technology may not be reliable, may not perform well, may negatively impact the rest of the infrastructure, and may be a maintenance nightmare.

On the other side, the training staff find that the information technology people want "heavy-handed" control of everything having to do with computers and technology. Working with IT slows everything down, as it seems to take forever to approve, test, and install hardware and software. The view of many training professionals is that IT will make them abandon promising learning innovations and experimentation in favor of a more conservative approach where everything must be pinned down in the form of "technology requirements." Furthermore, training often sees the IT organization as too fragmented into specialty groups such as networking, desktop, databases, hardware, application software, and security, each with its own myopic viewpoint—and often not working together. This fragmentation can make project approvals more like an endless string of paperwork and meetings—with nothing getting done. Everyone chimes in, but no one seems to own the overall solution. Training managers often perceive that IT is sabotaging their solutions by throwing out new obstacles that must be overcome at each encounter. At the end of the day, training may view IT as far too rigid and process bound—a sluggish bureaucracy that needs to be much more flexible, client-focused, and responsive. In short, they'd say, "Unless information technology becomes more responsive to our needs, they put us in a position to fail." The training group is concerned that a learning or performance solution might not be implemented in time, and may not meet the business need it's intended to address.

So, in many organizations, training and IT perceive each other as adversaries who put each other in jeopardy. It is little wonder that these two functions have difficulty collaborating.

## Risks of Maintaining the Status Quo and Benefits of Working Together

So why should they try collaborating? One could argue that IT and training have such different missions and personalities that it is only natural their views would diverge. That would be fine if these divergent views did not limit the effectiveness of both groups. But they do. Tension and dysfunction between IT and training pose many risks for the larger organization. Without a true collaboration with IT, a training group cannot sufficiently penetrate the organization to have the impact it needs to be successful. When a training group cannot work with IT, training, in turn, might try to entirely avoid IT. Training might engage its own outside vendors for IT services or build its own—and redundant—data centers and technical resources. Yet training must still go through the organizational network to deliver many of its services. As a result, IT cannot deliver the cost savings, reliability, and security needed by training applications, much less integrate learning into the workplace. So not only does IT fail to achieve its goals, but so does training.

Conflict between the two groups ultimately affects employees outside of both. With less immediate access to learning and information, and by not having content integrated into the workplace, employees waste time looking for the content they need or wait to attend classroom courses. As a result, the organization might fall behind in the marketplace, losing business to competitors whose employees, partners, and customers have immediate access to the precise tools, information, and training needed. Lack of cooperation between IT and training might also result in delays and longer time frames to deliver critical programs to large numbers of people, such as programs that must be taken by every worker in a business unit or the organization. This sluggishness also takes its toll in company competitiveness and agility. If the situation continues, the friction and conflict between training and IT will be seen as counter-productive, drawing attention and resources away from more critical areas. Eventually, the organization may try to end the tension through the expedient route of outsourcing one or both groups.

In other words, such an estrangement can no longer be tolerated. For technology-enabled learning to fully permeate the workplace, IT and training must cooperate. Beyond this basic imperative, both organizations realize a number of benefits by moving to a more collaborative relationship.

Multimedia-rich applications, such as video and simulation, require extensive system resources to run efficiently on users' systems. This, in turn, fuels an appetite for increased power and bandwidth, areas in which the IT organization can bring expertise and economies of scale. Because developing such technology-intensive applications often requires extensive design skills, training groups really do not have people to spare to work on upgrading technology services. But IT does, and often can upgrade networks more efficiently and effectively as a result. Most significantly, by letting IT focus on bandwidth, servers, and systems, training can focus on its core skill: designing and delivering learning and performance improvement. In turn, this strengthens training as it seeks to move from being a provider of courses to a group focused on improving organizational and individual performance.

IT benefits by building a strong partnership with training, too, if for no other reason than that e-learning, when done well, has demonstrated a return on investment in IT.

Four areas of mutual benefit seem to be the most immediately apparent. First, significant new learning and performance solutions like simulations, workflow-based training (training integrated into the workplace), and online coaching and tutoring systems provide IT with job enrichment opportunities, showcasing new and more sophisticated technologies in a more innovative and flexible manner. Training applications can serve as a bellwether for corporate networking requirements. The advanced technology needs of training often precede similar needs that follow in other business functions, such as corporate communications, sales and marketing, and HR.

The second set of benefits emerges from the seamless integration of e-learning systems into the enterprise IT architecture. Adoption of a single sign-on (also known as a simplified user log-in and authentication) increases network security and reduces the need for training to administer its own user accounts and passwords. Integration with corporate e-commerce platforms enables training to be sold to partners and customers while mitigating the need for the training department to handle its own billing and collection activities. Data integration with human resource information systems increases the completeness and accuracy of employee records, including training records. Integration with corporate portals brings training to the desktop of each person in the organization in the same familiar context as other enterprise content.

The third set of benefits emerges when new solutions and technologies are introduced. As training groups evolve into workplace learning and performance groups and increase their offering of non-training solutions such as knowledge management, communities of practice, and electronic performance support, IT will not only have additional production systems to support, but ones that are critical to the mission of the organization and that bring increased value to business operations.

The fourth—and most significant—benefit of collaborating is realized when new programs go live. Coordination between IT and training benefits end-users, especially when applications run well, necessary plug-ins and players are installed on the desktop, and IT is prepared to handle calls to the help desk. That simplifies use of a new learning application. Simplified use increases the likelihood of adoption, and only when people use learning applications do IT and training ultimately benefit.

# How to Achieve Collaboration

The growing need for interdependency must shape the future relationship between information technology and training. But how can two different cultures and years of non-collaboration be turned around? Based on our practical experience, we would like to offer the following nine concrete recommendations.

## Recommendation One: Recognize Existing Limitations, Even While Working to Alleviate Them

Keep in mind that bandwidth enables training impact and training impact funds bandwidth. In other words, the more technical capacity training has, the more training can do; and the more training can do, the more technical capacity it will need. It's only natural to want to shape e-learning into a more interactive, media-rich experience, especially when it enhances learning. But these requirements will, at least initially, put a strain on the IT infrastructure. In the short term, if the organization's capability is not yet ready to handle the desired level of sophistication, training should design programs for the current state while IT continues to find ways to advance network capacity. So training should focus on being ready to upgrade training applications when the infrastructure is ready to handle it, and IT should be upgrading its capacity to handle the training applications. All the while, training and IT must work much more closely to make this happen.

## Recommendation Two: Develop an e-Learning Technology Strategy, Iteratively and Jointly

Although recognizing the limitations of the other party and working to accommodate one another's needs is a healthy response, it should not be approached haphazardly. Efforts that mutually clarify expectations and establish clear responsibilities can strengthen understanding in a more concrete way. One of the most effective tools for doing so is by establishing a technology strategy, as described in Chapter 5.

In terms of strengthening the relationship between training and IT, the strategy should seek to carefully deploy e-learning technology, use it to solve increasingly bigger and more complex business problems, determine which components should be replicated and scaled, and, ultimately, enhance the infrastructure of the organization with each solution. If this is done well, both groups will share success, while keeping investment and implementation at a level that is manageable for the organization.

## Recommendation Three: Establish Work-Level Relationships, Partnerships, and Processes

Although a strategy sets out a longer-term plan and identifies responsibilities, it usually stops at defining what happens in the everyday environment. That's the purpose of work-level relationships, partnerships, and documented processes—to create the next level of detail in the relationship between IT and training. Some ideas for doing so include the following:

- Create a workshop, "boot camp," and other professional development opportunities for people from both organizations to attend together.

- Provide opportunities for the two groups to present relevant high-level visions and goals to one another.

- Cross-pollinate the viewpoints, values, and concerns of IT and training staffs by establishing cross-functional and interdisciplinary teams at the project level. These can start out at a relatively simple and straightforward level that enable IT and training staffs to achieve success through collaboration, then build on each successful project, progressing to more complex and difficult challenges.

- Integrate training analysis, design, development, delivery, and evaluation processes with IT planning and implementation to form a hybrid process that provides a clear path for IT and training to work together.

## Recommendation Four: Establish an Appropriate Governance Mechanism

As contracts can effectively mitigate the relationship among parties in a business agreement, so similar governance mechanisms can effectively mitigate the relationship between IT and training. More often than not, disagreements between IT and training arise not so much out of differences in goals, but out of differences in approach. Having a mutually agreed-on way to make decisions, resolve differences, allocate resources, and manage interdependent processes can help surface problems earlier, when they can be more easily resolved. In addition, a governance framework can ensure that what was learned from one experience is applied to future activities so that, over time, differences are mitigated, redundancies are eliminated, and productivity and innovation are enhanced. In some organizations, it may make sense to appoint an IT representative who has some formal reporting relationship to both the CIO and the CLO.

It is important, too, that the CIO and CLO form a collaborative relationship to provide strategic guidance and sponsorship for collaboration at lower levels. One critical aspect of the relationship between the CIO and CLO is to agree to support e-learning as a mission-critical business application that might require investment in the network, the desktop environment, and certainly in the IT and training people and processes that will drive success.

## Recommendation Five: Allow Time for Network Testing

Even with a strategic plan and strengthened work relationships and processes, training still needs to take additional measures to integrate its applications into the larger technology infrastructure of the organization. So even if a training group has already performed a variety of tests, including user acceptance testing, field testing, SME reviews, and debug testing on e-learning materials, the IT department will likely still want to test the compatibility and "load" of a new application on the network before a new e-learning application or technology is "certified."

To avoid last-minute problems, training should ask IT in advance which technical tests IT needs to do and how much time is needed to perform them. Training needs to further collaborate with IT by projecting the number of users who may access the application at a single time, designing use cases and test scripts for these tests, and assisting with the analysis of test results. Ideally, technical testing should be built into the process for designing and developing the approved courseware so that this step becomes part of the natural work flow.

## Recommendation Six: Learn Each Other's Languages

One of the core problems in the relationship between IT and training is that they speak different languages. The terms they use and the issues that matter to the two groups substantially differ.

To avoid talking past each other, IT and training must create a common lexicon of terminology, processes, and work flow. For example, a common misperception among IT professionals is that courseware is merely another type of data. In actuality, courseware is much more complex. It is a collection of mini-applications from multiple vendors using a wide array of tools that are usually integrated with an enterprise LMS based on loosely interpreted industry interoperability standards such as Sharable Content Object Reference Model (SCORM) and Aviation Industry CBT Committee (AICC). IT must develop a clearer understanding of e-learning courseware to work effectively with training. To do so, IT professionals should use training terminology to effectively and credibly communicate system specifications and requirements. Similarly, training professionals should gain experience in developing use cases and defining functional requirements that clearly communicate learning requirements in ways that an IT professional can appreciate and use. For example, IT needs to know the total number of projected users of an application as well as the expected number of concurrent users during peak use periods. This information helps IT specify the right sized server configuration and network bandwidth, among other things. Training will need to use IT jargon to effectively and credibly communicate these and other requirements.

## Recommendation Seven: Create a New Technical Liaison Position in the Training Group

In addition to the recommendations already mentioned, one of the best ways to build bridges between IT and training is to make that someone's job responsibility, perhaps called a "learning technology architect." The primary responsibility of someone in this job would be to build the bridges needed between IT and training by looking for opportunities to collaborate and avert misconceptions. More significantly, the learning technology architect (or whatever this person's job title would be) would take a longer-term approach to planning e-learning technology and would work closely with the infrastructure experts in IT to shape an organization's e-learning delivery capacity and with the instructional experts in training to understand their goals and translate them into a set of documented requirements that can be handed off to IT. With skills and knowledge from both IT and training, and with access to the leaders of both organizations, the person in this role could serve as a catalyst for teamwork, planning, and collaboration between the two groups.

### Recommendation Eight: Establish a Technology "Sandbox" for Experimentation with Leading-Edge e-Learning Platforms

The e-learning industry is rapidly evolving. Trainers must be able to experiment with new technologies to assess their value and appropriateness in delivering instruction and other productivity-improvement interventions. By equipping training with a private network and a set of servers, IT can enable training to test new tools and approaches without risking any negative impact to the enterprise network. This approach enables IT to monitor training's experimentation and helps establish a cooperative working relationship in which training and IT are collaborating from the outset, rather than IT learning about training's interest in developing a new technology platform after it is too late for sufficient planning and reliable execution.

### Recommendation Nine: Establish a Training–IT Forum

Even with these other eight measures in place, IT and training managers are still likely to need a mechanism for airing concerns and frustrations arising from the clash of these two professional cultures. These two groups can build a better understanding of each other and develop a much stronger collaborative framework through dialog and self-expression. But these activities need to take place on neutral, risk-free ground—away from data centers, training centers, and other workplaces associated with one of the two parties. The forum might have an online component, such as a blog or bulletin board, but probably needs to have an in-person component, too. The more talk that takes place between these two groups, the greater the opportunities for meaningful cooperation.

## Concluding Thoughts

For any training group to be successful, it must successfully build relationships with other groups in an organization. Building such a relationship with IT is essential to the success of e-learning and can serve as an example for working with other groups.

When building such a relationship, however, one key issue that trainers must address, justifiably or not, is their perceived lack of knowledge of the rest of the business. For years, many training groups have been criticized for a lack of business acumen—or understanding of the way business runs in general and the needs of the organization in particular—a charge that training leaders have worked hard to overcome. Now IT offers another criticism: a lack of technology savvy, that is, a failure to grasp the key technical concepts and issues needed to implement e-learning and related technologies in an organization. Working with the IT organization to overcome this latter perception may become a model for overcoming the former. The best practices that come out of a new relationship with IT can become catalysts for working closer with other business organizations.

Because technology seems to permeate everything an organization does these days, trainers developing a broader understanding of technology offers many benefits. Such an understanding broadens training professionals' view of operations, sales and marketing, manufacturing and the supply chain, and other business functions. Over time, this new level of awareness could lead to new opportunities to implement more technology-enabled learning within organizations.

Although presented grimly, the story used to open this chapter actually has a happy ending. Over the next six months after the story began, the IT and training groups established new processes for working together. A core team was formed to work out the deployment of the Sarbanes-Oxley training program. Admittedly, the members of this core team initially approached the relationship as adversaries. IT wanted training to remove the bandwidth-hogging rich media content from the program. Training wanted IT to find a way to handle it. Ultimately, the high level of executive sponsorship for online training became apparent to IT, which began to devise options for successfully mitigating network constraints. At the same time, training began to understand that running enterprise networks was much more complex than they were prepared to handle themselves. As the core team spent more time together, representatives of the two groups developed mutual respect and began to trust that they could work together successfully. IT demonstrated more of a "can-do" attitude, while training began relying more heavily on IT and stopped concentrating on technology deployment issues (focusing instead on its core strength—instructional design and delivery). The value of this improved relationship was really put to the test when the organization selected and deployed its first learning management system (LMS). Without collaboration between IT and training, this implementation would surely have faltered—or failed altogether. Today, these two groups are discussing plans to implement knowledge management and collaboration tools as well as a performance-centered redesign of the company's intranet.

As this organization learned, the relationship between training and IT is at a crossroads. Both groups understand the need to expand technology-enabled learning in the organization. Both agree on why learning technology is needed and see great advantages and benefits to the business if technology-enabled learning initiatives are successful.

What they often disagree on is how to make technology-enabled learning happen and who does what in the process. Continuing conflict in this relationship makes both groups weaker and increases the likelihood of one or both being downsized or outsourced, forcing internal and external clients to go directly to outside suppliers who can give them what they need. In some cases, training's stubborn reliance on doing things themselves is hurting the larger organization and the "our way or the highway" attitude of some IT groups doesn't help the situation.

To build the needed bridges, trainers must develop an appreciation for the professionalism that IT brings to the table and an understanding of the goals IT staffs have for enterprise technology management. At the same time, IT must develop an appreciation for the business value of learning technologies and an understanding of the goals trainers have for their e-learning programs.

Once training and IT professionals can successfully collaborate to deploy e-learning, just think what they can do together to enhance other information technology implementations. IT professionals possess a set of skills that many training organizations do not have: systems analysis and management. e-Learning programs can have more impact when IT professionals are involved in identifying the technology requirements and in ensuring the reliability, performance, and security of the solution. Likewise, training professionals bring to the table a set of core skills that many IT organizations do not have: human performance analysis and instructional design. By working more closely with training professionals, IT may eventually find great value from involving trainers in analyzing user performance requirements and advocating a performance-centered approach to user interface design, improving context-sensitive help systems, and strengthening the learning and performance value of any technology intervention.

Seems like a natural fit, right?

The time is now for IT and training people to recognize that the best possible future results from a mutual collaboration. The collaboration can start with something as simple as a lunch meeting at which common issues and disagreements can be discussed and joint opportunities can be identified. It can then move to some working agreements and the birth of a simple governance model. A demonstration project can be identified for which this newfound collaboration can be exercised. Small steps to be sure, but real, important progress will be the result. Get started!

# References

e-Learning Guild. (2005a, June 17). Who manages the LMS? What organization or department manages the operational/technical side of your enterprise LMS? [An eLearning Guild poll] Available: www.elearningguild.com/research/archives [Retrieved November 29, 2006.]

e-Learning Guild. (2005b, May 3). The relationship between e-learning and IT regarding e-learning technology deployment and management—Your group's relationship with IT/IS. [An e-Learning Guild poll] Available: www.elearningguild.com/ research/archives [Retrieved November 29, 2006.]

Wikipedia. (2006). Entry on Sarbanes-Oxley. Available: http://en.wikipedia.org/wiki/Sarbanes-Oxley_Act. [Retrieved November 29, 2006.]

◆ ◆ ◆

# Summary of Main Points

Readers should take away the following main ideas from this chapter:

- Practical information technology (IT) considerations can affect plans for e-learning and learning management technology.
    - The technology investment for e-learning is significant and, for the organization to receive the most value from it, e-learning must integrate with the existing enterprise

IT to avoid duplicate spending and, at the same time, make content conveniently available to learners on their desktops.

- Training applications require sophisticated networks, reliable servers, and 24/7 support to deliver learning to everyone who needs it, when they need it.

- But as organizations established networks and most workers received their own PCs over the past decade or so, training professionals have sought to distribute e-learning through these corporate intranets, extranets, and the Internet, rather than on dedicated work stations in a learning center.

- Further advancing these trends are enterprise applications such as learning management systems (LMS), learning content management systems (LCMS), virtual learning systems (VLS), and knowledge management systems (KMS), which are designed to be used on a user's own work station and at his or her own desk, rather than in a learning center.

- Many training organizations view reliance on IT as more of an obstacle than an enabler; some training groups try to work around the relationship by using vendors or creating their own technology capabilities.

- IT and training groups have a different view of technology:

  - IT organizations often see e-learning in the same way as they see other enterprise applications (that is, applications that affect and are used by a majority of people in an organization) in terms of technology—servers, applications, networks, and data. From this perspective, efficiency, reliability, and security are the critical goals to achieve. This happens through standardization, resource consolidation, careful planning, and rigorous process management.

  - Trainers see technology is an enabler for learning—a tool to be used, manipulated, and adjusted as the need arises.

Technology presents opportunities, such as the ability to introduce content published by outside vendors, provide solutions in a shorter time frame and apply approaches to learning that are less one-size-fits-all.

- If conflict exists, forces cry out for collaboration. These forces include:

- Reduced employee productivity

- Delays in implementing learning programs

- By letting IT focus on technology and training focus on learning, each can focus its attention on its core talents.

- Training applications also allow IT to:

    Showcase new and more sophisticated technologies in a more innovative and flexible manner

    Integrate training into other applications and simplify the use of training applications, through actions like adoption of a single sign-on and integration with corporate e-commerce platforms and HR applications

    Make training simple for end-users to use, so they adopt it

- The following recommendations can promote collaboration between IT and training:

- Recognize existing limitations, even while working to alleviate them

- Develop an e-learning technology strategy, iteratively and jointly

- Establish work-level relationships, partnerships, and processes

- Establish an appropriate governance mechanism

- Allow time for network testing

- Learn each other's languages

- Create a new technical liaison position in the training group

- Establish a technology "sandbox" for experimentation with leading-edge e-learning platforms

- Establish a training–IT forum

◆ ◆ ◆

# Guiding Questions for Discussion

- This chapter was written exclusively from the perspective of a corporate or government work setting. What are the relationships between IT and learning groups like in other types of organizations, such as universities, colleges, and schools? How are they similar to the situation described in this chapter? How do they differ? Why?

- The chapter makes reference to the fact that training managers need to understand technology better. What do you think training managers (and other managers responsible for e-learning) need to know about the technology?

- What do IT professionals need to know about training and e-learning?

- What is the nature of the current relationship between your learning and IT groups? Why does such a relationship exist? Which of the nine recommendations described earlier (if any) could you apply to strengthen the relationship?

| Learn More About It | |
|---|---|
| Books, Papers, Reports, and Articles | Barron, T. (2000, December). Getting IT support for e-learning. *ASTD Learning Circuits* (webzine). Available: www.learningcircuits.org/2000/dec2000/Barron.htm |
| | Cameron, B., Orlov, L.M., & Sessions, L. (2007, February 22). IT leadership maturity checkup: IT's operations are more mature than stakeholder relationships, strategy links. Available: www.forrester |

.com/Research/Document/Excerpt/0,7211,41041,00.html

Foreman, S. (2006). Who owns knowledge management? In M.J. Rosenberg (Ed.), *Beyond e-learning: Approaches and technologies to enhance organizational knowledge, learning, and performance* (pp. 153–156). San Francisco, CA: Pfeiffer.

Foreman, S., & Schroeder, D. (2007, April 11). *Pain in the LMS*. Presentation at The e-Learning Guild's Annual Gathering Conference and Expo, Boston, Massachusetts.

Hanson, W. (2006, February 18). IT and business alignment. *Government Technology*. Available: www.govtech.net/news/news.php?id=98496

Keefe, P. (2007, March). IT/business alignment: Can't we all just get along? *Optimize Magazine, 65*. Available: www.optimizemag.com/disciplines/corporate-culture/showArticle.jhtml;jsessionid=SNAYGGD1VNYTEQS NDLQCKH0CJUNN2JVN?articleID=198000363

# Part IV

# Design Issues

This part explores some of the design challenges that have arisen as our collective experience with e-learning has expanded. Chapters in this part include:

- Chapter 10, A Holistic Framework of Instructional Design for e-Learning by co-editor Saul Carliner, argues that ISD is a value system. Developed in the 1940s with few major changes since then, the value system it encodes no longer reflects the value systems of practicing instructional designers in industry, limits practice, and does not even consider project management. But because of its wide recognition and its flexibility in research, perhaps the model can be updated. This chapter then proposes such an update, labelled as a framework, because ISD is a methodology, not a model. The framework consists of three parts: design philosophies and theories, general design methodology, and instructional considerations. Among the implications of adopting this framework are practice that further focuses on human performance, teaching based on problems, and research that is focused on case studies.

- Chapter 11, Converting $e_3$-Learning to $e^3$-Learning: An Alternative Instructional Design Method by M. David Merrill, illustrates those instructional principles that can help designers avoid *enervative, endless,* or *empty* $e_3$-learning (pronounced e sub-three learning) and replace it with *effective, efficient,* and *engaging* $e^3$-learning (pronounced e to the third power learning). These first principles of instruction include the activation principle, the demonstration principle, the application principle, the task-centered principle and the integration principle. This chapter concludes with a brief description of an alternative method for designing more effective, efficient, and enabling $e^3$ instruction.

- Chapter 12, Design with the Learning in Mind by Patricia McGee, addresses the challenges of providing learners with the support needed to succeed in e-learning courses. Specifically, this chapter addresses the pedagogical, interpersonal, and cognitive supports that can support online learners. Within each area, system functionality illustrates how strategies, tactics, and organization can be enacted. For clarity, all examples are situated in a course management system (CMS).

# Chapter 10

# A Holistic Framework of Instructional Design for e-Learning

*Saul Carliner. Concordia University*

**About This Chapter**

This chapter answers the question, "How does instructional systems design (ISD) have to be adapted (if at all) to address the realities of the current contexts of learning and design, and the issues of e-learning?" In it, I describe the limitations of the current envisioning of instructional systems design, including problems with its designation as a model and how both the general context in which instructional designers work and the specific challenges posed by e-learning demand that our conception of instructional design be changed. I also observe, however, that, at its core, ISD is a value system and changing ISD means confronting long-held beliefs that might be in conflict with the realities of the design context.

# Introduction

Writing in *Training* magazine, Jack Gordon and Ron Zemke comment that instructional systems design (ISD), which guides the development of training materials, "is too slow and clumsy . . . produces bad solutions . . . [and] clings to a wrong world view" (2000). Some claim that ISD has limited trainers' perspectives. Those working in e-learning suggest that ISD no longer offers practical utility (Horton, 2002).

The problem is that no one has offered a comprehensive alternative. In this chapter, I do just that: offer an alternative framework for consideration. Before presenting it, however, I first define ISD and provide a brief history of it, providing a base of knowledge for those who have limited familiarity with ISD and a means of calibrating different understandings of it for those readers who are already familiar with the topic. Next, I argue that ISD is not a model; it is a value system and prescriptive methodology. Then, I identify nine practical problems with ISD, especially as it relates to instructional design. I close the chapter by proposing an alternate approach to ISD, one that, on the one hand is systematic but, on the other hand, acknowledges the realities of the real-world environments in which it will be used.

# What Is Instructional System Design?

Instructional systems design is the recommended process for designing, developing, and implementing learning programs (Carliner, Ribeiro, & Boyd, in press). It is a process that guides people who are developing learning programs (called *instructional designers*) in schools, academe, corporations, government agencies, and nonprofits.

ISD was first proposed during World War II. Researchers were asked to devise a means of preparing instructional materials that could be developed in the least amount of time and from which learners would take away the maximum amount of content. The U.S. government wanted to integrate the newly emerging military technologies into battle operations as quickly as possible. But the military recognized that it would not be possible without extensive training of the people who would use this technology (Deutsch, 1992; Reiser, 2001).

After the war, the American Institutes of Research continued work on ISD, and ISD received increasing recognition. By the 1970s, it formed the basis of practice in the training departments of many companies and the foundation of a large number of college curricula in education (Reiser, 2001). With increasing use came variations on the model. By 1991, Gustafson counted thirty-one versions of the models in the public domain, and in 1997, he noted forty. Additional models were developed for private use within various organizations.

Despite the numerous variations on the model, the most common models are essentially covered by the generic process known as ADDIE—an acronym constructed from these five broad phases of effort:

1. *Analysis,* during which instructional designers define the purpose and audience of the proposed learning program.

2. *Design,* during which instructional designers determine whether to buy a training program off the shelf or build their own. If buying a program off the shelf, instructional designers determine what tailoring is required to make the program suitable for use within their organization (if any). If building a program, instructional designers prepare detailed plans. Some represent this as a two-phase process, providing first a conceptual or high-level design followed by a complete or detailed design. Other models represent this as a one-step process.

3. *Development,* during which instructional designers prepare or adjust a learning program according to the plans developed in the design phase.

4. *Implementation,* during which instructional designers and their colleagues make a learning program available to its

intended learners. For classroom courses, this involves marketing the courses, scheduling classrooms and instructors, enrolling learners, and arranging for course materials to be available in the classroom. For e-learning and other types of self-study programs, this involves marketing, order fulfillment, scheduling reprints when necessary, and providing ongoing support to learners.

5. *Evaluation*, during which instructional designers (or others whom they commission) assess the effectiveness of the learning program in everyday use.

The instructional design process has wide acceptance within the professional community. For example, many corporate training departments require instructional designers to learn about ISD as part of their work-related training. An industry has grown up to support this need, with several companies and trade associations offering instructional design workshops.

Other entrepreneurs and researchers have tried to provide online assistance for some or all of the instructional design process—essentially automating ISD. For example, one effort is attempting to develop software that can automatically generate objectives and test questions, if someone provides the content (Clark, 1997). Designer's Edge, a software tool from Allen Interactions, structures the design process online and helps designers quickly generate learning modules in the now-retired tool, Authorware.

On the one hand, organizations that produce learning materials have invested extensive resources in ISD. Similarly, academic programs rely heavily on ISD as a theoretical base for their programs. Perhaps those practical considerations prevent people in the field from questioning ISD, because changes to it could ultimately require costly changes to work processes and academic curricula.

On the other hand, known problems exist. In his 1991 survey of ISD models, Gustafson observed that all instructional design models are prescriptive. That is, they are intended to guide practice by suggesting a methodology and issues to consider. None are based on a systematic observation of practice. Furthermore, he notes that, of all the models in use, only one had ever been tested to assess its effectiveness use in day-to-day practice. With time, the problems of applying ISD in everyday practice become increasingly clear, and practicing professionals have increasingly called for an overhaul. The rest of this chapter explores these issues. First, I explore the key problems with ISD as it currently is and as the problems relate to e-learning, then I propose a means to address these problems in a revamped approach to designing instruction.

# ISD Is a Value System

For my dissertation study, I conducted a qualitative study of the design of three permanent exhibitions in technology and history museums. After completing the research but before presenting it, I showed a preliminary draft of the completed study to a group of *auditors*, people in the field who would review the study to assess whether the conclusions were plausible given the data. Because this study was conducted in the field of instructional technology, all of the auditors were instructional designers. One part of the study was a comparison of the design process followed by museum exhibit designers and the Dick and Carey (1995) model of instructional systems design, which was then (and remains to this day) the dominant model of design taught in academic instructional and educational technology programs.

The auditors found that both processes are "linear [ones] that result in a finished product for an audience." Both processes are also "concerned with learning and operate on shared values." One of the most striking differences between the process used in museums and that in the Dick and Carey ISD model, however, is the lack of evaluation in the museum exhibit design process. "I admit, I'm an adherent of evaluation," noted one auditor, a trained instructional designer.

Especially troubling to the auditors was the absence of a criterion-referenced test of learning. I asked the auditor who raised the issue: How would museum staffs "test" museum visitors to quantify learning? Many visitors do not attend with that type of agenda, and exhibits are usually designed without any formal learning objectives. (In fact, one of the informants for the study commented, "An objective? What's an objective?" meaning that museum exhibit designers do not establish behavior objectives in the early phases of design as instructional designers do.)

Indeed, the absence of analysis and evaluation phases from the museum exhibit design process baffled these formally trained instructional designers. They assumed that these are required for any effective instructional program. Although the exhibits lacked the testing that instructional design models suggest is essential to instruction, the exhibits I studied were considered successes all the same. They were well-received by audiences; one was even recognized with several awards from museum organizations, and its schedule for school groups was usually fully reserved a year in advance. In other words, evaluation of the effectiveness of the exhibits occurred, but the type of evidence differed from the types of evidence that instructional designers are taught to value.

Furthermore, although instructional designers are taught that formal evaluation is essential to successful learning, research into everyday practice suggests that evaluation is advocated far more than it is actually practiced. For example, according to a meta-analysis by Arthur, Bennett, Edens, and Bell (2003), less than half of all workplace learning (38 percent) is tested for learning. Assessing long-term impact is even rarer.

That meeting of the auditors was a pivotal one in my own personal development as an instructional designer. I realized that the representation of the ISD process is more of a statement of beliefs about how instructional design *should* occur, rather than a statement about how the process actually does occur. Research evidence suggests ISD rarely happens the way that Dick and Carey recommend it. For example, several studies of practices by professionals in the field of instructional design have found that analysis and evaluation are minimally performed (Van Tiem, 2004; Wedman & Tesmer, 1993; Zemke & Lee, 1987), even though the people in the field believe that these tasks are important. Practical considerations limited their ability to perform these steps.

Why, then, do analysis and evaluation take half of the steps in the Dick and Carey model, leading a reader to believe that they represent as much as 50 percent of all instructional design activity? Analysis and evaluation activities are instructional designers' way of assuring our accountability to the organizations that sponsor our work. By documenting the need to analyze learning needs to make sure that the resulting program best meets the sponsor's needs as well as the need to evaluate learning programs to ensure that the programs actually accomplished what they set out to do, instructional designers document that their learning programs should provide tangible benefits to the organizations that sponsor these programs. Empirical evidence suggests, however, that either practical pressures of the workplace or a lack of pressure from sponsors to demonstrate these links leads to the rift between advocated and actual practice (Carliner, Qayyum, Sanchez-Lozano, Macmillan, van Barneveld, & Venkatesh, in preparation).

Museum exhibit designers have an entirely different type of accountability to their sponsors. Their sponsors are typically funding agencies such as national endowments for arts and humanities, which have established processes for funding museum exhibitions, whose costs can often run into the millions of dollars (U.S.)—several times the cost of even the costliest e-learning project. To avoid investing large sums of money in projects that are not feasible, funding agencies fund museum exhibits in two stages. In the first, designers prepare the storyline and blueprints for the exhibition. From that information, sponsors can determine whether the material is sufficiently compelling, the feasibility of the designs, and, because the designs are so complete, assess the completeness and accuracy of the proposed budget. With that information, funding agencies determine whether to fund the second phase, during which exhibition staffs build the proposed exhibit.

Looking again at the two processes, I realized that the ISD process does not include a request for funding. That's merely assumed.

In fact, instructional design projects rarely proceed unless they start with funding. (Designers might wish for more funding, but that's a different issue.) Although both types of projects actually receive funding, that the museum exhibit design process includes a phase for funding—and that the instructional design process does not—indicates that the funding process takes on more importance in one process than the other. In the case of museum projects, the lack of certainty of funding for building a project almost demands that it be acknowledged. Perhaps the certainty of funding before a project begins is why instructional designers do not even include funding as a phase in ISD, even though funding is just as vital to instructional design efforts as it is to the design of museum exhibits.

This taught me that a process represents what's important to the people documenting it, which might not include everything that occurs. In addition, to stress certain issues, people might over-document some parts of the process at the expense of others. Indeed, the empirical evidence suggests that the documentation of the ISD process over-emphasizes analysis and evaluation at the expense of design and development. For example, although the description of the Dick and Carey model suggests that more than one revision of draft learning programs might occur, the visual version of the process does not make clear just how extensive the drafting and revision process really is or suggest how much work it really is.

To find out how extensive this process is, consider the number of steps in the publications process in Figure 10.1. The publications process offers a good comparison because its goal is to produce a piece of usable documentation (Lasecke, 2006), a product that is similar to a piece of effective self-study e-learning. In the publications process, seven of the eleven steps are focused on development and production. Furthermore, Hackos (1994) suggests that, in a typical publications project, only 25 to 30 percent of a project is actually spent on analysis and design activities. In contrast, as much as 50 percent of a project might be invested in preparing the first draft of the content. Research also suggests that most publications go through two rounds of review and revision—twice as much as advocated by

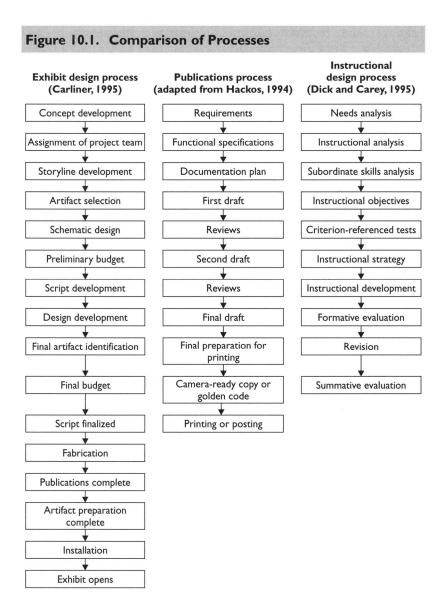

**Figure 10.1. Comparison of Processes**

| Exhibit design process (Carliner, 1995) | Publications process (adapted from Hackos, 1994) | Instructional design process (Dick and Carey, 1995) |
|---|---|---|
| Concept development | Requirements | Needs analysis |
| Assignment of project team | Functional specifications | Instructional analysis |
| Storyline development | Documentation plan | Subordinate skills analysis |
| Artifact selection | First draft | Instructional objectives |
| Schematic design | Reviews | Criterion-referenced tests |
| Preliminary budget | Second draft | Instructional strategy |
| Script development | Reviews | Instructional development |
| Design development | Final draft | Formative evaluation |
| Final artifact identification | Final preparation for printing | Revision |
| Final budget | Camera-ready copy or golden code | Summative evaluation |
| Script finalized | Printing or posting | |
| Fabrication | | |
| Publications complete | | |
| Artifact preparation complete | | |
| Installation | | |
| Exhibit opens | | |

the Dick and Carey representation of the model (Carliner, Qayyum, Sanchez-Lozano, & Macmillan, in preparation). In other words, the Dick and Carey model provides a partisan and incomplete view of the actual effort involved in producing learning materials, much less e-learning materials, which are significantly more writing- and graphics-intensive than materials for classroom courses and can involve extensive production of multimedia components. To represent time-consuming design, development, and revision in a small percentage of steps is in significantly underestimate their importance.

Reducing and simplifying these steps does not mean that they do not occur, or that the processes developed within organizations overlook these steps. That ISD overlooks these issues, however, suggests that the value system of the field is mis-aligned with the work of the field. The next section explores additional practical dimensions of this mis-alignment.

# Nine Reasons Why Instructional Systems Design Needs an Overhaul

As suggested in the last section, ISD is a value system that is closely held by instructional designers. To demonstrate its commitment to this value system, the training industry has invested extensive resources in ISD, and academic programs rely heavily on ISD as a theoretical base for their programs.

Although the value system is closely held, actual practice widely differs from advocated practice. In the mid-1980s, Zemke and Lee (1987) conducted a survey of ISD practice and found that few instructional designers make full use of ISD in practice. Some of the most widely performed tasks are writing objectives, development, and post-class surveys, while some of the least widely performed tasks are needs analysis and advanced evaluation—the phases that are emphasized most in ISD. Later studies (such as van Tiem, 2004, and Wedman & Tesmer, 1993) not only confirm these findings but show that the situation has not changed much with time.

That's because ISD is prescriptive—that is, describes the way instructional design theorists recommend that practice occur, as opposed to descriptive, that is, representative of everyday practice.

Not surprisingly, numerous specific issues with ISD have arisen over the years that characterize the nature of the gulf between theory and practice. As in many other spheres of life, people grow comfortable with this gulf between the ideals advocated and the realities experienced. This gulf between the ideal and the real also creates a cognitive dissonance for those who are entering the profession. The problems with ISD are not unique to e-learning, but the rise of e-learning has helped to make these problems all the more glaring.

The following sections describe some of the key issues with ISD. But because ISD is, at its core, a value system, confronting these specific problems and devising a response means challenging beliefs, some long- and tightly held. Such a process is easier said than done.

## One: Let's Get the Terminology Straight: Instructional Systems Design Is a Methodology, Not a Model

Although called a model, ISD is actually a methodology. A model provides a scheme for organizing phenomena that people observe in the world around them (dictionary.com, 2007). But ISD does not help practitioners organize a phenomenon that has been systematically observed. Indeed, some of the phenomena are not likely to occur naturally, such as designing evaluation instruments before designing actual learning materials. (It's not that this is a bad recommendation, it's that this is not something that is intuitive.)

Instead, ISD recommends a process for designing learning materials. The term "methodology" more aptly describes a recommended process.

## Two: ISD Represents Recommendations for Instructional Designers Working in the Mid-Twentieth Century

As noted earlier, ISD was first developed in the 1940s and emerged in its current form in the 1970s. In many instances, curriculum specialists (who are often educated with instructional designers and might not be instructional designers) would use instructional design models to help them effectively choose an off-the-shelf pro-gram, rather than design a new one.

A lot has changed since then. At the least, instructional design-ers are increasingly hired to design materials. At the most, each sector in which instructional design is practiced has been revolu-tionized. Consider the changes in primary and secondary educa-tion. In the early 1980s, businesses began taking an active interest in schooling and, as a result of that, school curricula have increas-ingly focused on preparation for the workforce, taken a back-to-basics approach, and are assessed with standardized tests. Scripted curricula have been introduced into some schools to teacher-proof education in an effort to ensure compliance with the curricula and performance targets for students (Kozol, 2005). Similar revolutions have occurred in workplace learning. Training departments in cor-porations have repositioned themselves as performance improve-ment centers, focused on providing prompt service to sponsors in helping them address the performance problems of their staffs. e-Learning has become increasingly pivotal to learning programs in all sectors, either as a primary means of providing learning pro-grams or as a means of supporting a classroom curriculum. This blending of e- and classroom learning has led to the development of more sophisticated curricula, ones that require more extensive design and coordination. In other words, both the circumstances underlying the design of learning and the actual materials designed have extensively changed since ISD was proposed.

What hasn't changed is ISD.

Although an excellent methodology holds up over time, and although the five general phases advocated by ADDIE are as crucial to instructional design today as they were three decades ago, some of the practicalities have changed. The sequence of phases should be condensed, and the specific issues addressed at each phase should broaden. For example, when ADDIE was first developed, the media selection addressed in the design phase primarily referred to the selection of already published learning resources. These days, it refers to the medium for presenting a message, such as text, audio, visual, or a combination. Similarly, the development phase assumed that most materials would be published as handouts for a classroom course or as a printed workbook, rather than as an online course. As a result, ISD did not anticipate a need for conducting technical tests of the programming to ensure that an e-course works as intended (that is, if one chooses A in response to a multiple-choice question, that text addressing choice A appears, not the text for choice B).

More significantly, ISD is a rigid process that presumes that all projects will receive the same level of attention and that such attention is necessary for all types of projects. That's at odds with trends in numerous spheres, which increasingly demand flexibility. Consider the business world, in which the time available to design and develop products is diminishing, and organizations demand that their staffs find ways to condense their development cycles. Consider, too, schools and universities, where students see education as a consumer service and faculty see their instructional designers in a similar light. Instructional designers in these environments feel a similar pressure to find processes that let them provide services in a more timely manner. More significantly, this rigidity is at odds with the nature of many instructional design assignments. For example, some assignments merely involve a brief update to some of the content in a learning program. Following a full ISD process in such an instance would be like following a full process for tailoring a suit when all that's needed is an adjustment to the hemline.

## Three: The Description of the Needs Assessment Phase Makes Inappropriate Assumptions

Specifically, the detailed descriptions of prescriptive processes for ISD make two assumptions that often add unnecessary time and complexity to many projects. The first assumption is that none of the information needed for a needs assessment has been gathered or, if it has been, the information is not useful because it was not collected by a learning professional. In her research on needs assessment, Rossett (1987) notes that many people do not perform some or all of the needs analysis because they receive the same information that they feel that they would learn from the analysis from others in their organizations. Instructional designers reason that, if others have already analyzed the audience or assessed the needs, doing so again would duplicate work and waste limited resources. Documented ISD needs to reach the same conclusions that practicing instructional designers have already reached.

Similarly, ISD assumes that instructional designers have limited knowledge of the content of the courses they are developing, as well as the audiences. This is one of the reasons why most instructional design models devote so much attention to needs analysis. The needs analysis process provides a framework for learning about a topic and its audience and brings instructional designers to a sufficient level of competence that they can design programs to teach others.

But this assumption is usually a false one. In many instances, instructional designers have abundant experience with the organization, audience, and content. Consider an instructional designer within a corporation who specializes in online sales training and has designed fifteen earlier e-learning programs. Or consider the school curriculum specialist who is designing materials for third-grade social studies and has five years of classroom experience teaching that subject. Most instructional designers are not new to their jobs. Even when they are, they might have been hired for their expertise. Consider a consultancy that specializes in online medical training, which specifically hires medical doctors to write all of its e-courses. Although these experienced instructional designers have to ask the same types of questions as less experienced designers, in many cases, the designers already know the answers. What they have to do is identify and validate their assumptions. That requires work, but not to the extent advocated by ISD.

## Four: ISD Works Best for Learning in the Psychomotor and Cognitive Domains of Learning

Although ISD is promoted as working for all types of learning, it actually works best for designing interventions that address the psychomotor and cognitive domains. That's because the field of instructional design still has much to learn about learning in the affective domain. Consider instructional objectives, which the methodology prescribes for each course, and that instructional designers express in observable and measurable terms. Such an approach works well for learning in the psychomotor and cognitive domains. In fact, the process of choosing the most precise observable and measurable behavior for a psychomotor or cognitive objective helps instructional designers better clarify what needs to be taught and how to test it. To address learning in the affective domain, the methodology suggests that instructional designers re-conceive of their affective goals in terms of the psychomotor and cognitive behaviors that a learner might exhibit if the affective goal truly characterized their beliefs (Mager, 1997). Although this approach clarifies some affective objectives, it overlooks others, especially ones that are more central to the learning context than the learning outcomes, such as modeling of good examples and creating a positive learning environment. Other models attempt to address these issues, but only address tightly defined situations, such as Keller's ARCS model, which is merely focused on gaining attention in a learning environment (Sung & Keller, 2001). ISD models provide neither frameworks for uncovering affective goals, nor templates for incorporating them into design plans.

## Five: ISD Assumes That Instructional Designers Will Only Design Courses

Although some instructional models acknowledge that training can occur without instruction (Dick & Carey, 1995; Dick, Carey, & Carey, 2000), most instructional design models implicitly assume that the end-product of the design effort will be a course, even when they suggest otherwise. Indeed, even the Dick and Carey model only describes how to prepare a course, even though it acknowledges that learners might be able to improve their performance through other interventions.

With the growing interest in knowledge management (see Chapter 4 of this book) and performance support (Gery, 2002) as viable approaches to transferring knowledge online and off, as well as the emergence of new genres of communication online (such as wizards, guided tours, frequently asked questions, tips of the day, electronic coaches, and discussion groups) (Price & Price, 2002; Redish, 2007), and the recognition that broader organizational issues often impede performance—to the point that a formal learning program will not change performance (Gilbert, 1996; Rummler & Brache, 1995), assuming that only a course can address an identified performance problem is no longer sufficient.

Furthermore, such an assumption prevents instructional designers from considering approaches to transferring knowledge that may be more effective, efficient, and economical. This is especially relevant to e-learning designers, because online solutions are often outside the traditional scope of thought of instructional designers. As a result, some instructional designers do not view online learning materials as having the same legitimacy as more traditional materials.

In addition, when learning moves online, possibilities also arise for supporting the transfer of learning to everyday behavior through other online supports, such as wizards and automatic reminders (among others).

As with learning in the affective domain, ISD models should provide frameworks for identifying other possible interventions and templates for incorporating them into design plans and integrating them into the entire learning program.

## Six: ISD Assumes That Instructional Designers Will Prepare Formal Courses

Not only is ISD focused on the design of courses, but a particular type—formal ones. A formal course is one in which the instructional designer specifies the objectives of the course for the learner and defines what successful completion looks like (usually represented as a criterion-referenced test).

But much learning is not formal. For personal learning, that's probably intuitive, but it's also true for learning at work, where as much as 70 percent of all learning is assumed to be informal.

Informal learning is learning in which the learner sets the objectives and determines for him- or herself when learning has been successfully completed. These goals often do not exactly match those of the instructional designer, and completion can occur after the learner thinks he or she understands the content, which might be long before the learner practices using the content or takes a quiz to assess his or her learning. This contrasts sharply with traditional notions of learning and is the truest application of putting the learner in control of learning, as is often advocated for e-learning (Horton, 2000).

Although the ability of e-learning to facilitate informal learning is loudly proclaimed (for example, Cross, 2006), ISD does not really cooperate. Objectives and evaluation do play a role in informal learning, but not the same role as in formal learning. In informal learning, objectives clarify the content of a unit of learning, so learners' expectations are appropriately set. The clearer the objective, the better learners can determine whether the content meets their needs. Similarly, criterion-referenced assessments are a tool to help learners determine for themselves whether they have mastered the content. Whether learners take advantage of this tool is their choice.

## Seven: Although Technically Neutral on the Choice of Instructional Strategy, ISD Tends to Favor Mastery Learning

As a consequence of its focus on formal learning, ISD also tends to favor one particular instructional strategy: mastery learning. Mastery learning receives its name from its goal of teaching and practicing content until learners master the material. It emerges from Gagnés (1985) nine events of instruction, beginning with gaining the learners' attention, continuing with a discussion of the purpose of the program and previewing the objectives, presentation then demonstration of the content, extensive practice that fades coaching and helps learners apply the concepts as "far" as possible, and closing with a test of learning. This model dominates classroom and online instruction for the workplace. Knowles recommends something similar for teaching adults (Knowles, Holton, & Swanson, 2005). Many introductory texts for designing e-learning recommend it, sometimes to the exclusion of other approaches.

The mastery model may be suitable for teaching technical skills, especially in the workplace and for learners who have a limited background with the content. But the approach limits creativity in some ways. For example, it has a rigid structure and promotes extensive (though unintentional) use of lecture-like techniques in the early part of the program (even though practice segments can be highly interactive). In some cases, learners already know the content, but just need some practice before testing. In other cases, this model is taught with rigid prescriptions that are more based in belief than in research or practice. For example, to overcome monotony in the presentation of content, some texts recommend a required interaction on every third screen of the course. Although well-intentioned, such pronouncements only create practical problems—such as asking irrelevant questions to ensure that interaction standards are met. Mastery learning is out of synch with the constructivist and problem-based approaches (such as Jonassen, 1997) that have been advocated with increasing support since the 1990s.

## Eight: Most ISD Models Do Not Have Steps for Estimating Costs, Budgets, and Staffing

All learning programs are designed with specified budgets and schedules, have staffing needs, and must be approved by a project sponsor (either internal or external), so these issues are integral to ISD. In fact, budget and schedule needs often play a crucial role in design choices, because some design options require more funding and time than others. When choosing options, instructional designers must balance educational needs with development resources available. Because their development schedules can run between six and eleven times longer than those for a traditional classroom courses (and development costs are similarly higher), these practical issues are especially relevant to e-learning courses.

Although Reiser (2001) notes that ISD includes management issues, the most key ones—setting of budgets, schedules, and quality guidelines—are noticeably absent from most ISD models. There's no phase for setting a schedule or budget. There's no phase for gaining approvals. At best, they're assumed to be integrated into other phases, rather than given phases of their own. If ISD is a value system, however, at face value, these practical issues are not valued.

## Nine: ISD Takes a One-Size-Fits-All Approach to Projects

That is, ISD assumes that all projects are new ones with an equal level of complexity. In reality, a wide variety of instructional design projects exist. Some are new, some are revisions. Some revisions are simple ones, requiring either a brief update of information or a quick fix to something in error. Some revisions are more complex than new courses, more like historic preservations that are intended to bring a building up to code while preserving the crumbling exterior of the original structure. Some projects are intended for the classroom, some are intended for presentation online.

Of those ISD projects destined for presentation online, a similarly large variety exists. Some are intended for synchronous use (that is, instructor and students are online at the same time) and others for asynchronous use (that is, instructor and students are not online at the same time). Of the asynchronous materials, some are primarily instructional (such as tutorials), some are primarily informational (such as online references), and some are intended to actually perform work for learners (such as smart online forms and wizards).

On the one hand, a broad process can probably address what's needed to analyze, design, and develop these materials. But the materials differ so much that no single process without variations can really encompass all of these.

That's what the next section of this chapter does. It proposes a broad framework for approaching instructional projects that provides some consistency among the different types of projects, while proposing more flexibility to address this broad range of projects and the different development needs they pose.

# ISD: An Updated Framework

To ignore the concerns with ISD is to condemn future practice to rote, formulaic approaches, in an era when e-learning and the adoption of the performance approach demand broader, more flexible, ones.

That demands that ISD change. Ideally, it would be broadened and deepened to reflect what has been learned about the design of instruction since the first models appeared sixty years ago, as well as what has been experienced in everyday practice.

So what should the updated model look like? It must have a broader scope, addressing not only the basic process of designing instruction, but also encompassing the underlying design philosophies and design techniques. It must address both formal and informal learning. If it is going to remain the dominant framework of instructional design, it must also acknowledge opposing viewpoints on instruction. Indeed, it has a responsibility to alert practitioners that such diversity exists.

A possible version of ISD would therefore have three parts, as shown in Table 10.1. The following sections describe specific issues in analyzing and implementing this revised model.

## A New Name

As mentioned earlier, what currently goes by the name "instructional systems design" and is labeled as a model is actually a *methodology*. The proposed revision incorporates a methodology, but also addresses design philosophies and approaches. Because it takes a broader approach, it is tempting to label this a "model."

But it is not a predictive model nor, in keeping with current discussions of post-modernism in ISD, does it attempt to provide a singular approach to designing instruction. Rather, it is a

| Table 10.1. A Revised Framework of Instructional Design for Performance Improvement | | |
| --- | --- | --- |
| **Design Philosophies and Theories** | **General Design Methodology** | **Instructional Considerations** |
| Science of how humans learn | Three-tiered approach based on the complexity of the project: | Issues to address: |
| Philosophy of how humans learn | • Bronze | • Educational |
| Theories underlying the approach to the instructional prob-lem | • Silver | • Business |
| The business of learning | • Platinum | • Practical |
| Related theories | Adaptations to the process: | Techniques to use |
| | • Analysis | • Formal learning |
| | • Design | • Problem-centered learning |
| | • Development | • Informal learning |
| | • Implementation | • Performance without learning |
| | • Evaluation | • Other HR interventions |
| | | Conventions |
| | | • Pertaining to the form |
| | | • Pertaining to the medium |

framework for considering instructional issues so that designers can identify, propose, and develop programs that are appropriate to the learning context. This framework identifies the different philosophies guiding the design of instruction and provides designers with a framework for contrasting them. It also identifies different instructional approaches and provides designers with a framework for considering them, too. In other words, this "structure" for considering instruction is actually a framework.

Furthermore, this framework is not so much systematic as it is holistic. It attempts to integrate the disparate, sometimes conflicting, issues in instructional design into a coherent whole. Rather than telling designers what to do, it provides designers with choices at appropriate times and suggests guiding theories that can help designers make appropriate choices.

Because this proposed approach is holistic rather than systematic, and a framework rather than a model, it should be called the "Holistic Framework for Instructional Design for Performance Improvement."

## Component One: Design Theories and Philosophies

If ISD is a value system and the number of value systems underlying the work rise, such as postmodernism (Solomon, 2000; Voithofer & Foley, 2002) and constructivism (Jonassen, 1991), then the starting point of any framework is acknowledging this plurality of value systems. Admittedly, most practicing instructional designers prepare courses without formally considering their beliefs about knowledge and learning. At an unconscious level, these beliefs do guide the work. For example, the instructional designer who believes that a course must include a number of exercises and, with each, learners receive decreasing levels of feedback, is actually designing according to the behaviorist approach and specifically applying the concept of fading. In contrast, the academic community is extremely conscious of instructional theories. Individuals often fiercely advocate for a favorite, as characterized by some of the lively debates between Merrill and Jonassen in the mid- and late-1990s.

Perhaps the academic community can inspire practicing professionals to care about their beliefs and how they affect the design of instruction. Most instructional designers and design theorists share certain basic beliefs about learning, such as:

- Learning represents a change in behavior, whether that behavior is psychomotor, cognitive, or affective.

- The structure of the human information processing system affects the amount and type of information learners can absorb at a sitting (cognitive load) (Cooper, 1990).

- Learners learn best when motivated to do so (Keller, 1987).

- Learners must be actively engaged with the learning content to apply it to practice (although different groups argue about the best placement and nature of these learning activities).

Where design theories differ is in the approach to presenting and sequencing learning activities. The constructivists like to place learners in situations in which they can build their own understanding, including outcomes that the designer had not anticipated (Bruner, 2002). The behaviorists are most comfortable with pre-defined learning outcomes. The performance improvement group acknowledges both approaches, but also acknowledges that people can master tasks without technically "learning" to do them (Gery, 1991, 1995, 2002).

These different theorists also take opposing views on the science of learning. Behaviorists believe that learning is like traditional sciences, with the principles of behavior and effective learning that can be uncovered through research. Constructivists believe that learning is a different type of discipline, that its science is not an exact one, and that very little about learning has been definitively researched.

While this debate rages in the pages of academic journals, most practicing instructional designers are aware only of the design process, not the belief system that guides it and the assumptions about learning inherent in those belief systems. In fact, some design courses are behaviorist and are labelled constructivist because they are interactive. A more complete framework would inform designers about the belief systems that underlie their decisions and how those beliefs influence the design of instruction and its ultimate effectiveness in the workplace.

Specifically, this first part of the instructional design framework would address:

- The study of how humans learn, cognitive psychology. It would not only describe the learning process, but also the physiology of learning that is increasingly guiding this discipline. Additionally, this topic area would address related applications, such as Bloom's taxonomy of knowledge, Gagné's conditions of learning and nine events of instruction, the hierarchy of knowledge (from data to wisdom), and similar applications.

- The different philosophies about the way that humans learn:

  - Behaviorist (promoting a change in behavior, building on the tradition of B.F. Skinner)

  - Constructivist (constructing a knowledge system, as advocated by David Jonassen [1991], among others)

  - Humanist (helping an individual reach full potential, building on the educational theories of Thomas Dewey)

  - Classical (transfer of knowledge, known in the vernacular as the "spray and pray" approach to learning because content is "sprayed" at learners and trainers "pray" that the content sticks)

- Theories underlying the approach to the instructional problem, such as (this is only a partial list):

  - Experiential learning, providing learners an opportunity to experience a learning challenge and use that experience to change behavior and develop insights

  - Human performance improvement, identifying the root cause of the problem—skills and knowledge, resources, or motivation—and developing an intervention to address it (Gilbert, 1996; Stolovich & Keeps, 1999)

  - Minimalism, providing learners with the least amount of material needed to affect a change in behavior (Carroll, 1990).

- Business factors underlying design considerations, especially those regarding the funding for learning programs, development schedules, and design guidelines.

Consider the last issue—design guidelines. An instructional designer might hope to design a simulation when revising an existing course on a software application. But the existing course relies solely on less labor-intensive drill-and-practice exercises. The simulation is both inconsistent with the existing course and costlier than the prevailing budget. Most likely, the suggestion will be nixed by management.

In other words, although many educators value learning for its own sake and might design e-learning programs accordingly, the organizations that fund learning often have more pragmatic issues in mind.

These practical issues are usually lumped together as "business factors" and always constrain learning, but most instructional design processes ignore the issue. Indeed, many instructional designers—especially those who do not plan to work in a corporate context—believe that business issues are irrelevant to their work. For example, one Ph.D. student recently commented: "I have a problem [about the need to read the] chapter about [the] business perspective . . . you know, corporate world is not my major interest."

The truth is, business realities such as budget and schedule dictate design choices, so a comprehensive framework must incorporate them. Specifically, the framework needs to identify the types of assets that organizations typically invest in learning (such as funds, staffing, technology, and facilities), the business principles that determine whether or not these assets are effectively used, and how organizations assess the return on investments in learning.

- Related concepts, such as modeling and gaming theory (for use in the construction of case studies, games, and simulations [Greenblat, 1988; Prensky, 2000]); computer-human interaction (for the design of e-learning and electronic performance support [Schneiderman, 1998]); artificial intelligence (International Artificial Intelligence in Education Society); and rhetorical theory (strategies for influencing learners, such as the influence of genre) (Berkenkotter & Huckin, 1995). Although it is often approached as a distinct discipline, instructional design is actually an interdisciplinary field that draws heavily from other disciplines. A complete framework of instructional design would acknowledge these disciplines and suggest how they influence our practice.

## Component Two: General Design Methodology

Rather than focusing on the process—ADDIE—first, the ISD framework should first focus on the complexity of the project. This, in turn, provides a framework for considering which tasks are necessary in design and development, and the level of flexibility needed. The following sections explore these issues. I first present a three-tiered approach to projects, then present the implications of this three-tiered approach to ADDIE.

### A Three-Tiered Approach to e-Learning Projects

To address the one-size-fits-all problem of ISD frameworks, e-learning entrepreneur Elliot Masie (2005) proposed that organizations classify e-learning projects into one of three tiers of effort and investment. When organizations launch an e-learning project, they would first identify its tier to determine how to approach it. The following sections elaborate on Masie's initially modest proposal. Each section defines tiers, provides examples of projects typical of that tier, describes the effort and investment typical of such projects, and identifies instructional design considerations for projects typical of that tier.

**Bronze—The Most Basic e-Learning Projects.** Bronze projects are the simplest in terms of their scope and, therefore, require the least instructional design effort. Masie suggested that bronze projects are ones that have either a limited impact on the organization, a limited number of learners (often fewer than one hundred), or are determined for other reasons to require limited instructional design effort.

In terms of technical skills, a typical bronze project first uses rapid e-learning tools in which the slides from an existing presentation are tweaked for appearance and clarity, then involves either recording of a narration or transcription of a lecture, and last involves adding a brief multiple-choice test to quickly assess understanding and a satisfaction survey to assess learners' reaction to the content. In most cases, learning professionals become involved in bronze projects late, after the decision to produce training has been made and often after the deadline has been decided, and when little time is available for anything other than completing the program.

Typical bronze projects include:

- Revisions to existing courses that only require simple updates to the technical content rather than a wholesale redesign of content, such as a quick revision to a university course for which a new edition of the textbook is now available (but requires few changes other than replacing the words "third edition" with "fourth edition")

- Courses whose primary purpose is to document existing processes that are used by a limited number of employees, such as the manufacturing processes used in a single plant by one or two teams, and for whom access to subject-matter experts is easy

- Courses compiled from noteworthy, one-time presentations by subject-matter experts the organization wants to make available on a "just-in-case" basis—just in case someone would like to view the presentation—but without the expectation that large numbers of learners would take them

Because most bronze projects are a low priority for the groups that produce learning materials, bronze projects are often produced by the subject-matter experts themselves. In fact, the emergence of rapid e-learning tools, such as Lectora and Breeze, and easy-to-use learning content management systems (LCMSs), such as Force10 and OutStart, and course management systems, such as Blackboard and Moodle, which let people develop and update content with little training on the software, has facilitated the growth of bronze projects.

Bronze projects are often produced as second- and third-priority projects on an as-available basis (that is, as the person assigned has time) and with limited resources. Most likely, they are produced without much, if any, needs assessment. Although they might have objectives, the focus in terms of development is often "What content has to be communicated?" rather than "What do learners need to do with the content?" Focusing on the content significantly speeds development, although it likely limits effectiveness. Bronze projects are often published with little or no formative evaluation.

Although instructional designers can take full responsibility for bronze projects, in most cases, they play a limited role. At the least, instructional designers provide some basic instruction for subject-matter experts on how to produce effective learning content, then leave subject-matter experts on their own to develop the content. At the most, instructional designers prepare templates and other resources to guide subject-matter experts through a fill-in-the-form-like approach to preparing the learning resources and review the resulting content to make sure that it is reasonably clear and conforms to formatting requirements.

Because bronze projects are produced on the quick, with little or no involvement from instructional designers, many instructional designers look down on such projects. Indeed, the large growth of bronze projects are seen to usurp instructional designers' jobs and de-skill the jobs of those remaining is of great concern to some.

But not all instructional designers look at these projects in this way. In some countries in which professional labor costs are relatively low, production of bronze projects represents a significant business opportunity and is one of the key reasons for the growth of outsourcing in e-learning.

But bronze projects offer benefits beyond outsourcing opportunities for some low-cost organizations. Because many bronze projects are low priority, they would not have been attempted when the majority of learning was presented in the classroom and technology-based instruction was assumed to require five to twenty-two times the effort of a classroom course. So another way of looking at bronze projects is that they make it possible for organizations to make training available that might not have been feasible in the past.

Indeed, in many cases, bronze projects are not intended to actually be used. They're like many of the reference books that people buy on impulse at a book sale—something that primarily is intended to sit on a shelf but that the reader knows is available should he or she ever want to read it. If there's a high likelihood that the content will never actually be used, why should an organization invest significant resources in developing it?

**Silver Middle-of-the-Road, Basic e-Learning Projects.** The next tier of e-learning projects is silver. Silver projects have either a high impact on the organization or a high volume of learners (between one hundred and one thousand), but rarely both, and, as a result, require a more significant investment of resources than do bronze projects.

In terms of technical skills, a typical silver project might involve some instructional design effort, including a limited needs assessment, the specification of well-articulated learning objectives, and the development of an attractive screen template and graphics. Instructional strategies, however, tend to be basic—silver projects often rely exclusively on adaptations of the mastery model of learning adapted from Gagné's (1985) nine events of instruction or games that rely on templates from other sources, such as Jeopardy. Organizations typically conduct verification tests to ensure that the e-learning programs work as expected, but often forgo pilot testing with learners because of the time and expense involved. In most cases, the learning professionals become involved in silver projects after leaders have decided that training is needed but when there is sufficient time to develop the e-learning program.

Typical silver projects include:

- Technical training courses, especially software and systems training, like the training for a new customer service system or for compliance training (where the requirement is that students take a course)

- Conversion of existing classroom courses to online formats, which involve reconceiving and redesigning content for a new medium, but for which most other aspects of the needs assessment, objectives, and assessment are already complete

- e-Learning materials intended for the general public but for which funding is limited, such as a web-based course on healthy eating that a public health department wants to develop

Because most silver projects involve some level of needs assessment, specification of learner outcomes, specification of an evaluation strategy, and moderate to complex instructional design strategies, they typically require that instructional designers play a central role in preparing them. In addition, because most of these courses require a more attractive visual appearance than bronze projects and more complex programming, they typically require that instructional designers not only have strong instructional design skills, a command of the subject matter, and an understanding of the impact of the content on the organization, but also strong production skills, such as skills in using web authoring tools like Dreamweaver and Flash.

However, silver projects typically have strong limits on resources, either tight schedules or budgets, or strong involvement by subject-matter experts whose understanding of instructional design is limited. As a result, instructional designers typically feel constrained in working on them. In some instances, they feel as though they could have produced stronger work had they had more development time or resources (such as funding for higher quality graphics or animation). In some other instances, instructional designers feel that existing standards and templates that were put into place to ensure consistency among learning programs and to increase the productivity of instructional designers limited the effectiveness of the resulting e-learning program. In still other instances, instructional designers feel that subject-matter experts failed to provide them with sufficient development time or dictated too much of the content or instructional strategy for the e-learning program to be as effective as it could have been.

The truth is, none of these issues is unique to e-learning. The same concerns have been raised about classroom training projects. Indeed, concerns about such issues have given rise to the movements within the field of educational technology to emphasize performance rather than learning, and within the field of workplace learning and development to emphasize a tighter alignment with sponsors and corporate goals. The belief is that, in doing so, learning projects might receive more resources and that subject-matter experts might better trust instructional designers to produce learning programs, and interfere less in development.

Although bronze projects might, in the future, be the most prevalent e-learning projects, silver ones typically consume most instructional designers' time.

**Platinum—The Most Extensive e-Learning Projects.** The top tier of e-learning projects is platinum. Platinum projects have both a high impact on the organization and a high volume of learners (over one thousand, but often in the tens of thousands). As a result, these projects not only require a significant investment of resources, but the return for such an investment is often so high that they can be easily justified.

In terms of technical skills, platinum projects require the most extensive instructional design and production skills. Because platinum projects often affect large numbers of students, sponsors have a vested interest in ensuring that the courses meet learners' needs and, therefore, invest extensively in needs assessment, specification of learning objectives, and development of evaluation instruments to ensure success. Similarly, because platinum courses often address both a high-impact topic and a wide variety of learners, they typically require complex instructional design that captures learners' interests, appeals to a variety of interests and learning styles, and ensures that learning "sticks." In many cases, this involves the development of sophisticated animations, videos, and simulations to enhance the learning experience and immerse students in the application of the content. In many cases, too, this involves the development of supplemental resources to support learners in applying the content, such as the development of job aids that accompany training courses and online tutors for academic courses.

Similarly, because of the large number of learners served by the course and the high need for them to master the content, not only do organizations invest in verification testing but also do up-front pilot testing. These pilot tests not only assess the likelihood that the learning content will achieve its objectives with the designated learners, but if it doesn't, they can be used to try to pinpoint what's not working so that it can be corrected before the e-learning materials go into wide use.

In addition, because most platinum projects have such a high requirement for success, instructional designers typically become involved in these projects early, when they can not only contribute to the design of the program but, more fundamentally, to the definition of what the project actually entails.

Typical platinum projects include:

- High-volume, off-the-shelf e-learning courses, including courses that are typically required in many academic programs, such as calculus, statistics, and Shakespeare; courses that are commonly taught in the workplace, such as diversity, safety, and MS Office applications; or common commercial courses, such as courses to teach pre-school children the alphabet

- Courses that support high-priority, organization-wide initiatives, such as a change management initiative, a major revamping of customer service processes, a new product launch, or a management initiative

- Courses that address an issue that carries a high liability cost, such as simulation of safety challenges in an airplane or safety procedures for performing dialysis

Because most platinum projects involve extensive needs assessment, use of creative and inventive instructional strategies, and pilot testing, they typically require the most extensive design resources of the three tiers of projects, often involving specialists in related fields. For example, in terms of needs assessment, many platinum projects benefit from the involvement of a performance consultant, an expert whose focus is broader than that of an instructional designer. Performance consultants might suggest that learning programs alone might not solve the underlying performance issue and that a combination of interventions (that is, projects) are needed that work together to help sponsors achieve the intended goals of their project (Robinson & Robinson, 1996; Watkins, 2007). Similarly, because the e-learning programs produced for platinum projects often involve the use of animation, video, and other media elements, these projects typically require production specialists such as directors and engineers. Indeed, one organization even hired illustrators from a major comic book franchise to illustrate its e-learning program (Driscoll & Carliner, 2005). To ensure the most reliable pilot tests, these projects require the specialized expertise of usability testers, who have the expertise to conduct usability tests and assess the results and translate them into tangible "action items" for improvement.

As a result of this need for highly specialized expertise, which is often beyond the scope of in-house training groups in corporations and government agencies, faculty development groups in universities, and curriculum development groups in schools, many organizations hire "boutique" shops to handle platinum projects. This troubles some staff instructional designers because they lose the opportunity to work hands-on on some of the most choice assignments. (Although technically outsourced, because firms are chosen for such projects based on their design expertise, they are not typically included in the broader discussion of outsourcing in the e-learning industry. Indeed, the cost of these firms is often high by industry standards because they bring unique expertise to the table.)

Not surprisingly, many of the projects that receive recognition in the various competitions for outstanding e-learning programs could be categorized as platinum. Indeed, they typically rank as the most common type of project that wins awards, even though they are the least common of all instructional design assignments.

Therein lies the paradox of platinum projects. On the one hand, because platinum projects most closely follow the instructional systems design processes taught in university programs and involve the most extensive allocations of resources, instructional designers typically deem them to be the ideal. Indeed, many representations of instructional systems design assume that designers work on platinum projects.

On the other hand, because they're rare, platinum projects are not typical of everyday instructional design projects. Indeed, as just noted, when platinum projects do arise, many organizations choose to hire an outside firm to develop them. So perhaps these projects are not necessarily the appropriate ones on which to base prescriptions of everyday instructional design practice.

### Implications of the Three Tiers of Projects

Besides their being non-representative of everyday instructional design projects, using platinum projects as the ones on which to base prescriptions of everyday practice also has a more damaging affect: it sets practicing professionals up for disappointment. By emphasizing the process followed on the platinum project as the ideal, expectations among instructional designers—especially those with less experience—is that their projects should follow this process. When the projects inevitably do not, instructional designers feel disappointment. At the least, they feel that they should have done more on a project. At the most, they feel that they have been less than competent on the job. The sad truth is that the project never warranted that much effort in the first place.

This idea of matching the work process to the scope of the project has particular implications for e-learning. The rise of rapid design tools and LCMSs has raised expectations that e-learning can be produced rapidly (as the name suggests). Groups outside of course production groups do not realize that "rapid" merely applies to the process of producing the content, not to scoping it out or designing it. Conducting a full needs assessment and evaluation (processes that cannot be sped up much by rapid e-learning tools) are perceived to slow down release of courses.

In other instances, organizations can afford to invest the time, but courses that either have a short shelf life or limited audience might not warrant the economic investment in sophisticated design like certain types of simulation-based experiential activities and games.

Penultimately, in emphasizing analysis and evaluation, the platinum instructional design process also de-emphasizes development and production, even though experience suggests that these account for the overwhelming majority of effort (as much as 75 percent) on most projects. Consider the implications of the ten-phase Dick and Carey model, which only allots two phases to development— development and revisions (one could argue that formative evaluation represents a third phase that is allotted to development). Every other phase refers to a form of planning (analysis, requirements, and design) or evaluation effort. This might have been sufficient for classroom instruction, in which the material is presented live and the instructor can make changes while a class is in session. But such an approach is not sufficient for the self-study and distance materials produced for e-learning. For example, because access to instructors is extremely limited, self-study materials must be understandable to all learners on the first "read through." (And even if learners have access to a help line or an e-mail address where they request clarifications to the content, chances are learners will not receive an immediate reply, as they would in the classroom).

Although the description of the Dick and Carey model suggests that more than one revision might occur, the visual version of the process does not make clear just how extensive the drafting and revision process really is, or suggest how much work it really is.

Perhaps, then, a revised model should be proposed. The more generic Analysis-Design-Development-Implementation-Evaluation model is useful, because it provides a consistent framework for all three tiers of projects, while affording instructional designers the flexibility to alter the process to specific projects.

Table 10.2 suggests how that model might be adapted.

| Table 10.2. Suggestions for a More Flexible Model of Instructional Design | |
|---|---|
| Analysis | Before advising instructional designers on how to conduct a full needs assessment, the design should first advise instructional designers to scope out the project. Based on that, all specific approaches to analyzing a project and defining its requirements could be recommended. For example, if a project is initially deemed to be a bronze project, the extent of analysis might be curtailed. |
| | In addition, if the project is a platinum one (perhaps even a bronze one), it might benefit from linking analysis and design into a cohesive process known as participatory design (Spinuzzi, 2005). In participatory design, instructional designers start by conducting a brief initial analysis—enough to design a simple prototype. They quickly show it to a group of people who are representative of the intended learners to hear their reactions. Based on the feedback, designers rework the designs on the spot and show the revisions to the same learners. The process continues until designers have a usable prototype. This process is also known as rapid prototyping. |
| Design | The extent of design—both in terms of the general effort as well as the range of solutions considered—should be tailored to the needs of the project. |
| | For example, if an instructional designer is working on a bronze project that is essentially a minor revision of an existing course, the designer should be encouraged to focus on consistency. Ensuring consistency is no easy effort unless the designer becomes intimately familiar with the existing program; changes in terminology, instructions, and visual design, for example, can be unintentionally introduced and can be startlingly disconcerting to learners. |
| | Similarly, if an instructional designer is working on a platinum project, the project most likely requires two levels of design: (1) high-level design, in which the designer identifies all of the components of the performance improvement system (not just the course, but all of the supporting materials, from job aids to follow-up) and (2) detailed design, in which the designer prepares in-depth plans for each screen, page, or |

| | Table 10.2. Suggestions for a More Flexible Model of Instructional Design, (*Continued*) |
|---|---|
| | slide in the course that identify the instructional strategy to be used as well as the specific content to be covered. |
| Development | Development often requires a much more extensive set of activities than most general instructional design tests offer, although most instructional design texts that are specifically intended for e-learning do a much more thorough job (Alessi & Trollip, 2000; Driscoll, 2000; Horton, 2002). Furthermore, designers must also consider variations on the development process to address unique production issues for the medium in use. For example, video production requires shooting and editing video and sound. Animation production requires illustration, animation, programming, and synching. |
| | That said, the extent of activities also varies with the extent of the project. For example, most bronze projects involve repurposing of existing content. Depending on the extent of repurposing and the amount of additional material needed, the project might only have go through two drafts rather than three. In contrast, most platinum projects involve the creation of new content. In addition to requiring three drafts, the processes must include reviews to ensure that the material is technically and editorially accurate. |
| Implementation | Most generic instructional design processes overlook this set of tasks. Implementation usually involves launching the course (usually through a management system of some sort), promoting the course (so people know that they can enroll in it), tracking and responding to learners' issues with the course (Carliner, 2002), and tracking enrollments in the course. When instructional designers work in large departments (often with scores of learning professionals) or when they develop courses for an external customer, they often do not have responsibility for these. When instructional designers work in smaller departments, they are also responsible for launching their own courses. |

**Table 10.2. Suggestions for a More Flexible Model of Instructional Design,** *(Continued)*

| Evaluation | As noted earlier, despite extensive coverage of evaluation in the trade press on learning, research suggests that, other than tracking "satisfaction," evaluation is only performed on a limited basis. Often, it is performed on platinum projects because organizations made an extensive investment in them. But some argue that organizations perform extensive evaluation on platinum projects because, with their high budgets and strong executive support, they have a higher likelihood of success.

A revised instructional design process might advise instructional designers to adjust their evaluation plans to those that are feasible within the scope of their project. Typically, this might include satisfaction surveys, self-assessments of learning, and self-assessments of transfer.

A revised instructional design process might also advise instructional designers to design instruments that give them more useful information. For example, satisfaction surveys can include questions about the relevance of the content and the likelihood of using it in the future.

In addition, a revised instructional design process might suggest ways to effectively use technology to capture evaluation data with the least amount of effort. For example, although systems might not track the scores of individual learners on post-course tests in their student records, the system might keep track of scores in general so that instructional designers have some idea how well students are mastering the content. The systems might also provide an analysis of how students are answering each question so that instructional designers might be able to track down learning challenges to specific areas of the content.

Similarly, a revised instructional design process might advise instructional designers to consider the automated capabilities of learning management technology so that they can conduct follow-up surveys on the transfer of learning. |

In addition to determining the extent of instructional design effort, starting a project by classifying it as bronze, silver, or platinum also helps a project manager appropriately staff it. Most bronze projects require the least instructional design effort. Their less complex nature and focus on production skills, rather than design instincts, means that they can be staffed by instructional designers with less experience. As a result, bronze projects make ideal projects for junior instructional designers because bronze projects introduce these new workers to the profession on simple projects that match their current level of knowledge and experience—and on which they are most likely to succeed. (That the number of these projects is growing and that they require less experience has broader and more troubling implications for the field; but in terms of staffing, the implications are more straightforward.)

Because they are moderately complex, most silver projects require more extensive instructional design effort than bronze projects do and they benefit when staffed by someone with a broader base of instructional design experience. These make ideal projects for intermediate instructional designers. They also make ideal "move up" projects for junior instructional designers who are ready for more challenging projects.

Because they are extremely complex and often highly political, platinum projects not only require the most extensive instructional design effort, but the most experienced instructional designers. The lead designer on a platinum project requires both extensive instructional design and organizational experience. Because platinum projects usually require several instructional designers, they also provide a number of developmental opportunities for intermediate and junior instructional designers. By working with a qualified senior designer, the intermediate and junior members of the team are exposed to the types of issues that arise on platinum projects without being accountable for project-related decisions.

This staffing approach stands in sharp contrast, however, to the way that most university programs teach instructional design. Most encourage students to approach each instructional design project as if it were a platinum level. Indeed, class projects that, in the real world, would be classified as silver projects at best are often treated as platinum projects. Approaching instructional design in the classroom as a platinum project has the key benefit of showing students the most extensive version of the process. In the process of teaching this approach, however, instructors also have a responsibility to inform students that the class project is intended to expose students to the entire process and then explain what might be more typical of a real-world project. (Of course, the best way is for the instructors to have extensive experience working on instructional design projects in the real world).

The last implication of the three tiers of projects pertains to the maturity of the organization's approach to ISD. In addition to assuming that all projects are of a similar scope, ISD assumes that all organizations approach ISD with a similar level of maturity. Studies of similar processes in other domains suggest otherwise (Hackos, 1994). For example, the process-maturity framework for software development suggests that organizations have different levels of control over their own internal processes, ranging from chaotic to self-reflexive. That is, despite many processes that have been advocated in the literature, some organizations do not have their own processes documented or, if they do, they might not follow the documentation that closely. Others follow their processes extremely closely and use project experience to strengthen those processes. In addition, because of cultural and contextual factors, different organizations follow their own documented processes more or less closely.

## Component Three: Instructional Considerations

This last component of an expanded framework of instructional design focuses on the tactical: addressing the instructional challenge identified in the needs analysis. Plass and Salisbury call this *instructional information design* (2002, p. 40). Others call it detailed design. Instructional designers focus on three categories of considerations when addressing the tactical: general issues, instructional approach, and conventions.

## General Issues

Although research might suggest, in certain instances, which instructional formats are most likely to achieve the intended results, often the research was conducted under ideal situations, where the only issues the researchers had to address were educational. For example, the types of issues that these researchers might have had to address include:

- Nature of the skill, such as comprehension, analysis, or evaluation
- Prior knowledge of learners
- Learning environment

In practice, instructional designers must also contend with two other sets of issues. The first are *business issues*. Specifically, issues such as schedules, budgets, available technology, and organizational initiatives affect the content an instructional designer can include and how the content is taught. For example, if an instructional designer believes that an online course should include sound, but the computers that learners will use to take the course do not contain sound cards, the course will not contain sound, no matter how apropos sound seems to the course.

Or consider the application of learning styles to a training course. To fully implement this, an instructional designer would need to prepare completely different versions of the same material; after all, a visual presentation substantially differs from a verbal presentation of the content. Realistically, developing separate versions of the same course is beyond the scope of most budgets, so most instructional designers compromise by trying to address as many learning styles as possible within the framework of a single course. (In fact, most research on the effectiveness of various instructional methods does not even consider the budgetary constraints of the course.)

The second additional set of issues pertains to *personal preferences*. Regardless of the cost-effectiveness of e-learning, the practical reality is that an instructional designer who is techno-phobic is less likely to choose an electronic approach than one who is techno-phonic (that is, embraces technology). A more significant issue is the instructional designer's previous experience. If the designer has faced a situation like the current one before and had good luck with a particular approach, the designer is likely to choose it.

## Instructional Approach

After sorting through these general issues, the instructional designer must choose an instructional approach, such as mastery learning, discovery learning, case-based learning, gaming-simulation, learning without instruction, and other interventions that improve performance.

As noted earlier, some popular ISD models imply that the use of mastery learning is a learning strategy. Others do not suggest an approach; they don't suggest any instructional approaches that may be used. These models merely tell designers when to make these decisions. That seems like a significant oversight. After all, if the heart of instructional design is designing instruction, the model should help designers make decisions about instruction (or at least direct them to helpful frameworks of thinking and resources).

Furthermore, an instructional designer is only as effective as the "bag of tricks" he or she brings to a particular challenge. By including the "bag of tricks" in the framework, the model implicitly suggests the value of broad experience to instructional designers.

## Convention

The third category of instructional considerations pertains to something called *convention,* which refers to the expectations that learners bring to various learning experiences (Kostelnick & Roberts, 1998). For example, one of the many conventions in asynchronous e-learning tutorials is bookmarking, the ability to leave a course and resume it at the point at which the learner left off. Instructional designers need not include the ability to bookmark but risk upsetting learners unless instructors alert learners in advance that they plan to break with this convention.

In addition, some of the conventions come from the instructional context—that is, what learners expect to learn—and some come from the online context—that is, as a standard convention of working online. An instructional convention might be a break in a webinar. An online convention might be the forward and back buttons at the bottom of the screen. Such conventions are studied in the field of human factors.

Conventions are rarely documented, but that does not prevent learners from expecting them. By explicitly alerting designers to conventions as part of the design process, designers can "design in" these conventions or, if they choose to ignore the conventions, can do so purposely and manage the expectations of learners accordingly (Kostelnick & Roberts, 1998).

# Concluding Thoughts

If this adapted framework of instructional design gains acceptance in practice, it would benefit the design of e-learning and affect both practice and teaching in the broader realm of educational technology. At the least, this design framework might broaden the discussion of design from its almost single-note discussion of methodology (and corollary presentation of checklists of activities) to a more complete consideration of instructional problems—adequately defining them and crafting appropriate and realistic solutions. This framework also introduces economic, technical, political, and philosophical issues into the consideration of designs, rather than merely focusing on instructional issues. Certainly instructional considerations are paramount, but the reality is that the choice of solutions is often affected as much by these other factors as by instructional issues. To ignore their role in design is to provide incomplete guidance to instructional designers.

At the most, this design framework might influence education, practice, and research in educational technology. In education, this approach suggests that the movement away from process-oriented approaches to teaching instructional design to problem-centered approaches (Dabbagh, Jonassen, Yueh, & Samouilova, 2000) needs to continue. This is happening in academia, but most training programs on ISD in industry tend to take the process-oriented approach. In addition to problem-centered courses, education and training in ISD might also offer workshop-like approaches, in which learners critique existing work and, in the process, explore the impact of specific design choices.

In academia, the broader framework also suggests that programs might stress content outside of the discipline (especially in fields like communication and cognitive psychology) and add more courses on the business of instructional design—not just project management (already a part of many programs) but courses that also address strategy, business models, marketing, and strategy— issues that have as strong an impact on design choices but that are rarely addressed formally.

In practice, this framework could have an impact in three ways. First, by including a focus on performance, this framework could help designers focus their efforts on end results, rather than the activities of learning. One complaint with ISD is that "the underlying framework . . . has displaced the more critical focus on results" (Zemke & Rossett, 2002, p. 31). The second implication to practice is a move away from rigid applications of a cookbook-like approach to design now known as ISD to appropriate applications of learning and business principles. One of the flaws with the cookbook approach advocated now is that many implementations of it reward adherence to the model rather than the end results. (And in some cases, the resulting instruction should not be rewarded.) This framework rewards end results. The last implication to practice is a related issue: replacing the cookbook-like approach with guiding questions. Doing so allows practice to become more flexible because the model merely states the outcomes that must be achieved, not the means of reaching the outcome.

In research, this framework suggests the need for the continued growth of case study research. It suggests some of the issues that these cases should address: not just what happened, but also:

- The philosophical framework underlying the designer's work
- The design activities involved
- The complexity of the project

- The maturity of project management in the organization
- The balancing among educational issues, business issues, and personal preferences that occurs during design
- The design strategies used
- The conventions identified or ignored
- The technology platform

At some point, one or more researchers might analyze case studies to assess how well this framework meets the needs of practicing professionals and make further adjustments to it.

Another impact of this broadened framework is that it would tie up loose ends of conversation in our field: new ideas that emerged since ISD was first introduced (like the Kirkpatrick model, the principles of andragogy, and e-learning) and substantive dichotomies of thought (such as the behaviorist/constructivist/cognitivist splinter among theorists) and bring a workable holism back to our field.

The penultimate impact is that we instructional designers should feel empowered to reassess this framework every ten years and, rather than merely criticize it, either suggest ways to improve it or offer a viable alternative. After all, this framework is a living one.

The last impact is that it acknowledges that instructional design is ultimately a value system. This framework makes those values transparent.

# References

Alessi, S.M., & Trollip, S.R. (2000). *Multimedia for learning: Methods and development*. New York: Allyn & Bacon.

Arthur, W., Bennet, W., Edens, P.S., & Bell, S.T. (2003). Effectiveness of training in organizations: A meta-analysis of design and evaluation features. *Journal of Applied Psychology, 88*(2), 234–245.

Berkenkotter, C., & Huckin, T. (1995). *Genre knowledge in disciplinary communication: cognition/culture/power*. Mahwah, NJ: Lawrence Erlbaum Associates.

Bruner, J. (2002.) *About constructivism*. Found at http://tip.psychology.org/bruner.html

Carliner, S. (1995). *Every object tells a story: A grounded model of design for object-based learning*. Doctoral dissertation. Atlanta, GA: Georgia State University.

Carliner, S. (2002). *Designing e-learning*. Alexandria, VA: ASTD Press.

Carliner, S., Qayyum, A., Sanchez-Lozano, J.C., & Macmillan, S. (In preparation). *The value of technical communication: What technical communication managers track, what technical communication managers report*.

Carliner, S., Qayyum, A., Sanchez-Lozano, J.C., Macmillan, S., van Barneveld, A., & Venkatesh, V. (In preparation). *The value of training: What training managers track, what training managers report*.

Carliner, S., Ribeiro, O., & Boyd, G. (In press). Educational technology. In N.J. Salkind, (Ed.), *Encyclopedia of educational psychology*. Newbury Park, CA: Sage.

Carroll, J. (1990). *The Nurenberg funnel: Designing minimalist instruction for practical computer skill*. Cambridge, MA: MIT Press.

Clark, R. (1997). Keynote presentation. New Media Instructional Design Symposium. Influent Technology Group. Chicago, Illinois, July 24, 1997.

Cooper, G. (1990). Cognitive load theory as an aid for instructional design. *Australian journal of educational technology, 6*(2), 108–113.

Cross, J. (2006). *Informal learning: Rediscovering the natural pathways that inspire innovation and performance*. San Francisco, CA: Pfeiffer.

Dabbagh, N.H., Jonaassen, D.H., Yueh, H-P, & Samouilova, M. (2000). Assessing a problem-based learning approach to an introduction instructional design course: A case study. *Performance Improvement Quarterly, 13*(3), 60–83.

Deutsch, W. (1992). Teaching machines, programming, computers, and instructional technology: The roots of performance technology. *Performance & Instruction, 31*(2), 14–20.

Dick, W., & Carey, L. (1995). *Systematic design of instruction* (4th ed.). Reading, MA: Addison-Wesley.

Dick, W., Carey, L., & Carey, J. (2000). *The systematic design of instruction* (5th ed.). Reading, MA: Addison-Wesley.

Dictionary.com. (2007). Definition for model. Available: http://dictionary.reference.com/browse/model [Retrieved January 15, 2007]

Driscoll, M.P. (2000). *Psychology of learning for instruction* (2nd ed.). Needham Heights, MA: Allyn & Bacon.

Driscoll, M., & Carliner, S. (2005). *Advanced web-based training: Adapting real-world strategies in your online learning*. San Francisco, CA: Pfeiffer.

Gagne, R.M. (1985). *The conditions of learning and theory of instruction* (4th ed.). New York: Holt, Rinehart, and Winston.

Gery, G. (1991). *Electronic performance support systems*. Tolland, MA: Gery Performance Press.

Gery, G. (1995). Attributes and behaviors of performance-centered systems. *Performance Improvement Quarterly, 8*(1), 47–93.

Gery, G. (2002). Keynote address. Online Learning 2002. VNU Business Media. Anaheim, California, September 23, 2002.

Gilbert, T. (1996). *Human competence: Engineering worthy performance*. Silver Spring, MD: ISPI.

Gordon, J., & Zemke, R. (2000). The attack on ISD. *Training, 37*(4).

Greenblat, C.S. (1988). D*esigning games and simulations: An illustrated handbook*. Newbury Park, CA: Sage.

Gustafson, K.L. (1991). *Survey of instructional development models* (2nd ed.). Syracuse, NY: ERIC Clearinghouse on Information Resources.

Hackos, J.T. (1994). *Managing your documentation projects*. Hoboken, NJ: John Wiley & Sons.

Horton, W. (2000). *Designing web-based training: How to teach anyone anything anywhere anytime*. Hoboken, NJ: John Wiley & Sons.

Horton, W. (2002). Keynote address to the 18th Wisconsin conference on distance teaching and learning. Madison, Wisconsin, August 15, 2002.

Jonassen, D.H. (1991). Objectivism vs. constructivism: Do we need a new philosophical paradigm. *Educational Technology Research and Development, 39*(3), 5–14.

Jonassen, D. (1997). Instructional design model for well-structured and ill-structured problem-solving learning outcomes. *Educational Technology: Research and Development, 45*(1), 65–95.

Keller, J. (1987). The systematic process of motivational design. *Performance and Instruction, 26*(8), 1–7. www.learningcircuits.org/2001/sep2001/karrer.html.

Knowles, M.S., Holton, E.F., & Swanson, R.A. (2005). *The adult learner: The definitive classic in adult education and human resource development* (6th ed.). San Francisco, CA: Butterworth-Heinemann.

Kostelnick, C., & Roberts, D. (1998). *Designing visual language: Strategies for professional communicators*. New York: Allyn & Bacon.

Kozol, J. (2005). Still separate, still unequal. *Harper's, 311*(1864), 41–54.

Lasecke, J. (2006). Stop guesstimating, start estimating. *Intercom, 53*(2), 7–9.

Mager, R. (1997). *Preparing instructional objectives*. Atlanta, GA: Center for Effective Performance.

Masie, E. (2005, September 14). Keynote address to the Ottawa Centre for Research and Innovation, Ottawa, Ontario.

Plass, J.L., & Salisbury, M.W. (2002). A living systems design model for web-based knowledge management systems. *Educational Technology Research and Development, 50*(1), 35–57.

Prensky, M. (2000). *Digital game-based learning*. New York: McGraw-Hill.

Price, J., & Price, L. (2002). *Hot text: Web writing that works*. Indianapolis, IN: New Riders Press.

Reiser, R. (2001). A history of instructional design and technology: Part II: A history of instructional design. *Educational Technology Research and Development, 49*(2), 57–67.

Robinson, D., & Robinson, J. (1996). *Performance consulting: Moving beyond training*. San Francisco, CA: Berrett-Koehler.

Rossett, A. (1987). *Training needs assessment*. Englewood Cliffs, NJ: Educational Technology Publications.

Rummler, G., & Brache, A. (1995). *Improving performance: How to manage the white space on the organization chart*. San Francisco, CA: Jossey-Bass.

Schneiderman, B. (1998). *Software psychology: Human factors in computer and information*. New York: Scott, Foresman.

Solomon, D.L. (2000). Towards a post-modern agenda in instructional technology. *Educational Technology Research and Development, 48*(4), 5–10.

Spinuzzi, C. (2005). The methodology of participatory design. *Technical Communication, 52*(2), 163–174.

Sung, S.H., & Keller, J. (2001). Effectiveness of motivationally adapted computer-assisted instruction on the dynamic aspects of motivation. *Educational Technology Research and Development, 49*(2), 5–22.

Stolovich, H., & Keeps, E. (Eds.). (1999*). Handbook of human performance technology: Improving individual and organizational performance worldwide* (2nd ed.). San Francisco, CA: Pfeiffer.

Van Tiem, D.M. (2004). Usage and expertise in performance technology practice: An empirical investigation. *Performance Improvement Quarterly, 17*(3), 23–44.

Voithofer, R., & Foley, A. (2002). Post-IT: Putting postmodern perspectives to use in instructional technology—a response to Solomon's "Towards a post-modern agenda in instructional technology." *Educational Technology Research and Development, 50*(1), 5–14.

Watkins, R. (2007). *Performance systems design*. Amherst, MA: HRD Press.

Wedman, J., & Tesmer, M. (1993). Instructional designer's decisions and priorities: A survey of design practice. *Performance Improvement Quarterly, 6*(2), pp. 43–57.

Zemke, R., & Lee, C. (1987). How long does it take? *Training, 24*(6), 75–80.

Zemke, R., & Rossett, A. (2002). A hard look at ISD. *Training, 39*(2), 26–35.

◆ ◆ ◆

# Summary of Main Points

Readers should take away the following main ideas from this chapter:

- Instructional systems design is the recommended process for designing, developing, and implementing learning programs (Carliner, Ribeiro, & Boyd, in press). It is a process that guides people who are developing learning programs (called *instructional designers*) in schools, academe, corporations, government agencies, and nonprofits.

- ISD was first proposed during World War II and emerged in its current form in the 1970s.

- Numerous versions of ISD exist, but the most generic is a five-phase process known as ADDIE: analysis, design, development, implementation, and evaluation.

- ISD is a value system that represents what instructional designers feel is important about instructional design, not what they actually do.

- Instructional design needs an overhaul so that its recommendations more closely match actual practice. Specific issues include:

  - It is a methodology (that is, a step-by-step process), rather than a model (a representation of an observed phenomenon).

  - It represents recommendations for instructional designers working in the mid-20th century. The realities of instructional designers have substantially changed since then, including new pressures for creation of content, more flexible approaches to design, and contextual issues.

- The description of the needs assessment phase assumes that no information has been collected and that instructional designers have no experience with the content or the learners; this conflicts with practice

- ISD works best in the psychomotor and cognitive domains of learning and offers limited assistance with the affective domain.

- ISD assumes that instructional designers will only design courses when the performance paradigm in general and e-learning in particular increase opportunities for providing other means of building performance.

- ISD assumes that instructional designers will only produce formal courses when the growth of e-learning opens opportunities for informal learning. Formal learning refers to learning experiences in which the instructional designer determines the objectives and what successful completion looks like. Informal learning refers to learning experiences in which the learner determines the objectives and when learning has been successfully completed.

- ISD tends to favor the mastery approach to learning, a behaviorist instructional strategy.

- Most ISD models do not have steps for estimating costs, budgets, and staffing, even though these are critical factors in design.

- ISD takes a one-size-fits-all approach to projects, in which the extent of design activity is the same among all projects, regardless of whether or not it's needed.

◆ ◆ ◆

# Guiding Questions for Discussion

- What are the major deficiencies of that instructional designers cite with instructional systems design (ISD)?

- Do you believe that ISD should be replaced? Why or why not?

- Do you feel that the proposed framework addresses the current challenges with the design of e-learning? Why or why not?

| Learn More About It | |
| --- | --- |
| Links | Encyclopedia of Educational Technology (available online to members of the Association of Educational Communications and Technology at www.aect.org) |
| Books, Papers, Reports, and Articles | Consider these classic texts on instructional design: Dick, W., Carey, L., & Carey, J. (2000). *The systematic design of instruction* (5th ed.). Burlington, MA: Addison-Wesley. Smith, P.L., & Ragan, T.J. (2004). *Instructional design* (3rd ed.). Upper Saddle River, NJ: Prentice-Hall. Also consider these classic texts exploring the deeper theories and beliefs of instructional design: Alessi, S.M., & Trollip, S.R. (2000). *Multimedia for learning: Methods and development.* New York: Allyn & Bacon. |
|  | Reigeluth, C.M. (1999). *Instructional-design theories and models, volume II: A new paradigm of instructional theory.* Mahwah, NJ: Lawrence Erlbaum Associates. Reiser, R.A., & Dempsey, J.V. (Eds.). (2002). *Trends and issues in instructional design and technology.* Upper Saddle River, NJ: Merrill. Seels, B.B., & Richey, R.C. (1994). *Instructional technology: The definition and domains of the field.* Washington, DC: Association for Educational Communications and Technology. |

# Chapter 11

# Converting e$_3$-Learning to e$^3$-Learning

## An Alternative Instructional Design Method

*M. David Merrill, Utah State University and Florida State University*

**About This Chapter**

How can instructional designers avoid *enervative, endless,* or *empty* e$_3$-learning (pronounced e sub-three learning) and replace it with *effective, efficient,* and *engaging* e$^3$-learning (pronounced e to the third power learning)? This chapter explores how and illustrates those instructional principles that can help. It starts by describing e$_3$- and e$^3$-learning. Next, it proposes how to achieve e$^3$-learning through the application of the first principles of instruction, which include the *activation, demonstration, application, task-centered,* and *integration* principles. This chapter concludes with a brief description of the pebble-in-the-pond model, an alternative method for designing more effective, efficient and enabling e$^3$ instruction.

## Introduction

There is a trivial debate raging in the world of words: Should the term *e-learning* be hyphenated? When the term *e-learning* starts a sentence, should the *e* be capitalized? And what does the *e* stand for anyway? Is e-learning educational game learning? Is e-learning edutainment learning? Is e-learning email or epistle learning?

For whatever else the *e* represents, it is apparent from even a superficial examination of instruction offered over the Internet that way too many of the websites that claim to be instructional are in fact not. Easy-to-use tools and inexpensive availability of server hosting makes it possible for anyone with even minimal computer skills to uncritically shovel information onto the Internet and call it instruction. There are even well-funded projects[1] that are assisting faculty to uncritically transfer their course materials, effective or not, to open-source sites on the Internet so that they are readily available to anyone. Are such repositories of notes, syllabi, PowerPoint presentations, and videos really instruction? Can we naïvely assume that college professors obviously know how to organize effective learning materials?

## e$_3$-Learning: Enervative, Endless, and Empty

This chapter suggests that for many of these so-called e-learning sites the *e* must stand for *enervative, endless,* or *empty* learning. The adjective *enervative* means "to weaken or destroy the strength or vitality of" something (www.answers.com, an online Houghton-Mifflin dictionary). In this case, *enervative-learning,* rather than promoting skill acquisition, actually interferes with the learning that should occur.

---

[1]See the URL for the William and Flora Hewlett Foundation, www.hewlett.org. This foundation is sponsoring a number of projects designed to make open source educational materials available. At this writing these projects include MIT Open Course Ware; Open Learning Initiative, Carnegie Mellon University; Open Learning Support, Utah State University; Sharing of Free Intellectual Assets (SOFIA), Foothill-DeAnza Community College District; SAKAI Educational Partners Program; and Harvard University Library Open Collections Program.

The adjective *endless* means "tiresomely long, seeming without end," or boring. *Endless-learning* is too repetitive leading to boredom. *Endless-learning* is too passive, devoid of interaction, allowing learners to disengage thereby failing to gain the desired skill acquisition.

The adjective *empty* means "without contents that could or should be present."*Empty-learning* fails to implement those instructional strategies that have been found to be necessary for learning to occur. Too much so called e-learning is merely information transferred to the Internet without appropriate demonstration, practice, feedback, learner guidance, or coaching. Information alone is not instruction.

This chapter refers to *enervative, endless,* or *empty* learning as e₃-learning (pronounced e sub-three learning).

## Enervating Learning

Figure 11.1 is a depiction[2] of the menu screen for an online course. In the original screen a medieval scholar is leafing through an ancient manuscript. His hand is on a stack of scrolls. Clicking on the various medieval buildings in the foreground takes the learner to the different activities of the course. The original shows the name of the course in the small window at the lower center of the drawing.

What do you think this course is about? See the footnote for the answer.[3]

Is the medieval theme related to the topic of the course? Does this unrelated theme motivate the student? Or does this unrelated theme make learning more difficult?

The designers of this course are under the assumption that a theme is motivating for the learners. This course also contains a

---

[2]The original screen is a very well-executed colored drawing and is copyrighted. It is difficult to get permission to reproduce an original drawing to use as a bad example. Our illustration is an original drawing that is merely a depiction showing the components and layout of the original sufficient for the purpose of our discussion.

[3]Auto Damage Estimation

**Figure 11.1. Irrelevant Themes**

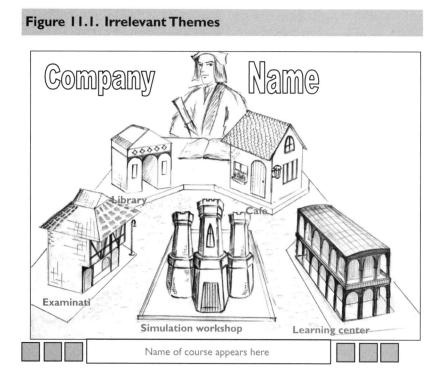

game in which knights joust with each other. The knights advance when the learner determines the correct estimation for a damaged part of an automobile. This medieval theme is carried throughout the instruction in various learning activities.

What do you think of when you see a medieval monk with scrolls? What does a castle or other medieval building activate in your mind? Probably not automobile damage estimation. The medieval theme of this course activates a schema or mental model in the head of the learner. The schema activated by the medieval theme is unlikely to have anything to do with estimating damage to automobiles. Learners have limited capacity for mental processing. This course requires learners to simultaneously activate two different, unrelated schemas: medieval schema and automobile damage schema. Trying to work with two schemas simultaneously significantly increases cognitive load. The result is that any increase in motivation is more than offset by an increase in learning difficulty because of the increase in cognitive load. Unrelated themes make learning the intended content more difficult. Our medieval theme is an example of *enervative-learning,* an instructional practice that actually makes learning more difficult.

Consider Figure 11.2. This is one display from an online course on workplace safety. When this display is presented, a voice reads the text at the left to the learner. As the text is read, the graphic at the right changes to correspond to the text. The second image is of the skeleton; the next image is a close-up of the vertebrae and disks.

When text is being read out loud, where does the learner look? Probably not at the image. Most learners follow the written text as it is being read. Humans are linear processors. We cannot look at two things at the same time. When our eyes are focused on the text, we cannot simultaneously look at the graphic. If we glance at the graphic, we lose our place in the text. Research (Clark & Mayer, 2003; Mayer, 2001) has shown that when a presentation contains three elements—graphic, text, and audio reading the text—that

## Figure 11.2. Inappropriate Uses of Multimedia Elements

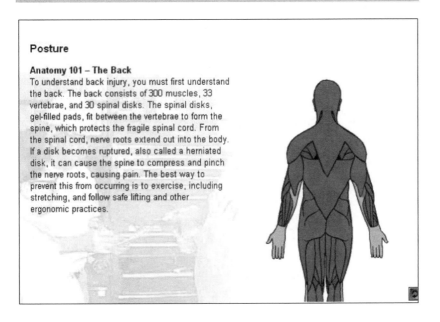

**Posture**

**Anatomy 101 – The Back**
To understand back injury, you must first understand the back. The back consists of 300 muscles, 33 vertebrae, and 30 spinal disks. The spinal disks, gel-filled pads, fit between the vertebrae to form the spine, which protects the fragile spinal cord. From the spinal cord, nerve roots extend out into the body. If a disk becomes ruptured, also called a herniated disk, it can cause the spine to compress and pinch the nerve roots, causing pain. The best way to prevent this from occurring is to exercise, including stretching, and follow safe lifting and other ergonomic practices.

there is a decrement in learning. It is better to have the graphic with audio and no text or the text and graphic with no audio than it is to have all three. Yet how often do e-learning courses read the text to learners when there is a graphic on the screen. Violating known principles of multimedia instruction interferes with learning and results in enervative learning.

## Endless Learning

The soccer game depicted in Figure 11.3 is designed to teach English listening vocabulary to non-English-speaking youth. An auditory message in their native language instructs learners to "Find the word *red*" by clicking on the speaker below each player and listening to the spoken word. The game can be used for any vocabulary matching; in this case the words are color words. When the learners hear the matching word, they are directed to click on the corresponding player. If they are correct, the player scores and the goalie pounds his fists on the ground. If they are incorrect, the player misses the net and the goalie jumps up and down in

**Figure 11.3. Edutainment**

celebration. Each response is timed and a running score is kept for the student.

Obviously, the purpose of this edutainment game is to find a way to motivate the student to learn the vocabulary words. Do you think that learners will find this game motivating? How many times is it entertaining to see the goalie pound the ground when the player scores? Repetitive feedback becomes boring. Is it more fun to see the goalie upset when there is a score or to see him celebrate when the ball misses the net? Too many so-called educational games violate the basic rules of effective games: challenge, increasing skill levels, and competition. The result is a boring exercise for which the learner quickly loses interest. Poorly designed games, far from motivating, actually create boredom and appear, even to young learners, to be irrelevant. Ineffective activities that are thought to motivate too often result in endless boring learning.

One of the most prevalent forms of online instruction is a textbook online.

Figure 11.4 is a small quotation from an online first aid course comprised of a frequently used digitized first aid manual. While it is convenient to have the information available online, it does not

**Figure 11.4. Online Book**

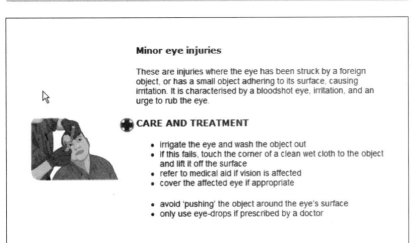

**Minor eye injuries**

These are injuries where the eye has been struck by a foreign object, or has a small object adhering to its surface, causing irritation. It is characterised by a bloodshot eye, irritation, and an urge to rub the eye.

**⊕ CARE AND TREATMENT**

- irrigate the eye and wash the object out
- if this fails, touch the corner of a clean wet cloth to the object and lift it off the surface
- refer to medical aid if vision is affected
- cover the affected eye if appropriate

- avoid 'pushing' the object around the eye's surface
- only use eye-drops if prescribed by a doctor

make for engaging instruction. Online electronic reference materials are not instruction.

## Empty Learning

Figure 11.5 is a representation of a single display from a course on office safety.

This course is an illustrated lecture on the Internet. In this lecture the audio and text are used more effectively than in the course represented in Figure 11.2. This instruction presents only bullet points from the audio rather than reading the entire text. Following each lesson in this course the student is asked to answer five multiple-choice or short-answer remember-what-I-told-you questions. Figure 11.6 lists a couple of sample questions for one module in this course.

Of course, there is a place for tell-and-ask instruction; however, tell-and-ask falls short of enabling learners to acquire the desired skills. Appropriate application exercises would better assess whether or not learners have acquired the skill of promoting office safety. Rather than merely asking learners to remember the rules, better application would require them to make adjustments in a real or simulated office. This application exercise would require

**Figure 11.5. Tell-and-Ask Instruction**

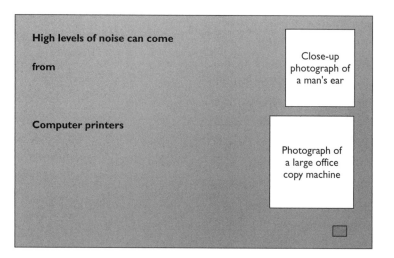

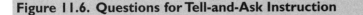

**Figure 11.6. Questions for Tell-and-Ask Instruction**

**Select the appropriate answer for each question or enter the**

**answer in the blank provided. When you are done, click the**

**button to submit your answers, register your answers and find out**

**your score.**

1. Which methods below identify ways to reduce office

equipment noise?

    a.  Relocating equipment to other rooms.

    b.  Using insulating dividers or pads.

    c.  Installing carpet and drapes.

them to first recognize a problem and then take corrective action. Rather than merely remembering the general rule, they would have to apply the rule in a specific situation. It should be obvious to the reader that applying the rules of office safety in several different situations would be an even more effective application. Adding appropriate application to this rather effective online lecture would convert it from empty learning to more effective learning.

Perhaps the most common approach to teaching computer applications is the use of *Simon Says* demonstrations. Do you know the game *Simon Says* or perhaps *Mother May I?* In Simon Says instruction, learners are directed to click on a particular menu or button ("Click on the copy tool"), as illustrated in Figure 11.7. If they click some other place on the screen, they are told, "No, this is not the copy tool," and then some prompt such as an arrow shows them where to click.

Some programs call Simon Says demonstrations *simulation*. While the instruction may simulate the actions of the computer program to a limited extent, this is certainly not simulating the kind of performance

**Figure 11.7. Simon Says Instruction**

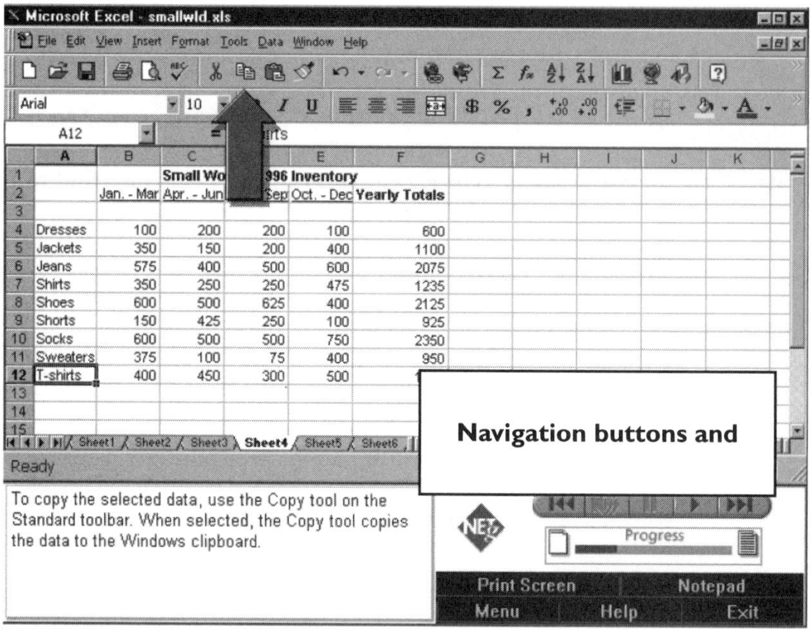

that will be required of learners later when they use the program to do real-world tasks. After you have completed a Simon Says demonstration of the commands for some computer application, do you feel like you can use the tool to create a spreadsheet? Is Simon Says really an example of application? Why is merely clicking on each of commands in a program an inefficient way to acquire the necessary skills? Simon Says can be an effective first demonstration of particular commands. At least it does get the student to actually click on the appropriate place on the screen. But all computer applications involve more than merely knowing the individual commands. It is necessary to be able to select the appropriate command in a given situation. It is necessary to know a sequence of appropriate commands to accomplish some sub-task within an application. More appropriate application would require learners to actually do a whole real-world task that requires a combination of the commands from a given program. Simon Says may be a first good step in effective instruction, but by itself it is still empty, incomplete learning.

# e³-Learning Is Efficient, Effective, and Engaging

How can we avoid $e_3$-learning? What characterizes $e^3$-learning? There are many instructional design models, theories, and procedures identified in the literature. I reviewed many of these theories and related research and found that most agree on five important instructional principles that promote effective, efficient and engaging $e^3$-learning (Merrill, 2002a, 200b, 2007, in press).

These first principles of instruction are summarized as follows:

- The *activation principle*: learning is promoted when learners activate relevant cognitive structures by being directed to recall, describe, or demonstrate relevant prior knowledge or experience.

- The *demonstration principle*: learning is promoted when learners observe a demonstration of the skills to be learned that is consistent with the type of content being taught. Demonstrations are enhanced when learners receive guidance that relates instances to generalities. Demonstrations are enhanced when learners observe media that is relevant to the content.

- The *application principle*: learning is promoted when learners engage in application of their newly acquired knowledge or skill that is consistent with the type of content being taught. Application is effective only when learners receive intrinsic or corrective feedback. Application is enhanced when learners are coached and when this coaching is gradually withdrawn for each subsequent task.

- The *task-centered principle*: learning is promoted when learners are engaged in a task-centered instructional strategy that teaches task components in context and involves learners in a progression of whole tasks.

- The *integration principle*: learning is promoted when learners integrate their new knowledge into their everyday lives by reflecting on, discussing, and defending their new knowledge and skill. Integration is enhanced when learners publicly demonstrate their new knowledge or skill.

# Australian First Aid

## Demonstration Course

We have examined snippets from courses that involve $e_3$-learning, but what characterizes an $e^3$-learning course? Consider selections from the following course from St. John Ambulance Australia titled Australian First Aid (1996, Version 1.5, Commonwealth Bank): "The aims of this course are to provide you with the confidence and skills to treat the injured in a range of emergency situations."

The course consists of four introductory lessons: (1) Aims of First Aid, (2) Accident Prevention, (3) First Aid Essentials, and (4) The First Aid Kit; twenty-nine tutorials that provide instruction in specific first aid procedures; two guided case studies demonstrating first aid in real-world emergency situations; twenty practice case studies that require learners to demonstrate first aid skills in real-world emergency situations; ten test case studies; and four supplementary test case studies.

Learners must complete each of the four lessons before they can begin the practice case studies. The guided case studies teach learners how to navigate the simulations in the case studies. The tutorials cover the skills needed for the case studies. Before each case study, learners are given a list of the tutorials that they should complete before undertaking the case study. Learners can complete the tutorials and practice case studies in any order. Learners must complete all twenty of the practice case studies before they can begin the test case studies.

A few selected segments of this course will be described in this paper to illustrate those first principles of instruction that make this instruction more effective, efficient, and engaging.

## Opening Simulation

After registration the course begins with a brief simulation, as shown in Table 11.1.

**Table 11.1. Opening Simulation**

| Learner Action | System Response | |
|---|---|---|
| Click on next button after registration | *Audio:* I'm a qualified first-aider, but I need your help. Could you find a phone box and call for an ambulance. This woman is unconscious, but she is breathing. She needs medical help urgently. | *Graphic:* The learner sees a photograph of a street scene where someone has collapsed. An officer is kneeling beside the victim and pointing out of the screen toward the learner. There are a couple of bystanders standing behind the officer, one with his hands on his hips and the other with his hand on his head looking as if they don't know what to do. There are numerous other pedestrians walking on the sidewalk behind the four figures in the foreground. |
| Click the forward arrow | *Text (overlays photo):* Will you need to place coins or a phone card in the public telephone? <br><br> *Buttons:* <br>   YES <br>   NO | *Graphic:* Close-up photograph of a public phone in a phone booth. |
| Click NO | *Audio:* Call for help by clicking on the buttons on the telephone to call the correct number. | |
| Click any numbers other than 000 | *Text:* Incorrect. You have dialed xxx. In Australia, you must dial 000 to get emergency service. Please dial 000. | |

**Table 11.1. Opening Simulation, (Continued)**

| Learner Action | System Response | |
|---|---|---|
| Click numbers on phone—000 | *Audio:* Which emergency service to you require? | *Buttons:* Fire Brigade Ambulance Police |
| Click button— Ambulance | *Audio:* Tone—Ambulance service. Don't hang up until I tell you! What is your location with nearest cross street? | *Graphic:* Information card displayed near the telephone, which includes the address, phone number, and other information. *Buttons:* Three choices for the address and cross street |
| Click button— Martin Place near Elizabeth Street | *Audio:* How many casualties are involved? | *Buttons:* One Two Three |
| Click button—One | *Audio:* What type of injuries? | *Buttons:* Possible heart attack Collapsed in street Unconscious but breathing |
| Click button— Unconscious but breathing | *Audio:* Are any other emergency services required? | *Buttons:* YES NO |
| Click button—NO | *Audio:* What is the number of the phone you are calling from? | *Buttons:* 02 309 019P2 02 309 0192 02 309 091P2 |

| Table 11.1. Opening Simulation, (Continued) | |
| --- | --- |
| **Learner Action** | **System Response** |
| Click button—<br>02 309 019P2 | *Audio:* An ambulance is on<br>its way. You may hang up<br>now. Siren sounds. |

*Narrator Audio:*

The importance of the part you have just played in this simulated first emergency should never be underestimated. But the reality is that there will always be more bystanders than effective first-aiders. Completion of this exciting CD-ROM package accompanied by qualified trainers during a special one-day practical course conducted by St. John's ambulance will equip you with skills and knowledge to provide life-saving first aid to the injured or acutely ill. First aid is one of the most important of all life skills. Acute illness or sudden injury have no respect for age or status, place or time, and many of us will be called on to deal with emergencies among our family, friends, or even total strangers.

What is the purpose of this opening simulation? Does it help learners recall emergency situations from their own experiences when first aid was needed? Does it provide a reason why learners may want to take the course? Does it help motivate learners to acquire the skills taught in the course? When considering the responses to these questions, consider, again, the Activation Principle.

*Activation Principle:* Learning is promoted when learners activate relevant cognitive structures by being directed to recall, describe, or demonstrate relevant prior knowledge or experience.

## Lesson 2: Accident Prevention

Lesson 2 is described in Table 11.2. This lesson stresses prevention by presenting a number of situations and asking the learner to identify potentially dangerous conditions.

Is this lesson teaching about potential accidents or merely focusing learners' attention on dangers that may exist around them? Is this lesson helping learners recall situations from their own experience? Is this lesson helping students activate those

**Table 11.2.  Lesson 2: Accident Prevention**

| Learner Action | System Response | Graphic |
|---|---|---|
| Click on Lesson 2 on main menu | *Audio:* Please click on items that represent a potential danger. | *Graphic:* Photograph of a typical kitchen. Various dangerous situations are included in the photograph, including knives close to the edge of a counter, cleaning supplies sitting out on the floor, dishes sitting on a dish cloth that drapes over the edge of the counter, a pan on the stove with the handle pointing into the room, etc. |
| Learner clicks on a potential danger in the photograph. | (Similar interaction for each of the potential dangers. If learners do not find them all, a message reminds them that there are more dangers.) | *Text:* Sharp knives lying around loose are a temptation for children and a potential hazard for adults. Make sure that they are kept in a drawer or purpose made holder. |
| (Similar to above) | (Similar to above) | *Graphic:* Shop with dangerous items lying around. |
| (Similar to above) | (Similar to above) | *Graphic:* Pool area with dangerous situations present. |

mental models that provide context for the first skills to be taught? When considering the responses to these questions, consider the instructional principles that promote $e^3$ learning.

## First Aid Guided Case Study

The guided case studies are simulations (micro-worlds) that place learners in real-world situations and ask them to make appropriate first aid decisions to respond to the emergencies presented. The format is a "Simon Says" type demonstration. The system indicates the step that is next and directs learners to take this step. If learners perform some other action, the system indicates that the step was incorrect and again directs learners on which step to take.

Figure 11.8 illustrates the interface for the guided and practice case studies. A menu on the right of the screen represents the first aid actions that learners can take. Clicking a button on this menu pops up a list of specific actions learners can select. For example,

**Figure 11.8. Interface Design for Case Study Simulations**

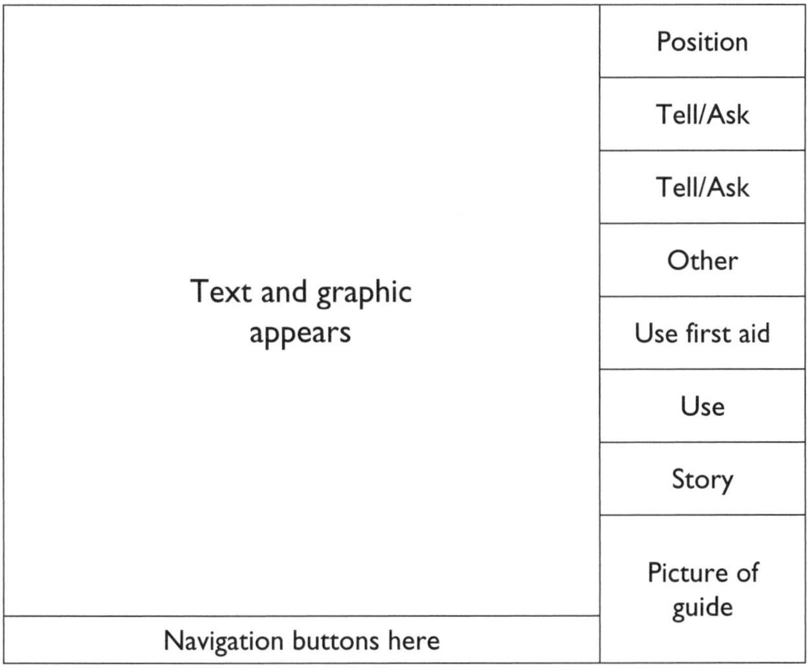

| Text and graphic appears | Position |
| | Tell/Ask |
| | Tell/Ask |
| | Other |
| | Use first aid |
| | Use |
| | Story |
| | Picture of guide |
| Navigation buttons here | |

clicking the button *Position Casualty* pops up the following list of actions: *lie in stable side position, lie in alternate side position, lie flat on back, . . ., sit down, sit (head between legs), . . ., bend over the back of a chair.* In the guided case study, only the button that is appropriate is active. Table 11.3 describes the first guided case study.

| Table 11.3. Interaction for Guided Case Study | | |
| --- | --- | --- |
| **Learner Action** | **System Response** | **Graphic** |
| Select guided case study from the menu | *Audio:* At the beginning of each case study, you will be given a list of the tutorials that cover the material you need to know to complete the case study. It is a good idea to view the tutorials before beginning the case study. You can view the tutorials at any time by clicking the tutor button at the bottom of the screen and then selecting the tutorial you want to view. | *Text:* This case study deals with materials covered in the following tutorials:<br><br>• DRABC action plan<br>• Side position<br>• EAR<br>• CPR |
| Click next | *Audio:* You are working in your office when you hear one of your colleagues call out and then collapse. There is one other person around and you have a first aid kit and a telephone available. | *Graphic:* shows an office worker lying face-up on the floor with a colleague kneeling beside him. It is obvious that the victim is unconscious. |

| Table 11.3. Interaction for Guided Case Study, Cont'd | | |
|---|---|---|
| **Learner Action** | **System Response** | **Graphic** |
| | The first thing you must do is check to see whether there is any danger to yourself, to anyone else nearby, or to the casualty. Click on the Other Action button, then select check for danger. | |
| Click button—Other Action—check for danger | *Audio:* When you think it is safe to assist the casualty, you must then check to see whether the person is conscious. Click on either the Tell/ Ask Casualty or Other Action button and select a way to check for a response. | *Text (overlays graphic):* You do not see anything that could be dangerous to yourself, to others, or to the casualty. Select the next step. |
| Click button—Other Action—gently shake casualty | *Audio:* The casualty did not respond, so you must move him into the correct position for an unconscious person. Click on the Position Casualty button, then select a position from the list. | *Text (overlays graphic):* You gently shake the casualty, but he does not respond. Select the next step. |
| Click button—Position Casualty—stable side position | *Audio:* The next step of the DRABC action plan is to clear and open the | *Graphic:* Casualty is shown turned into the stable side position. |

| Table 11.3. Interaction for Guided Case Study, Cont'd | | |
|---|---|---|
| **Learner Action** | **System Response** | **Graphic** |
| | casualty's airways. However, before doing this you should put on a pair of gloves from the first aid kit. | *Text (overlays graphic):* Correct. You roll the casualty into a stable side position. |
| | Check on the Use First Aid Kit Item, then select gloves from the list. | Select the next step. |

The Guided Case study continues by having learners engage in additional required first-aid actions, each followed by text and an audio message. When appropriate, the graphic is changed to reflect the situation.

◆ ◆ ◆

| | | |
|---|---|---|
| After the last step is completed: | *Audio:* You check the casualty's pulse and breathing after one minute, then every two minutes. | *Text:* Summary |
| | | [picture from case] Check for danger and response. |
| | A siren is heard, indicating the arrival of the ambulance. | [picture] Roll casualty into side position, clear and open airway, and check for breathing. |
| | When the ambulance arrives, the ambulance officers take over the resuscitation. | [picture] Roll casualty onto back, and give five full breaths in ten seconds. |
| | At this point, you should wash your hands thoroughly with soap and water. | [picture] Check circulation, and have someone telephone for medical aid. |
| | | [picture] Begin CPR, and continue until ambulance arrives. |

> Demonstration Principle: Learning is promoted when learn-
> ers observe a demonstration of the skills to be learned
> that is consistent with the type of content being taught.
> Demonstrations are enhanced when learners observe
> media that is relevant to the content.

This guided case study demonstration shows two things: First, the first aid actions to take when someone collapses (see the summary) and second, how to use the navigation commands of the simulation interface. This demonstration teaches the principles of first aid by *showing* rather than by merely *telling*. While the above storyboard does not show the actual photographs used in this instruction, the descriptions indicate that these photographs illustrated the first aid procedures that were being taken. They were not superfluous pictures included to promote "motivation." The photographs actually carry some of the instructional information. For example, the illustration of the *stable side position* shows how the patient should appear when positioned in this way.

When general information is merely presented (told) to learners, they have no option but to memorize the information and hope that it can later be recalled when it is needed. However, seeing the information demonstrated in specific situations enables the learner to form a mental model of the skills being taught. Demonstration is one key to effective and efficient learning. While information can be presented more quickly than appropriate demonstrations can be, the resulting learning is not efficient or effective because too much of the information is forgotten and cannot be used at a later time. Including appropriate demonstrations would seem to take more instructional time, but often the inclusion of appropriate demonstrations makes it easier for learners to grasp what is being taught, resulting in instruction that is actually more efficient.

## Tutorial on Facial Injuries

In our example, the learner goes next to the sample case studies and selects a case for a bleeding nose from the main menu. When advised to complete tutorials first, the learner goes to the tutorial described in Table 11.4.

| Table 11.4. Tutorial on Facial Injuries | |
| --- | --- |
| **Learner Action** | **System Response** |
| Select Bleeding Nose from the practice case-study menu. | *Text:* You should complete the following tutorials before undertaking this case study:<br><br>DRABC Action Plan<br><br>Facial Injuries |
| The learner decides to complete the tutorials before completing the practice case study. | |
| Click on DRABC Action Plan from tutorials menu. | *Text:* DRABC Action Plan Tutorial<br>This tutorial covers the following topic areas:<br><br>Introduction to the principles of DRABC<br><br>The DRABC Procedure |
| Click Next | *Text:* From time to time you may hear people say that they have done a first aid course but are not sure if they remember what to do. This is not unusual, because some people don't get much opportunity to practice and because first aid covers so many different situations and possibilities.<br><br>There is, however, a simple plan of action that provides an easy-to-remember, five step, "must do" procedure known as the DRABC Action Plan. |
| Click Next | *Text:* The initials DRABC stand for (items in list appear one by one) Danger, Response, Airway, Breathing, Circulation. |
| Click Next | *Text:* (The list moves to the left of the screen and each item is highlighted in turn.) Place the cursor over the title highlighted in blue and click the mouse button. |
| Click on Danger | *Text:* (Color of the word danger changes to red.) As soon as you become aware that a first aid situation exists and before you do anything, you must immediately look at the whole scene to see whether there is any Danger: to yourself, to any bystanders, or to the casualty. |

| Table 11.4. Tutorial on Facial Injuries, Cont'd | |
|---|---|
| **Learner Action** | **System Response** |
| Click Next | *Text:* Always check for danger … |
| | To yourself—You can be of no help to anyone if you become a casualty yourself. |
| | To any bystanders—Your task will become much more difficult if the people watching become casualties as well. |
| | To the casualty—There is no point working on an injury if the casualty is still at risk from passing cars or falling rocks, etc. |
| Click Next | *Graphic:* Photograph of a person lying on the floor of what looks like a shop. There is an electric drill lying next to him, still plugged into an electrical outlet. On the workbench above the person is an object hanging partially off the workbench. | *Text* (next to the graphic): You hear someone cry out and then a thump, so you go to see what has happened. You see a person lying unmoving on the floor, and you can smell hot electrical wiring. <br><br> Click on anything you think might be dangerous to yourself, to other people, or to the casualty. |
| Click on electric drill in photograph. | *Graphic:* same as previous. <br> *Text:* Correct. The casualty may have suffered an electric shock from the power drill, so before approaching him you should made sure the switch is off and the plug is disconnected. | |
| Click Next | *Graphic:* same as previous. <br> *Text:* You turn off the power and move the drill away from the casualty. However, there is something else that could be dangerous and which should be removed. | |

## Table 11.4. Tutorial on Facial Injuries, Cont'd

| Learner Action | System Response |
| --- | --- |
| Click on object on the workbench. | *Graphic:* same as previous<br><br>*Text:* Well done. Very often people are so intent on what is happening on the ground that they miss the hazards above them. Remember, always look up. |
| Click Next | *Graphic:* same as previous<br><br>*Text:* You remove the overhead hazard. It will now be safe for you to approach the casualty and check for response. |

A similar presentation is used for the other four terms of the DRABC Action Plan: response, airway, breathing, circulation.

After the learner has completed the DRABC tutorial he or she goes to the tutorial on facial injuries.

| Learner Action | System Response |
| --- | --- |
| Click on Facial Injuries | *Text:*<br><br>Facial injuries are those involving the facial features listed below:<br><br>    The eye<br>    The ear<br>    The nose<br>    The jaw<br>    The teeth<br>    Click on a facial feature. |
| Click on the nose from tutorials listed on the main menu. | *Text:* Injuries to the Nose<br><br>The three most common injuries to the nose are:<br><br>Objects in the nose<br>    (explanation here omitted)<br><br>Bleeding nose<br>    Some people, particularly children, have a tendency for<br>    their nose to bleed frequently and for no apparent |

**Table 11.4. Tutorial on Facial Injuries, Cont'd**

| **Learner Action** | **System Response** | |
|---|---|---|
| | reason. Others will receive bleeding noses from blows in fights or sports.<br>Broken nose<br>(explanation here omitted) | |
| Click on Bleeding Nose | *Graphic:* girl sitting in a chair holding her nose. | *Text* (next to graphic):<br>Bleeding nose. A bleeding nose is one of the most common first aid problems and yet it is one most often incorrectly managed. The correct procedure is for the casualty to:<br>Pinch the soft part of his or her nose and breathe through his or her mouth.<br>Tilt the head slightly forward. |
| Click Next | *Graphic:* girl sitting with head slightly forward and holding a cold wet towel to her forehead | *Text* (next to graphic): It also helps to apply cold, wet towels or an ice pack to the back of the casualty's neck and forehead in order to reduce circulation in surface blood vessels. |

Do the two tutorials described here implement the demonstration principle? Are learners shown what to do rather than merely being told the action to take? Do the demonstrations include relevant graphics that actually carry part of the instructional load? Could this demonstration be improved to more adequately demonstrate the skill being taught? How?

Now consider the Application Principle:

> Application Principle: Learning is promoted when learners engage in application of their newly acquired knowledge and skill that is consistent with the type of content being taught. Application is effective only when learners receive intrinsic or corrective feedback. Application is enhanced when learners are coached and when this coaching is gradually withdrawn for each subsequent task.

Do the two tutorials described here implement the application principle? Are learners given the opportunity to apply the skill that they were just taught? Which tutorial lacks adequate application? What could be done to provide more adequate application for this tutorial? Do the tutorials provide intrinsic feedback? Intrinsic feedback allows learners to see the consequences of their actions. Could learners see the consequences of their actions in the application that is provided by these tutorials? Do the tutorials provide corrective feedback? Corrective feedback informs learners of the quality of their performance and shows them how they did or should have performed the procedure. Is there corrective feedback provided for these tutorials? How could more effective corrective feedback be employed? Is there any coaching available for the skills being taught? How could coaching be included in these tutorials?

Lack of relevant practice, consistent with the real-world application of the skill, is perhaps one of the most common problems in instruction. Merely answering multiple-choice questions that require learners to remember what they were told is not appropriate practice. While remembering is a component of all application, actually using the newly acquired knowledge and skill to complete a task results in far more effective learning.

## Case Study Practice: Bleeding Nose

The case study practice is a variety of specific emergency situations. There are twenty individual case studies. Some of these include scalded arm, sprained ankle, insect in the ear, drowning infant, splinter in eye, etc.

Each of these case studies is a simulation that places learners in a real-world situation and asks them to make appropriate first aid decisions to respond to the emergency presented. The format is a semi-open simulation wherein there are multiple alternative actions open to learners on any given screen. As in the guided case studies, a menu at the right of the screen represents the actions to be taken. Each of the buttons pops up a list of actions learners can select (see Table 11.5). Unlike the guided case study, in the practice case studies all of the buttons are active and learners can take any of the actions listed. The feedback is appropriate for the action taken. Often this feedback includes advice about what learners should have done or may want to do next. Usually, the appropriate actions can be taken in any order. Table 11.5 describes the interaction for the bleeding nose case study.

Does this case study require application? How does coaching occur? Is there corrective feedback showing or telling learners the action they should have taken? In the tutorials recommended for this case study, learners should have learned how to treat a nose bleed and other facial injuries. The case study allowed them to apply their knowledge in a somewhat real-world situation. The learner in our example did not perform perfectly, but the system provided intrinsic feedback when appropriate, showing the learner what happens as a result of certain actions and corrective feedback by showing or having learners take the correct action. In this course, the level of coaching remains constant across the case studies because learners are allowed to complete these case studies in any order. Would a more effective coaching strategy be to decrease the amount of coaching with each subsequent case study?

Topic-centered instructional strategies typically teach task components in a hierarchical fashion by teaching all the related skills

| Table 11.5. Case Study: Bleeding Nose | | |
|---|---|---|
| **Learner Action** | **System Response** | |
| After completing the tutorials the learner goes back to the exercise case study. | | |
| Select Bleeding Nose from the course menu. | *Text:* You should complete the following tutorials before undertaking this case study:<br><br>Facial Injuries<br><br>Communicable Diseases | |
| Click Next button. | *Audio:* You are walking by a high school when you see a young boy who looks as if he has been in a fight. There is no one else nearby and no telephone, but you have a small first aid kit with you. Select your first action. | *Graphic:* A young man about ten or eleven years old has obviously been in a fight. His nose is bleeding and he looks frightened. |
| The learner is unsure how to start interacting with the tutorial, so he clicks on the Expert Advice button. | | |
| Click on Expert Advice | *Audio:* The first thing you must do is check to see whether there is any danger to yourself, to others nearby, or to the casualty. Click the Other Action button and then click Check for Danger. | |
| Click button—Other Action—Check for Danger. | *Text:* You do not see anything that could be dangerous to yourself, to others, or to the casualty.<br><br>Select your next step. | |
| Click Position Casualty button . . . sit with his head slightly forward. | *Text:* Yes, the casualty should sit with his head slightly forward. | *Graphic:* Close-up of young man's face showing the bloody nose and a black eye beginning to develop. |

| Table 11.5. Case Study: Bleeding Nose, Cont'd | |
| --- | --- |
| **Learner Action** | **System Response** |
| Click on Tell/Ask Casualty . . . to apply pressure to his nose. | *Text:* He asks you what part of his nose he should hold. Click on the part of the casualty's nose to which he should apply pressure. |
| Click on the soft part of the boy's nose in the picture. | *Text:* Correct, the casualty should pinch the soft part of his nose. |
| Click button—Tell/Ask Casualty . . . not to blow his nose. | *Text:* Correct. You tell casualty that he should not blow his nose. Select your next step. |
| Click button—Tell/Ask Casualty . . . to breathe through his mouth. | *Text:* Correct. You tell casualty to breathe through his mouth rather than his nose. Select your next step. |
| Note that there are many different paths through the simulation, many of which are alternate correct paths. | |
| Click button—Other Action . . . wait to see if the bleeding stops. | *Text:* You can do more to try and control the bleeding before waiting to see whether it stops. Try again. Select your next step. |
| Click button . . . Other Action . . . Look closely at casualty's face | *Text:* The casualty's nose is bleeding, but it is not swollen or bruised. A bruise is forming around his eye, but the eye itself does not look as if it is damaged. Select your next step. |
| Click button—Use Other Item . . . water | *Text:* Question. What do you want to use water for?<br>    Wash blood off casualty<br>    Wash your hands<br>    Dampen towel<br>    Click on your answer |

## Table 11.5. Case Study: Bleeding Nose, Cont'd

| Learner Action | System Response | |
|---|---|---|
| Click . . . wash your hands | *Text:* Correct. When possible you should wash your hands before and after managing a casualty.<br><br>Select your next step. | |
| Click button—Use Other Item . . . towel | *Text:* Yes. You could place a cold wet towel on the back of the casualty's neck to try to control the bleeding nose.<br><br>Select your next step. | |
| Click button—Other Action . . . take casualty to doctor. | *Text:* Medical aid may not be necessary. It may be possible for you to control the bleeding nose simply by using first aid.<br><br>Try again. Select your next step. | |
| Click button—Other Action . . . wait to see if bleeding stops. | *Text:* Wait. You have not treated the bruised eye. What should you do to manage this injury?<br><br>Select your next step. | *Graphic:* Photograph shows a wet towel on the back of the casualty's neck. |
| Click button—Use First Aid Kit Item . . . ice pack. | *Text:* Correct. You get an ice pack and wrap it in a cloth. For example, you could wrap it in a triangular bandage. Click and drag the ice pack to the area where you would use it. | |
| Click and drag ice pack to the black eye. | *Text:* Correct: The casualty must hold the ice pack against his forehead and over the bruise near his eye. It should stay for twenty-nine minutes.<br><br>Select your next step. | *Graphic:* Photograph close-up of casualty's face. Graphic of ice pack below picture. |
| Click button—Other Action . . . wait to see if bleeding stops. | *Text:* Question. After a minute, the casualty tells you he thinks the bleeding has stopped. Should he release the pressure from his nose?<br><br>YES   NO   Click your answer. | |

| Learner Action | System Response |
|---|---|
| **Table 11.5. Case Study: Bleeding Nose, Cont'd** | |
| **Learner Action** | **System Response** |
| Click NO | *Audio:* Tell casualty that if his nose starts bleeding again after he lets go to apply pressure for another ten minutes. If it starts again, he should see a doctor. He should also apply ice to the bruise for twenty minutes every two hours for twenty-four hours. |
| | Remember to wash your hands after you have completed your first aid. |
| Click Next | *Text:* Summary |
| | Check for danger |
| | Have casualty sit with head slightly forward, applying pressure on the soft part of his nostrils. He should not blow his nose. Place a cold, wet towel or ice pack wrapped in a cloth on back of casualty's neck. |
| | Apply an ice pack (wrapped in cloth) to the bruised area around the casualty's eye. |

of one type and then the related skills of another type, chapter by chapter, until all of the component skills have been taught. Learners are then given a task to which they can apply their skills as a final project in a course. A topic-centered approach is often characterized as the "you won't understand this now, but later it will be very important to you" approach to skill development.

A contrast to the topic-centered approach is a task-centered one, which represents the Task-Centered Principle:

> Task-Centered Principle: Learning is promoted when learners are engaged in a task-centered instructional strategy. A task-centered instructional strategy is enhanced when learners undertake a progression of whole tasks.

Figure 11.9 illustrates a task-centered instructional strategy: (1) rather than teaching topics out of context, a task of the type learners are learning to do is demonstrated right up-front;

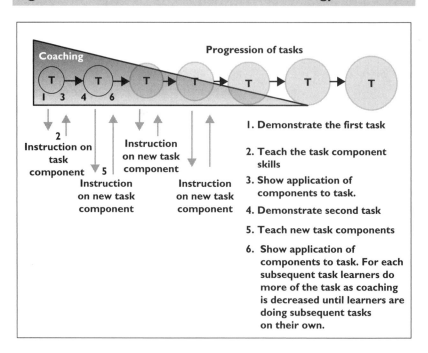

**Figure 11.9. Task-Centered Instructional Strategy**

(2) learners are then given instruction—presentation, demonstration, application—of the skills required to do this task; this instruction does not teach all there is to know about a given topic or component skill, but only what learners need to know to complete the task; (3) the whole task is revisited at this point and learners are shown how these component skills were applied to complete the task or solve the problem; and (4) a new task is then given to the learners. Learners are asked to apply their newly acquired skills to this task. In addition, they are taught additional skills or more detail for the initial skills that are required for this new and slightly more complex task. Again learners are shown or asked to recognize how the previous and new skills are used to complete the task. This cyclical procedure is repeated for each new task in the progression, with the learners required to do more and more of the task as they acquire skill, while the instructional system demonstrates less and less. Eventually, learners are expected to complete the next task in

the progression on their own. If the progression of tasks is carefully chosen and sequenced, when learners have demonstrated their ability to satisfactorily complete one or more whole tasks without coaching or additional demonstration, they have acquired the desired skill intended by the goals of the instruction. A minimal task-centered strategy is a single worked task. However, a truly effective task-centered instructional strategy involves a progression of increasingly complex tasks and a corresponding decreasing amount of learner guidance and coaching.

In the first aid course, the case studies are equivalent to the tasks in Figure 11.9. The guided case studies are a demonstration of a whole task, applying first aid in an emergency situation (1). The tutorials are instruction on task components (2 and 5). The exercise case studies require learners to apply the component skills to a new situation (4 and 6). This course deviates from an ideal task-centered instructional strategy in that the exercise case studies are not sequenced according to complexity. In the first aid course, learners can take the exercise studies in any order. Acquiring component skills without knowing how these skills will be incorporated into real-world tasks often makes the learning seem irrelevant and therefore empty or boring and endless. However, when learners are engaged in real-world tasks right from the outset of the instruction, they have a context for these component skills and they can immediately see their relevance.

## Other Parts of First Aid Course

During the course, learners' performance is recorded on a floppy disk to be sent to St. Johns when learners are registered for the course. The CD-ROM course is followed by an on-site day when learners have an opportunity to engage in a series of role-playing case studies treating various injuries. Upon completion of both the CD-ROM version of the course and the practicum experience, learners are certified in first aid.

Knowing that at the end of their study they will have to demonstrate their first aid skill in an all-day on-site experience adds significant motivation to learners to effectively acquire the skills being taught. When learners know that they will be required to actually demonstrate their newly acquired skills, the instruction becomes more important to them. As a result, the learners are more likely to be actively engaged in the learning. This practicum demonstrates the Integration Principle:

> Integration Principle: Learning is promoted when learners integrate their new knowledge into their everyday world by publicly demonstrating their new knowledge or skill.

## Summary

Do you feel that this demonstration course is effective? Efficient? Engaging? Effective, efficient, and engaging courses implement the first principles of *activation, demonstration, application,* and *integration* using a *task-centered instructional strategy.*

Australian First Aid is not a perfect example of e³-learning, but comes much closer than most courses. Not every tutorial has effective demonstration and application, but many do. The progression of real-world tasks is not carefully sequenced, but this is still an excellent example of teaching component skills in the context of real-world problems. How does your course compare? What would be required to adapt your course to e³-learning?

# A Pebble-in-the-Pond Model for Designing e³-Learning

How does designing e³ instruction differ from more standard instructional design methods? In earlier work, I suggested a pebble-in-the-pond model for instructional development (Merrill, 2002a). This approach differs from the accepted analysis, design, development, implementation, and evaluation (ADDIE) model of instructional design in a couple of significant ways.

Too often in the ADDIE Model, the content is only outlined during the analysis phase and the actual development of the content to be taught takes place in the development phase of the process. The pebble model suggests that the content should be specified up-front and that this content be used for the remainder of the development process. This model also advocates a task-centered instructional strategy, as previously described. The usual model of instruction is to have individual modules—or even whole courses—focused on component skills required for some complex task. All of the knowledge or skill for one of these component areas is taught in the corresponding module. A task-centered approach starts with a complex problem. In the module for this problem, all of the component knowledge and skill relevant to the problem is taught. The component skills are taught in the context of the problem. Then another real-world complex problem is taught, and all of the component skills are taught again, elaborating and expanding the skill as required for this second, more complex problem. This process is repeated with all of the component skills being visited for each subsequent problem in the progression of complex real-world problems. This represents a considerable departure from conventional curriculum design.

The pebble model also recognizes the importance of front-end analysis to determine whether or not instruction is needed. The description here assumes that it has been determined that instruction is an appropriate solution to an existing problem. The description here assumes that it has been determined that there are learners who lack the knowledge and skill necessary to accomplish some real-world tasks.

The pebble model is illustrated in Figure 11.10.

The first step, the initial splash, in the pebble model is to select a *specific complex real-world task,* the pebble to be cast into the development pond. This task should represent the type of task learners should be expected to be able to do after they have completed the instruction. In order to select this task, the designer/developer should complete several intermediate steps: (1) select the audience for the instruction; (2) identify the task appropriate for this audience; (3) then actually create the task, not merely a description of the task but the actual task itself, which involves gathering all the materials, data, and specific information that are required to complete the task; and (4) do the task, complete the task, and record in detail all the activities necessary to

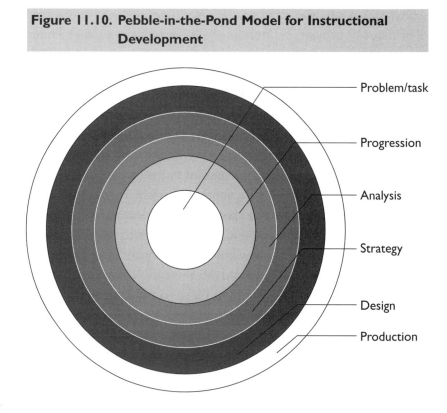

Figure 11.10. Pebble-in-the-Pond Model for Instructional
Development

- Problem/task
- Progression
- Analysis
- Strategy
- Design
- Production

complete the task. This task solution will later be used either
to demonstrate the task to the students or to use as a template
against which to judge the adequacy of the students' performance
as they complete the task.

The second step, the first ripple in the pond, is to identify a *progression* of specific complex real-world tasks from the same class of
tasks as the initial task. There are again several sub-steps in selecting and preparing this progression: (1) identify potential tasks for
the progression; (2) create and work each of these tasks, as was
done for the first task; (3) sequence these tasks on the basis of complexity, difficulty, or amount of component skill required (It should
be noted here that this progression is not a series of sub-tasks that
are all parts of a more complex task, but rather, each of these tasks
should be a complete complex task that belong to the same class as
the other tasks in the progression); (4) check for content coverage,

making sure that by the time learners have completed each of the tasks in the progression they will have acquired the necessary component knowledge and skill to complete yet-to-be-encountered complex tasks in the future; and (5) modify the tasks, rearrange the sequence, and make adjustments that are necessary to ensure the coverage of the subject-matter content.

The third step, the next ripple in the development pond, is instructional *component analysis:* (1) for each task in the progression, carefully determine the instructional components (knowledge and skill) required to work the task; (2) determine what information, demonstration, guidance, application, feedback, and coaching are necessary for learners to acquire the knowledge or skill represented by the instructional component; and (3) carefully show how each knowledge or skill component is used in completing the related whole task.

The fourth step is to (1) determine the overall instructional *strategy* that will be used; (2) determine the instructional strategy that will be used to teach each of the components; (3) integrate the instructional components with the tasks; and (4) provide the necessary wrap-around overview, summary, transitions, and navigation. Note that the content has all been specified prior to the determination of the instructional strategy to be used in the pebble model. This is a deviation from the more traditional ISD models.

The fifth step is to *design* the instructional interface: (1) determine the delivery vehicle (While the title of this paper is e-learning, I have interpreted the e to mean effective, efficient, and enabling. These principles are relevant to many delivery systems not just online learning); (2) once a delivery system has been selected, it is necessary to determine the look and feel for the instruction; (3) script and storyboard the content that has been previously specified so that it can be programmed into whatever delivery system you have selected; (4) develop the relevant multimedia required for your instruction: graphics, video, audio, text, etc.; (5) determine navigation and prepare the necessary navigation buttons; and (6) determine instructional management, including record-keeping, registration, cooperation, and learner control.

The final step is to *produce* the course: (1) all the content should be specified, placed into an effective strategy, and specified in appropriate storyboards and scripts and (2) all the instructional strategy should be specified prior to production. If the pebble model is used, then you can avoid problems if graphic artists design your instruction and programmers program your instruction.

The pebble-in-the-pond model is designed specifically to facilitate the implementation of first principles of instruction.

## Concluding Thoughts

We are frequently told that we live in the Information Age. The rise of the Internet is one of the wonders of the modern world. The click of a button enables us to reach information on almost any subject. Often this information is labeled instruction. Many of these sources are called courses. However, merely labeling a website instruction does not make it so. Charging tuition, calling it a course, or even asking a few multiple-choice questions does not turn information into instruction.

Are you considering the acquisition or development of interactive, multimedia, or e-learning to meet your training needs? Beware! Too many courseware vendors are under-prepared in instructional design. It is not necessary to be certified to hang out a shingle and offer your services as a courseware developer. A clever name, an impressive title, experience in a subject matter, experience in computer graphics, or experience in computer programming cannot substitute for expertise in the development of consistent instructional strategies that teach. Too many of these vendors deliver enervative, endless, empty $e_3$-learning.

However, you can protect yourself. You can learn to look beneath sales hype to the underlying effectiveness of a given instructional product. You can acquire the skill necessary to look beneath the production quality of the product to the underlying instructional strategies and determine whether the product is really effective, efficient, engaging $e^3$-learning. You can learn to recognize and recommend instructional design methods that are more likely to produce $e^3$-learning.

# References

Clark, R.C., & Mayer, R.E. (2003). *e-Learning and the science of instruction.* San Francisco, CA: Pfeiffer.

Mayer, R.E. (2001). *Multimedia learning.* Cambridge, UK: Cambridge University Press.

Merrill, M.D. (2002a). A pebble-in-the-pond model for instructional design. *Performance Improvement, 41*(7), 39–44.

Merrill, M.D. (2002b). First principles of instruction. *Educational Technology Research and Development, 50*(3), 43–59.

Merrill, M.D. (2007). First principles of instruction: A synthesis. In R.A. Reiser & J.V. Dempsey (Eds.), *Trends and issues in instructional design and technology.* Columbus, OH: Merrill Prentice Hall.

Merrill, M.D. (in press). First principles of instruction. In C.M. Reigeluth & A. Carr (Eds.), *Instructional design theories and models* (Vol. III). Hillsdale, NJ: Lawrence Erlbaum Associates.

◆ ◆ ◆

# Summary of Main Points

Readers should take away the following main ideas from this chapter:

- Much current e-learning could be characterized as $e_3$-learning (pronounced e sub-three learning). These three are:

  - *Enervative,* which, rather than promoting skill acquisition, actually interferes with the learning that should occur.

  - *Endless,* which leads to boredom by being too passive, devoid of interaction, allowing learners to disengage, thereby failing to gain the desired skill acquisition.

- *Empty*, which fails to implement those instructional strategies that have been found to be necessary for learning to occur and may be, at its worst, information alone—transferred to the Internet without appropriate demonstration, practice, feedback, learner guidance, or coaching. Information alone is not instruction.

- In contrast, e³-learning (pronounced e to the third power learning) is effective, efficient, and engaging. It applies these five instructional principles:

  - The *activation principle:* learning is promoted when learners activate relevant cognitive structures by being directed to recall, describe, or demonstrate relevant prior knowledge or experience.

  - The *demonstration principle:* learning is promoted when learners observe a demonstration of the skills to be learned that is consistent with the type of content being taught. Demonstrations are enhanced when learners receive guidance that relates instances to generalities. Demonstrations are also enhanced when learners observe media that is relevant to the content.

  - The *application principle:* learning is promoted when learners engage in application of their newly acquired knowledge or skill that is consistent with the type of content being taught. Application is effective only when learners receive intrinsic or corrective feedback. Application is enhanced when learners are coached and when this coaching is gradually withdrawn for each subsequent task.

  - The *task-centered principle:* learning is promoted when learners are engaged in a task-centered instructional strategy that teaches task components in context and involves learners in a progression of whole tasks.

  - The *integration principle:* learning is promoted when learners integrate their new knowledge into their everyday lives by reflecting on, discussing, and defending their new knowledge and skill. Integration is enhanced when learners publicly demonstrate their new knowledge or skill.

- One way of ensuring implementing $e^3$-learning is through the Pebble-in-the-Pond Model for instructional development. This approach differs from the accepted ADDIE model by:

    - Specifying content up-front and using this content for the remainder of the development process

    - Advocating for a task-centered instructional strategy

- Under the pebble model, instructional design works like this:

    - Select a *specific complex real-world task*—the pebble to be cast into the development pond.

    - Identify a *progression* of specific complex real-world tasks from the same class of tasks as the initial task.

    - Perform an instructional *component analysis.*

    - Determine the overall instructional *strategy* that will be used, as well as the instructional strategy that will be used to teach each of the components. Integrate these with the task and provide the necessary wraparound overview, summary, transitions, and navigation.

    - *Design* the instructional interface.

    - *Produce* the course.

# Guiding Questions for Discussion

- Do you feel that the demonstration course described in this chapter is effective? Efficient? Engaging?

- How does a course that you recently developed compare? Does it already represent e³-learning? If so, how? If not, what would be required to adapt your course to e³-learning?

## Learn More About It

**Links**  http://cito.byuh.edu/Merrill

www.mdavidmerrill.com

Online task-centered course based on first principles of instruction:

Mendenhall, A., Buhanan, C.W., Suhaka, M., Mills, G., Gibson, G.V., & Merrill, M.D. (2006). *Introduction to entrepreneurship: How to start your own business,* http://cito.byuh.edu/entrepreneur/main.swf

Online lectures with PowerPoint slides on first principles, pebble-in-the-pond, and a task-centered instructional strategy (90 minutes):

Merrill, M.D. (2006). *A task-centered instructional strategy part 1: First principles,* http://cito.byuh.edu/merrill/Merrill_1/Merrill-1.html

Merrill, M.D. (2006). *A task-centered instructional strategy part 2: Knowledge analysis,* http://cito.byuh.edu/merrill/Merrill_2/Merrill-2.html

Merrill, M.D. (2006). *A task-centered instructional strategy part 3: A knowledge object for a whole task,* http://cito.byuh.edu/merrill/Merrill_3/Merrill-3.html

**Books, Papers, Reports, and Articles**

Mendenhall, A., Buhanan, C.W., Suhaka, M., Mills, G., Gibson, G.V., & Merrill, M.D. (2006). A task-centered approach to entrepreneurship. *TechTrends, 50*(4), 84–89.

Merrill, M.D. (2006). Hypothesized performance on complex tasks as a function of scaled instructional strategies. In J. Enen & R.E. Clark (Eds.), *Handling complexity in learning environments: Theory and research* (pp. 265–281). Amsterdam: Elsevier.

Merrill, M.D. (2006). Levels of instructional strategy. *Educational Technology, 46*(4), 5–10.

# Chapter 12

# Design with the Learning in Mind

*Patricia McGee, The University of Texas at San Antonio*

**About This Chapter**

Evidence suggests that the design of online learning programs often favors those who would already succeed at them. This chapter explores the question: "How can online learning programs be designed so that all types of learners are appropriately supported and can succeed with them?" In it, I describe the specific types of support that online learners require and how designers can meet these needs for support. I first explain why online learners need special support. Then I describe the pedagogical, intra- and interpersonal, and cognitive supports needed by online learners. I close with some ideas about thinking about and conferring with learners before designing online learning experiences, so that resulting learning programs truly support learning.

## Introduction

In 1993 I took my first online course as I pursued a graduate degree. I had never been "on" the Internet, never "surfed" websites, nor did I know how to do so. When I received the instructor's directions for the first assignment via the postal service, I was lost.

I didn't even have access to the Internet. I had to find a service provider, figure out how to configure a Mac SE, and then figure out how to navigate the rather cumbersome and entirely text-based black-and-white screen interface that served as our course "environment." At that time, operating systems and browsers were less uniform than they were ten years later and therefore, understandably, the instructor could only provide generic directions and support rather than step-by-step instructions. In 1993, the Internet was not populated with help-desk-type resources for confused users to find answers to problems, adding to the complexity of the course. This course experience was, perhaps, the most stressful, frustrating, and exhilarating learning experience I have ever had. It was *real*, and I was motivated to overcome the persistent and enduring barriers that plagued me for the first three weeks of the course. In this case, it was the instructor support, patience, and her learning design that saved me. As I have since designed my own courses, studied online course design and implementation, and taught others about teaching online, I find that we online educators still overlook many practical strategies that can support and comfort the online learner. Perhaps we do so because online learning challenges our traditions of formal learning.

Maeroff (2003) believes online learning does challenge us, in part, because it allows an accessible and optional way for people to learn. Although he believes not all learners are prepared for or capable of learning through current systems and configurations of online learning, for some it is a good fit and, most significantly, it may provide opportunities that are otherwise unavailable. However, no online learner has the same supports he or she would have in a traditional learning environment. Those of us responsible for designing instruction and instructional delivery mechanisms must therefore consider the context and nature of learning in a "classroom of one." So not only must the needs of a generation reared on digital games and communication devices be met, but the same systems and learning designs must also accommodate older learners who are now required to embrace lifelong learning. One of the ways to do so is by providing appropriate supports for different types of students, supports that are situated in the design of both the learning experience and the environment.

But what specific types of support do online learners need, and how can designers meet these needs for support? This chapter describes them. It describes the pedagogical, intra- and interpersonal, and cognitive supports that can assist the online learner. Within each area, this chapter illustrates strategies and tactics that instructors can use either within their general instructional designs or with the use of a learning/course management system (L/CMS). The chapter closes with thoughts about the importance of gathering information about learners before designing online learning experiences, so that the resulting learning programs truly support learning.

# Providing Support for Learning

Because online learning in situated in technology, it is tempting to rely on technology for requisite learner supports. However, it is my position that technology can only support learning if the instructional design underlying the learning program is informed and comprehensive. If we look at the problems and barriers that learners experience in online learning—the academic skills, technical abilities, and motivation of the learner; organization and support of interaction; and inadequate time for study (Berge & Muilenburg, 2000; Muilenburg & Berge, 2005)—and how theory and research inform the design of learning experiences, we find that learning-centered systems and instructional designs are preferred and recommended (McGee, Carmean, & Jafari, 2005; Sloan, 2007).

One approach to learning-centered systems is "distributed learning"—a model in which learning resources might be physically located in separate places but are combined together to create a cohesive program that addresses learners' needs—which White and Baker (2004) see as most appropriate for working adults who are motivated to achieve educational goals. They identify the most successful online learner as one who has determined that online learning best suits his or her life needs and is willing to take responsibility for the learning. However, given the increasing reliance on distributed learning in higher education and industry, we cannot assume that learners enter into the learning experience with the necessary skills and predisposition. Many online programs use pre-assessment instruments to help potential students determine their likely success in an online class. However, a study of the use of such instruments in higher education revealed that such surveys only serve as self-selecting instruments that no doubt encourage the learner with the "right" qualities and discourage the learner with the "wrong" attributes to take an online course (McGee, 2002).

In other words, pre-assessments only confirm existing characteristics of the learner; they do not help learners who have weak skills to overcome their inadequate capabilities. Table 12.1 identifies pedagogical, inter- and intrapersonal, and cognitive solutions to address this. The next several sections discuss them.

## Pedagogical Supports

Pedagogical supports are strategies and tools that are embedded within, or associated with, the instructional design of a learning experience. The supports articulated in this section include individualization, personalization, and feedback and are drawn primarily from Keller's (1987) motivation theory, Attention-Relevance-Confidence-Satisfaction (ARCS[1]), and the more recent work on deeper learning principles (see APA, 1997; Carmean, 2002; Dabbagh, 2003; Weigel, 2002).

*Individualization* requires that the instructional designer and course instructor identify and understand the implications of the learner's unique characteristics (Reeves, 1996) that may be associated with habits of mind (Costa & Kallick, 2000), intelligence (Gardner, 1999), age (Tapscott, 1999), gender (Venkatesh & Morris, 2000), or culture (Collis, 1999).

Individualization requires that, for some tasks and activities, the learner be allowed to make choices. This can be accomplished

---

[1]ARCS examples and descriptions as they may relate to technology-mediated learning can be found at View by Theory http://ide.ed.psu.edu/idde/ARCS.htm.

**Table 12.1. Solving Learning Challenges**

| Problem | Solution | Type | Illustration |
|---|---|---|---|
| Attrition | Varied supports available just in time and just in need | Cognitive | Automated responses to email, technology-graded assessments, acknowledgments of progress and accomplishments |
| Isolation | Accessible and seamless information and communication tools (ICTs); social interactions | Intrapersonal and interpersonal | Learning teams, relevant and active course interactions and participation |
| Lack of self-direction | Social networks and collaboration through which self-direction will develop (Dunlap & Grabinger, 2003) | Intrapersonal, pedagogical | Community ICTs, visual and social presence activities, mentoring, learning teams, peer critique |
| Limited management skills | Deadlines, course overviews, clear expectations | Pedagogical, cognitive | Course map, rolling deadlines, rubrics |
| Varied learning preferences | Choices in assignments, ICT interactions, modalities | Pedagogical | Collaborative assignments, student-generated products, communication through visuals, video, audio, or text |

in a variety of ways. Pre-testing for prior knowledge can help articulate the choices a learner has. For example, in an L/CMS like Moodle or Blackboard, an instructional designer can set up a pre-test as students enter the course for the first time to determine whether students enter into the course missing some background knowledge or ability. The results could be assessed by the system for comparison against criteria that establish baselines for novice, intermediate, and advanced levels of expertise. Based on the assessment, the system could recommend a path through the course that would address a (address a learner's) learner's entering level of knowledge and ability (Bransford, Brown, & Cocking, 2000). Not only could designers use such an assessment to provide paths through the content (as is most common), but it might even suggest multiple paths through a course that direct learners to appropriate levels of activities. The novice level indicates the baseline achievement expected in a course. Pre-testing helps the instructor and the learner assess where they fall in the continuum, and assignments that are appropriately organized by abilities can identify criteria for completion for each level.

Individualization also is a strategy that can support multiple modalities as indicated through learning style or intelligence (Campbell, Campbell, & Dickinson, 2003). Although much of adult learning has been directed by andragogy theory, less attention has been paid to style or intelligence (Gardner, 1993, 1999). By providing options of how work is completed or articulated, individual preference can be supported while still adhering to rigorous standards of performance.

Most courses are designed long before designers and instructors know who the students are. But by considering in advance the differing levels of learner knowledge and ability, designers can create learning programs that identify where learners are in the knowledge and ability continua and provide several paths through the course so that learners can accomplish the objectives for the course in a way that is appropriate to their own unique needs.

*Personalization* makes the learners feel that they are more than an email address to the instructor. Using names in communications, both one-on-one and in group discourse, makes learners feel acknowl-edged. White believes that the effort to recognize the person behind the learning, which he calls "person building" (2000, p. 8), is essential to developing a well-educated person. This requires that we keep in mind the entire person, not just the fact that the person is a student in the course, but whether he or she is young, old, working, a full-time student, married with children, single with two jobs, and so on. Learning online should afford flexibility so that formal learning fits into the individual's schedule, rather than the learner fitting into the learning experience. If not, we have only replicated what brick-and-mortar campuses have institutionalized.

There are many ways we can personalize the learning experi-ence, and learning software such as L/CMSs and Web 2.0 appli-cations (O'Reilly, 2005) can support this effort. For example, many experts suggest having students post pictures and biographical statements so participants in online courses can know something about their classmates. Similarly, experts suggest holding "getting to know you" events, which provide a more direct meet-and-greet experience. In order to build deeper understanding among class members, it is best to allow students to use what they know about each other to make decisions. For example, if students are assigned a group task, they can be asked to choose team members who have complementary skills. Activities such as discussions or chats can be designed to reflect the opposing viewpoints and perspectives represented in the group; students learn not only about the content but also about the person representing a position.

*Feedback* differs from interaction in that it helps the learner and the instructor obtain information about the learner's performance. The feedback is usually substantive, communicating both what is working well and where additional work is needed. It goes beyond grades or points on an assignment because, alone, grades or points do not communicate what is understood or not. Feedback can also come from peers, self-critiques, technology, and instruments designed to elicit information about experience and knowledge acquisition. Peer, self, and instructor critiques and interaction can be supported in a variety of ways in both training and course-based learning. Blogs and wikis can be used for FAQs, journaling, or group logs. (See Chapter 8 for a more in-depth discussion of blogs and wikis.) Feedback can even be provided through handheld devices, which can be used for data collection, storage, and transportation. Software that allows for the easy interchange of data between these handheld devices and L/CMSs on institutional computers is readily available and continues to improve. Field-based employees and mobile learners have increased market development of such software (Thibeault, 2005).

Feedback is a two-way interaction and just as important for the instructor as for the learner. The Distance Education Learning Environments Survey (DELES)[2] is a validated instrument designed to determine instructor support, student interaction and collaboration, personal relevance, authentic learning, active learning, and student autonomy. If completed by students and the instructor during an online course, the results provide a clear and insightful analysis of how learner experiences may differ from that intended by the instructor.

## Intrapersonal and Interpersonal Supports

Learning requires *intrapersonal* abilities, which are those related to an understanding of the self. Assessments of intrapersonal abilities are grounded in both meta-cognition about what we do and do not know and reflection about our actions and decisions (see Driscoll, 1994). It is easy to make the assumption that online learners are reflecting about their work as they proofread, write, communicate, and interact with others. There is evidence that communicating online does support meta-cognition (see Dobrovolny, 2003); however, such cognitive activity is challenging to ensure or document.

Fortunately, the development of tools that are situated in thinking have expanded the options for doing so. Writing tools and strategies situated in a variety of technologies support meta-cognition

---

[2]See http://insight.southcentralrtec.org/ilib/deles/actual

and reflections. Software that can help analyze writing and thinking patterns is readily available, even if not required for online learning. For example, Microsoft Word™ provides a reviewing and summarizing function that can be used to track and document thinking patterns. Reviewing documents as they change over time as well as progress throughout the writing process, and using the summarizing function, can help the learners "see" the patterns in their own writing. Additionally, developments in discussion thread analysis software[3] can allow learners to extract patterns in threaded discussions and better identify important points in their own submissions as well as the conversation as a whole.

Self-critique is a metacognitive tactic that also helps learners better understand their abilities and progress. This may take the form of a pre- and post-test on content knowledge or skills. Rubrics, which provide students with criteria against which to compare their work, can be made available at the introduction of an assignment to assist with self-critique as students work on a task.

*Interpersonal* supports ensure that group interaction and communication are seamless and meaningful. These are perhaps less evident in L/CMSs but critical when students only communicate and interact virtually. We assume that if there is an exchange of information between individuals that each person is supporting the other, but this may not be the case. Although historically online learning is derived from text-based correspondence courses, an important difference is that online learning supports two types of interaction: not only peer-to-instructor interaction common in correspondence courses, but also peer-to-peer interaction. The plethora of information and communication tools (such as Web 2.0 tools) that support interpersonal interaction are not necessarily designed for that purpose; they are primarily designed for communication. Interaction is more complex, requiring thoughtful configurations

---

[3]Examples of discussion analysis software are Copernic Summarizer (www.copernic.com), Text Analysis (www.megaputer.com), Theme Weaver (http://alg.ncsa.uiuc.edu/do/index), and Threader (www1.cs.columbia.edu/~swan1/doc_run.html).

and applications that can support both instructional objectives and learner needs and wants. Supports for interaction must focus on expectations, parameters, and application.

- Expectations for collaboration should be evident to all participants and situated in the context of the interaction and communication. For example, criteria for the performance of a task should not be separated from where and when that task will occur.

- Parameters for collaboration can help articulate expectations by stating the duration of an event (which can be set as a function within an L/CMS), the quantitative nature of the interaction (number of posts, length of product, etc.), and the tools that can or should be used to accomplish the task.

- In traditional courses or training modules, application is a means of providing a variety of collaborative options, whether they occur within an L/CMS or are generated and worked on externally. Learners may possibly select the medium for interaction, the duration, or the means in which collaboration is evidenced. When learners are involved in the process of determining how collaboration occurs, interpersonal skills are used and, most likely, improved.

## Cognitive Supports

Cognitive supports must be present in not only what the learners are asked to do but also in how they do it and what tools they are asked to use. Cognitive supports should alleviate cognitive load and provide just-in-time information, advance and visual organizers, and cognitive connections. Table 12.2 lists a variety of tools that can be used independently or within an L/CMS as cognitive supports.

One of the key challenges in designing online learning is to make sure that learners do not become overwhelmed with content or directions. One significant way to avoid this problem is by starting learning programs with tools that help learners see the bigger

**Table 12.2. Sample Cognitive Tools**

| Type | Description | Example |
|------|-------------|---------|
| Adaptive Tools | Support individualized cognitive needs that may be at odds with the delivery system | CAST, Magic Paper™ (http://icampus.mit.edu/MagicPaper/)<br><br>Spoken language dialogue systems (SLDSs) |
| Assessment Tools | Provide formative and self-assessment activities | iMOAT™ (http://web.mit.edu/wac/evaluation/imoat.html)<br><br>Respondus™ (www.respondus.com/products/respondus.shtml) |
| Virtual Environments | Allow learners to collaborate, practice, and experiment | Croquet™ (www.opencroquet.org/)<br><br>COSE (www.staffs.ac.uk/COSE/) |
| Virtual Tutors | Content or skill-based programs that encourage self-directed learning | AVID™ (www.avidonline.org/)<br><br>XTutor™ (http://icampus.mit.edu/xTutor/)<br><br>ATutor (www.atutor.ca/acollab/index.php) |
| Virtual Study Aids | Allow learners to improve general learning skills | StudyMate™ (www.respondus.com/studymate/samples.shtml)<br><br>Online Writing Lab (http://owl.english.purdue.edu/) |

picture and develop expectations about what they're going to learn and how long it might take.

Advance organizers provide a preview of the learning experience, describing what an upcoming unit is about and the order in which the content will be covered. Advance organizers help learners prepare for an online learning experience and can alleviate stress by building expectations and helping learners connect their existing knowledge with what is about to be learned.

Visual organizers are a special type of advance organizer that can make a primarily text-based experience more appealing. Ideally, students should be allowed into a course environment prior to the start of a course, but often institutional policy prohibits this. Such a limitation does not prevent course information and overviews from being made available prior to the activation of the course. For example, a course map can be made available to students prior to the course start date. The map is designed as a matrix and intended to provide a high-level overview of the course. Table 12.3 provides an example.

Just-in-time supports are critical to the learner working alone and removed from people and non-digital resources. Such supports can be conceptualized in a variety of ways, from human interaction and relationships (such as peer coaching) to technologies that allow the learner to be more autonomous and empowered to have ownership of his or her learning. Within L/CMSs, just-in-time supports can be thought of in terms of how items are linked and displayed within the typically frame-based interface. Rather than have an activity page open in a new browser window, it may be more effective to open within a frame, so that an FAQ or instruction for an activity is visible and readily available to the learner. Online instructors typically answer the same questions from learners repeatedly, so a page, discussion area, or pop-up window that links to categories of standard concerns saves time and can reduce learner frustration while facilitating self-directed learning.

Or an instructor might use these frequent questions to redesign the instructions on assignments so that learners' needs are addressed as they start to perform an assignment, mitigating the need to consult an external source.

Within assignments, instructors might also link to supports. For example, in a reading assignment for an academic class, rather than merely listing the readings for the week, the instructor might provide a narrative that introduces the readings and links to them (or directs readers to offline resources). In a training course, an instructor might provide students with access to a software tool that will help them perform a task (and their jobs) more efficiently.

**Table 12.3. Course Map Excerpt***

| Week | Date | Topic | Location | Reading | Due |
|------|------|-------|----------|---------|-----|
| 1 | Aug. 26 | Course overview | HSS 3.03.18 | | (1) Personal data |
| 2 | Sept. 2 | ICTS used in education and training | Online | (1) Text, CH 6 and 7 | (1) Be prepared to discuss group project |
| 3 | Sept. 9 | Barriers | FS 3.536 | (1) Hi-ed *Using Information Technology to Enhance Academic Productivity*. See barriers<br><br>(2) *Educational technology: An extended literature review*<br><br>(3) K-12 *e-Learning synthesis: Instructional technology systems*. This NCREL article identifies a number of conditions and resources that should be present for eLearning but which apply to K-12 and industry. | (1) Needs Assessment posted to *Needs Assessment Discussion* (10 pts.) |

*Underlined text indicates hyperlink to elaborated instructions or resource.

413

Just-in-time supports are especially needed for learners who are far from centralized learning resources. For example, academic students who are in remote locations with no access to the school bookstore must have the ability to order textbooks well in advance of a course so they have the text on the course start date. Similarly, remote trainees who must have access to confidential corporate information have to be provided with access codes before the start of a training course so that they can access systems covered in the course.

Cognitive connectors are devices that help the learners make connections between content and their own experiences. Traditionally, these types of cognitive supports would include metaphors and imagery (which describe new content in a way that might be familiar to learners), matrixes and concept maps (which help learners visualize how aspects of the content relate to each other), mnemonics (which help learners remember content), and frames (which help learners organize new concepts) (West, Farmer, & Wolff, 1991).

For online learning, cognitive connectors can provide a starting point for making connections and then triggering behaviors. For example, when using lecture-type presentations with audio narration, a link to a notepad can prompt the viewer to take notes. Instructor-prepared templates of matrixes, frames, and concept maps help to scaffold a cognitive strategy that the learners may eventually adopt for their own benefit in subsequent learning activities.

# Concluding Thoughts

Informed, systematic, and pervasive learner supports are more than strategies to help the learners acquire knowledge; they deliver the message that the learner is the center of the experience. Providing such a message with current instructional delivery systems is a challenge, however, because many are not intuitive, intelligent, or truly as adaptive to the online learner as an instructor-directed traditional classroom can be. Such intuitiveness, intelligence, and adaptivity should be our goal in designing online instructional systems and learning experiences. Doing so requires more than knowing the tools available, however. It involves designers and instructors learning about their learners' needs and asking learners what they feel they need in order to succeed in learning online—then taking this data and designing learning experiences that address the needs identified.

Clearly, much has been written about the support of the online learner, and this short chapter could only draw attention to a few areas. But if designers and instructors address these key areas, they can help learners feel more comfortable in a virtual environment and, I hope, more successfully complete the learning experience.

# References

American Psychological Association (APA). (1997). *Learner-centered psychological principles: A framework for school redesign and reform.* Washington, DC: American Psychological Association.

Berge, Z.L, & Muilenburg, L. (2000, September/October). Designing discussion questions for online, adult learning. *Educational Technology,* pp. 53–56.

Bransford, J.D., Brown, A.L., & Cocking, R. (Eds.). (2000). *How people learn: Brain, mind, experience, and school.* Washington, DC: National Academy Press.

Campbell, L., Campbell, D., & Dickinson, D. (2003). *Teaching and learning through multiple intelligences* (3rd ed.). New York: Allyn & Bacon.

Carmean, C. (2002). *Learner-centered principles.* Retrieved February 16, 2007, from www.educause.edu/MappingtheLearningSpace/2594

Collis, B. (1999). Designing for differences: Cultural issues in the design of WWW-based course-support sites. *British Journal of Educational Technology, 30*(30), 201–215.

Costa, A.L., & Kallick, B. (Eds.). (2000). *Activating and engaging habits of mind.* Washington, DC: Association of Supervision and Curriculum Development.

Dabbagh, N. (2003). *The intersection and alignment of learner-centered instructional strategies in online learning and their implementation using course management systems.* Presentation at NLII Next Generation CMS, Tucson, Arizona. Retrieved April 10, 2003, from www.educause.edu/asp/doclib/abstract.asp?ID=NLI0330

Dobrovolny, J. (2003). Learning strategies. *ASTD Learning Circuits.* Available: www.learningcircuits.org/2003/oct2003/dobrovolny. htm [Retrieved February 16, 2007]

Driscoll, M.P. (1994). *Psychology of learning for instruction.* New York: Allyn & Bacon.

Dunlap, J.C., & Grabinger, R.S. (2003). Preparing students for lifelong learning: A review of instructional features and teaching methodologies. *Performance Improvement Quarterly, 16*(2), 6–25.

Gardner, H. (1993). *Multiple intelligences: The theory in practice.* New York: Basic Books.

Gardner, H. (1999). *Intelligence reframed.* New York: Basic Books.

Goodyear, P. (2003). Psychological foundations for networked learning. In C. Steeples & C. Jones (Eds.), *Networked learning: Perspectives and issues* (pp. 49–76). London: Springer.

Gunstone, R., & Northfield, J. (1992). *Conceptual change in teacher education: The centrality of metacognition.* ERIC Document Service ED 348 342.

Keller, J.M. (1987). Development and use of the ARCS model of motivational design. *Journal of Instructional Development, 10*(3), 2–10.

Ludwig-Hardman, S. (2003). Learner support services for online students: Scaffolding for success. *International Review of Research in Open and Distance Learning.* Retrieved March 10, 2003, from www. irrodl.org/content/v4.1/dunlap.html.

Maeroff, G. (2003). *A classroom of one: How online learning is changing our schools and colleges.* New York: Palgrave Macmillan.

McGee, P. (2002). *Distance learning supports: The intentionality of pre-assessment surveys.* Paper published in the proceedings of the 6th Annual e-Learn Conference. Montreal, Canada.

McGee, P., Carmean, C., & Jafari, A. (Eds.). (2005). *Course management systems for learning: Beyond accidental pedagogy.* New York: IDEA Group Publishing.

Muilenburg, L.Y., & Berge, Z.L. (2001). Barriers to distance education: A factor-analytic study. *The American Journal of Distance Education, 15*(2), 7–22. Retrieved February 17, 2007, from www.emoderators.com/zberge/fa_ajde_050401.shtml.

Muilenburg, L.Y., & Berge, Z.L. (2005). Student barriers to online learning: A factor analytic study. *Distance Education: An International Journal, 26*(1), 29–48.

O'Reilly, T. (2005). *What is web 2.0?* Available: www.oreillynet.com/pub/a/oreilly/tim/news/2005/09/30/what-is-web-20.html/ [Retrieved August 31, 2007]

Reeves, T.C. (1996). *A model of the effective dimensions of interactive learning on the world wide web.* Paper presented at Ed-Media 96 and Ed-Telecom 96, Boston, Massachusetts.

Sloan Consortium. (2007). Effective practices. Available: www.sloan-c.org/effective/browse.asp [Retrieved February 15, 2007]

Tapscott, D. (1999). *The rise of the net generation: Growing up digital.* New York: McGraw-Hill.

Thibeault, J. (2005). *Learning on the go.* Retrieved April 26, 2005, from www.pdaed.com/vertical/features/learning.xml.

Venkatesh, V., & Morris, M.G. (2000). Why don't men ever stop to ask for directions? Gender, social influence, and their role in technology acceptance and usage behavior. *MIS Quarterly, 24,* 115–139.

Weigel, V. (2002). *Deep learning for a digital age: Technology's untapped potential to enrich higher education.* San Francisco, CA: Jossey-Bass.

West, C.K., Farmer, J.A., & Wolff, P.M. (1991). *Instructional design: Implications from cognitive science.* Boston, MA: Allyn and Bacon.

White, C. (2000). Students and faculty respond to online distance courses at Grant MacEwan Community College. *T.H.E. Journal Online, 27*(9), 66–70.

White, K.W., & Baker, J.D. (2004). *The student guide to successful online learning.* Boston, MA: Pearson.

◆ ◆ ◆

## Summary of Main Points

Readers should take away the following main ideas from this chapter:

- Online learners need support to successfully complete courses and achieve the learning objectives.

  - Many instructional designers and instructors of online learning experiences overlook practical strategies for doing so.

  - Perhaps they do so because online learning challenges traditions of formal learning through accessible and optional ways for people to learn.

  - In response, online learners need pedagogical, intra- and interpersonal, and cognitive supports.

- Technology can only support learning if the instructional design underlying the learning program is informed and comprehensive.

  - Design should be learning-centered, which anticipates and addresses the needs of learners, so that learners have the greatest opportunity to achieve the objectives for the learning program.

  - One approach to learning-centered systems is distributed learning, where learning resources might be physically located in separate places but are combined to create a cohesive program that addresses learners' needs.

  - Design must also recognize that learners do not enter into the learning experience with the necessary skills and predispositions.

- Table 12.4 (see below) summarizes the pedagogical, intra- and interpersonal, and cognitive supports needed by online learners.

- To design a course that appropriately places learners at the center of the learning experience involves designers learning about their learners' needs and asking learners what they feel they need to succeed in online learning—then taking this data and designing learning experiences that address the needs identified.

**Table 12.4. Categories of Support**

| Category of Support | Description | Types |
|---|---|---|
| Pedagogical Supports | Strategies and tools that are embedded within or associated with the instructional design of a learning experience | Individualization<br><br>Personalization<br><br>Feedback |
| Intrapersonal and Interpersonal Supports | Interpersonal supports are grounded in both meta-cognition about what people know and don't know, and in reflection about actions and decisions<br><br>Interpersonal supports ensure that group inter-action and communica-tion are seamless and meaningful | Writing tools and strategies<br><br>Self-critique<br><br>Expectations<br><br>Parameters<br><br>Applications |
| Cognitive Supports | Cognitive supports alleviate cognitive load | Just-in-time information, advance and visual organizers<br><br>Cognitive connections |

◆ ◆ ◆

# Guiding Questions for Discussion

- Describe three learning experiences for which you felt the most supported. How were you supported and why did these supports work for you?

- Consider a learning experience that was both frustrating and challenging for you. What kind of support might have helped to alleviate what you experiences?

**Learn More About It**

Links          Connectivism, www.connectivism.ca/

National Learning Infrastructure Initiative (NLII) Online Learning Resources

CM/KM/LMS, www.educause.edu/ CM%2FKM%2FLMS/946

Learner Centered Principles and Practices, www.educause.edu/LearnerCenteredPrinciplesand Practices/ 940

New Learners, www.educause.edu/NewLearners/683

We-Learning: Social Software and e-Learning, www.learningcircuits.org/2003/dec2003/kaplan.htm

# Part V

# Issues of Theory and Research

This part explores some of the challenges that arise in transferring learning theory, which has primarily been developed for application in the classroom, to the online environment, as well as issues with the research—including a call for a radically different approach to research on e-learning. Chapters in this part include:

- Chapter 13, Revisiting Learning Theory for e-Learning by Gretchen Lowerison, Roger Côté, Philip C. Abrami, and Marie-Claude Lavoie, explores the ways that learning theories have had to be adjusted to the realities of teaching online and whether certain popular approaches to learning, such as constructivism, can effectively work in a self-study online environment.

- Chapter 14, Design Research: A Better Approach to Improving Online Learning by Thomas C. Reeves, Jan Herrington, and Ron Oliver, explores what should happen with research in online learning in the light of several major meta-analyses that have essentially concluded that "no significant differences" exist between distance and classroom instruction, adding that "It hardly needs saying that the largely pseudoscientific research studies reviewed for these meta-analyses fail to provide practitioners with much needed guidance for improving the design and use of online learning." In this chapter, the authors propose a different approach to research called design research, which

(1) addresses pressing complex problems in real contexts in close collaboration with practitioners; (2) integrates known and hypothetical design principles with technological affordances to render plausible solutions to these real world problems; and (3) involves conducting cycles of rigorous and reflective inquiry to test and refine innovative learning environments as well as to define new design principles. This chapter explores what design research is, provides a rationale for it, presents strategies for conducting it, and suggests ways to overcome challenges to design research.

# Chapter 13

# Revisiting Learning Theory for e-Learning

*Gretchen Lowerison, Roger Côté,*
*Philip C. Abrami, and Marie-Claude Lavoie,*
*Centre for the Study of Learning and Performance,*
*Concordia University*

## About This Chapter

As David Merrill laments in Chapter 11, designs for e-learning often fall short of their potential. He proposed one model for addressing this. In this chapter, we explore other issues surrounding this problem. Specifically, this chapter explores the question, "How can learning theory inform designs for e-learning?" In it, we first review the three key theories of how learners learn. Next, we explore specific approaches to designing e-learning that represent each of the theories. Then we discuss efforts to identify the design approaches taken in e-learning. We close this chapter by offering suggestions for the future development of designs for e-learning.

# Introduction

The history of educational technology is replete with examples of promising technologies that were embraced with naïve enthusiasm, only to be later discredited and discarded either because interest was not widespread and sustained and/or because early implementations were poorly conceived, impractical, and not readily scalable. e-Learning has maintained this tradition. Its early proponents believed that the use of computer technology in education and training could change the way people teach and learn. They promised that, with the aid of computers, education had the potential to shift teaching and learning from an instructor-led, didactic, linear learning environment to one that is student-centered, resource-rich, collaborative, and active, promising dramatic changes in learning (Bransford, Brown, & Cocking, 2000; Jonassen & Reeves, 1996; Laurillard, 2002). The combination of computer technology and the Internet were intended to give educators and trainers the opportunity to bring a larger, more diverse set of learning resources and opportunities to students. More than a replacement for the classroom, e-learning could offer alternate means of supporting and facilitating learning (Weigel, 2002). Early researchers in e-learning (then commonly referred to as computer-based training) even had names for the use of computers in education: cognitive technology (Pea, 1985); technologies of the mind (Salomon, Perkins & Globerson, 1991); and mindtools (Jonassen, 1996).

As the use of e-learning grew, people in educational technology realized that a gap in understanding existed between how people learn with computer technology and how people design for learning. In terms of learning, however, no such gap exists. Research comparing the effectiveness of learning with computer support with that in classrooms has to date shown, overall, no practical or large difference (Bernard, Abrami, Lou, Borokhovski, Wade, Wozney, Wallet, Fiset, & Huang, 2004). In short, the potential of e-learning as a transformative tool for learning is not being realized (Weigel, 2002).

In many cases, the problem emanates from the people involved. Some problems derive from the developers of the applications.

When designing computer applications for learning, pedagogy is often not factored in; these decisions are left up to the implementer instead (Govindasamy, 2001), with variable results (Wozney, Venkatesh, & Abrami, 2006). Even when instructors are involved, Bates and Poole (2003) comment that they are generally ill-equipped to design instruction suitable for computer technology. The end result is instruction that is centered more on technology than on pedagogy (Mayer, 2001).

Some problems derive from learners. They may be unprepared for a new learning environment. Learners can be resistant to taking responsibility for learning and be overwhelmed by the amount of information and resources available to them online (Bonk & Cunningham, 1998). Moreover, the focus tends to be on the "e," with a strong focus on the technology, rather than on the "learning" (Romiszowski, 2005).

Some problems derive from researchers, who do not necessarily understand the features and processes that make the technology and its applications effective, efficient, and sustainable (Jonassen, 2003). The end result tends to be e-learning environments that focus on distribution of information (Zemsky & Massy, 2004).

But on a more fundamental level, the problems may emanate from a limited understanding of learning theory and how it applies to e-learning. Learning theories such as behaviorism, cognitivism, and constructivism encapsulate ideas about how people learn that are translated into instructional strategies. Different strategies are used to produce different learning outcomes (Gagné, Briggs, & Wager, 1992) and are intended to be used purposefully by instructional designers when they design learning programs. The learning theory used to frame the design of instruction is dependent on the desired learning outcomes. On a practical level, however, designers often find translating these theories into detailed designs for learning programs to be difficult, and blending several strategies together to achieve a larger goal even more difficult.

This chapter explores how learning theory can inform more effective designs for e-learning and proposes a tool for doing so. We first review the three key theories of how learners learn. Next, we explore specific approaches to designing e-learning that represent each of the theories. Then we discuss efforts to identify the design approaches taken in e-learning. We close this chapter with an application of these concepts: some general templates that can be used to design e-learning that are consistent with the IMS Learning Design specification (see www.imsglobal.org/learningdesign/index.html).

## How Do We Learn?

Before considering learning theory as it specifically relates to e-learning, we would first like to review some of the key theories that explain how people learn. Theories of learning range from those that propose that knowing is the result of objective experience (behaviorism), knowing is the mental processing of information (cognitivism), and knowing is subjectively constructed (constructivism). Mayer (2003) likens these perspectives to the following metaphors: strengthening a connection (the behaviorist perspective); adding files to a file cabinet (the cognitivist perspective); and building a model (the constructivist perspective).

In recent years, learning-theory-driven applications of technology have shifted from behaviorist to constructivist (Jonassen & Reeves, 1996). In the behavioral view of computer-based instruction, the instructor's role is to transmit information to the learner in small manageable chunks and provide immediate feedback to the learner's responses. In computer-based instruction designed from the cognitivist view, the instructor's role is to help learners encode new information, form meaningful links with prior knowledge, and facilitate the process of retrieval for maximum use and transfer. In a constructivist-oriented learning environment, the instructor's role is to guide the learner through dialogue, scaffold new concepts (that is, build support for them), and provide additional support for learning (Jonassen, 1999). Instruction is still very important. The designer's responsibility in using technology is to create learning tasks and conditions that facilitate understanding, while the learner's responsibility is to take advantage of what is offered (Laurillard, 2002). Table 13.1 summarizes the three approaches, which are described in more detail below.

## Table 13.1. Three Approaches to Learning

|  | **Behaviorism** | **Cognitivism** | **Constructivism** |
|---|---|---|---|
| Learning is achieved through … | Transmitted information | Acquisition of knowledge | Construction of knowledge |
| Learning is believed to be … | A change in behavior | Built on previously learned materials | A change in meaning |
| Teaching is … | Instructor-centered | Instructor-centered | Student-centered |
| Process of learning | Passive | Active | Active |

## The Behaviorist Approach

Behaviorism holds that instruction is most effective when learners are rewarded as they progress incrementally toward larger learning goals. Common tactics used to implement behaviorism include the following:

- Designing instruction based on performance objectives, which is intended to create effective, measurable instruction. The objectives state the behavior to be mastered in observable and measurable terms, as well as the conditions under which the behavior should be performed and the level of acceptable performance.

- Providing immediate, regular feedback and evaluation to determine the extent to which the material has been learned (Dick & Carey, 1990).

- Tailoring instruction to accommodate individual learners' preferred pace of learning.

The behavioral approach to instructional design is prescriptive and places emphasis on well-defined learning objectives. Mager (1984) emphasizes that effective instructional design should answer these three general questions: (1) Where are we going? (2) How will we get there? and (3) How will we know when we have arrived? Mager (1984) supports the idea of criterion-referenced instruction (CRI). This approach stresses the relationship between learning goals and learning tasks. The first component of CRI is to define the learning objectives for the program. Second are specific learning tasks that address those objectives. Third, assessments that directly relate to the specified learning objectives. Other supporters of this approach include Dick and Carey (1990) and Skinner (1968).

Critics of behaviorism claim that this method results in the learning of lower-order skills such as rote learning (Bloom, 1956; Weigel, 2002) and that it does not teach for understanding (Winn, 1990).

## The Cognitivist Approach

Cognitivist instructional design models go a step further by addressing how learners cognitively process learning material and designing instruction to support that (Reigeluth, 1987). The cognitivist instructional design process shares elements with the behavioral process in that it is highly structured with explicit learning objectives. Both behaviorists and cognitivists see knowledge as something that is real, objective, and measurable. Unlike behaviorists, however, cognitivists are concerned with the active processing of information and how knowledge is organized in the brain, often likening processing and storage activities in the human brain to those of computers (Mayer, 2003).

The cognitivist approach places emphasis on strategies that build mental models. A good example of this is the idea of advanced organizers (Ausubel, 1978). Advanced organizers allow the learners to organize their knowledge, facilitating the process of connecting new information with information already stored in memory (Smith & Ragan, 2005). Knowledge results when information is received, stored, and retrieved—each time building on previously stored knowledge (Marshall, 1998).

Two approaches to cognition are situated cognition, which emphasizes learning that is rooted in real situations, and distributed cognition, which proposes that cognition occurs within environments, including social environments, in which various cognitive resources are placed.

Critics of cognitivism claim that, because knowledge is acquired in fact form from the instructor by the learner, it may be difficult for learners to internalize the information and make it personally meaningful (Brown, Collins, & Duguid, 1989). It is sometimes difficult to ensure that learners are cognitively actively engaged in the learning process (Duffy & Cunningham, 1996). The linear, hierarchical nature of instruction, often with an emphasis on well-designed problems, may make complex learning difficult (Wilson, Jonassen, & Cole, 1993). Critics also claim that, even when cognitivism is an effective form of learning, it is not especially efficient, requiring more learning time—especially when compared to behaviorist approaches (Driscoll, 2005; Ertmer & Newby, 1993).

## The Constructivist Approach

In contrast to both the behaviorist and cognitivist approaches to learning is the constructivist approach. Constructivism is based on the belief that knowledge is subjectively constructed, often within a social context and, consequently, constructivist learning environments provide learners with the tools and resources needed to build their own knowledge.

Constructivist approaches to learning emerge from post–positivist philosophies and beliefs that learning is most effective when the learners can set and meet their own learning goals in an environment that is flexibly or even automatically adaptive to their individual learning needs (Alexander & Murphy, 1998; Jonassen, Howland, Marra, & Crismond, 2008; Laurillard, 2002; Wagner & McCombs, 1995).

An effective learner-centered learning environment focuses on the process of learning rather than on the process of transmitting facts from instructor to learner. Learners actively construct meaning through exploration, communication, and reflection (Jonassen, Howland, Marra, & Crismond, 2008; Laurillard, 2002). This illustrates the change in teaching and learning from the traditional didactic instructor-led behaviorist and cognitivist approaches to the more learner-centered, constructivist learning environment (Lambert & McCombs, 2000).

Critics of constructivism emphasize that the lack of specific learning objectives and clear measurable learning outcomes reduces the effectiveness of the method (Dick, 1992). Dick also points out that the method can be time-consuming and problematic with respect to assessment. Constructivism may be especially ill-suited to learning situations in which the learner lacks intrinsic interest or otherwise is unwilling or incapable of taking responsibility for learning (Dick, 1992). Critics also claim that constructivist pedagogy may ignore the learner's need to have foundational knowledge from which to build on and may not be suitable to all learning domains (Molenda, 1991).

## Instructional Design Frameworks

The instructional design framework informs the design process of learning materials. The goal of instructional design is to put learning theory into practice. Whether intended for academic or industry learners, the potential exists for designs that more actively engage learners and that make more effective use of the capabilities of the computer. It is important to look at these frameworks critically, because although they may give direction to designers, they usually do not provide specific pedagogical answers. The following sections explore different frameworks of instructional design for e-learning. But first, it defines the concept, e-learning, to make sure that all readers are working with a common definition.

### Definitions of e-Learning

Definitions of e-learning vary. We define e-learning to include any element of teaching and learning that involves digital material and information communication technologies (ICT). e-Learning can comprise 100 percent of the teaching and learning environment or can be part of a blended approach with a combination of face-to-face and digital elements.

Generally, there are three ways that computer technology can be used in education: (1) as a tool for the instructor to organize or present material in keeping with the paradigm of teacher-directed instruction; (2) as something that individuals can learn from, in effect an alternate delivery system; and (3) as something that individuals can learn with—a pedagogical tool embodying the principles of student-centered learning (Jonassen, 2003).

The potential benefits of e-learning may include increased access to information (Bonk & Cunningham, 1998); increased flexibility of learning environments (Spiro, Feltovich, Jacobson, & Coulson, 1991); personalized instruction (Alonso, Lopez, Manrique, & Vines, 2005); reduced cognitive load (Salomon, 1983); increased learner control (Jonassen, 2003; Laurillard, 2002); and authentic learning (Bransford, Brown, & Cocking, 2000). Although e-learning provides an alternative way to teach and learn (Alonso, Lopez, Manrique, & Vines, 2005; Weigel, 2002), educators typically convert existing print-based materials into electronic format and offer what Weigel refers to as "post-a-lecture" and "host-a-discussion" (2002, p. 2). This method maintains a teacher-directed approach to instruction.

## Behavioral Models of Instructional Design

As noted earlier in this chapter, instruction designed according to the behaviorist approach holds that instruction is most effective when learners are rewarded as they progress incrementally toward larger learning goals. Because, at their core, computers are engineered devices that operate on a series of explicit instructions, they seem well-suited to behavioral approaches to designing instruction. This section reviews two specific behavioral designs: directed instruction and programmed instruction.

### Directed Instruction

Directed instruction is associated with traditional, didactic teaching and is often contrasted with student-centered learning and open learning environments (Hannafin, Land, & Oliver, 1999). In directed instruction, the instructor articulates learning objectives, then breaks them into their component tasks and works students through them in a hierarchical fashion, leading students incrementally from the "bottom up." Recognizing and mastering key concepts is made easier for students by isolating each component, allowing learners to master one component before learning the next, and providing students with explicit, teacher-directed instruction and practice (Hannafin, Land, & Oliver, 1999).

Directed instruction relies heavily on an engineering paradigm in which teaching and learning activities are designed using structured templates, and internal conditions conducive to learning are fostered by engineering external conditions. Mastery of content is viewed as the ability to produce correct responses. The instructional designer or instructor adopts the role of "learning engineer" and learning plays the part of raw materials (Hannafin, Land, & Oliver, 1999). Computer technology can enhance directed instruction through (1) increased access to information, (2) explicit prompts, (3) access to multiple examples, (4) increased opportunities for feedback regarding right and wrong responses, and (5) increased opportunities for practice. As well, the computer can offer learners relief from cognitive loading thereby freeing up working memory (Kirschner, Sweller, & Clark, 2006).

### Programmed Instruction

Programmed instruction originated when behavioral principles were applied to the problem of academic instruction—a method pioneered by B.F. Skinner (1968). The approach is equally applicable to computer-based and paper-based settings (Burton, Moore, & Magliaro, 1996). In programmed instruction, instruction consists of content broken down into learning units and arranged into "frames" presented with increasing difficulty. Salient features of Skinner's approach are immediate, frequent assessment, and feedback; learners cannot progress to the next frame until they have demonstrated mastery by successfully completing the objective of the task.

To address issues such as boredom due to incremental progress and linear structure, or learners at various levels of competence, branching instructional programs were developed that permitted fast learners to skip ahead and directed struggling learners to remedial material. The increasing prevalence of computer-based learning environments allowed for more complex branching, automatic record-keeping, more complex graphics, and synthesized speech.

Drill-and-practice software, representative of programmed instruction, is extremely, common today (Burton, Moore, & Magliaro, 1996; Driscoll, 2005).

## Cognitive Models of Instructional Design

As noted earlier in this chapter, cognitivist instructional design models address the way learners mentally process learning material. This section reviews two cognitivist approaches: Gagne's three-part instructional theory and Merrill's Instructional Transaction Theory.

### Gagné's Theory

Gagné's instructional theory (Gagné, Briggs, & Wager, 1992) is made up of three components: a taxonomy of learning outcomes, conditions of learning, and nine events of instruction. The taxonomy of learning outcomes refers to Gagné's belief that it is important to distinguish the varying domains of capabilities that human beings can acquire. The nine events of instruction suggest a formal structure to lessons beginning with gaining the learner's attention and continuing through a variety of activities to practice and assess the skills taught in increasingly less familiar contexts (called far transfer of learning, because the learning is transferred beyond the original context in which it was taught).

Gagné's theory bridges the behaviorist and cognitivist theories. Although the characteristics of this theory of instructional design tend to focus on instructor control, with prescribed learning events that are external to learners, Gagné also addresses the needs of individual learners. Gagné's model makes the assumption that knowledge is objective, external, and predefined and can be transmitted from knowers to learners. Learners are passive recipients of information. This method of instructional design is most effective when the overall goal of learning is to acquire facts or perform a procedure in a prescribed way. Gagné's theory is less supportive of creative thinking or personal knowledge building and understanding.

### Merrill's Instructional Transaction Theory

M. David Merrill's (1999) instructional transaction theory (ITT) is intended to guide more effective instructional design, improve development efficiency, especially the development of microworlds and simulations, enable more effective learner guidance, and allow for instruction that adapts to individual learners in real time.

ITT starts with the concept of knowledge objects, which take one of four different forms: entities, properties, activities, or processes. Knowledge objects, which contain raw information that learners need to reach an instructional goal, have attributes (such as name and media type) and descriptions of purpose, plus other descriptors that can be defined by a user. As envisaged by Merrill, stored knowledge objects will be selected and arranged into meaningful learning experiences by associated but separate instructional algorithms ("transactions") that specify instructional strategy elements like presentation, practice, and learner guidance. The principal pedagogical features of Merrill's transaction model are a learning outcome classification scheme; a common framework for specifying knowledge structure, presentation, practice, and learner guidance; and Gagné's assumption of unique conditions of learning for different learning outcomes (Merrill, 1999).

Merrill's transactions amount to a new schema for classifying and achieving instructional outcomes. According to him, transactions can support the learning of both hard skills in well-structured domains, and soft skills in ill-structured domains.

## Constructivist Models of Instructional Design

As noted earlier in this chapter, constructivist approaches help learners set and meet their own learning goals in environments that are flexible or even automatically adaptive to their learning needs. Constructivist approaches are based on the belief that knowledge is personally constructed, and constructivist learning environments provide learners with the ability to build their own knowledge. This section reviews two constructivist approaches: the learner-centered framework and problem-based learning.

### The Learner-Centered Framework

Within the learner-centered framework, the instructor's role is that of a guide who facilitates learning, rather than one who passes knowledge on to learners. To this end, instructional designers must ensure that the conditions for learning are in place so that learners can take advantage of them (Laurillard, 2002). The conditions for learning must be meaningful to learners, provide learning challenges at an appropriate level, promote critical thinking, be situated, offer learning flexibility, occur within a social framework, and takes into account learner diversity (McCombs, 2000).

Bonk and Cunningham (1998) suggest that effective design for learner-centered instruction involves:

- Providing conditions for active cognitive reorganization

- Providing access to raw materials

- Promoting learner autonomy by focusing on learning that is personally meaningful

- Facilitating cognitive framing though effective organization of materials

- Eliciting and building on prior knowledge

- Encouraging questioning and dialogue

- Encouraging exploration that results in knowledge construction

- Providing opportunities for learners to become self-regulated

- Offering assessment based on authentic products such as portfolios or other higher-order tasks.

In the learner-centered approach, learners becomes an active agent in the learning and design process (Hannafin & Land, 1997; Laurillard, 2002). Learner interactivity and collaboration must be built into the instructional model (Wagner & McCombs, 1995). e-Learning, through the flexibility, versatility, and customizability of computer technology, can complement learner-centered designs by giving learners access to rich learning environments that address individual learning needs. These needs can include access to a variety of learning materials, opportunities for hands-on activities and simulations, scaffolding in the form of prompts and guidance, and increased opportunity for learner collaboration. As a result, these environments can provide opportunities for constructing, evaluating, reflecting on, and revising ideas (Herrington & Oliver, 2000; Jonassen, 2003).

By giving learners increased opportunities to interact with the learning environment, the instructor, and other learners, learning shifts from being a passive, decontextualized experience to one that is active, contextual, and in the learner's control (Bruning, Schraw, Norby, & Ronning, 2004). For this reason, it is important for developers to create learning environments that facilitate higher-order thinking skills. They can do so by providing opportunities for learners to engage in critical thinking, analysis, inference making, and problem solving through the technology's ability to situate learning in the context of challenging, complex, and realistic problems.

## Problem-Based Learning

In problem-based learning (PBL), a problem or case lies at the heart of the learning experience and drives learning and meaning-making. This is in contrast to objectivist and cognitivist learning approaches, in which problems are merely used as examples of previously taught principles or procedures. In constructivist PBL, students learn domain-specific knowledge and skills in order to solve a problem, not vice versa. Various interpretive and intellectual support systems (for example, modeling, coaching, and scaffolding) surround the central problem. The problem should be ill-defined or ill-structured; some aspects should be emergent and defined by learners (Jonassen, 1999).

The real key to learner engagement and motivation in PBL is learner ownership of problem. For that to happen, learners must feel that the problem is interesting, appealing, and engaging. The problem must perturb learners: they must be intrinsically motivated to solve it. Finally, the problem must be authentic. A minority of design theorists believe this means faithfully replicating the performance of specific real-world tasks. Most constructivist educators, however, believe "authentic" simply means that the problem presents the same type of cognitive challenges and activity structure as problems in the real world. Activity theory might be used to analyze this underlying activity structure (Jonassen, 1999).

While computer technology is not required for the facilitation of PBL, it is well-suited for this type of learning activity. Representing authentic problems can be accomplished in a variety of ways—not the least through narrative. But simulation and micro-worlds are especially powerful approaches (Jonassen, 1999). In addition, the interpretive and intellectual support systems that PBL depends on, related cases, information resources, cognitive tools, conversation and collaboration tools, and social and contextual support systems, are likely to be more effective if they take advantage of ICT and the Internet.

## Some Concluding Thoughts About Constructivist Learning

The transition from teacher-centered to learner-centered approaches is progressing slowly. Many implementations of constructivist learning environments fail to fully utilize what constructivist learning is (Clark, 2006). More fundamentally, however, many instructional designers simply rely on more familiar approaches to design. "The traditional pedagogical approaches to learning generally remain unchanged, in spite of the fact that the introduction of the new medium typically demands new instructional methods" (Jochems, van Merriënboer, & Koper, 2004, p. ix).

Bonk and Cunningham (1998) offer recommendations for the design and development of e-learning in support of the learner-centered perspective. Their suggestions include (1) the establishment of community between learner and instructor; (2) go beyond using technology only as a means of delivery of information; (3) offer choice and variety of learning activities; (4) establish the instructor's role as a guide and facilitator, rather than a transmitter of information; (5) provide timely, constructive public and private feedback; (6) make use of computer-assisted communication to encourage peer mentoring; (7) allow learners to build their knowledge though the use of recursive assignments; (8) encourage activities that enhance thinking, such as writing and reflection; (9) make use of the expansive collections of resources available on the web through guided activities; (10) pay careful attention to task structure and expectations to help learners manage their time and their learning goals; (11) use assessment in the form of portfolios and dimensional scoring schemes to measure the meeting of learning objectives (low to high) on different components or skill sets required to complete the task; and (12) make use of the interactivity and flexibility that computer-based tools offer to personalize the learning experience for each learner.

Finally, constructivism eschews objective and formulaic design principles, challenges learners to be self-regulated, and works best when levels of intrinsic interest are high.

# Technology-Driven Instructional Design

In this section we consider some new developments in e-learning that have the potential to build on design approaches rooted in learning theory. First, we provide an in-depth definition of learning objects, which are segments of pedagogically and contextually independent, self-contained instruction. The current attraction of learning objects is focused on the idea that they can be reused and sequenced into new instructional scenarios and learning contexts (Jones, 2004). Next, we discuss the IMS Learning Design, which provides a framework for using learning objects. We believe that a renewed emphasis on well-articulated instructional design derived from learning theories will enable these new developments to achieve their potential and avoid the pitfalls of being technologically rich and pedagogically poor.

## About Learning Objects

There are many definitions for them. The broadest definition is from the Institute of Electrical and Electronics Engineers (IEEE). In its proposed standard, IEEE (2002) defined an LO as "any entity, digital or non-digital, that may be used for learning, education or training." Wiley (2000) narrowed the definition as "any digital resource that can be reused to support learning." In its most basic form, a learning object can be any content in digital form that facilitates some valued learning in some computer-based media context. This would mean that a learning object could be anything from a selection of text or video to an entire instructional unit (Polsani, 2003).

Learning objects, from an instructional design perspective, represent the opportunity to customize instruction without having to replicate and reinvent core content. Instead of textbooks or pre-packaged materials as "one size fits all," LOs theoretically allow maximum flexibility in customizing content and pedagogy to suit the demands of the situation and the individual needs of the learner. In an ideal situation, it should be possible for an instructional designer to build learning materials by browsing and selecting the relevant learning object to meet a desired learning outcome and needs of the learner. This ideal forms the basis of learning object repositories like Multimedia Educational Resource for Learning and Online Teaching (MERLOT) (www.merlot.org), Co-operative Learning Object Exchange (CLOE) (www.cloe. on.ca/), and LearnAlberta (www.learnalberta.ca/), which hope to transform teaching and learning in higher education. Cisco's (2000) reusable learning object project serves as an example of a successful implementation of learning objects.

This potential is certainly appealing, but the LO approach may foster a tendency for instructional designers to seek to create objects that suit technological needs rather than learning or pedagogical needs (Romiszowski, 2005). As a result, learning objects have attracted technological and pedagogical controversy (Bennett, 2005). Farrell, Liburd, and Thomas (2004) address the issue of how to sequence learning objects to support learner differences and learner control consistent with constructivism and learner-centered principles. They argue that, in a work environment, people often do not have the time to engage in a full-blown course and instead rely on just-in-time learning. In this type of learning situation, learning material built on a learning object framework seems ideal—learners can choose and take just what's needed.

Developers of learning objects use the term "reusable" or "repurposing" to emphasize the fact that the objects can be grouped and regrouped (Cisco, 2000). However, people often have difficulty locating and retrieving evaluation information regarding the pedagogical effectiveness of each object prior to download.

Nesbit, Belfer, and Vargo (2002) point out that common questions asked by learners and instructors when searching a repository are "Is it the right type?" "Is it the best I can find?" and "How should I use it?" Research has indicated that, in some cases, developers of learning objects may be reluctant to upload carefully constructed learning objects for others to use, making them essentially unavailable (Koppi, Bogle, & Bogle, 2005). Learning objects that do appear need to be carefully coded so that they can be effectively retrieved. Learning object repositories themselves generally lack guidelines for instructional use (McGee, 2004).

One key tool for coding learning objects so potential users can easily find them is meta-data. Meta-data standards, or the criteria and categories for labeling LOs, allow designers to locate learning objects based on a set of keywords. The IEEE describes meta-data as a set of "relevant characteristics of the learning object to which it applies" (IEEE 1484.12.1, 2002). Other standards for specifying meta-data include Dublin Core, UK LOM, CanCore, and Normetic.

The different standards offer a slightly different focus, making them relevant for different purposes. But meta-data for learning objects stresses fields such as interactivity, learning resource type, interactivity level, typical age of learner or user, typical amount of time required to use the object, language and similar descriptive fields. The CanCore website provides a collection of links and resources on this topic (www.cancore.ca). Consider why meta-data is helpful. Initially, few learning objects were designed with a specific pedagogy in mind. So someone searching for a learning object based on pedagogical use such as collaboration, problem solving, or critical thinking, would yield low results.

An approach that also places a greater emphasis on constructivist principles is Jonassen and Churchill's (2004) activity-centric meta-tagging schema. According to the authors, contemporary theoretical conceptions of learning all share the idea that learning is an activity. In this paradigm, learning objects act as catalysts for thinking in an activity-based learning system and as media for constructing learning artifacts. Learning object tagging should therefore describe the thinking processes they support. A learning object itself is not reused: it is reused within an activity. Jonassen and Churchill explicitly reject learning objects as information ("information is not instruction"), learning objects as teaching objects ("teaching is not learning"), and learning objects as practice and assessment ("ability to apply knowledge cannot be tracked, it must be reflected in artifacts and examined qualitatively through reflection in context").

Rather, Jonassen and Churchill (2004) believe that learning objects should be described in multiple dimensions: as information objects (conceptual models or representations), conversation objects (for collaboration or argumentation), learning objects (this refers to artifacts of the learning process only), thinking objects (for creative, critical, or meta-cognitive thinking), knowledge objects (ranging from declarative to experiential to strategic), and activity objects (which embody component skills or reasoning).

## IMS Learning Design

The IMS Global Learning Consortium has attempted to address the issue of pedagogical evaluation of learning objects within instructional design with the development of the IMS Learning Design (IMS-LD) framework. Based on educational modeling language (EML) developed at the Open University of the Netherlands (OUNL), IMS-LD provides a framework of elements that can describe any design of a teaching-learning process in a formal way.

IMS-LD identifies four issues related to effective design: (1) the nature of knowledge; (2) the nature of learning; (3) motivation; and (4) social exchange. Although learning material is most often designed with specific learning objectives in mind, it is also often very specific to the situation or context of those learning objectives (Koper, 2005). To address this, Koper recommends an "if–then–with" formula for designing instruction: If given situation "S," then use learning design method "M" in consideration with probability of success "P" (2005, p. 6).

IMS-LD is based on a theater analogy wherein elements such as roles, acts, stage environment, role parts, sequences, and conditions are specified within a script. Roles are performed by actors—in this case the actors' roles are those of instructor and learner. Acts serve as divisions between distinct instructional components. The stage environment becomes the learning environment. Role parts refer to the activities of the actors—the role of the instructor and the learner. The sequence of activities describes the order, in time, of learning events. Finally, the conditions refer to specific situations of the learning activity. Other factors include the specificity of the script, which can range from detailed to improvisation; realization of the model of the play, where the same script can be staged differently; the scripting language, which can be any genre; and the constraints of the medium, which refer to inherent limitations. Just like theater, in which a play is written by a skilled playwright and interpreted by a director and actors, instructional design is often written by instructional designers and interpreted by instructors and learners.

In the learning design framework, general bibliographic factors, situational factors, learning outcomes, and learning objectives are contained within a database. This allows an instructional designer to search for relevant learning elements based on the context of the desired learning outcomes. Situational factors can be divided into learning outcomes and learning conditions. Learning outcomes refer to effectiveness, efficiency, attractiveness, and accessibility, whereas learning conditions refer to the learning objectives, learner characteristics, and the characteristics of the setting and media. Koper (2005) includes the value of the learning designer into the equation.

Learning design needs to be comprehensive, specifying how, when, and why learning material is made available. It should support blended learning; be flexible in describing multiple theories; be able to describe various learning conditions; be able to identify, isolate, de-contextualize and exchange parts; be standardized with other notation; be able to be processed automatically; and be applicable in different settings (Koper, 2005).

## Implications for Instructional Design

A major problem faced today is that mediocre or uninformed designs from other learning environments are being adapted for e-learning. We propose that templates based on sound, widely accepted pedagogical models should be used to create e-learning, no matter what specification is chosen as the digitization platform.

In this chapter, we have identified IMS-LD as a suitable structure for modeling learning programs; thus the templates that we propose can be implemented in IMS-LD. We are including representations of behaviorist, cognitivist, and constructivist instructional designs (Figures 13.1, 13.2, and 13.3). The tool used to complete the templates was LICEF's MOTPlus 1.4.2.5, the only graphical modeling tool for learning design.

These basic representations allow for a successful implementation of pedagogy within a learning context. Once users are able to identify which pedagogy is best suited to their particular situation, assuming that they have the requisite background knowledge and follow the best practices embodied in the LD models, they will contribute to the pedagogical effectiveness of their implementation. It is important to recognize that matching pedagogical models to situations is no simple matter, and that this step itself demands further study and supporting techniques and technology.

## Concluding Thoughts

Learning theories are a fundamental part of sound pedagogy. As we have demonstrated here, for pedagogy to be truly part of new educational media and e-learning, it must be a large consideration in the design as well as in the implementation of e-learning.

In a student-centered approach, effective computer-enhanced instruction must be meaningfully suited to the pedagogy or goals of the learning task, thereby allowing active learner engagement and complex learning (Abrami, 2001). It is essential that we focus

# Figure 13.1. Behaviorist Learning Design Template

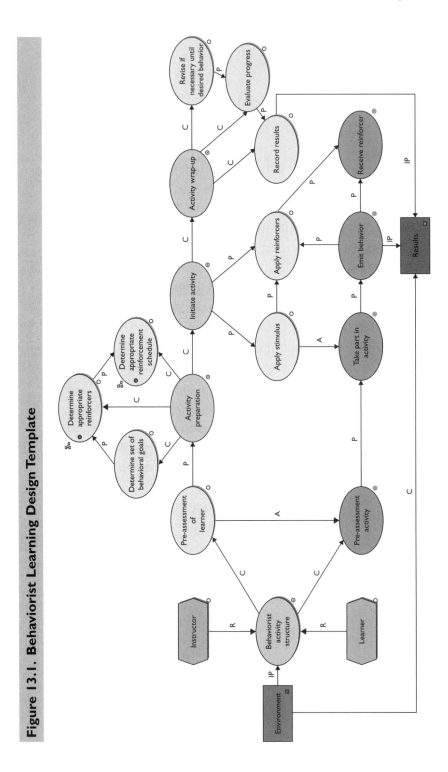

**Figure 13.2. Cognitivist Learning Design Template**

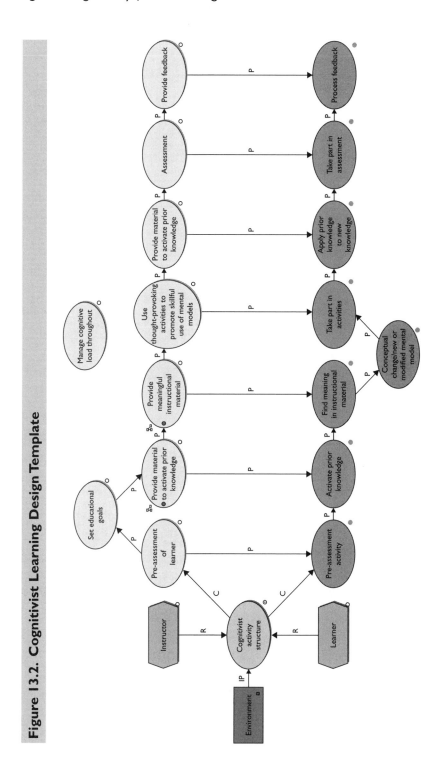

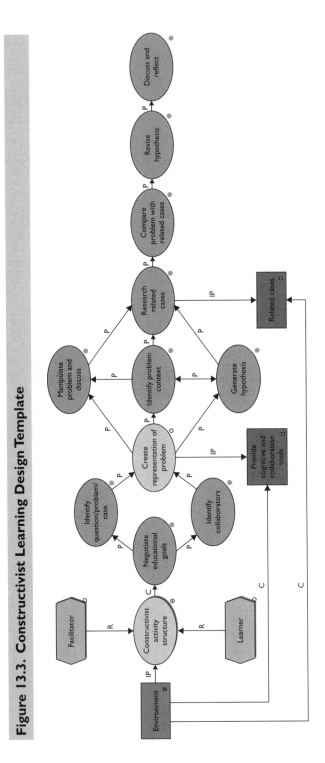

**Figure 13.3. Constructivist Learning Design Template**

on the effects of learning with technology rather than the effects of learning from technology (Salomon, Perkins, & Globerson, 1991). As Bransford, Brown, and Cocking (2000) have pointed out, a central question should be how technology can best support the way learners learn.

We have demonstrated that templates based on sound pedagogy are possible. However, there are several key issues that must be considered. First, validation of these models is very difficult because most designers have their own style and interpretation of how these templates should be completed. Each template is an approximation of a best practice. Another difficulty is matching the right pedagogy to each situation. How do we select templates? How do we teach instructors to select the right templates? Finally, there are not yet any functional LD "players" at the time of this publication and, therefore, it is difficult to verify and concretize these templates.

# References

Abrami, P.C. (2001). Understanding and promoting complex learning using technology. *Educational Research and Evaluation, 7*(2–3), 113–136.

Alexander, P.A., & Murphy, P.K. (1998). The research base for APA's Learner-Centered Psychological Principles. In N. Lambert & B.L. McCombs (Eds.), *How students learn: Reforming schools through learner-centered education.* Washington, DC: American Psychological Association.

Alonso, F., Lopez, G., Manrique, D., & Vines, J.M. (2005). An instructional model for web-based e-learning education with a blended learning process approach. *British Journal of Educational Technology, 36*(2), 217–235.

Ausubel, D. (1978). In defense of advance organizers: A reply to the critics. *Review of the Educational Research, 48,* 251–257.

Bannan-Ritland, B., Dabbagh, N., & Murphy, K. (2000). Learning object systems as constructivist learning environments: Related assumptions, theories, and applications. In D.A. Wiley (Ed.), *The instructional use of learning objects: Online version*. Retrieved April 4, 2005, from http://reusability.org/read/chapters/bannan-ritland.doc

Bates, A.W., & Poole, G. (2003). *Effective teaching with technology in higher education: Foundations for success*. San Francisco, CA: Jossey-Bass.

Bennett, S. (2005). Using related cases to support authentic project activities. In A. Herrington & J. Herrington (Eds.), *Authentic learning environments in higher education* (pp. 120–134). Hershey, PA: Idea Group, Inc.

Bernard, R., Abrami, P., Lou, Y., Borokhovski, E., Wade, A., Wozney, L., Wallet, P., Fiset, M., & Huang, B. (2004). How does distance learning compare with classroom instruction? A meta-analysis of the empirical literature. *Review of Educational Research, 74*(3), 379–434.

Bloom, B.S. (Ed.). (1956). *Taxonomy of educational objectives: The classification of educational goals: Handbook I: Cognitive domain*. New York: McKay.

Bonk, C., & Cunningham, D. (1998). Searching for learner-centered, constructivist, and sociocultural components of collaborative educational learning tools. In C. Bonk & K. King (Eds.), *Electronic collaborators: Learner-centered technologies for literacy, apprenticeship, and discourse* (pp. 25–50). Mahwah, NJ: Lawrence Erlbaum Associates.

Bonk, C.J., & Dennen, V.P. (1999). Getting by with a little help from my pedagogical friends. *Journal of Computing in Higher Education, 11*(1), 3–28.

Bransford, J.D., Brown, A.L., & Cocking, R.R. (Eds.) (2000). *How people learn: Brain, mind, experience, and school*. Washington, DC: National Academy Press.

Brown, J.S., Collins, A., & Duguid, P. (1989). Situated cognition and the culture of learning. *Educational Researcher, 18*(1), 32–41.

Bruner, J. (1966). *Towards a theory of instruction*. Cambridge, MA: Harvard University Press.

Bruning, R.H., Schraw, G.J., Norby, M.M., & Ronning, R.R. (2004). *Cognitive psychology and instruction* (4th ed.). Upper Saddle River, NJ: Pearson Merrill Prentice Hall.

Burton, J.K., Moore, D.M., & Magliaro, S.G. (1996). Behaviorism and instructional technology. In D.H. Jonassen (Ed.), *Handbook of research for educational communications and technology* (pp. 46–67). New York: Simon & Schuster.

Cisco Systems. (2000). Reusable learning objects strategy: Definition, creation process, and guidelines for building. Available: www.reusablelearning.org/Docs/Cisco_rlo_roi_v3-1.pdf [Retrieved April 2, 2002]

Claik, J.M., & Paivo, A. (1991). Dual coding theory and education. *Educational Psychology Review, 3,* 149–210.

Clark, R. (2006, September 28). Keynote presentation to the conference of the Montreal chapter of the International Society for Performance Improvement, Montreal, Quebec.

Deci, E.L., Koestner, R., & Ryan, R.M. (1999). A meta-analytic review of experiments examining the effects of extrinsic rewards on intrinsic motivation. *Psychological Bulletin, 25,* 627–668.

Dick, W. (1992). An instructional designer's view of constructivism. In T.M. Duffy & D.H. Jonassen (Eds.), *Constructivism and the technology of instruction: A conversation* (pp. 91–98). Hillsdale, NJ: Lawrence Erlbaum Associates.

Dick, W., & Carey, L. (1985). *The systematic design of instruction.* Glenview IL: Scott Foresman.

Dick, W., & Carey, L. (1990). *The systematic design of instruction* (3rd ed.). New York: HarperCollins.

Dickey, M.D. (2005). Engaging by design: How engagement strategies in popular computer and video games can inform instructional design. *Educational Technology Research & Design, 53*(2), 67–83.

Driscoll, M.P. (2005). *Psychology for learning and instruction.* Boston, MA: Pearson Education.

Duffy, T.M., & Cunningham, D.J. (1996). Constructivism: Implications for the design and delivery of instruction.

In D.H. Jonassen (Ed.), *Educational communications and technology* (pp. 170–199). New York: Simon & Schuster.

Ertmer, P.A., & Newby, T.J. (1993). Behaviorism, cognitivism, constructivism: Comparing critical features from an instructional design perspective. *Performance Improvement Quarterly, 6*(4), 50–72.

Farrell, R., Liburd, S., & Thomas, J. (2004). Dynamic assembly of learning objects. *Proceedings of the 14th World-Wide Web Conference (WWW '04)*, New York City.

Gagné, R.M., Briggs, L.J., & Wager, W.W. (1992). *Principles of instructional design* (4th ed.). Orlando, FL: Harcourt Brace Jovanovich.

Govindasamy, T. (2001). Successful implementation of e-learning: Pedagogical considerations. *The Internet and Higher Education, 4*(3), 287–299.

Hannafin, M.J., & Land, S.M. (1997). The foundations and assumptions of technology-enhanced student-centered learning environments. *Instructional Science, 25,* 167–202.

Hannafin, M., Land, S., & Oliver, K. (1999). Open learning environments: Foundations, methods and models. In C.M. Reigeluth (Ed.), *Instructional-design theories and models: A new paradigm of instructional theory, Volume II.* Mahwah, NJ: Lawrence Erlbaum Associates.

Herrington, J., & Oliver, R. (2000). An instructional design framework for authentic learning environments. *Educational Technology Research & Development, 48*(3), 23–48.

IEEE. (2002, July). Draft standard for learning object metadata. Available: http://ltsc.ieee.org/wg12/files/LOM_1484_12_v1_Final_Draft.pdf [Retrieved October 15, 2004]

Jochems, W., van Merriënboer, J., & Koper, R. (2004). Preface. In W. Jochems, J. van Merriënboer, & R. Koper (Eds.), *Integrated e-learning: Implications for pedagogy, technology and organization.* New York: RoutledgeFalmer.

Jonassen, D.H. (1996). *Computers in the classroom: Mindtools for critical thinking.* Englewood Cliffs, NJ: Prentice Hall.

Jonassen, D.H. (1999). Designing constructivist learning environments. In C.M. Reigeluth (Ed.), *Instructional-design theories and models: A new paradigm of instructional theory, Volume II*. Mahwah, NJ: Lawrence Erlbaum Associates.

Jonassen, D.H. (2000). Transforming learning with technology: Beyond modernism and post-modernism or whoever controls the technology creates the reality. *Educational Technology, 40*(2), 21–25.

Jonassen, D.H. (2003). *Learning to solve problems with technology: A constructivist perspective*. Upper Saddle River, NJ: Merrill.

Jonassen, D.H., & Churchill, D. (2004). Is there a learning orientation in learning objects? *International Journal on e-Learning, 3*(2), 32–41.

Jonassen, D.H., Howland, J., Marra, R.M., & Crismond, D. (2008). *Learning with technology* (3rd ed.). Upper Saddle River, NJ: Merrill/ Prentice Hall.

Jonassen, D.H., & Reeves, T.C. (1996). Learning with technology: Using computers as cognitive tools. In D.H. Jonassen (Ed.), *Handbook of research for educational communications and technology*. New York: Macmillan.

Jones, R. (2004). Designing adaptable learning resources with learning object patterns. *Journal of Digital Information, 6*(1), Article No. 305. Retrieved December 18, 2005, from http://jodi.tamu. edu/Articles/v06/i01/Jones/

Kirschner, P.A., Sweller, J., & Clark, R.E. (2006). Why minimal guidance during instruction does not work: An analysis of the failure of constructivist, discovery, problem-based, experiential, and inquiry-based teaching. *Educational Psychologist, 41*(2), 75–86.

Koper, R. (2005). An introduction to learning design. In R. Koper & C. Tattersall (Eds.), *Learning design: A handbook on modelling and delivering networked education and training* (pp. 3–20). Berlin and Heidelberg: Springer-Verlag.

Koppi, A.J., Bogle, L., & Bogle, M. (2005). Learning objects, repositories, sharing and reusability. *Open Learning, 20*, 83–91.

Lambert, N., & McCombs, B.L. (Eds.). (2000). *How students learn: Reforming schools through learner-centered education.* Washington, DC: American Psychological Association.

Laurillard, D. (2002). *Rethinking university teaching: A framework for the effective use of educational technology* (2nd ed.). London: Routledge.

Lave, J., & Wenger, E. (1991). *Situated learning: Legitimate peripheral participation.* New York: Cambridge University Press.

Mager, R.F. (1984). *Preparing instructional objectives* (2nd ed.). Belmont CA: Fearon-Pittman.

Marshall, H.H. (1998). Teaching educational psychology: Learner-centered and constructivist perspectives. In N. Lambert & B.L. McCombs (Eds.), *How students learn: Reforming schools through learner-centered education.* Washington, DC: American Psychological Association.

Mayer, R.E. (2001). *Multimedia learning.* Cambridge, UK: Cambridge University Press.

Mayer, R.E. (2003). *Learning and instruction.* Upper Saddle River, NJ: Merrill Prentice-Hall.

McCombs, B.L. (2000). *Assessing the role of educational technology in the teaching and learning process: A learner-centered perspective.* The Secretary's Conference on Educational Technology 2000. Retrieved June 28, 2001, from www.ed.gov/Technology/techconf/2000/mccombs_paper.html.

McGee, M.K. (2004, November). The relearning of elearning. *Information Week, 1014,* 16.

Merrill, M.D. (1991). Constructivism and instructional design. *Educational Technology, 39,* 45–53.

Merrill, W.D. (1999). Instructional transaction theory (ITT): Instructional design based on knowledge objects. In C.M. Reigeluth (Ed.), *Instructional-design theories and models: A new paradigm of instructional theory, Volume II.* Mahwah, NJ: Lawrence Erlbaum Associates.

Molenda, M. (1991). A philosophical critique on the claims of constructivism. *Educational Technology, 31*(9), 44–48.

Nardi, B.A. (Ed.). (1996). *Context and consciousness: Activity theory and human computer interaction.* Cambridge, MA: MIT Press.

Nesbit, J.C., Belfer, K., & Vargo, J. (2002). A convergent participation model for evaluation of learning objects. *Canadian Journal of Learning and Technology, 28*(3), 105–120.

Oliver, R. (1999) Exploring strategies for on-line teaching and learning. *Distance Education, 20,* 240–254.

Pea, R.D. (1985). Beyond amplification: Using the computer to reorganize human mental functioning. *Educational Psychologist, 20*(4), 167–182.

Polsani, P.R. (2003). Use and abuse of reusable learning objects. *Journal of Digital Information, 3*(4). Available: http://jodi.ecs.soton.ac.uk/Articles/v03/i04/Polsani/

Reigeluth, C.M. (1987). Educational technology at the crossroads: New mindsets and new directions. *Educational Technology Research and Development, 37,* 67–80.

Romiszowski, A.J. (2005). How's the e-learning, baby? Factors leading to success or failure of an educational technology innovation. *Educational Technology, 44*(1), 5–27.

Russell, D.R. (2002). Looking beyond the interface: Activity theory and distributed learning. In M.R. Lea & K. Nicoll (Eds.), *Distributed learning: Social and cultural approaches to practice.* London: Routledge/Falmer.

Salomon, G. (1983). The differential investment of mental effort in learning from different sources. *Educational Psychologist, 18,* 42–50.

Salomon, G., Perkins, D., & Globerson, T. (1991). Partners in cognition: Extending human intelligence with intelligent technologies. *Educational Researcher, 20*(3), 2–9.

Schank, R.C. (1996). Goal-based scenarios: Case-based reasoning meets learning by doing. In D. Leake (Ed.), *Case-based reasoning: Experiences, lessons and future directions* (pp. 295–347). Cambridge, MA: AAAI Press/The MIT Press.

Skinner, B.F. (1968). *The technology of teaching*. New York: Appleton-Century-Crofts.

Smith, P.L., & Ragan, T.J. (2005). *Instructional design* (3rd ed.). Hoboken, NJ: John Wiley & Sons.

Spiro, R.J., Feltovich, P.J., Jacobson, M.J., & Coulson, R.L. (1991). Knowledge representation, content specification, and the development of skill in situation-specific knowledge assembly: Some constructivist issues as they relate to cognitive flexibility theory and hypertext. *Educational Technology, 31*(9), 22–25.

Sweller, J., & Chandler, P. (1994). Why is some material difficult to learn? *Cognition & Instruction, 12*, 185–233.

Vygotsky, L. (1978). *Mind in society*. Boston: MA, Harvard University Press.

Wagner, E.D., & McCombs, B.L. (1995). Learner centered psychological principles in practice: Designs for distance education. *Educational Technology, 35*(2), 32–35.

Weigel, V.B. (2002). *Deep learning for a digital age: Technology's untapped potential to enrich higher education*. San Francisco, CA: Jossey-Bass.

Wiley, D.A. (2000). Connecting learning objects to instructional design theory: A definition, a metaphor, and a taxonomy. In D.A. Wiley (Ed.), *The instructional use of learning objects: Online version*. Available: http://reusability.org/read/chapters/wiley.doc [Retrieved March 17, 2004]

Wilson, B.G., Jonassen, D.H., & Cole, P. (1993). Cognitive approaches to instructional design. In G.M. Piskurich (Ed.), *The ASTD handbook of instructional technology* (pp. 21.1–21.22). New York: McGraw-Hill.

Winn, W.D. (1990). Some implications of cognitive theory for instructional design. *Instructional Science, 19*, 53–69.

Wozney, L., Venkatesh, V., & Abrami, P.C. (2006). Implementing computer technologies: Teachers' perceptions and practices. *Journal of Technology and Teacher Education, 14*(1), 173–2007.

Yan, Z., Hao, H., Hobbs, L.J., & Wen, N. (2003). The psychology of e-learning: A field of study. *Journal of Educational Computing Research, 29*(3), 285–296.

Zemsky, R., & Massy, W. (2004). Thwarted innovation: What happened to e-learning and why. A final report for The Weatherstation Project of the Learning Alliance at the University of Pennsylvania in cooperation with the Thomson Corporation. Available: www.irhe.upenn.edu/Docs/Jun2004/ ThwartedInnovation.pdf [Retrieved February 15, 2005]

◆ ◆ ◆

## Summary of Main Points

Readers should take away the following main ideas from this chapter:

- More than a replacement for the classroom, e-learning could offer alternate means of supporting and facilitating learning.

  - As the use of e-learning grew, people in educational technology realized that a gap in understanding existed between how people learn with computer technology and how people design for learning.

    The focus in e-learning tends to strongly favor technology over learning

  - On a more fundamental level, the problems might emanate from a limited understanding of learning theory and how it applies to e-learning.

- Learning theories encapsulate beliefs about how people learn and are translated into instructional strategies, such as behaviorism, cognitivism, and constructivism.

  - In turn, these different strategies are used to produce different learning outcomes and are intended to be used purposefully by instructional designers when they design learning programs.

- Designers often find translating these theories and strategies into detailed designs for learning programs to be difficult, and blending several strategies together to achieve a larger goal is even more difficult.

- Three dominant approaches to learning include:

  - Behaviorism, which holds that instruction is most effective when learners are rewarded as they progress incrementally toward larger learning goals. Two design approaches to behaviorist instruction include Direct Instruction and Programmed Instruction.

  - Cognitivist instruction advocates for highly structured lessons with explicit learning objectives; sees knowledge as something that is real, objective, and measurable; and is concerned with mental models and how knowledge is organized in the brain.

    Two design approaches to cognitivist instruction include situated cognition and distributed cognition.

  - Constructivism is based on the belief that knowledge is socially constructed, and constructivist learning environments provide learners with the ability to build their own knowledge. Two design approaches to constructivist instruction include the Student-Centered Framework and Problem-Based Instruction.

  - e-Learning can comprise all of a teaching and learning environment, or it can comprise one part of it—"blended" with classroom instruction and a variety of digital elements.

- Learning objects represent the opportunity to customize instruction without having to replicate and reinvent core content.

  - To help users identify the approach taken in a given learning object, the IMS Global Learning Consortium has proposed an approach, known as IMS Learning

Design (IMS-LD), that labels the teaching and learning processes embedded in a learning object in a formal and consistent way.

> IMS-LD identifies four issues related to effective design: (1) the nature of knowledge, (2) the nature of learning, (3) motivation, and (4) social exchange. IMS-LD is based on a metaphor of a street theatre, whose "script" includes roles, acts, stage environment, role-parts, sequences, and conditions. IMS-LD is intended to be comprehensive, specifying how, when, and why learning material is made available and can support a variety of learning contexts, including blended learning.

- Templates based on sound, widely accepted pedagogical models should be used to create e-learning, no matter what specification is chosen as the digitization platform.

◆ ◆ ◆

# Guiding Questions for Discussion

- Do you have a preferred approach to designing instruction, such as behaviorist, cognitivist, or constructivist? If so, why do you favor that approach?

- This chapter suggested that e-learning can be designed to support any of the three general approaches. Provide examples for each of the three. How do these learning programs represent a given approach (for example, why is a particular e-learning program an example of constructivist learning)?

- Review the three templates provided in the latter part of the chapter. How might you use these when designing e-learning programs? What would be the advantages of these templates? Disadvantages?

| Learn More About It | |
|---|---|
| Links | Extensive collection of summaries on theories of learning is available from the TIP Database: Explorations in Learning & Instruction: The Theory Into Practice (http://tip.psychology.org/) |
| | For more information on the IMS Global Learning Consortium, please visit www.imsglobal.org/learningdesign/index.html |
| Books, Papers, Reports, and Articles | One of the preferred textbooks on learning theory: Driscoll, M.P. (2004). *Psychology of learning for instruction* (3rd ed.). Boston, MA: Allyn & Bacon. |
| | One of the most comprehensive compendiums of instructional design theory: Reigeluth, C. (Ed.). (1999). *Instructional design theories and models: A new paradigm of instructional theory* (volume 2). Mahwah, NJ: Lawrence Erlbaum Associates. |

# Chapter 14

# Design Research

## A Better Approach to Improving Online Learning

*Thomas C. Reeves, The University of Georgia,*
*Jan Herrington, University of Wollongong,*
*and Ron Oliver, Edith Cowan University*

### About This Chapter

It hardly needs saying that the largely pseudoscientific research studies reviewed for these meta-analyses fail to provide practitioners with much-needed guidance for improving the design and use of online learning. Another approach exists. It is called design research, and this chapter explores it. Specifically in this chapter, we recommend a design research agenda that has the potential to enhance the effectiveness and worth of online learning. We first describe the rationale for design research, next present design research strategies, and then suggest how to overcome challenges to design research. We conclude by suggesting how readers might become more actively involved in design research in a variety of roles, from academic researcher to consumer of e-learning.

# Introduction

It is regrettable, if not pathetic, that quasi-experimental comparisons of online learning environments with traditional classroom learning environments continue to be published in refereed journals when we have known for nearly twenty-five years that such media comparison studies are useless (Clark, 1983). The most recent large-scale meta-analysis of these types of media comparisons was reported in the *Review of Educational Research* by Bernard, Abrami, Lou, Borokhovski, Wade, Wozney, Wallet, Fiset, and Huang (2004) to address the question: "How does distance education compare to classroom instruction?" Although the researchers found over one thousand quasi-experimental comparisons of distance education courses with face-to-face instruction courses in the refereed research literature published between 1985 and 2002, their review only included 232 studies because the majority of the published studies did not meet the criteria for inclusion in the meta-analysis. Indeed, Bernard and his colleagues (2004) reported that most of the comparison studies they found were "of low quality" (p. 416).

The final outcome of their meta-analysis was essentially "no significant differences" between distance and classroom instruction. These results were similar to the dismal findings of most other large-scale reviews of educational technologies (for example, Dillon & Gabbard, 1998; Fabos & Young, 1999). It hardly needs saying that the largely pseudoscientific research studies reviewed for these meta-analyses fail to provide practitioners with much needed guidance for improving the design and use of online learning.

There is a better way.

The purpose of this chapter is to describe and recommend a "design research" agenda that has the potential to enhance the effectiveness and worth of online learning. The key points addressed in this chapter are:

- The rationale for design research,
- Design research strategies, and
- Overcoming challenges to design research.

# The Rationale for Design Research

Although most online learning proponents decry the lack of significant differences found between online and classroom instructional methods, some in the distance education world actually seem to regard such results as a point of pride. Hundreds of studies that have shown no significant differences in academic achievement between distance education instruction (including online learning) and traditional face-to-face instruction are listed on a website called the "No Significant Differences Phenomenon" (www.nosignificantdifference .org/). The creator of this site and author of a book with the same name, Thomas L. Russell (1999), maintains that this research record proves that distance education is just as effective as traditional classroom instructional methods. Given the lamentable outcomes of our education and training systems at all levels, this hardly seems acceptable, much less a point of pride.

Dabbagh and Bannan-Ritland (2005) provide an excellent synthesis of the implications of previous online learning research, but ultimately conclude that:

> The field of online learning (and educational research in general) is beset with criticisms of the research efforts conducted thus far, and reading the research is often an exercise in patience because of the need to weed through the various approaches and results. Reading research is also often associated with negative perceptions such as conflicting results and trivial topics. (p. 70)

Meanwhile, online learning is growing at an amazing pace. Commercial institutions such as the University of Phoenix Online and Laureate Education (formerly Sylvan Learning Systems) already enroll tens of thousands of online learners, while traditional institutions ranging from large research intensive universities (such as www.umassonline.net/) to community colleges (such as www.rio .maricopa.edu/) are rushing to put courses and whole degree programs online. According to the most recent estimates from the Sloan Foundation's (2004) survey of online learning penetration, more than 2.6 million post-secondary students were learning online in the United States as of the fall of 2004. These figures do not even begin to encompass the hundreds of thousands of people learning online in Australia, China, Europe, India, and around the globe.

If the research base is as poor as it obviously is, what are designers and instructors of online learning using to guide their practice? The answer is anecdotal information. There is a virtual cottage industry in books, journals, magazines, workshops, conferences, and online support for designing online learning environments as well as for teaching and learning online. Unfortunately, very few of these resources are based on rigorous research. Two of the best-known online learning experts, Rena M. Palloff and Keith Pratt (1999), state as much in the preface of their best-selling book, *Building Learning Communities in Cyberspace: Effective Strategies for the Online Classroom*:

> Although computer-mediated learning is currently under study in many venues, very little scientific research has been conducted regarding the efficacy, benefits, or pitfalls of a computer-mediated approach to education. Within the next few years, the results of studies should become increasingly available. In the meantime, much of what is written about and shared— including what is in this book—is anecdotal and based on the experiences of instructors and students. (p. xvi)

The prediction that more research should be forthcoming made by Palloff and Pratt (1999) has certainly been realized, but very little of it stands up to serious scientific scrutiny (Reeves, 2005). Neither the aforementioned pseudoscientific media comparison studies nor the ever-burgeoning qualitative studies of synchronous and asynchronous learning environments tell practitioners enough about how to design and implement online teaching and learning. This inadequate research base provides precious little guidance regarding the most effective alignments of educational objectives, content, subject-matter expertise, instructional methods, learning tasks, technological affordances, and assessment strategies for online learning.

Despite a rosy future for online learning predicted by Duderstadt, Atkins, and Van Houweling (2002), Pittinsky (2003), and others, our current state of evidence-based knowledge about this topic is woefully inadequate, and as others have noted, the research findings are often contradictory (Dabbagh & Bannan-Ritland, 2005).

We cannot wait any longer for traditional quantitative and qualitative research approaches to provide stronger research-based design principles for online learning. An entirely different research approach is needed. To provide enhanced guidelines for designing and implementing effective online teaching and learning environments, there is an urgent need for what has been labeled "design research" (Laurel, 2003), "design-based research" (Kelly, 2003), "development research" (van den Akker, 1999), "design experiments" (Brown, 1992; Collins, 1992), and "formative research" (Newman, 1990). The three critical characteristics of "design experiments," as described by Brown (1992) and Collins (1992), are:

- Addressing pressing complex problems in real contexts in close collaboration with practitioners;

- Integrating known and hypothetical design principles with technological affordances to render plausible solutions to these real world problems; and

- Conducting cycles of rigorous and reflective inquiry to test and refine innovative learning environments as well as to define new design principles.

There are major differences between the philosophical framework and goals of traditional educational technology research methods, both predictive and interpretive, and design-based research approaches. Van den Akker (1999) clarifies the differences:

> More than most other research approaches, development research aims at making both practical and scientific contributions. In the search for innovative "solutions" for educational problems, interaction with practitioners . . . is essential. The ultimate aim is not to test whether theory, when applied to practice, is a good

predictor of events. The interrelation between theory and practice is more complex and dynamic: is it possible to create a practical and effective intervention for an existing problem or intended change in the real world? The innovative challenge is usually quite substantial, otherwise the research would not be initiated at all. Interaction with practitioners is needed to gradually clarify both the problem at stake and the characteristics of its potential solution. An iterative process of "successive approximation" or "evolutionary prototyping" of the "ideal" intervention is desirable. Direct application of theory is not sufficient to solve those complicated problems. (pp. 8–9)

# Design Research Strategies

The key strategies for design research are straightforward, but profoundly different from traditional approaches to online learning research. Researchers wishing to engage in design research to improve the state of the art of online learning should:

1. Work closely with practitioners to define important pedagogical outcomes that online learning is intended to address. The rationales for online learning may include extending learning opportunities to learners who would not otherwise have them, improving the quality of teaching and learning, reducing costs (or even making profits), and/or increasing the efficiency of an educational system.

2. Create a prototype online learning environment that addresses these outcomes. Throughout the online learning prototyping and refinement stages, emphasize content and pedagogy over technology. Give special attention to supporting meaningful interactions for learners as well as nurturing the development of substantive online learning communities.

3. Test and refine the online learning environment until the pedagogical outcomes are reached. This will not be realized in weeks or months, but in most cases will take years to

accomplish, especially for higher-order outcomes such as problem solving and lifelong learning.

4. Reflect on the process continuously to extract reusable design principles that can inform the design and implementation efforts of other educators and researchers. These design principles will also enhance your own online learning development projects in the future.

A hypothetical scenario is the best way of illustrating how these design research strategies might actually be put into action. Imagine that a group of faculty members at a highly rated school of public health at a research intensive university in North America has received funding from a private foundation to put a master's of public health (MPH) degree online. The target audience for this degree program consists of health workers in Spanish-speaking countries in South America. While it is well known that there is a shortage of public health officers with advanced degrees in South America, the specific set of competencies needed by these professionals is unclear.

The North American academics could have decided to convert their existing MPH courses to online formats without making substantive changes to content or the pedagogical dimensions of the learning environments (Reeves & Reeves, 1997). Or they could have looked at how other health-related online learning programs are designed and emulate them. Alternatively, they could have sought to build their online MPH courses using the heuristics and design guidelines drawn from anecdotal reports and the limited implications of existing research studies. But instead they decide to employ design research as a basis for developing, implementing, and systematically refining this online design program.

The first design research strategy is to identify a group of practitioners with whom to define the critical outcomes that this new MPH program should target. In this case, the North American faculty members decide to collaborate with health care workers in the Ministry of Health in Peru as well as with medical faculty members of one of Peru's top public universities. Through face-to-face meetings and an extensive review of the literature, the North and South American collaborators identify the major outcomes that graduates of the new online MPH program will be expected to achieve. Among the thirty major competencies defined are:

- Design a surveillance system for disease conditions important to public health.

- Apply a risk assessment process, including exposure assessment, and the degree of uncertainty in assessing a given disease outbreak.

- Implement an action plan to improve existing and potential methods of immunization and other disease prevention procedures.

- Evaluate the processes and outcomes of social and behavioral interventions on the health of communities, families, and individuals.

The second strategy involves developing prototype online learning environments. Working with online learning design experts from Australia and the United States, the collaborators decide to utilize authentic tasks as the defining pedagogy in these online courses (Herrington, Reeves, Oliver, & Woo, 2004). For example, in a survey methods and statistics course, the students will be tasked with actually going out into their local communities to collect data concerning the rates of infant immunization, with the goal of learning how to collect data and analyze statistics in the process. The following semester in a health promotion course, they will use the data from the earlier course to plan and implement a public health education campaign focusing on young mothers in their community. Although authentic tasks such as these have the potential to provide real service to the participating communities, collecting data *in situ* and applying it to a real health campaign inevitably involves risks, and so the online courses are designed to provide learners with access to experts who provide guidance and feedback. The learners are also integrated into online learning communities for learner-to-learner support.

The third strategy requires the prototype learning environments to be implemented while collecting the data needed to make critical decisions for enhancing the design and implementation of these online courses. The collaborators conduct numerous small-scale and large-scale studies to test and refine the prototype public health courses. Quantitative, qualitative, and mixed-methods (Creswell, 2003) are used to provide the evidence needed to make progress toward reaching the critical outcomes. For example, a qualitative investigation of student attitudes toward the online courses might reveal that, although students value the authentic tasks, they find that the workload required is too heavy for them to also maintain the part-time jobs they need to hold to survive financially. Accordingly, the collaborators might decide to cut back on the number of required courses per semester or seek funds to provide students with living stipends.

The fourth and last strategy is to reflect on the findings of the various tests and evaluations to tease out feasible design principles that can be shared with others. The findings about student feelings of being overloaded when undertaking online courses defined by authentic tasks might support the specification of a design principle that online courses should clearly state the time-on-task allocations expected for learners, both online and in the field.

Is this scenario realistic? Peru is a country with enormous health challenges, including high rates of infant mortality and abbreviated life spans, especially among the indigenous people inhabiting squatter settlements around Lima or surviving at a subsistence level in remote Andean villages. It cannot be expected that the development of an online MPH program will enable improvements in these conditions overnight, but through design research, closer and closer approximations of the critical outcomes will be attained. Once Peru (or any other developing country) is provided with a cadre of well-trained public health officers, progress can be expected. The type of online learning program envisioned here, developed via long-term collaborative design research, has enormous potential to accomplish the two most desirable rationales for online learning in this case, that is, extending educational opportunities where they would otherwise not exist and enhancing the methods and results of teaching and learning.

# Overcoming Challenges to Design Research

Shifting online learning researchers away from traditional quantitative and qualitative studies won't be easy. Frankly, the ultimate goal of the research agenda of many people in academe is simply to enhance one's academic career. If this is the case, then the traditional approaches may provide faster rewards with respect to the publications needed to achieve academic promotion and tenure. However, if one's research agenda is primarily concerned with having socially responsible impact, then design research is highly recommended. In any case, design research may well be our only hope to stop the conduct of futile media comparison studies or the proliferation of sterile qualitative investigations. If we do not adopt design research, online learning research is at risk of continuing to be essentially inconsequential and increasingly irrelevant.

The good news is that we believe that academics can engage in design research and win the publish-or-perish game as well. Design research is such a new approach to educational inquiry that many journal editors and reviewers are unfamiliar with it. Reviewers may confuse the method with simple software evaluations. Editors may unfairly conclude that the *research* aspects of studies have suffered at the expense of the *development*. Hence, design researchers must be creative in their efforts to disseminate the findings of their endeavors. First, they should regularly present in-progress reports of their design research initiatives at international conferences such as ED-MEDIA (www.aace.org/conf/) and ASCILITE (www.ascilite .org.au/) as well as at discipline-specific conferences. Second, they should maintain a series of numbered interim reports of their findings on the design research project website. Third, from time to time, they should submit syntheses of their conference papers and interim reports to both print and online journals. Fourth, at the conclusion of a major design research cycle, they should publish a book and associated web resource to summarize the methods, results, and design principles emerging from the project. This requires rigorous attention to dissemination, but such attention helps to encapsulate the findings of each iterative cycle or stage into a whole and substantial contribution to the online learning community, in the form of frameworks or guidelines for others to apply.

# What You Can Do

If you are reading this book, we assume that you are interested in online learning as a researcher, developer, instructor, administrator, or consumer. If you are a researcher, we encourage you to reinvent yourself as a design researcher. The poor state of online learning research cannot be isolated from the widespread perception that educational research as a whole has been a failed enterprise. The U.S. Department of Education under the current federal administration of President George W. Bush has repeatedly proclaimed its agreement with the conservative Coalition for Evidence-Based Policy (2002) that "over the past thirty years the United States has made almost no progress in raising the achievement of elementary and secondary school students . . . despite a 90 percent increase in real public spending per student" (p. 1). Their solution to the crisis in educational research is to urge educational researchers to adopt the experimental clinical trials methods employed by medical researchers (Slavin, 2002). We concur with Olson (2004) that this recommendation is ill-advised because double blind experiments, although certainly feasible in medicine, are impossible in education. We also agree that the viability of randomized controlled trials in education is poor, given that implementation variance in education reduces treatment differences, causal agents are under-specified in learning, and the goals, beliefs, and intentions of students and teachers affect treatments to an extent much greater than the beliefs of patients affect medical treatments.

If you are a developer, we recommend that you align yourself closely with a vigorous team of researchers and practitioners to engage in design research. Online learning developers can no longer depend on their own creativity and anecdotal heuristics alone, but instead should engage in design research to develop and refine innovative, effective, and efficient e-learning environments.

If you are an instructor who also has research responsibilities, design research provides an approach to using your research time in a socially responsible manner. In a manner akin to what Shulman (2001) calls the "scholarship of teaching," design research is a rewarding activity with short-term and long-term payoffs. Even if you are an instructor with no allocated time for research, you can play a collaborating role in significant design research projects.

If you are an administrator, we strongly encourage you to reconsider the criteria used for academic promotions to include demonstrated impact on societal problems such as reducing inequitable access to education. It is not enough to tally the numbers of refereed journal publications academic staff publish or the dollar amounts of research grants they attract. In the social sciences, especially education, impact must be demonstrated.

Finally, if you are a consumer, we plead with you to demand better than you are receiving as a participant in most existing online learning programs. The status quo should not be tolerated when the teaching and learning opportunities provided online can be so much better, provided they are developed under the aegis of design research protocols. "No significant difference" is simply no longer acceptable.

# References

Bernard, R.M., Abrami, P.C., Lou, Y., Borokhovski, E., Wade, A., Wozney, L., Wallet, P.A., Fiset, M., & Huang, B. (2004). How does distance education compare to classroom instruction? A meta-analysis of the empirical literature. *Review of Educational Research, 74*(3), 379–439.

Brown, A.L. (1992). Design experiments: Theoretical and methodological challenges in creating complex interventions in classroom settings. *Journal of the Learning Sciences, 2*, 141–178.

Clark, R.E. (1983). Reconsidering research on learning with media. *Review of Educational Research, 53*(4), 445–459.

Collins, A. (1992). Towards a design science of education. In E. Scanlon & T. O'Shea (Eds.), *New directions in educational technology* (pp. 15–22). New York: Springer.

Creswell, J.W. (2003). *Research design: Quantitative, qualitative, and mixed method approaches* (2nd ed.). Thousand Oaks, CA: Sage.

Dabbagh, N., & Bannan-Ritland, B. (2005). *Online learning: Concepts, strategies, and application.* Upper Saddle River, NJ: Pearson Education.

Dillon, A., & Gabbard, R. (1998). Hypermedia as an educational technology: A review of the quantitative research literature on learner comprehension, control and style. *Review of Educational Research, 68*(3), 322–349.

Duderstadt, J.J., Atkins, D.E., & Van Houweling, D. (2002). *Higher education in the digital age: Technology issues and strategies for American colleges and universities.* Westport, CT: American Council on Education and Praeger.

Fabos, B., & Young, M.D. (1999). Telecommunications in the classroom: Rhetoric versus reality. *Review of Educational Research, 69*(3), 217–259.

Herrington, J., Reeves, T.C., Oliver, R., & Woo, Y. (2004). Designing authentic activities in web-based courses. *Journal of Computing in Higher Education, 16*(1), 3–29.

Kelly, A.E. (2003). Research as design. *Educational Researcher, 32*(1), 3–4.

Laurel, B. (2003). *Design research: Methods and perspectives.* Cambridge, MA: MIT Press.

Newman, D. (1990). Opportunities for research on the organizational impact of school computers. *Educational Researcher, 19*(3), 8–13.

Olson, D. (2004). The triumph of hope over experience in the search for "what works": A response to Slavin. *Educational Researcher, 33*(1), 24–26.

Palloff, R.M., & Pratt, K. (1999). *Building learning communities in cyberspace: Effective strategies for the online classroom.* San Francisco, CA: Jossey-Bass.

Pittinsky, M.S. (Ed.). (2003) *The wired tower: Perspectives on the impact of the internet on higher education.* Upper Saddle River, NJ: Prentice Hall.

Reeves, T.C. (2005). No significant differences revisited: A historical perspective on the research informing contemporary online learning. In G. Kearsley (Ed.), *Online learning: Personal reflections on the transformation of education* (pp. 299–308). Englewood Cliffs, NJ: Educational Technology Publications.

Reeves, T.C., Herrington, J., & Oliver, R. (2005). Design research: A socially responsible approach to instructional technology research in higher education. *Journal of Computing in Higher Education, 16*(2), 97–116.

Reeves, T.C., & Reeves, P.M. (1997). The effective dimensions of interactive learning on the WWW. In B.H. Khan (Ed.), *Web-based instruction* (pp. 59–66). Englewood Cliffs, NJ: Educational Technology Publications.

Russell, T.L. (1999). *The no significant difference phenomenon.* Montgomery, AL: International Distance Education Certification Center.

Shulman, L. (2001). Inventing the future. In P. Hutchings (Ed.), *Opening lines: Approaches to the scholarship of teaching and learning.* Menlo Park, CA: Carnegie Publications.

Slavin, R.E. (2002). Evidence-based education policies: Transforming educational practice and research. *Educational Researcher, 31*(7), 15–21.

Sloan Consortium. (2004*). Entering the mainstream: The quality and extent of online education in the United States, 2003 and 2004.* Retrieved April 4, 2005, from www.sloan-c.org/resources/).

van den Akker, J. (1999). Principles and methods of development research. In J. van den Akker, N. Nieveen, R. M. Branch,

K.L. Gustafson, & T. Plomp (Eds.), *Design methodology and developmental research in education and training* (pp. 1–14). Amsterdam, The Netherlands: Kluwer Academic Publishers.

◆ ◆ ◆

# Summary of Main Points

Readers should take away the following main ideas from this chapter:

- In general, the research on online learning is poor:
  - It is characterized by quasi-experimental comparisons of online learning environments with traditional classroom learning environments that do not stand up to scientific scrutiny and ultimately fail to provide practitioners with much-needed guidance for improving the design and use of online learning.
  - At the same time, online learning is growing at an amazing pace.
  - Designers and instructors of online learning are using anecdotal information to guide their practice, supported by cottage industry in books, journals, magazines, workshops, conferences, and online support for designing online learning environments as well as teaching and learning online.
  - This inadequate research base provides precious little guidance regarding the most effective alignments of educational objectives, content, subject-matter expertise, instructional methods, learning tasks, technological affordances, and assessment strategies for online learning.
- About design research:
  - Provides an alternative to this quasi-experimental approach

- Is known as design research (also design-based research, development research, design experiments, and formative research).

- Critical characteristics include:

  Addressing pressing complex problems in real contexts in close collaboration with practitioners

  Integrating known and hypothetical design principles with technological affordances to render plausible solutions to these real-world problems

  Conducting cycles of rigorous and reflective inquiry to test and refine innovative learning environments as well as to define new design principles

- Design research aims to make both practical and scientific contributions.

- The key strategies for design research include:

  - Working closely with practitioners to define important pedagogical outcomes that online learning is intended to address.

  - Creating a prototype online learning environment that addresses these outcomes. Throughout the online learning prototyping and refinement stages, emphasize content and pedagogy over technology.

  - Testing and refining the online learning environment until the pedagogical outcomes are reached. This will not be realized in weeks or months, but in most cases will take years to accomplish, especially for higher-order outcomes such as problem solving and lifelong learning.

  - Reflecting on the process continuously to extract reusable design principles that can inform the design and implementation efforts of other educators and researchers.

- Design research does not necessarily provide rewards with respect to the publications needed to achieve academic promotion and tenure as more traditional research does.

- In response, design researchers should:
  - Regularly present in-progress reports of their design research initiatives at international conferences and discipline-specific conferences
  - Develop websites for their design research projects and publish a series of numbered interim reports of their findings
  - Submit syntheses of their conference papers and interim reports to both print and online journals
  - At the conclusion of a major design research cycle, publish a book and associated web resource to summarize the methods, results, and design principles emerging from the project
- In terms of what readers can do:
  - Researchers can reinvent themselves as design researchers
  - Developers can align themselves with a vigorous team of researchers and practitioners to engage in design research
  - Instructors who also have research responsibilities can become involved in a design research project
  - Academic administrators can reconsider the criteria used for academic promotions to include demonstrated impact on societal problems

◆ ◆ ◆

# Guiding Questions for Discussion

- Review three refereed publications reporting quantitative and qualitative research findings related to online learning. Discuss the implications of these publications for practitioners.

- It is suggested above that the criteria for academic rewards such as promotion or tenure must be revised if design research is to be supported in higher education. Discuss what else will have to change in academe to accommodate what amounts to a major paradigm shift in how educational research is conducted.
- What are the implications of design research for commercial developers of online learning programs?

### Learn More About It

Links        Here are links to resources about design research and authentic tasks:

Columbia Center for New Media Teaching and Learning Design Research Resources: www.ccnmtl .columbia.edu/designresearch/

Design-Based Research Collective: www.designbasedresearch.org/

Design-Based Research Special Interest Group of the Canadian Institute for Distance Education Research: http://cider.athabascau.ca/CIDERSIGs/DesignBasedSIG/

*Educational Researcher* Special Issue on Design Research: www.aera.net/publications/?id=393

Example of Design-Based Research applied to online learning: www.telscenter.org/research/ research%20update/perspectives_newstyle/ designprinpers.html

Authentic Task Design: www.authentictasks.uow.edu.au/

# Part VI

# Economic Issues and Moving Forward

This part explores some of the economic issues that have affected the growth of e-learning in academic and corporate environments, as well as predictions for the future of e-learning. Chapters in this part include:

- Chapter 15, Is e-Learning Economically Viable? by Patrick Lambe, which explores how the evaluation of e-learning and its economic impact have evolved over the past several years from simplistic ROI considerations to metrics that are closely aligned with a business strategy, and thereby can be justified and tracked over time. Specifically, this chapter explores why investments in training and e-learning are not equivalent; the need for infrastructure investments in e-learning; and the a variety of economic benefits to e-learning, such as productivity and quality improvement, meeting a market requirement, providing access to new markets, as a means of leveraging human capital or as a means of reducing business risk.

- Chapter 16, e-Learning: Today's Challenge, Tomorrow's Reality by co-editor Saul Carliner, which explores three emerging trends in e-learning: a more responsive e-learning, e-learning by assignment, and e-learning as a way of life.

# Chapter 15

# Is e-Learning Economically Viable?

*Patrick Lambe, Straits Knowledge*

## About This Chapter

One of the early pieces of hype around e-learning was that it would lead to significantly reduced learning costs. Somehow, it didn't. This chapter explores how, in response, a growing, and more nuanced, approach to evaluating e-learning in general, and its economic impact in particular, have emerged. I first explain why investments in training and e-learning investments are not equivalents. Next I survey a range of different applications of e-learning and show how measurement of impact varies for each, depending on the nature of the business strategy that is being supported by e-learning.

## Introduction

As Margaret Driscoll notes in Chapter 2, early justifications of e-learning focused on its supposed "anywhere, any time" capabilities, and its potential cost savings in time, travel, and scalability of investment, as compared with face-to-face training. (Marc Rosenberg, who co-wrote Chapter 9, makes the same point in his 2000 book).

However, large enterprises soon found that technology investments required to make e-learning available "anywhere, any time" were also high and, even after calculating the cost savings from replacing a face-to-face course, discovered that demonstrating a positive return on investment (ROI) was still difficult.

In retrospect, the optimism was a bit exuberant (a point also explored by Margaret Driscoll in Chapter 2). Some of the key reasons that large enterprises had difficulty demonstrating a positive ROI were:

- The instability and immaturity of the technology—thus requiring replacements and additional investments before the initial ones could bring about a return

- A slowness to realize that the effectiveness of e-learning differs from that of classroom training—so the two are not necessarily equivalent

- Inappropriate models used to justify the investment in e-learning, especially ones focused on productivity improvements and cost reductions

In the end, some organizations found that e-learning turned out to be more expensive and provided less predictable outcomes than were initially expected.

In this chapter, I argue that the reason large organizations had these difficulties is that their models for evaluating the performance and financial impact of e-learning were as naïve as their understanding of the technology and as immature as their ideas about how to effectively deliver learning with technology. After all, the ultimate impact of e-learning is with the people who use it—and how that learning ultimately has an impact on the performance of those individuals and the institutions that invest in the learning. Few of the early ROI models really considered this.

I also explore the growing, and more nuanced, approach to evaluating e-learning in general and its economic impact in particular. Specifically, in this chapter I first explain why attempts to calculate the return on e-learning investments did not work. I do so by explaining why investments in training and e-learning are not equivalents. Then I explore responses to this problem by surveying a range of different applications for e-learning and showing how measurement of impact varies for each, depending on the nature of the business strategy that is being supported by e-learning. While doing so, I demonstrate that no single metric works for every type of business strategy and close by noting. TXhe metric tracked needs to be appropriate to the reason for investing in e-learning.

# Why Initial Attempts to Evaluate Investments in e-Learning Did Not Work

During the dot-com boom of the late 1990s, the justifications for investing in e-learning primarily focused on their potential to scale back training budgets. Organizations could realize savings through a reduction in training time (because e-learning courses often take less time than their classroom equivalents to complete and learners can complete courses at their desks, avoiding travel time) as well as savings in travel-to-training expenses—the airfare, hotel and lodging expenses that can often double the total cost of a single training class.

Implicit in these justifications is that classroom training activity could be easily interchanged with e-learning modules: that they were functional equivalents. I call this the *Myth of e-Learning as a Replacement for Training*. Although studies that compare the effectiveness of classroom and mediated learning have consistently shown that the two are equally effective (Bernard, Abrami, Lou, Borokhovski, Wade, Wozney, Wallet, Fiset, & Huang, 2004; Russell, ongoing), the materials used in the academic studies underlying these meta-analyses were often designed appropriately for the medium, and were primarily conducted in an academic environment. The actual experience of most organizations, especially ones who provide workplace learning, show the research to be profoundly naïve of actual practice (Davis, 2001).

Although certain types of, and some elements of, face-to-face training can be conducted effectively through electronic means, other types and elements cannot. Similarly, although some courses transfer from the classroom to an online environment with little change, many require a redesign before they can work effectively online. Consider the instance of rapid e-learning courses. They earn their name by rapidly converting classroom courses to online ones as follows: using authoring tools for the purpose, an instructor records the lecture of a classroom course on a computer while advancing the slides online. The entire program is recorded; quizzes and tests are added; and the recorded program is made available to learners, usually through a learning management system. Although efficient, the courses are often perceived as boring by the intended users, and usage rates have been astonishingly low. (One organization that produced fifty-four such courses found that, after a year, each only had, on average, four users.)

One of the primary reasons for this is that, as human beings, we find it difficult to sustain attention to each other without periodic interaction, whether by eye contact, body language, or verbal interaction. The reason why converted-to-video lectures of more than about twenty minutes are more "boring" than live lectures is the same reason why a lecturer who never makes eye contact and never modulates her delivery to the signals provided by her audience is a boring lecturer. Both are autistic (Lambe, 2002). To compensate for this, the duration of delivery needs to be shortened and appropriate motivational scaffolding needs to be built around the module (Day, Foley, Groeneweg, & van der Mast, 2004).

In other words, although both delivery modes might be able to present the same teaching content in exactly the same way, this equivalent level of learning does not necessarily happen with the same exact course. To translate effective classroom instruction into an effective e-instruction, the traditional training framework needs to be analyzed, disassembled, and reconstructed. Often, the result is not an entirely online course but, rather, a new hybrid comprising both face-to-face and technology-mediated elements called blended learning.

Different training needs have differing degrees of knowledge complexity and richness, which have a direct impact on the relative ease of knowledge transfer and the degree to which the knowledge can be made explicit in a modular e-learning format. Insights from knowledge management have revealed that knowledge is often layered with different levels of complexity and context dependency. David Snowden's (2000, 2004) ASHEN Framework, for example, decomposes knowledge into a gradient of increasing richness and complexity, which also corresponds to a gradient of relative ease of transfer:

- Artefactual or explicit knowledge embedded in things such as documents and tools is information rich and easily transferable through e-learning modules

- Skills, which can be differentiated into informational content supplemented by structured practice with feedback

- Heuristics, which are simple rules of thumb that people pick up through repeated exposure to the nuances of specific contexts, can be communicated through anecdotes and examples, but are rarely internalized well without exposure to the same contexts, so shared local context is just as important as the informational content

- Experience, which can only be developed internally over time through repeated exposure to a specific practice, can be accelerated if trainers provide well-structured and guided practice scenarios

- Natural talent, which cannot be communicated in any form but is part of the natural ability of a learner.

Human beings operate across all of these layers, so gifted trainers can modulate their teaching activities to tune into the range of knowledge needs and opportunities presented by the current audience, including being able to leverage the degree of experience and natural talent present among trainees. e-Learning modules cannot respond naturally across these different layers because the medium is highly insensitive to the specific context and background of its learners. e-Learning is only naturally effective at the artefactual level and in the informational portion of skills transfer.

For other layers of knowledge complexity, considerable analysis and design work is necessary to compensate for the natural constraints of the medium (whereas a face-to-face trainer will instinctively compensate).

This analysis and design activity involves additional costs that are hard to quantify in advance because each training requirement has different mixtures of knowledge types. This imposes a restructuring mortgage on the process of adopting e-learning. The Myth of e-Learning as a Replacement for Training does not anticipate or accommodate this important fact, and results in unrealistic expectations about both the investment required and the likely outcomes (Davis, 2001).

More significant than the fact that training and e-learning are not interchangeable learning products is the fact that the investment models for training and e-learning are polar opposites. Training budgets are typically recurrent budgets accounted for as an operations or infrastructure cost. In the context of training, therefore, discussions about return on investment (ROI) have traditionally had little relevance. It would be like seeking the ROI on groceries in a personal budget or of stationery supplies in a business. Both are costs of doing business.

In contrast, IT system investments are typically large capital expenditures with smaller recurrent maintenance and upgrade budgets, as well as an amortization mechanism as the system ages over time. In the face of large capital investments for technology, ROI has always been an important consideration, particularly because technology investments have traditionally been justified on the basis of the increases in productivity they promise.

Hence the indirect support of ongoing operations that has traditionally characterized the investment of training is not a sufficient justification for an e-learning project, because e-learning involves a technology investment. Furthermore, because technology investments are justified by the improvement in productivity that they are projected to offer, the training function is faced with becoming accountable to a productivity justification model that it has rarely had to account for before. Lacking experience with determining

ROI in general, and ROI for technology investments in particular, training groups fell prey to the temptation to calculate the economic viability of proposed investments in e-learning based on productivity measures; that seemed to be the accepted approach that worked for other groups in the organization that justified similar types of investments, and they lacked the experience to realize that this model was inappropriate.

However, no one considered whether such an approach to ROI really made sense for learning activities. Several fundamental questions were not asked:

- Can these activities produce outcomes that can be directly observed and measured in this way?

- Are learning activities most appropriately measured in this way?

- Can learning activities provide benefits other than direct productivity-related benefits?

## Assessing the ROI of e-Learning in the Context of Strategic Objectives It Is Intended to Support

If measuring improvements in productivity fails to provide a meaningful approach to evaluating the ROI of an e-learning program, what works? The following sections explore the answer to that question. In them, I look at some of the most common ways that organizations deploy e-learning to support their strategic objectives and show how measurement of viability and impact can be approached. Specifically, I look at the ways to measure the viability and impact of e-learning in support of these specific strategic objectives:

- Productivity improvement

- Quality improvement

- Leveraging human capital

- Risk reduction

- Basic qualification to remain in the marketplace

- Access to new markets

When looking at the ways to measure the viability and impact of e-learning in these instances, I explore the use of three assessment techniques: contingent valuation, outcomes-based evaluation, and most significant change (MSC) evaluation. But before exploring any of these, I first consider the nature of the infrastructural investment in e-learning and why both the investment and impacts need to be measured differently.

## Why Investments and Impacts of e-learning Need Their Own Measurements

A good understanding of the economics of e-learning involves realizing that e-learning is an infrastructure phenomenon. My definition of infrastructure is similar to—but slightly broader than—that used by Patti Shank, L. Wayne Precht, Harvey Singh, Jim Everidge, and Jane Bozarth in Chapter 5 and is outlined in greater detail in Lambe (2007). When referring to infrastructure, I mean the composite of technology systems, business processes, work culture, and control mechanisms that make up the way an organization operates and does its work. Infrastructure is distinct from assets and resources insofar as an existing infrastructure enables or constrains the performance of assets, such as specific technologies, people, and availability of time. If e-learning were merely a resource or asset, it would be an interchangeable part that could be plugged into an organization and become operational at the flick of a switch. But that's not the case. In fact, as some of the early implementers of large-scale e-learning initiatives discovered, it introduces significant problems of change management because e-learning is more than an interchangeable, plug-and-play part. Making e-learning work involves more than integrating technology systems. It also involves re-gearing work processes, tuning into soft work cultures, and deeply integrating the needs of business and work processes. In contrast, although going to a training class might disrupt a work schedule to make workers available for training, the class requires no other deep integration. And, although making training stick does require broader change in the workplace, research suggests that organizations still offer classroom training without these related changes (Broad & Newstrom, 2001).

This highlights another important difference between training and e-learning. Training has established for itself a distinct niche and role within an organization's infrastructure. It is compartmentalized and relatively easy to manipulate. In contrast, e-learning pervades the entire infrastructure. As part of the information technology (IT) network of the organization, learning content is potentially available at any point in the flow of work, in any business process and as part of any decision. But corresponding attitudes, processes, workflows, habits, and routines necessary for the exploitation of this content are not natively present in the surrounding infrastructure and must be deliberately worked in and fostered.

Recognizing the role of infrastructure in e-learning has two significant implications for discerning its economic impact or viability. First, because an infrastructure is a complex interweaving of diffuse and diverse elements ranging from "hard" technology to "soft" culture, attributing specific outcomes to specific interventions may be extremely difficult.

Some contexts are easier to see than others. For example, provision of new product training for a sales force offers an opportunity to see a direct link between the input (learning content) and output (sales performance) if no other sales-supporting initiative has been put into place at the same time. But a transformation of health and safety training may involve a number of different interventions; the results (such as fewer incidents) may not be observed for a considerable time, cannot easily be attributed to a single input, and may be influenced by the inherited learning models prior to the transformation. Infrastructure is generally opaque when linking causes to effects, and this substantially contributes to its apparent inertia in the face of change.

Second, any infrastructure-related initiative, such as e-learning, has an absorption or integration cost that is extremely difficult to anticipate, precisely because of the opacity of infrastructure. In laymen's terms, an absorption or integration cost is the cost of change management, such as unanticipated costs associated with the technology, like the cost of providing tutoring support to learners (which is a cost that most organizations do not consider when deciding to launch an e-learning effort) or that, despite the availability of learning to workers anywhere at any time, if the work environment does not support transferring the learning to the job, learners will not become more productive. As a result, in addition to investing in e-learning, organizations must also invest in efforts intended to transfer learning to the job. Whatever these unanticipated change management costs are, they are universally under-anticipated. The consequence is that advance predictions of economic benefits from e-learning are usually over-estimated and the post-implementation results have usually disappointed executives, reducing their confidence levels in a variety of learning-related issues, starting with the mechanisms for assessing the viability of a proposed e-learning investment.

Recognizing the infrastructural aspect of an e-learning initiative is highly advantageous for three reasons. First, it focuses executives' attention at the beginning of the project on likely integration and adaptation issues with a greater level of precision than if the metaphor of a plug-and-play box is used. Second, e-learning initiatives that seek to unlock the constraints of an existing infrastructure are likely to have fewer challenges in installation and implementation because they are simpler than those that attempt to graft a complex e-learning system onto an existing infrastructure. In the latter situation, the grafted e-learning system will have more numerous points of integration and, as a result, more issues to address. This is why small, highly localized, and focused initiatives always have higher success levels than large-scale enterprise-wide initiatives. The smaller initiatives impinge upon, and depend on, fewer elements of the infrastructure for their success.

The third implication of recognizing e-learning as an infrastructure initiative is that a simplistic ROI model would be inappropriate for all but the most tightly defined productivity-oriented initiatives.

For example, simplistic ROI assumes that a quantifiable output can be attributed to the effect of a quantifiable input. But as we have seen, infrastructure often renders the relationships between inputs and outputs opaque. In many cases, the establishment of an infrastructure is not about a single input and output, but several, often unrelated, ones. Attributing the initiative to just one of them seems to underestimate the larger benefits. Moreover, a complex system has a variety of inputs that affect a variety of outputs—many of which are unrelated to one another or that affect a variety of situations. Purely quantifiable and objective measures are increasingly inadequate for capturing the full range of value that such an infrastructure might create.

So metrics such as *contingent valuation* and *outcomes-based evaluation* (which I describe in detail in a moment) are increasingly being applied for measuring the impact of other intangible, knowledge-based interventions, such as public library services or knowledge-based ecological systems. A methodology called *Most Significant Change* (MSC)—originally developed for broad-based development and community-oriented projects—tracks "softer" impact measures in terms of whether an initiative satisfies the agendas of interested parties and stakeholders. As with enterprise infrastructure projects, project impact must satisfy diverse stakeholder agendas. The MSC technique is especially good at identifying the points at which these agendas are aligned. Because of the similarities of such initiatives to e-learning, especially because all three approaches to evaluation relate to diffuse, infrastructure-related projects, perhaps they could be used for measuring the impact of e-learning, too. The basic lesson here is that, when an initiative is a complex one, as many infrastructure initiatives are, then the evaluation mechanism must match the nature of the complexity being evaluated. Simple evaluation mechanisms can only measure simple things.

The key premise of the contingent valuation model is that it measures infrastructures at two different levels. One measure focuses on the value created by the entire ecological system. The other measure focuses on the inter-relations and functionality of the parts as valued by key stakeholders at different points in the ecosystem. An ecological system includes all of the facilitating and constraining facets of the environment (in this case, the technology infrastructure) (Macmillan, 2007). The concept is not unique to technological infrastructure; the concept also applies to the design of classrooms. Contingent valuation was originally developed in 1993 by Nobel-prize-winning economists Kenneth Arrow and Robert Solow for the purpose of quantifying the value of ecological systems. It has been applied by a number of public and national libraries as a method of demonstrating the direct and indirect economic impact of the intangible services they provide, such as knowledge supply. The method involves identifying key groups that obtain value from the service and then quantifying the economic impact as well as the value perception of those services. This is partly achieved by asking the stakeholders to consider what value they would lose if the service were not provided to them. For example, in libraries, they would identify the key stakeholders who receive value from the knowledge supply services provided by libraries, then ask these stakeholders to quantify how losing those services might affect them (British Library, 2004; Missingham, 2005).

However, it is also possible to take a narrower approach that is focused on objectives. This is known as outcomes-based evaluation. Outcomes-based evaluation is similar to criterion-referenced instruction. Both start by identifying objectives at the beginning of the project—even before considering alternative solutions—and, after the solution is implemented, assessing the extent to which the objectives have been achieved. In the case of using an outcomes-based approach to assessing infrastructure projects, the entering objectives are strategic business objectives that the infrastructure is mobilized to support. The assessment explores the extent to which these objectives were achieved. Outcomes-based evaluation has several strengths, particularly (but not exclusively) for commercial organizations, because it encourages the e-learning initiative to support specific strategic objectives and define the measures of accountability for its success. Because the objectives are strategic business objectives for which the organization is most likely already conducting assessment, existing measurement systems, such as the balanced scorecard, can be deployed. Also worth noting is that, although productivity improvement is one possible type of strategic objective, it is by no means the only one.

A third evaluation method is the most qualitative of the three. Named the Most Significant Change evaluation method, it collects numerous specific examples of significant impact on the recipients of an intervention, typically through a story gathering exercise, asking the recipients of the service, "What is the most significant change in your (working) life as a result of this initiative?" The collected stories are then prioritized and filtered by different levels of stakeholder and project sponsors. For example, in a commercial organization, the impact stories may be collected from the users of the e-learning system and prioritized. A preliminary selection is then made by operational managers, and a final selection is made by the company's directors. For each selection, the selectors explain why the impact example is important to them, thus revealing the priorities and agendas of all the key stakeholder groups within the human infrastructure for a change. The Most Significant Change was originally developed for human development projects for which there are diverse stakeholder and sponsor agendas, and for which quantitative evaluation methods provided little support (Davies & Dart, 2005).

With that in mind, the next several sections explore how one might assess the return on investment for an e-learning infrastructure that supports a variety of different business objectives. Figure 15.1 shows a process for approaching the types of issues described in these upcoming sections. The first of these sections explores e-learning in support of productivity improvement.

## e-Learning for Productivity Improvement

When e-learning is intended to support the improvement of productivity, it is ultimately aimed, in economic terms, at ensuring that the output per time or dollar spent is the same or greater than before the e-learning program was introduced. At the least,

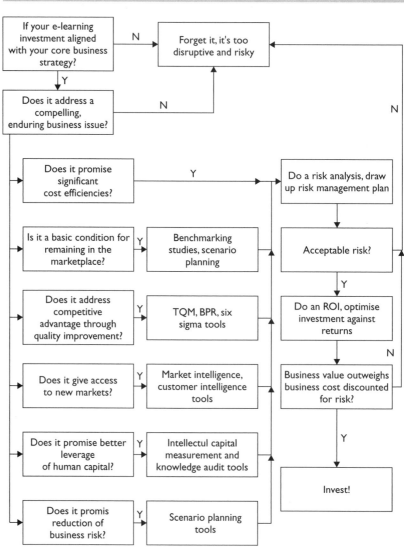

**Figure 15.1. Decision Tree for Assessing the Business Impact of Investments in e-Learning**

© Straits Knowledge 2002. Used with permission.

an effective investment should result in an equivalent level and quality of output. At most, one or both are improved. For the most part, e-learning in terms of productivity improvement is based on the productivity of the learning staff—not the learners.

Examples of e-learning in support of productivity improvement include:

- More people have access to learning for the same budget outlay or less

- The sales force of an organization takes product training by e-learning, thus reducing time spent in classroom and out of the field, away from customers

The stakeholders in such an effort are:

- Business owners of the product or service being addressed by the learning

- Participants in the learning program, who are evaluated and rewarded on productivity targets

Points to leverage such an e-learning infrastructure include standard productivity and performance reporting systems; performance bonuses and commissions; and existing intranets and mobile computing infrastructures.

Measurement questions include:

- How is ROI calculated?

- To what degree do stakeholders attribute any productivity gains to the e-learning (pre- and post-initiative)?

- What alternatives to e-learning exist as an aid to productivity improvement, and how much would they cost (pre- and post-initiative)?

- Have there been any quality or effectiveness gains or losses as a result of deploying e-learning? If yes, can these be quantified? How? Can specific examples of improvements be collected from key stakeholders?

## e-Learning for Quality Improvement

When e-learning is intended to support a strategic quality improvement initiative, e-learning is integrated into the workflow through performance support systems at the specific points in a business process. These processes need improvements in speed, accuracy, or consistency, or have vulnerabilities in quality can be mitigated by providing e-learning support. This e-learning support can help workers perform more effectively or can be aimed at customers to help them effectively buy and use complex products and services.

Examples of e-learning in support of quality improvement include:

- A medical clinic that provides healthcare workers with mini-modules about the diagnosis and treatment of a specific conditions, based on symptoms, patient history, and medications

- A vendor of enterprise resource planning (ERP) software, which provides e-learning on its public site to help small and medium enterprises to understand how its products can support their businesses, and to help them make purchasing decisions appropriate to their needs

The stakeholders in such an effort are:

- Business owners of the product or service being addressed

- Quality audit and control departments, which have overall responsibility for quality in businesses

- Business process improvement teams, which have similar responsibilities

- Customers and potential customers of complex products and services, who would be users of the service

Points to leverage such an e-learning infrastructure include:

- Quality audit and control systems

- Standard operating procedures and standards such as ISO 9000

- Business process reengineering and Six Sigma (a type of quality control) projects

- Marketing and customer service processes and initiatives

- Internet website and sales force deployment

- Product information and manuals

Note that some of these leverage points are not necessarily in the technology itself, but comprise other parts of the ecological system that supports e-learning in the organization.

Measurement questions include:

- What improvements in speed, consistency, or accuracy does e-learning enable? By what amount and degree of seriousness are customer-facing errors (that is, errors that customers would notice) reduced?

- To what degree do stakeholders associate the quality of their performance or their purchasing decision (if customers) with the support provided by e-learning?

- What alternatives to e-learning exist as an aid to quality improvement, and how much would they cost (pre- and post-initiative)?

- Have there been any productivity or sales impacts as a result of deploying e-learning, and can these be quantified? If so, how are they quantified? Can specific examples of improvements be collected from key stakeholders?

## e-Learning for Leveraging Human Capital

When e-learning is intended to help an organization leverage its human capital, it refers to the ability to attract, develop, and retain talent and experience in employees so that the organization realizes a competitive advantage. In globally dispersed organizations, e-learning tools can connect employees and executives through collaboration software, giving them access to common learning resources in support of their work. Some e-learning provides professional development opportunities that might not be otherwise available and is widely valued by employees, such as access to personal development courses like time management and effective negotiations, as well as access to online academic courses. In other instances, e-learning supports leadership and management development programs. Such programs are usually blended and include face-to-face components for establishing and strengthening relationships across the organization, but e-learning components can extend the impact of these sessions and sustain collaborative learning across distances and time. Leveraging human capital is especially important in knowledge-intensive industries, especially those in which much of the knowledge is intrinsic and lies within the minds of the workers.

Examples of e-learning in support of leveraging human capital include:

- A knowledge management project in a large multinational organization that captures the more challenging leadership experiences of senior retiring executives, packages them in modules as business simulations, and uses them as the basis for online leadership development projects.

- A series of modules on common engineering standards that a global engineering firm asked its experts to prepare and make available on its global intranet as a support tool for its project teams that are distributed throughout the world and work virtually. These modules are included in a collaborative project space so that engineers in different countries can discuss their application in different contexts, and each project space has access to the company's subject-matter experts.

The stakeholders in such an effort are human resource directors and the senior management team, executives and managers, functional specialists and subject-matter experts, and knowledge managers, all of whom play multiple roles—sometimes commissioning pieces of the system, sometimes using the system.

Points to leverage such an e-learning infrastructure include:

- Knowledge management projects, particularly knowledge audits, expertise directories, and intellectual capital measurement systems

- Leadership and management development programs

- Global intranets

- Collaborative technologies and tools

- Virtual team working and project management processes

- Recruitment, induction, performance review and promotion processes

As in the last section, note that some of these leverage points are not necessarily in the technology itself, but comprise other parts of the ecological system that supports e-learning in the organization.

Measurement questions include:

- To what degree is the reuse of expertise and tacit knowledge of an organization's human capital enabled through e-learning?

- What economic or competitive advantage is reaped by the reuse of expertise through the e-learning system?

- To what degree do employees attribute their personal development and learning to the support provided by e-learning? Can specific examples of improvements be collected from key stakeholders?

- To what degree do stakeholders associate the re-application of knowledge with their e-learning support?

- What alternatives to e-learning exist as an aid to human capital development, and how much would they cost (pre- and post-initiative)?

## e-Learning and Risk Reduction

When e-learning is intended to support the reduction of risks throughout an organization, it is used to avoid or mitigate risks in volatile and uncertain business environments, in markets that are subject to rapid deregulation, in capital and infrastructure-intensive industries such as pharmaceuticals, and in industries in which the pace of innovation is high. Because the requirement for authoritative and coordinated knowledge of the inherent risks in the environment is high, e-learning can help by allowing the enterprise to disseminate up-to-date knowledge of the environment and corporate policies that respond to these environmental conditions quickly, widely, and in a way that is customized to particular job roles.

Examples of e-learning in support of risk reduction include:

- An insurance company updating its product training materials on the fly as regulatory changes take effect, and as competition with banks for the same market segments intensifies. The company can use learner records on its LMS to demonstrate that all employees have been trained in compliance with regulatory requirements.

- A pharmaceutical company requiring its research and development teams to compile e-learning modules summarizing current research projects and their progress to share across the entire company. This creates greater visibility for risk and success factors in projects, subjects projects to greater professional scrutiny, and fosters cross-fertilization of ideas.

The stakeholders in such an effort are legal and compliance teams, risk managers, business development teams, directors of research and development, investors, and business owners of products and services addressed by the e-learning effort.

Points to leverage such an e-learning infrastructure include:

- Legal and compliance processes
- Standard operating procedures and operating guidelines
- ISO 9000 processes
- Training department processes
- Risk assessment and management processes
- Corporate intranets
- Content publishing capabilities
- Processes for funding and structuring research and development efforts

Measurement questions include:

- What risks have been avoided or mitigated through the timely provision of knowledge through e-learning, and can their impact be quantified? If so, how? Can specific examples of improvements be collected from stakeholders?

- What disadvantage would have accrued from the absence of e-learning?

- To what degree do stakeholders attribute their avoidance or mitigation of risk to the support provided by e-learning?

- Are close competitors using e-learning to help manage their risks, and what impact does it appear to have on their competitive performance?

- What alternatives to e-learning exist as an aid to risk avoidance, and how much would they cost (pre- and post-initiative)?

## e-Learning as a Basic Qualification to Remain in the Marketplace

When e-learning is intended to provide a basic qualification to remain in the marketplace, it is simply providing a ticket to compete. The concept is best described by John Chambers of Cisco. When asked if he had calculated the ROI of his e-learning drive, he is reported to have responded, "Who calculates ROI on their telephone systems? If we don't have one, we can't do business. e-Learning is fundamental to the way we operate."

Examples of e-learning as a basic qualification to remain in the marketplace include:

- Using e-learning to address fast-evolving technology and software products which, when combined with large distributed sales forces, require speedy and frequent production and dissemination of product information in a form that learners can easily consume

- Using e-learning in high-turnover call centers to gain advantages of speed, market share, accuracy and consistency, productivity and profitability

The stakeholders in such an effort are business owners of the product or service being addressed by the learning initiative, employees who cannot effectively function without easy access to information about products and service information, and executives of strategic planning.

Points to leverage such an e-learning infrastructure include:

- Strategic and business planning cycles
- Intelligence about competitors
- Benchmarks of competitors
- High reliability intranet and broadband access
- Content publishing capabilities
- Performance support systems

Measurement questions include:

- What is the competitive intensity of our market? How costly is it to compete in this market in relation to the potential profiles?
- Are competitors using e-learning to gain competitive advantage? How many competitors are doing so, and what advantage do they acquire?
- To what degree do stakeholders associate their effectiveness with their e-learning support?
- What alternatives to e-learning exist as an aid to functional effectiveness and how much would they cost (pre- and post-initiative)?
- Have there been any competitive gains or losses as a result of deploying e-learning, and can these be quantified? If so, how? Can specific examples of improvements be collected from key stakeholders?

## e-Learning for Access to New Markets

When e-learning is intended to support access to new markets, their existing infrastructure usually possesses sparse knowledge resources and experience in the new area of need, whether that area of need be a new geographic area, a new product line, or a new vertical market. In such a situation, learning needs are pervasive across the organization, from design, procurement, and production, to marketing, sales, and service. e-Learning can help by making available packaged information and knowledge content across the enterprise, presented in forms that are appropriate to the different functional roles.

Examples of e-learning in support of access to new markets include:

- A consortium of small and medium enterprises in Scotland, who subscribe to a shared e-learning platform hosting resources, modules, and case studies focused on acquiring new business in the European Union

- A large multinational organization that specializes in consumer products and provides a global management development program that includes e-learning modules on multi-cultural awareness, simulations, and case studies on doing business in different countries, and online collaborative projects

The stakeholders in such an effort are business owners of the product or service being addressed, country and regional managers, sales teams and sales managers, business development managers, and partners in any joint ventures.

Points to leverage such an e-learning infrastructure include:

- Business development cycle
- Legal processes
- Global intranets
- Competitive intelligence processes and systems
- Strategy and business planning cycle
- Localization systems and processes
- Recruitment and overseas posting of employees
- New employee orientation, as well as ongoing training and development processes

Once again, note that some of these leverage points are not necessarily in the technology itself, but comprise other parts of the ecological system that supports e-learning in the organization.

Measurement questions include:

- To what degree can the establishment of new offices or marketing campaigns be accelerated or made less costly through the use of e-learning?

- To what degree, and how quickly, is the experience gained by executives who pioneer the entry into a new market recycled and reused by other executives?

- To what degree do stakeholders associate the speed and effectiveness of their entry into a new market with their e-learning support?

- What alternatives to e-learning exist as an aid to market entry, and how much would they cost (pre- and post-initiative)?

- Have there been any sales or market share impacts, or any avoidance of risk as a result of deploying e-learning, and can these be quantified? If so, how? Can specific examples of improvements be collected from key stakeholders?

## Concluding Thoughts

The current widespread disillusionment about e-learning has resulted from over-optimistic and naïve approaches to large-scale e-learning implementations in enterprises. The difficulties, costs, and challenges have been routinely underestimated, inappropriate systems have been purchased, and ill-defined objectives combined with overly simplistic value measurement regimes have produced cynicism about the promise of the technology. Furthermore, executives and experts have not been able to discriminate true causal factors of success from accidental ones.

Creating a better, more discriminating set of tools for measuring the economic value impact of e-learning will help executives warrant their investments with greater confidence and guide their initiatives with greater precision. The ground covered in this chapter maps out the ways in which a closer linking of e-learning to business strategy, combined with clear performance and impact targets, recognition of key infrastructure opportunities, and a system for engaging and soliciting measurement data from stakeholders, can cumulatively enhance its economic viability and recover some of the promise that e-learning has lost.

# References

Bernard, R.M., Abrami, P.C., Lou, Y., Borokhovski, E., Wade, A., Wozney, L., Wallet, P.A., Fiset, M., & Huang, B. (2004). How does distance education compare to classroom instruction? A meta-analysis of the empirical literature. *Review of Educational Research, 74*(3), 379–439.

British Library. (2004). *Measuring our value: Results of an independent economic impact study commissioned by the British Library to measure the Library's direct and indirect value to the UK economy.* London: British Library.

Broad, M.L., & Newstrom, J.W. (2001). *Transfer of training: Action-packed strategies to ensure high payoff from training investments.* New York: Perseus.

Davies, R., & Dart, J. (2005). *The most significant change (MSC) technique: A guide to its use.* London: Care International.

Davis, K. (2001). What e-learning can learn from history. *USDLA Journal, 15*(10), 22–28.

Day, J., Foley, J., Groeneweg, R., & van der Mast, C. (2004). *Enhancing the classroom learning experience with web lectures* (GVU Technical Report; GIT-GVU-04–18). Atlanta, GA: Georgia Institute of Technology.

Lambe, P. (2002*). The autism of knowledge management.* Available: www.greenchameleon.com/thoughtpieces/autism.pdf

Lambe, P. (2007). *Organising knowledge: Taxonomies, knowledge and organisation effectiveness.* Oxford, UK: Chandos.

Macmillan, S. (2007). *Development of writing for research purposes: An ecological exploration of graduate level non-native English speaker writing process.* Doctoral dissertation. Montreal, Canada: Concordia University.

Missingham, R. (2005). *Libraries and economic value: A review of recent studies.* Canberra, Australia: National Library of Australia.

Rosenberg, M. (2000). *e-Learning: Strategies for delivering knowledge in the digital age.* New York: McGraw-Hill.

Russell, T. (Ongoing publication). No significant difference website. www.nosignificantdifference.org.

Snowden, D. (2000, 2004). The ASHEN model: An enabler of action. *Knowledge Management, 3*(7). Re-edited in 2004 and released under Creative Commons license at www.cognitive-edge.com/ceresources/articles/7_Organic_KM_1_of_3_ASHEN.pdf

◆ ◆ ◆

## Summary of Main Points

Readers should take away the following main ideas from this chapter:

- One of the main reasons that large enterprises had difficulty demonstrating a positive ROI for early e-learning efforts was because their models for evaluating the performance and financial impact of e-learning were as naïve as their understanding of technology and as immature as their ideas about how to effectively teach with technology. In the end, organizations found that e-learning turned out to be more expensive and provide less predictable outcomes than were initially expected.

- Initially, organizations justified e-learning by focusing on reduction in training time (because e-learning courses often take less time than their classroom equivalents to complete and learners can complete courses at their desks, avoiding travel time) and savings in travel-to-training expenses—the airfare, hotel, and lodging expenses that can often double the total cost of a single training class.

- Implicit in these justifications is that classroom training activity could be easily interchanged with e-learning modules: that they were functional equivalents. They are not.

- This is known as the Myth of e-Learning as a Replacement for Training.

- Not only are classroom and e-learning different products, but they are economically justified in different ways.

- Training budgets are typically recurrent budgets accounted as an operations or infrastructure cost.

- In contrast, e-learning is an information technology (IT) investment, and these are typically large capital expenditures with smaller recurrent maintenance and upgrade budgets attached, and an amortization mechanism as the system ages over time. ROI has always been an important consideration for IT projects.

- No one considered whether such an approach to ROI really makes sense for learning activities.

- Because e-learning is an infrastructure project (an infrastructure is the composite of technology systems, business processes, work culture, and control mechanisms that make up the way an organization operates and does its work), there are two significant implications:

  - Because an infrastructure is a complex interweaving of diffuse and diverse elements ranging from "hard" technology to "soft" culture, attributing specific outcomes to specific interventions is extremely difficult.

  - Any infrastructure-related initiative, such as e-learning, has an absorption or integration cost that is extremely difficult to anticipate, precisely because of the opacity of infrastructure. In laymen's terms, an absorption or integration cost is the cost of change management, such as unanticipated costs associated with the technology.

- As a result, a simplistic ROI model would be inappropriate for all but the most tightly defined productivity-oriented initiatives.

  - Contingent valuation measures infrastructures at two different levels. One measure focuses on the value created by the entire ecological system. The other measure focuses on the inter-relations and functionality of the parts as valued by key stakeholders at different points in the ecosystem. An ecological system includes all of the facilitating and constraining facets of the environment (in this case, the technology infrastructure).

- Outcomes-based evaluation starts by identifying objectives at the beginning of the project—even before considering alternative solutions—and, after the solution is implemented, assessing the extent to which the objectives had been achieved.

- Most Significant Change (MSC) is a methodology for identifying the different agendas and value perceptions of stakeholders. It is especially useful for projects with many stakeholders whose support is necessary for an initiative and to find the outcomes that satisfy the majority of those stakeholders' agendas.

- Alternative measures explore e-learning in support of specific strategic objectives:

  - Productivity improvement which, in economic terms, is aimed at ensuring that the output per time or dollar spent is the same or greater than before.

  - Quality improvement, in which e-learning is integrated into the workflow and through performance support systems at the specific points in a business process that need improvements in speed, accuracy, or consistency, or where vulnerabilities in quality can be mitigated by providing support through e-learning support.

  - Leveraging human capital, in which e-learning is used to help attract, develop, and retain talent and experience in employees so that the organization realizes a competitive advantage.

- Risk reduction, in which e-learning is intended to avoid or mitigate risks in volatile and uncertain business environments, in markets that are subject to rapid deregulation, in capital and infrastructure-intensive industries such as pharmaceuticals, and in industries in which the pace of innovation is high.

- As a basic qualification to remain in the marketplace, in which e-learning essentially provides a ticket to compete in a marketplace.

- Access to new markets, in which e-learning addresses the sparse knowledge resources and experience in the new area of need in an organization, whether that area of need be a new geographic area, a new product line, or a new vertical market.

◆ ◆ ◆

# Guiding Questions for Discussion

- List two or three different e-learning initiatives that you know about. Are they infrastructure projects or highly focused niche projects? How has this affected their success in your view? (If possible, ask people who have been involved in these projects, if you don't have personal knowledge of these initiatives.)

- Take a look at your organization's current strategic plan (or ask your boss about it). Which of the six types of strategic objectives listed earlier appear in it? Choose one of them and try to envision how e-learning could support that objective.

- Identify your key stakeholders for this e-learning initiative and your infrastructure "touch points." Go talk to the stakeholders, check out the relevant infrastructure leverage points, and draw up a list of key measurement questions that you will need to answer to be confident about whether or not your initiative creates value.

| **Learn More About It** | |
|---|---|
| Links | The following websites are intended to appeal to a management audience and often include articles on ROI and other issues associated with the return on e-learning programs: |
| | CLO Magazine (www.clomedia.com) |
| | www.hr.com |
| | www.TrainingOutsourcing.com |
| Books, Papers, Reports, and Articles | Phillips, J. (2003). *Return-on-investment in training and performance improvement programs* (2nd ed.). New York: Butterworth-Heinemann. |
| | Davies, R., & Dart, J. (2005). *The most significant change (MSC) technique: A guide to its use.* London: Care International. |
| | Horton, W. (2001). *Evaluating e-learning.* Alexandria, VA: ASTD. |

# Chapter 16

# e-Learning

## Today's Challenge, Tomorrow's Reality

*Saul Carliner, Concordia University*

---

### About This Chapter

If you have read this book sequentially (or close to it), by now, you might be convinced that e-learning failed to live up to its initial expectations, but that it has not been a failure either. Within the framework of this more realistic set of expectations, this chapter answers the question: "What can learning specialists expect of e-learning in the coming years?" Building on the analyses of the preceding chapters, I specifically explore three emerging trends in e-learning: a more responsive e-learning, e-learning by assignment, and e-learning as a way of life.

---

## Introduction

Each of the previous chapters in this book has explored a different aspect of "the e-learning that wasn't." The chapters in Part II explored how e-learning failed to live up to expectations in both industry and academe. The chapters in Part III explored how e-learning proved to be a more daunting technology challenge than expected—in terms of the infrastructure, standards, and the use of learning objects. Most significantly, these chapters explored how interpersonal issues, especially the relationships between the learning and information technology (IT) groups, affect the technology of learning. The chapters in Part IV explored how e-learning has failed to rise to the design challenges it poses, and the chapters in Part V explore how e-learning places demands for broader approaches to theory and research that, until now, have not been met. Finally, the first chapter in this sixth part of the book explored how e-learning failed to provide the promised economic benefits.

Ouch! After reading that summary, one might conclude that e-learning is a failure.

But that would be an overstatement. If each chapter addressed how e-learning failed to live up to the expectations for it, each also explained why some of those expectations might have been unrealistic in the first place and suggested, as well, the many ways in which e-learning has succeeded. These successes have admittedly been more modest than the initial predictions. But with hype like "e-learning is the next killer app" in the early days of the dot-com boom, the industry set up e-learning to disappoint.

Within these more modest expectations, however, what can learning specialists expect of e-learning in the coming years? That's what I explore in this chapter. Building on the analyses of the preceding chapters, I specifically explore three directions in e-learning: a more responsive e-learning, e-learning by assignment, and e-learning as a way of life.

## The Three Directions of e-Learning

At the beginning of the 1990s, experts predicted two trends in food. (I promise to show the connection to e-learning in a moment.) One trend in food was an emphasis on healthy eating. To encourage it, lower-fat versions of popular foods would be developed, such as low-fat ice cream and fat-free potato chips. The other trend in food was in response to all of this healthy eating; to congratulate themselves, people would indulge in new lines of premium foods—ones that were even less nutritious than their 1980s counterparts, such as higher-fat ice creams (think Ben & Jerry's) and gourmet potato chips (think Cape Cod chips).

When asked about the trends in e-learning, the contributors to this book saw a similar dichotomy. On the one hand, almost every one of them saw the quality of e-learning improving and becoming more responsive to learners. On the other hand, almost every one of them also saw the emergence of less expensive, less thoughtful e-learning. In addition, the contributors saw one other trend that might help to reconcile this dichotomy: e-learning as a way of life. The next sections individually explore each of these trends.

## Trend One: A More Responsive e-Learning

Although e-learning always had the potential to actively engage learners and provide a customized, learner-centered experience, many early efforts failed to do that. It's not that the designers and developers set out to fail, they merely didn't succeed.

In some instances, the designers and developers did not understand the capabilities of the technology. For example, many designers did not realize that they could easily set up drag-and-drop exercises that would simulate, to some extent, the experience of setting up equipment. So designers opted instead for multiple choice and similar types of questions. Other designers did not realize that, through the use of recordings, guest speakers might be used in online tutorials and opted, instead, for long text passages.

In other cases, the limited library of examples and teaching ideas limited designers. Familiar only with the few examples of high-design, high-budget simulations shown at trade shows and conferences, designers often lamented the lack of budget to create good simulations, not realizing that a combination of a problem-based approach to learning and effective storytelling techniques could lead to similarly engaging learning environments, even if they lacked the eye appeal of the video and graphics. Similarly, because most early e-learning textbooks emphasized an approach to designing instruction that applies Gagné's (1985) nine events of instruction, few designers experimented with other approaches to learning, such as discovery learning or electronic performance support (although interest in these ideas was always strong).

Most significantly, many e-learning designers focused their efforts primarily on designing courses, and many were surprised when they encountered a range of problems during implementation, from small oversights (such as trying to avoid monotony by varying the wording of instructions and, in the process, confusing learners) to major blunders that were often beyond the scope of the course content, but that had a significant effect on acceptance (such as failing to market an e-learning course, then wondering why no one took it).

Research shows that experienced designers primarily work by instinct (for example, Rowland, 1993, 2004; van Tiem, 2004), so perhaps the challenge with some of these early applications of e-learning was that individual and collective instincts around e-learning had not been honed.

Now they have been. As a result, designers have a more mature approach to e-learning. As Patrick Lambe observes, "e-Learning content design will be less constrained by the old . . . school of instructional design, and there will be more adventurous design work using e-learning modules less for teaching content and more for engaging or supporting practice (modules become much more like tools)" (personal correspondence, 2005).

Lambe is one of several contributors who believe that e-learning is moving into informal domains. Lambe and Marc Rosenberg both see e-learning increasingly used for knowledge management and performance support, especially in the workplace. Organizations will increasingly rely on their internal systems to provide meaningful content to workers at the time and in the context of need. The content will take different forms. Although sometimes it will be in the form of tutorials, the content might also provide practice, reminders, quick facts, advice, and similar types of useful information. Rosenberg notes that the move to this type of learning represents a cultural shift for most organizations, and Lambe suggests how they might respond: by moving training out of the training organization and into the line organizations, so that learning content is developed as closely as possible to the place where it is created. Rosenberg adds that organizations will be sensitive to all of the non-technical issues associated with making e-learning a success. These issues include finding electronic alternatives to an instructor throwing out candy to the class, assuring nervous managers that e-learning really can help workers develop their skills, and resolving a myriad of copyright issues with e-learning in university curricula (from the use of copyrighted material in an electronic classroom [rules differ because the class can be recorded] to resolving copyright issues with course content).

This move to provide content on demand—also known as informal learning, workflow-based learning, and performance support—is but one of many attempts to make the material more meaningful to learners in the contexts in which it will be used. Gretchen Lowerison, Roger Côté, Phil Abrami, and Marie-Claude Lavoie anticipate that this increased learner-centeredness will be evident in all e-learning, even material intended to be taken as more traditional courses. Through the development projects in his research center, Abrami has worked to create environments in which learners are not only the center of the work, but have tools to assess themselves and adjust their learning in response (self-regulated learning).

But these learner-centered environments need not be solitary ones. Alphie's Alley, developed by Abrami's Centre for the Study of Learning and Performance at Concordia University, is a performance support system for two—an elementary-aged learner who is trying to improve reading skills and a tutor who is usually a volunteer and guided in his or her efforts by an electronic performance support system.

The use of systems to provide helpful advice during learning and to facilitate interpersonal communication is also likely to increase in the coming years. Intelligent agents, like the ones used by Amazon.com to recommend products, are finding their way into learning programs so that learners can have a tailored learning experience. Similarly, Web 2.0 technologies, like those described by Patti Shank, are working their way into learning contexts. For example, many university instructors are assigning projects in which students develop entries for the Wikipedia. Others are using blogs to conduct virtual class conversations. In addition, Brent Wilson notes that synchronous learning tools—especially virtual classrooms—are playing an increasingly important role in e-learning now, and will do more so in the future.

One of the most significant issues for e-learning is interoperability. Although initial attempts at establishing standards fumbled, the increasing reliability of standards, along with the growing use of open source software, especially in primary, secondary, and higher education, should promote the increased interchange of learning materials. In fact, this might facilitate the exchange more than the establishment of learning repositories, in which interest seems to have waned. Through this interchange of materials comes the interchange of ideas and, ultimately, a further honing of our design instincts.

## Trend Two: e-Learning by Assignment

Although most of this book's contributors saw positive developments in the design of e-learning, most also observed that, just as organizations are learning how to design and implement effective e-learning, they also are looking for ways to do so "on the cheap."

Margaret Driscoll expressed concern that the increased use of informal learning might result in reduced use of training, because employers will decide that workers already have access to the content. In other words, organizations will use content that is developed for other purposes, such as users' guides and references, as learning material (an approach known as "repurposing content").

David Merrill agrees, but observes that much of that content in the workplace—both informal and formal—will be developed by subject-matter experts, whom he labels "instructional-designers-by-assignment" (personal correspondence, 2005). Instructional-designers-by-assignment prepare content as an adjunct responsibility of their work, usually with little or no training in how to train others.

This raises several concerns. Because instruction is a secondary responsibility of instructional-designers-by-assignment, most instruction will be designed rapidly (called rapid e-learning), such as converting existing PowerPoint presentations to Adobe Breeze with recorded narration. Because they are expert in the content, these instructional-designers-by-assignment are not likely to be questioned about their instructional choices, which could easily be poor ones, as they are not trained in instructional design.

Others question the role of instructional designers in such an environment. Several contributors wondered what more traditional instructional designers might do if engineers, programmers, and others with technical knowledge are actually developing the learning content. Most likely, instructional designers will find themselves in the same situations that many technical writers did earlier in this decade—that of production wonk. These people take the material produced by others and prepare it for publication by copyediting it, running it through an authoring tool, and verifying that it runs correctly online. In some instances, instructional designers might also prepare templates for the SMEs to use. Although this is honest work, it hardly uses the skills that most instructional designers possess. More significantly, rather than requiring that instructional designers participate in projects as early as possible—as advocated by the performance technologists in the profession—this support of instructional-designers-by-assignment limits most of our work to the final stages of an effort, when our influence will be most limited.

Because they will likely be unsatisfied with this role, Brent Wilson suggests that instructional designers might need to wage a struggle for control of content: "The learning profession (instructional designers, distance-learning specialists) needs to assert its role in articulating standards, roles, and values that should be reflected in professional products and practices." But he adds, "My fear is that a weak professional presence will continue to plague e-learning initiatives" (personal correspondence, 2005).

## Trend Three: e-Learning as a Way of Life

In contrast to these two starkly different alternatives is a third trend, e-learning as a way of life. Matthew Davis, the acquisitions editor who contracted with Patti and me to write this book, was the first person I heard verbalize this observation.

In practical terms, e-learning as a way of life means that e-learning will become part of the standard repertoire of all learning groups and most learning professionals and will regularly be offered as one of the choices for presenting content. The cultural barriers to adoption and acceptance will be lowered and, as a result, managers, learners, and learning professionals alike will not consider e-learning as something special and different, just a choice. Although some learning professionals will certainly choose to specialize in e-learning, generalists are more likely to include it in their bags of tricks and will develop increasing comfort moving back and forth between e- and other forms of learning.

Perhaps the prospect of this integration of e-learning into the mainstream of learning prompted the initial excitement over blended learning. In its most common implementation, blended learning usually involves linking e-learning and classroom learning.

Perhaps, too, the idea of e-learning as a way of life might also help to reconcile the two other perspectives on e-learning. Because e-learning can be quick and easy to produce, organizations can provide more of it. But because many of the tools enable subject-matter experts to produce their own e-learning, instructional designers need not develop all of it themselves. In some cases—such as material with low volumes of learners and low impact on a large organization—it does not make much sense to invest full instructional design resources. Instead, it might make sense for us to help instructional-designers-by-assignment do their work most effectively. We can provide them with templates, some production assistance, and consciousness raising about the importance of learning and how they can be most effective in their task.

Similarly, for courses of high interest and that affect large numbers of learners, making sure that the instruction is "right" is essential and, freed of the responsibility for developing all of the material available, instructional designers can focus our talents on those projects for which our efforts are most needed.

Perhaps, more than anything, this differentiation of roles is the future of e-learning. e-Learning—like all other online ventures—is making learning more democratic, not only in who receives it, but also who designs and delivers it.

## References

Gagné, R.M. (1985). *The conditions of learning and theory of instruction* (4th ed). New York: Holt, Rinehart, and Winston.

Rowland, G. (2004). Shall we dance? Designing for organizational performance and learning. *Educational Technology Research and Development, 52*(1), 33–48.

Rowland, G. (1993). Designing and instructional design. *Educational Technology Research and Development, 41*(1), 79–91.

Van Tiem, D. (2004). Interventions (solutions) usage and expertise in performance technology practice: An empirical investigation. *Performance Improvement Quarterly, 17*(3).

◆ ◆ ◆

## Summary of Main Points

Readers should take away the following main ideas from this chapter:

- Each of the previous chapters in this book has explored a different aspect of "the e-learning that wasn't":
    - It failed to live up to expectations in both industry and academe.
    - The technology proved to be more daunting than expected—in terms of the infrastructure, standards, and the use of learning objects.
    - It failed to rise to the design challenges it poses.
    - It places demands for broader approaches to theory and research that, until now, have not been met.
    - It has failed to provide the promised economic benefits.

- But perhaps e-learning has failed to live up to expectations because the initial expectations weren't all that realistic to begin with.

- But e-learning is hardly a complete failure, either. Rather, perhaps a combination of outsized expectations and an un-honed design instinct have limited our ability to effectively implement e-learning.

- Now that the learning industry has some experience with e-learning, we can expect three significant trends to affect it in the coming years:

    - At one end of the spectrum is a more responsive e-learning. As a result, e-learning will (1) take more varied forms than the formal tutorial; (2) encompass content that is available on demand; (3) provide more learner-centered environments; and (4) provide better interoperability—that is, e-learning that is designed on one platform and can be used on others.

    - At the other end of the spectrum is "e-learning by assignment":

        Organizations increasingly turn to subject-matter experts to develop e-learning programs "on the cheap," such as using users' guides and references as learning content (known as repurposing content) and converting existing PowerPoint presentations to recorded presentations (known as rapid e-learning).

        Merrill labels subject-matter experts who develop courses as part of their technical assignments as instructional-designers-by-assignment.

        Instructional-designers-by-assignment not only take jobs from instructional designers, but affect the job quality for those positions that remain.

    - e-Learning as a way of life, in which e-learning will become part of the standard repertoire of all learning groups and most learning professionals, and will regularly be offered as one of the choices for presenting content. The cultural barriers to adoption and acceptance will be lowered and, as a result, managers, learners, and learning professionals alike will not consider e-learning as something special and different, just a choice. Learning that blends e- and classroom learning exemplifies e-learning as a way of life.

◆ ◆ ◆

# Guiding Questions for Discussion

- This chapter starts by saying that early implementations of e-learning were a disappointment and suggests that unrealistic expectations and a lack of experience caused the situation. What is your impression of the early installations of e-learning? Do you believe they were a disappointment? Why? What evidence supports this belief?

- This chapter closes by suggesting three trends in e-learning: a more responsive e-learning, instructional-design-by-assignment, and e-learning as a way of life. What trends do you see? How do those trends affect instructional designers?

**Learn More About It**

Links      Keep up with industry developments through:

Association for the Advancement of Computers in Education (www.aace.org), a professional association that brings together computer scientists, educational technologists and academics, and professionals who all share the common interest in e-learning

Stephen Downes' blog (www.downes.ca), a private blog that tracks issues and trends in e-learning

Educause (www.educause.edu), an association for advancing technology in higher education *e-Learn Magazine* (www.elearnmag.org), an online magazine that explores applications and challenges in e-learning and publishes an annual trends issue

*e-Learning Post* (www.elearningpost), a private blog that tracks developments in e-learning and related fields

*Learning Circuits* (www.learningcircuits.org), the American Society for Training and Development's online webzine about e-learning for workplace learning professionals; includes special issues of interest to buyers of e-learning products and services

| Books, Papers, Reports, and Articles | The following printed resources provide insights from which the future of learning in general—and e-learning in particular—can be inferred: |
| --- | --- |
| | ASTD Annual State of the Industry reports. (Authors vary by year.) |
| | *Training* magazine's annual industry survey. (Published in the January issue each year.) |

# Index

# About the Editors

**Saul Carliner, Ph.D.,** is an associate professor in the graduate program in educational technology at Concordia University in Montreal a member of the Centre for the Study of Learning and Performance, and a member of the Canadian Council on Learning's Work and Learning Knowledge Centre. His research interests include emerging forms of online communication for the workplace, the management of workplace learning and communication groups, and the process for designing and developing learning content. He has received research funding from the Social Sciences and Humanities Research Council of Canada, Canadian Council on Learning, and Hong Kong University Grants Council. Also active in industry, Saul has consulted for organizations such as Alltel, Berlitz, Chubb Insurance, Microsoft, IBM, 3M, Wachovia, and several Canadian, U.S., and state government agencies.

He has published six books and over seventy-five articles and serves on the editorial boards of the *Canadian Journal of Learning and Technology, Information Design Journal,* and *Performance Improvement Quarterly.*

He is a Certified Training and Development Professional, board member of the Canadian Society for Training and development, past research fellow of the American Society for Training and Development, and a fellow and past international president of the Society for Technical Communication. Website: http://education.concordia.ca/~scarliner/

**Patti Shank, Ph.D.,** is the president of Learning Peaks LLC, an internationally known instruction and information design consulting firm that provides instruction, training, and performance support solutions to government, corporate, nonprofit, and higher education clients. She has contributed numerous chapters to training and instructional technology books and is co-author of *Making*

*Sense of Online Learning* (Pfeiffer, 2004) and the editor of *The Online Learning Idea Book* (Pfeiffer, 2007).

Patti is frequently invited to speak at instructional design, training, and instructional technology conferences. She was an award-winning contributing editor for *Online Learning Magazine* and is regularly quoted in trade journals. Her articles are found in eLearning Guild publications, Adobe's Resource Center, Magna Publication's *Online Classroom*, *Training Media Review*, and elsewhere. She was awarded the Certified Performance Technologist (CPT) designation, and her research on new online learners won an EDMEDIA (2002) best research paper award. Website: www.learningpeaks.com

# About the Contributors

We are proud of the diversity of contributors to this volume. Our authors represent a diversity of uses of e-learning, including experts focused on the K through 12, higher education, and workplace learning and performance. Our authors also represent a diversity of views, including the research-based approaches of academe, the practical approaches of industry, and in-between. Our authors represent, too, geographic diversity, with authors from Asia, Australia, Europe, and North America. Most significantly, each of our authors has a unique body of learning, research, and experience influencing his or her perspective on e-learning. The following biographies briefly describe the experiences and perspectives that our contributors bring to this volume.

**Philip C. Abrami, Ph.D.,** is a professor in the Department of Education at Concordia University and the director of the Centre for the Study of Learning and Performance. His research interests include social psychology of education, small group learning in virtual learning communities, the uses of technology for learning, and meta-analysis. He has published numerous journal articles in *Review of Educational Research, Educational and Psychological Measurement, Contemporary Educational Psychology, Educational Research and Evaluation,* and elsewhere, and contributed many chapters in educational psychology, measurement, and technology texts. Abrami's texts include *Statistical Analysis for the Social Sciences: An Interactive Approach* (2000) and *The Student Ratings Debate: Are They Valid and How Can We Best Use Them: New Directions for Institutional Research* (2001). Website: http://doe.concordia.ca/cslp/

**Jane Bozarth, M.Ed.,** is the e-learning coordinator for the state of North Carolina and a popular presenter at training industry events. Author of *e-Learning Solutions on a Shoestring: Help for the Chronically Underfunded Trainer,* Bozarth frequently publishes in both trade and academic journals and is a regular contributor to *Training* magazine. A graduate of the University of North Carolina at Chapel Hill, she holds a master's degree in training and development/technology in training and is presently completing her doctorate in adult education/training and development at North Carolina State University. Her research interests include reflective practice in training and development, espoused theory of training practice versus theory in use, and emotional sources of resistance to e-learning among workplace trainers.

**Pat Brogan, Ph.D.,** has held various jobs in the high-technology sector, including senior management positions at Apple, Macromedia, Raychem, Giga Information Group, and IBM. Currently, Brogan works for Anystream, a company that makes lecture capture software, and serves as an adjunct faculty member at Santa Clara University. She has worked in the field of technology and learning for over a decade and has written and researched various areas of learning performance improvements through technology. She is also actively involved in working with technology programs for at-risk youth, serving on the board of the Intel clubhouse program, and acting as a volunteer sexual assault counselor.

**Lee Christopher** is the e-learning manager for Arapahoe Community College. She holds an M.Ed. from Tulane University, an M.F.A. in writing and poetics from Naropa University, and is currently completing doctoral studies at Capella University. Also, as an adjunct faculty member at Regis University, Metropolitan State College of Denver, Naropa University, and Arapahoe Community College, she enjoys teaching writing. Her research interests include instructional design, distance education, and digital storytelling in the online classroom.

**Roger Côté** is a graduate of the master's program in educational technology at Concordia University in Montreal, Quebec. His research interests include project management, modeling and simulation, and instructional applications of artificial intelligence. While completing his degree, he worked as a member of the Canadarm 2 training team at the Canadian Space Agency and as a research assistant for the Centre for the Study of Learning and Performance. He holds a master's degree in history from the University of Western Ontario and has experience in web application and content development. His website is www.rogercote.com.

**Margaret Driscoll, Ed.D.,** is a managing consultant in IBM Global Services, Client Enablement Services Practice. She is author of *Web-Based Training* and co-author of *Advanced Web-Based Training: Adapting Real-World Strategies in Your Online Learning,* both published by Pfeiffer. She is a featured speaker at national and international training events. Her work has appeared in *Performance Improvement, Training and Development, Chief Learning Officer,* and *Communications Week.* Driscoll is a regular contributor to ASTD's *Learning Circuits.* She is an adjunct professor at Suffolk University in Boston and Teachers College of Columbia University in New York City.

**Jim Everidge, MBA,** is president and CEO of Rapid Learning Deployment (rapidLD), a learning systems integrator in Atlanta. rapidLD provides a suite of learning consulting services, including learning strategy, vendor selection, and deployment services. Under his leadership, the team at rapidLD has participated in over three hundred learning system implementations at organizations such as AT&T, Wal-Mart, Best Buy, and UPS. Tools implemented include learning management suites, collaboration and testing tools, and learning content management tools. He has been a regular speaker for the eLearning Guild, Interwise Online Seminars, and other industry-specific venues. His undergraduate technical degree is from Auburn University and his graduate business degree is from The University of South Alabama. Website: www .rapidld.com.

**Steve Foreman** is president of InfoMedia Designs, a provider of e-learning infrastructure consulting services and technology solutions to Fortune 500 companies and founder of Q Innovation, provider of collaborative knowledge exchange and performance support software products. Since establishing his consulting practice in 1983, Foreman has spent more than twenty years working with forward-looking companies to find new and innovative ways to apply computer technology to support human performance. His work includes enterprise learning and knowledge management strategy, LMS selection and implementation, e-learning process design, and the creation of innovative online environments that blend working and learning and clearly improve productivity. His websites include both Q Innovation, www.qinnovation.net, and InfoMedia Designs, www.infomediadesigns.com.

**Jan Herrington, Ph.D.,** is associate professor in IT in education at the University of Wollongong, Australia. Recent research and development interests have focused on the design of web-based learning environments for higher education, mobile learning, and the use of authentic tasks as a central focus for web-based courses. She was awarded the Association of Educational Communications and Technology (AECT) Young Researcher of the Year Award in Houston in 1999 and won a Fulbright Scholarship in 2002 to conduct research at the University of Georgia in the United States. The authentic tasks web page (developed with Tom Reeves and Ron Oliver) can be accessed at www.authentictasks.uow.edu.au.

**William Horton** has been designing network-based education since 1971 when he was an undergraduate at MIT. He has authored over a dozen books on using technology to educate and inform, including *Designing and Writing Online Documentation, Leading e-Learning, Evaluating e-Learning, Using e-Learning,* e-*Learning Tools and Technologies,* and e-*Learning by Design.* He is a registered Professional Engineer, a fellow of the Society for Technical Communication, and a recipient of ACM's Rigo Award and IEEE's Alfred N. Goldsmith Award. He has designed courses on subjects ranging from delivering anesthesia to discovering spiritual vision. His clientele ranges over Europe, Asia, the Middle East, and the Americas. Website: www.horton.com.

**Patrick Lambe** is one of Asia's most respected knowledge management and e-learning consultants, teachers, and researchers. He is founder of the consulting firm Straits Knowledge, president of the Information and Knowledge Management Society, and adjunct professor in the master's program in Knowledge Management at the Hong Kong Polytechnic University. Mr. Lambe regularly reviews papers for established knowledge management. He is the author of *The Blind Tour Guide: Surviving and Prospering in the New Economy* (2002) and *Organizing Knowledge: Taxonomies, Knowledge Management and Organization Effectiveness* (2007).

**Marie-Claude Lavoie** holds an M.A. in educational technology from Concordia University, where her research interests included mobile learning and educational modeling languages. She also holds a B.Sc. in interactive arts with a concentration in interactive design from the Simon Fraser University School of Interactive Arts and Technology (SIAT). She is currently working at Bluestreak Technology as head of Technical Writing and Training. Website: www.mclavoie.com.

**Gretchen Lowerison** is a lecturer and Ph.D. candidate in educational technology at Concordia University in Montreal, Canada. Her research interests focus on the role that computer technology and pedagogical support play in facilitating learning in formal and informal learning environments. Other interests include student-centered learning, goal orientation, and perceived competence.

**Patricia McGee, Ph.D.,** is an associate professor of instructional technology in the College of Education and Human Development at the University of Texas at San Antonio. Director of several technology and training grants, she has worked as research faculty through the Office of Naval Research and the EDUCAUSE Learning Initiative (formerly NLII) researching emerging technologies and learning systems, particularly those used in distributed learning environments, resulting in a book, *Course Management*

*Systems for Learning: Beyond Accidental Pedagogy*. McGee is an active consultant and invited presenter in the areas of strategies for faculty support, designs of new systems, and strategies for pedagogically sound applications of digital tools and resources. She earned a Ph.D. in curriculum and instruction with a cognate in instructional technology from the University of Texas at Austin.

**M. David Merrill, Ph.D.,** is an instructional effectiveness consultant, a visiting professor at Florida State University and Brigham Young University-Hawaii, and professor emeritus at Utah State University. Since receiving his Ph.D. from the University of Illinois in 1964, he has served on the faculty of George Peabody College, Brigham Young University—Provo, Stanford University, the University of Southern California, and Utah State University. He is internationally recognized as a major contributor to the field of instructional technology, has published many books and articles in the field, and has lectured internationally. Among his principle contributions: TICCIT authoring system, component display theory, elaboration theory, instructional transaction theory, automated instructional design and ID based on knowledge objects, and first principles of instruction. He was honored to receive the Lifetime Achievement Award from the Association of Educational Communications and Technology.

**Ron Oliver, Ph.D.,** is the Foundation Professor of Interactive Multimedia at Edith Cowan University in Western Australia. He has wide experience in the design, development, implementation, and evaluation of technology-mediated and online learning materials. He uses technology extensively in his own teaching and his ideas and activities are all typically grounded in practical applications. Oliver has won a number of awards for his innovative teaching and research, including the inaugural Australian Award for University Teaching for the use of multimedia in university teaching. Website: http://elrond.scam.ecu.edu.au/oliver

**Patrick Parrish** is production manager with the COMET® Program, providing instructional design management supporting the creation of education and training for operational meteorologists in government, military, and private positions. Parrish holds an M.A. in instructional technology and is currently completing his doctorate in educational leadership and innovation at the University of Colorado at Denver. He has published in *Educational Technology Research & Development, Educational Technology, TechTrends*, and the forthcoming *Handbook of Visual Languages for Instructional Design* and has presented on instructional design and technology at many national and international conferences and workshops. His interests include design process, technology innovation, and the aesthetic nature of teaching and learning. Website: www.comet.ucar .edu/~pparrish.

**L. Wayne Precht, M.S.,** is the assistant director for Development in the Learning Applications Development and Support unit of University of Maryland University College, where he leads the development team for the WebTycho online learning platform. In his more than fifteen years in higher education, Precht has worked on successive generations of e-learning platforms at UMUC, starting with fifty students using the mainframe-based PLATO™ system through the current WebTycho™ project with its sixty thousand worldwide students taking more than 100,000 accredited classes this semester alone. He is currently an architect for the follow-on system expected to be available in 2008.

**Thomas C. Reeves, Ph.D.,** is a professor of instructional technology at The University of Georgia. After completing his Ph.D. at Syracuse University, he spent a year as a Fulbright lecturer in Peru. His research interests include evaluation of instructional technology, socially responsible educational research, mental models and cognitive tools, authentic learning models, and instructional technology in developing countries. In 2003, he was the first person to receive the Fellowship Award from the Association for the Advancement of Computing in Education. His *Interactive Learning Systems Evaluation* book (with John Hedberg) was published in 2003. Website: http://it.coe.uga. edu/~treeves/

**Marc J. Rosenberg, Ph.D.,** is a management consultant and speaker in training, organizational learning, e-learning, knowledge management, and performance improvement. He is the author of the best-selling book, *e-Learning: Strategies for Delivering Knowledge in the Digital Age* (McGraw-Hill). His new book is *Beyond e-Learning: Approaches and Technologies to Enhance Organizational Knowledge, Learning, and Performance* (Pfeiffer). Rosenberg is past president of the International Society for Performance Improvement (ISPI). He holds a Ph.D. in instructional design, plus degrees in communications and marketing, and the Certified Performance Technologist (CPT) designation from ISPI. He has spoken at The White House, keynoted at professional and business conferences, authored more than forty articles and book chapters, and is a frequently quoted expert in major business and trade publications. Website: www.marcrosenberg.com.

**Harvey Singh** is the CEO of Instancy, Inc., which develops Web 2.0-based enterprise learning and knowledge management solutions. He is internationally recognized as one of the key thought leaders in technology-enabled learning, performance support, and knowledge management. Previously, Singh served as the chief learning technology officer at Centra Software after the company he co-founded, MindLever, was acquired by Centra Software, a leader in collaborative learning. Singh served as an advisor to e-learning standards organizations such as ADL/SCORM and IMS and is frequently invited to speak at national and international training conferences and to contribute to books, magazines, and webzines on the topic of enterprise learning. He has graduate degrees in both computer science and educational technology from Stanford University and a bachelor's degree in computer science from North Carolina State University. Website: www.instancy.com.

**Brent G. Wilson, Ph.D.,** is a professor of information and learning technologies at the University of Colorado Health Sciences Center in Denver, where he directs the research lab in Innovative Designs of Environments for Adult Learners (http://thunder1.cudenver .edu/ideal/index.html). His research has focused on helping educators design effective learning resources and helping learners make effective use of those resources—in a variety of school and non-school settings. He has published four books and a variety of articles on topics related to performance improvement, learning technologies, and instructional design. Website: www.cudenver .edu/~bwilson

# What will you find on pfeiffer.com?

- The best in workplace performance solutions for training and HR professionals

- Downloadable training tools, exercises, and content

- Web-exclusive offers

- Training tips, articles, and news

- Seamless on-line ordering

- Author guidelines, information on becoming a Pfeiffer Affiliate, and much more

# Discover more at www.pfeiffer.com